Watteau and the Cultural Politics of Eighteenth-Century France

In *Watteau and the Cultural Politics of Eighteenth-Century France,* Julie Anne Plax engages in an interdisciplinary examination of several categories of Watteau's paintings – theatrical, military, *fêtes,* and signboards. Arguing that Watteau consistently applied coherent strategies of representation aimed at subverting high art, she shows how his paintings toyed ironically with conventions and genres and confounded traditional categories. Plax connects these strategies to broader cultural themes and political issues that Watteau's art addressed throughout his career, thereby revealing the substantial unity of his oeuvre. Using a wide array of visual and verbal primary resources to illuminate the richness of the visual culture of eighteenth-century Paris and the last years of Louis XIV's reign, *Watteau and the Cultural Politics of Eighteenth-Century France* contributes substantially to the current reassessment of the period.

Julie Anne Plax is associate professor of art history at the University of Arizona, Tucson. A scholar of eighteenth-century painting, she has contributed to *Eighteenth-Century Studies* and *Source.*

Watteau and the Cultural Politics of Eighteenth-Century France

JULIE ANNE PLAX

University of Arizona

CAMBRIDGE
UNIVERSITY PRESS

PUBLISHED BY THE PRESS SYNDICATE OF THE UNIVERSITY OF CAMBRIDGE
The Pitt Building, Trumpington Street, Cambridge, United Kingdom

CAMBRIDGE UNIVERSITY PRESS
The Edinburgh Building, Cambridge CB2 2RU, UK http://www.cup.cam.ac.uk
40 West 20th Street, New York, NY 10011-4211, USA http://www.cup.org
10 Stamford Road, Oakleigh, Melbourne 3166, Australia
Ruiz de Alarcón 13, 28014 Madrid, Spain

First published 2000

Printed in the United States of America

Typefaces Sabon 10.25/13.5 pt. and Cochin *System* QuarkXPress [CS]

A catalog record for this book is available from the British Library.

Library of Congress Cataloging in Publication Data
Plax, Julie Anne.
Watteau and the cultural politics of eighteenth-century France / Julie Anne Plax.
p. cm.
Includes bibliographical references and index.
ISBN 0-521-64268-X (hb.)
1. Watteau, Antoine, 1684–1721 – Criticism and interpretation.
2. Watteau, Antoine, 1684–1721 – Themes, motives. I. Title.
ND553.W3P65 2000
759.4 – dc21 99-37851
CIP

ISBN 0 521 64268 X hardback

Contents

Illustrations

Acknowledgments

In the process of researching and writing this book I have received aid and encouragement from a number of people. Foremost, I would like to acknowledge my debt of gratitude to my husband, Kenneth Plax. Without his critical and editorial advice, and support in moments of doubt, this book would never have seen the light of day. Patricia Crown, who was my dissertation advisor at the University of Missouri–Columbia, introduced me to the pleasures of eighteenth–century art and shaped my thinking in important ways. I shall always appreciate her support and her guidance. I would like to thank Thomas Crow and Norman Land, both of whom influenced the direction my work has taken. Mary Sheriff also merits a special word of thanks for her scholarly and collegial generosity; she read the manuscript in several different incarnations, provided critical insights, and offered her support of the project.

Many others played a role in the creation of this book, sometimes unwittingly. Conversations with friends and colleagues helped to clarify my thinking and offered new perspectives. Shared information made living and researching in Paris more productive and pleasurable. I wish to acknowledge gratefully the following friends and colleagues: Vivian Cameron, Candace Clements, Roy Gary, Nancy Goldberg, Melissa Hyde, Kevin Justus, Sura Levine, Noël Maffray, Paula Rea Radisich, Wendy Wassyng Roworth, and my colleagues at the University of Arizona.

I owe a great debt to the Department of Art History and Archaeology at the University of Missouri–Columbia for its financial support through my graduate study and dissertation research. Thanks also to the Kress Foundation, whose support contributed to my graduate career and my dissertation research. The University of the South supported my work in the form of travel and research grants. I owe a special thanks to Brown Patterson, who was the dean when I was there. The University of Arizona provided funding for research through a grant I received in 1992 from the Small Grants for Research Program from the Office of the Vice President for Research, through a Faculty of Fine Arts Summer Research and Professional Development Incentive Grant in 1994 and in 1998. I am grateful to have received a University of Arizona Provost's Author Support Fund Award, which offset the expenses for photographs and the permissions to reproduce them. I wish to thank Peter Harrington, Curator of the Anne S. K. Brown Military Collection, for his help both when I was researching the collection and later acquiring photographs. I thank Jennifer Laffoon for her photographic expertise, and Susan Greenberg for her careful, thoughtful editing.

Last but not least I wish to acknowledge my parents, Anne and Warren Finkbeiner, and my in-laws, Mildred and the late Jakob Plax, for all their support and acts of kindness through the years, and my daughter Irene for providing so much delight in my life.

Introduction

THE WORK OF WATTEAU is mythic: frequently, it is described as enchanting, ambiguous, and mysterious. This is the work of the Watteau celebrated by the Goncourts; however, this is the Watteau who in the scholarship of the last fifteen years or so has been more and more supplanted by the "historical" Watteau – an artist rooted in and responding to a particular historical place and time and engaging his contemporaries about matters of political, social, and cultural consequence. In this book I want to further historicize Watteau, his works, and the eighteenth-century viewers.

The "historical" Watteau I have reconstructed was situated at a social, cultural, and aesthetic confluence, in the crepuscular era of Louis XIV's decline, when the king's hegemony had not, certainly, dissipated, but when it was no longer as effective as it had been either. It was a time when the authority of the Crown was in crisis and, during the regency of Philippe d'Orléans, when the shifting bases of political and cultural authority were up for grabs; it was also a time when the boundaries between social classes were in flux, as were the criteria for how those boundaries were to be determined and understood. These struggles were often played out on a cultural and aesthetic battlefield, and I argue in this book that Watteau participated in those struggles.

Watteau's personal experiences suggest that he rode on a number of the crosscurrents of the period. Watteau was from Valenciennes, a town in northern France that was culturally more Flemish than French, but he carved out his career in Paris. In the Parisian milieu, he experienced a number of cultural realms; he absorbed not only the popular culture of the street and the fair and the salons of wealthy collectors and connoisseurs but also the official high culture of the Royal Academy of Painting and Sculpture. As an artist Watteau was trained in the northern tradition; he apprenticed with Claude Gillot, who was known as a painter of theatrical scenes, and with Claude III Audran, who was a fashionable Parisian decorator. In addition, through the collections of his friends and patrons Watteau had access to the works of the great European masters. In short, Watteau was in a position to understand a variety of highly coded practices and discourses – in art as well as in life – and the overlap between the two.

Watteau's position inevitably affected his art. Yet I would not wish to imply that I therefore believe Watteau's work to have been purely a product of his social experience; nor would I assert that Watteau remained immune to the world in which he lived. I merely insist that Watteau was alive to his surroundings and that he responded to them in some ways to which we can gain access. Of course, art historians, critics, and commentators of various stripes have shared this conviction for almost three centuries now, offering an enormous range of interpretations of both Watteau the man and the paintings he left behind; and the library, veritable and venerable, that has swelled around Watteau is a testament to that conviction. I believe nonetheless that the library still has room for additions (as if the work of an artist as pivotal and controversial as Watteau might ever be exhausted!), including mine, which I do not pretend to be either comprehensive or definitive.

Rather, I have explored one area in which I believe the conjunction of Watteau the man living a historical moment and Watteau the painter proves especially revealing of both Watteaus: his techniques of representation. I argue here that Watteau confounded, inverted, and toyed ironically with preexisting genres, conventions, traditions, and practices in his painting. I further argue that he did so in consistent ways throughout his career. This unconventional manipulation of the cultural, social, and painterly codes of representation mixed things up, broke down boundaries, and brought the construction and meanings of the codes themselves – and who controlled them – into question. I would like therefore to add another word to the list of adjectives applied to Watteau's paintings that has not heretofore been found there: *subversive.*

We customarily associate the term *subversion* with conscious efforts to overthrow or undermine a political regime, and I do not think it would be inconsistent to suggest that Watteau's techniques have a powerful political undertow, even if I argue here that the political content is more elliptical than modern viewers are accustomed to interpreting. I want to make clear, however, that I do not see Watteau as having worn the Phrygian cap prematurely. Rather, I think Watteau deployed strategies that were formally subversive and were informed by a perspective that was politically charged and critical of the policies specific and general of the regime because the historical moment required that he use them: at the end of the reign of Louis XIV they offered the surest means for him to express his ideas. I repeat, moreover, that Watteau's chosen field of battle was culture; thus, to the degree that Watteau engaged politics directly, they were cultural politics he engaged.

In order best to open to view Watteau's subversive strategies and their internal consistency within his oeuvre, I have organized this book into four independent, yet mutually supportive chapters. Each chapter focuses on a different category of subject matter and represents a different phase in the artist's career. I have consciously limited the scope of my project to a thorough, sustained analysis of individual works or groups of works. I address not only the subject or theme of these works but also the narrative structuring of the imagery and, most important, how Watteau's subversive manipulations of form and genre connected to contemporary social, cultural, and political issues.

In chapter 1 I focus on an early theatrical work that has not been the object of great interest before, *Departure of the Italian Comedians in 1697*, executed sometime between 1703 and 1709. The importance of the theater and theatricality to Watteau's paintings has already been well explored; here I explore the subject and its representation in relation to specific political events and to a larger crisis of political authority. In chapter 2 I examine a group of military subjects done between 1709 and 1714 and how Watteau's play of conventions and allusions helped to articulate a change in military values and practices in a time when *gloire* was no longer a viable possibility. In chapter 3 I discuss Watteau's *fêtes galantes* and analyze in detail Watteau's reception piece, *Pilgrimage to Cythera.* Here I suggest that Watteau's free appropriation of divergent cultural discourses structurally reproduces and documents the very process by which cultural transformations and social redefinitions occurred. In chapter 4 I approach *Gersaint's Signboard* in relation to urban experience, to the legitimization of a new class of collectors and dealers, and to a system of artistic production and consumption. I also interrogate the dealer Gersaint's account of the creation of the *Signboard,* written twenty-two years after the fact, as a personal and professional rewriting of history.

The works in the first two chapters, *Departure of the Italian Comedians in 1697* and the military paintings, have not been extensively studied. I want to bring out the hitherto unexplored richness and complexity of these works as well as to create enough of a context for them so that the nuanced meanings of the images will become apparent. I metaphorically liken my task here to that of "cleaning" a painting – a process during which specific meanings and connections emerge from beneath a layer of generalized observations and inattention.

By contrast, the works discussed in the last two chapters have been the subjects of a vast amount of research, much of which I rely upon for my own interpretive ventures – in particular, Thomas Crow's reading of Watteau's *fêtes galantes* in *Painters and Public Life in Eighteenth-Century Paris,* Norman Bryson's interrogation of narrative structure in *Word and Image: French Painting of the Ancien Régime,* and Robert Neuman's reading of *Gersaint's Signboard* in his 1984 article in the *Gazette des beaux-arts,* "Watteau's *L'Enseigne de Gersaint* and Baroque Emblematic Tradition."[1] In my examination of these paintings I amplify their cultural context: it is my hope that my work deepens interpretations that extend both the number of ripples caused by these paintings and the size of the splash they made.

Here, as in the first two chapters, Watteau's paintings act as springboards for an interdisciplinary interrogation of the milieus in which the paintings were produced and received: the question I continually pose is What significance would certain elements, themes, arrangements of forms, and narrative structures have had for the eighteenth century? In an attempt to answer this question, I have relied on a wide range of textual and visual primary sources and have sought among them both expected and unexpected intertextual connections or relationships. I construct a vantage point from which new insights, complications, and nuances of past interpretations are made possible.

Yet to say that I construct a vantage point is perhaps misleading since it suggests a single, commanding overview. Rather (to shift metaphorical gears), I wish to evoke the cultural and mental horizons that shaped the making and reception of the works of art. Hans-Robert Jauss utilizes the term "horizon of expectations" to describe how the boundaries of a reader's experience in and of the world condition his or her response to a literary text; in turn, the literary text may reaffirm those boundaries, or change them.[2] The metaphor of a horizon is appropriate, for it implies both a fixed space beyond the edges of which is the unseen and, hence, the unknown and a flexible space that shifts depending upon one's particular position in society and in history. In short, I want to restore the works to the situations that shaped their intelligibility and dictated their form. These words are paraphrased from Roger Chartier, whose work on the reception of texts has greatly influenced my work on the interpretation of images.[3] Like Chartier, I seek out the common assumptions and practices that would have created a shared community of interpretation for an image, the institutional constraints that limited possibilities in a work's production or reception, and the ways in which the work functioned actively as a vehicle for the construction and reproduction of social identities. The general contours that shape this shared community of interpretation are, of course, predicated upon individual texts, documents, objects, and images from the past; the contours are the result of the accretion of individual elements rather than an expression of some informing spirit.

We must acknowledge, however, that we are always working from secondhand representations, that we can create only incomplete pictures, informed, yet always fragmentary. But is this any different from the way we make sense of the world in the here and now? Whether in the past or the present, individuals can operate in their world only through the preexisting patterns of belief, practices (including language), and perceptions. We maneuver within and against any number of signifying discourses, or ideologies (class, gender, legal, corporate/professional, aesthetic), that shape our identity and position in that world. My thinking about these matters as I have tried to explain the significance of Watteau's work in an eighteenth-century context benefited greatly from the work of a few scholars in particular.

Raymond Williams's work on the sociology of culture has been critical to my thinking about the dynamic relationship between social relations and cultural change, especially his formulation of dominant, emergent, and residual cultural forms.[4] His work has allowed me to see how these signifying discourses, or systems of meaning, simultaneously respond to and are shaped by a particular constellation of social relations and interests at any given time. These discourses or ideologies can overlap and elide, clash and compete. Williams's work, and Chartier's work on appropriation,[5] helped me to get at the interplay of low and high culture, to remain sensitive to the ebb and flow of power in the midst of social and cultural change, and to be alert to some of the ways new systems of producing meaning could develop.

Robert Darnton's work on the way ordinary people make sense of the world, especially his emphasis on the way people think with things, has been extremely helpful to me.[6] My understanding of the visual culture of eighteenth-century Paris, for example, is rooted in a recognition of a material world that contained its own epistemology and language. Pictorial narrative strategies, like those Watteau consistently relied upon, would have been less accessible to me without the illumination of Darnton's insights.

Chartier, Williams, and Darnton have provided what amount to some theoretical wellsprings for my conclusions; some waters, however, remain troubled. Throughout this book I allude to the reactions to various plays, spectacles, paintings, and so on, of the eighteenth-century audience. The identity of this audience is not only remote but is also, to some degree, speculative, for there is actually very little concrete evidence about it that might sustain the statistical generalizations from which contemporary social historians prefer to argue. Nevertheless, I am convinced that enough information is available about Watteau's friends, about his immediate milieu, and about those persons who collected his work to allow me to make informed speculations concerning the contours of his audience. For example, we know that Watteau was friends with two dealers who promoted his work – Sirois, and Sirois's more prominent son-in-law, Edme Gersaint. One can safely assume that there would be an overlap between the dealers' clientele (whose identities can be partially reconstructed through later sales catalogues, inventories, and letters) and the hypothetical audience for Watteau's works. We know as well that Watteau was part of a circle of collectors and amateurs who gathered around the wealthy banker Pierre Crozat. Watteau lived in Crozat's household for several periods during his time in Paris, and he was present at social gatherings whose participants we can identify with a high degree of certainty. In addition, through Claude Gillot, Watteau would have been acquainted with a theatrical milieu. If we cannot always pinpoint the identity of every member of this audience, we can determine the various circles in which Watteau moved that would have constituted the possible audience pools. We can also construct representative types and make informed assumptions about what they would have brought to and found in Watteau's paintings.

Lacking a statistical base, I have tried to define the shape and composition of the audience for Watteau's paintings as well as for the other cultural productions I have interpreted in this book through informed extrapolation based on what is known and on the little indirections, recurrent puns, and thematic circumlocutions great and small that occur in a hundred different primary sources. Scholars in every discipline in the arts and the humanities who have immersed themselves in the sources for years will understand me when I offer about the eighteenth-century audience a paraphrase of what a justice of the U.S. Supreme Court said about pornography: "I may not be able to define it, but I know it when I see it." It is thus my hope that the reading of Watteau's works that I offer here will be persuasive to my own contemporaries and will reflect, however faintly, Watteau in his own era.

CHAPTER ONE

Watteau's *Departure of the Italian Comedians in 1697* and the Battle of the Theaters

Much has been made of the theatricality in Watteau's paintings. Figures costumed as Mezzetins, Harlequins, Gilles, and other characters from the Italian Comedy inhabit his painterly world. They dance and make music in spaces that invoke the stage and its conventions. Embodying the performative nature of social ritual, Watteau's *fêtes galantes* echo the importance of the theater in the early eighteenth century. Not only was there a growing "taste" for the theater in segments of the society that ranged from the street to the elite, but there was also a theatricalization of society itself. The theater provided structures or models for "acting" in the world, and for a particular kind of aestheticization of life. Theatrical performances may have influenced and even suffused daily life, but the interchange between performers and spectators was not only merely of actors imposing their medium upon a passive audience, for the other side of the stage constituted a type of public forum. The audience, speaking in a communal voice, engaged in a cultural dialogue with the performers that not only commented on the formal aspects of the performance and on the references to contemporary events and practices that were embedded within it but also absorbed, reshaped, and transformed future performances.

If one reads Watteau's paintings as cultural productions that both partake of and comment upon the contemporary social and cultural scene, the presence of this theatricality is not surprising, for in the late seventeenth and early eighteenth centuries the theater was a major battleground upon which contending forces fought to determine who would control and define cultural forms and practices. Sometime between 1703 and 1709, Watteau depicted one of the major skirmishes in this battle: Louis XIV's suppression of the Italian Comedians in 1697. The painting, entitled *Departure of the Italian Comedians in 1697*, henceforth referred to as *Departure* (fig. 1), has been lost, and we know it only through the engraving by Louis Jacob and through two copies, one of which, at the University of Missouri Museum of Art and Archaeology, has been cut down (fig. 2).[1]

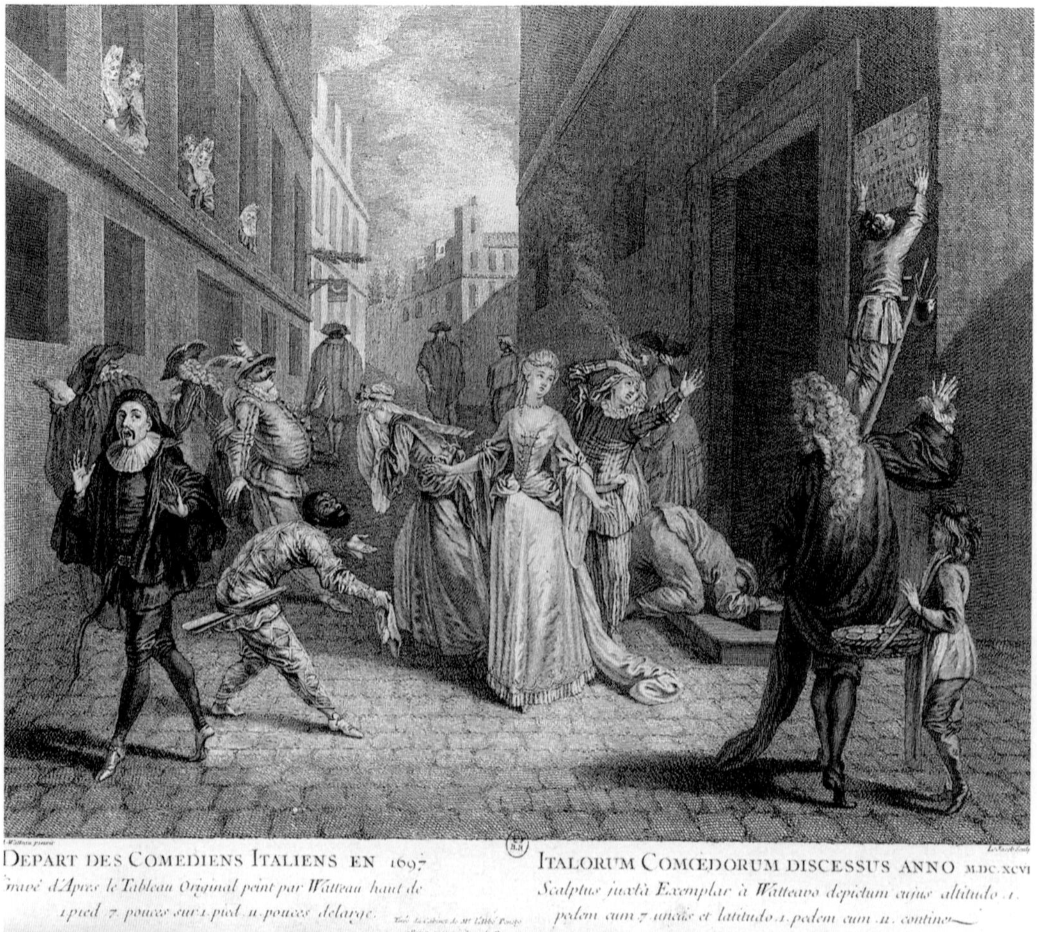

1. Louis Jacob, engraving after Antoine Watteau, *Departure of the Italian Comedians in 1697 (Départ des Comédiens Italiens en 1697)*, engraving announced 1729, painting between 1703 and 1705, Bibliothèque Nationale de France, Paris. Cliché, Bibliothèque nationale de France, Paris.

The painting of this subject is something of an anomaly in Watteau's work. Of the 129 easel paintings Jean de Jullienne had engraved after Watteau's works, only two qualify as "*sujets historiques*" in Dacier and Vuaflart's classification of the engravings by subject.[2] On only one other occasion did Watteau contribute to official history by representing a specific event from the recent past, *Louis XIV Presenting the Cordon Blue to M. de Bourgogne* (fig. 3).[3] Within Dacier and Vuaflart's classification – which also includes portraits, landscapes, satires, and mythological, religious, and military subjects – the vast majority of the works (96) falls under the nebulous appellation "informal, Arcadian, theatrical or gallant scenes and figures of different characters, that is to say, that which represents the art of Watteau in its most original and personal."[4] Implicit in the definition of this last category is the notion of uniqueness. Watteau created a whole range of subjects that are somehow different from the more commonly accepted and readily recognized genres. Articulating just what that difference is, however, and just what might unify such a seemingly disparate body of works, caused Dacier and Vuaflart much difficulty, for they ultimately fall back on Watteau's personal genius as the source of this uniqueness. As this classification should suggest, the subject matter, and hence the meanings, of the majority of Watteau's works are ambiguous and difficult to pin down.

This ambiguity makes *Departure* even more atypical, for it appears to be emphatically straightforward. The title defines the subject; there is a clear correspondence between what we see and the text supplied by the title.[5] Watteau illustrates – and here "illustrates" is a key word – the event with exactitude. There is none of that uneasy unaccountability that marks the *fêtes galantes* of Watteau's mature work. Because the painting shows nothing that cannot be explained within the context of the event, *Departure* has lain outside the traditional literary and scholarly discourse on Watteau that capitalizes on the perceived mood, mystery, and melancholy of his paintings and his life. The Goncourt brothers' *L'art au dix-huitième siècle* (1856–75) provided the cornerstone for discourse, which Norman Bryson refers to as "Watteau writing."[6] Firmly grounded in the ancient Greek tradition of *ekphrasis* (a written description of a work of visual art), the Goncourts verbally evoked Watteau's images: "A poetry as unique as it is delightful, the poetry of sumptuous ease, of the colloquies and songs of youth, of pastoral recreations and leisurely pastimes, a poetry of peace and tranquility amid which the movements even of a garden swing die faintly away . . . a boldness of gesture orchestrated like a ballet for the occasion."[7] The Goncorts' rhapsodic parallel poetry is alluring and has persisted even in recent scholarship precisely because it reflects how we experience Watteau's paintings as mood and contradictory sensations.[8] As Bryson discusses, this experience of the paintings as mood is the effect of a particular narrative strategy in which enough questions are raised and situations set up, but not enough information is provided to answer the questions or resolve the situations. The viewer, or the writer, must explore the possibilities engendering reverie as a form of thought and of language. "Watteau writing" perpetuates the mythic Watteau: a man whose imagination and genius remain the sole source of a unique and original genre of painting – the *fête galante. Departure* does not lend itself to this type of *ekphrasis,* and in part this may explain why the work has received only cursory interest.

Although *Departure* is uncharacteristic of what we generally perceive Watteau's work to be, it is not viewed as remarkable or even unusual. It is discussed in stylistic terms as being exemplary of the influence of Watteau's first

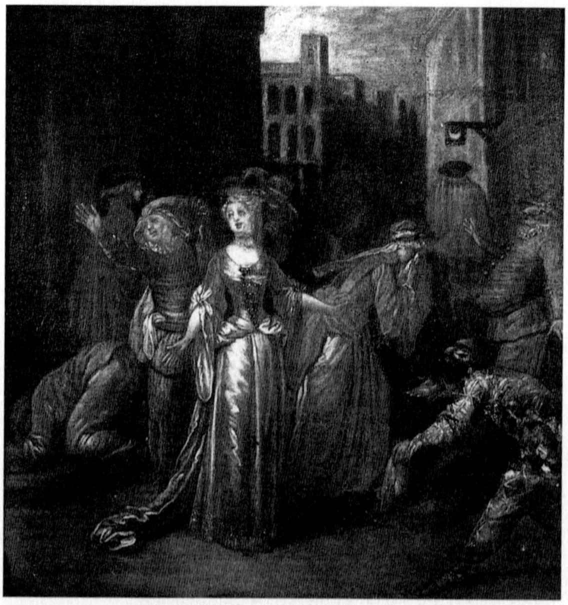

2. Attributed to François-Joseph de la Pierre, *Departure of the Commedia dell'Arte from Paris*, Museum of Art and Archaeology, University of Missouri – Columbia.

master, Claude Gillot. Most of the scholarly discussion of *Departure* either focuses on questions of attribution – was the painting by Watteau, or by Gillot, or, the most accepted view, a collaboration between the two – or uses the work illustratively to accompany a discussion of the Italian Comedians. But what might the eighteenth-century viewer have perceived in Watteau's representation of this particular event? We can restore much of *Departure*'s meaning by placing it within the larger, ongoing battle for cultural control. Indeed, if one considers the implications of the departure of the Italian Comedians within that context, Watteau's representation of their banishment, produced sometime between seven and eleven years after the event and witout firsthand observation, takes on a charged meaning. Our perception of the work changes. Rather than seeing the work as straightforward illustration or objective chronicling, we begin to view the work as something complex, controversial, and, in the end, subversive. We begin to notice certain internal inconsistencies and contradictions. We are made aware of how Watteau, even at this early stage in his career, ironically manipulated existing genres and their conventions to undermine the assumptions on which they are based and to reveal an unexpected meaning.

An examination of Watteau's *Departure* is instructive. First, in this work, which has a clearly identifiable subject and seemingly documentary quality, it is easier to isolate the narrative and pictorial strategies the artist used to produce meaning – mixing things up – than it is in Watteau's later, more "original," and ambiguous works. Second, and more important, *Departure* illustrates the process of cultural mediation: Watteau's pictorial and narrative strategies are not just his own unique invention; they are historically conditioned, articulating some of the collective values and concerns of a culture and society in a state of transformation. Last, an understanding of *Departure* and its loaded meaning helps to explain the vogue for things theatrical in painting.

Watteau painted *Departure* sometime during his apprenticeship under Claude Gillot from 1703–4 until 1708–9.[9] Louis Jacob engraved a copy of it in 1729 for the corpus of engraved works after Watteau, drawn up and marketed

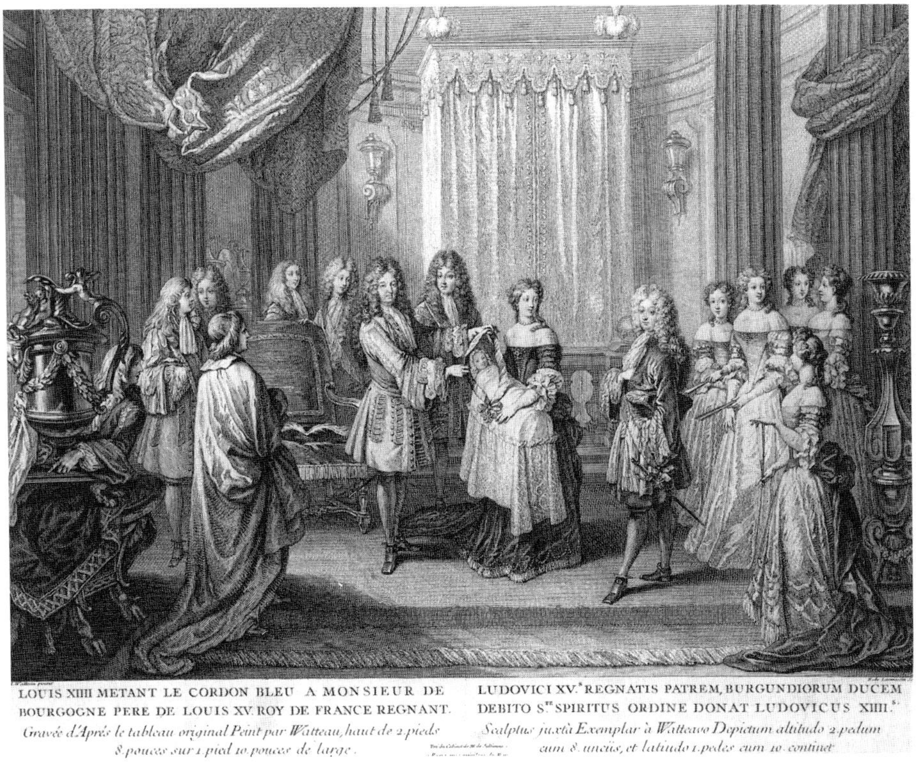

3. Nicolas de Larmessin II, engraving after Antoine Watteau, *Louis XIV Presenting the Cordon Blue to M. de Bourgogne (Louis XIV Mettant le Cordon Bleu à Monsieur de Bourgogne)*, engraving announced 1729, painting c. 1710, Anne S. K. Brown Military Collection, Brown University Library, Providence, RI.

by Jean de Jullienne after Watteau's death.[10] The legend on the engraving indicates that the painting belonged to Abbé Penetti, secretary to Abbé Franchini, who was the Florentine envoy at the French court. Abbé Penetti was a friend of Pierre-Jean Mariette, one of Watteau's principal patrons, and he acted as a messenger between Mariette and his Florentine correspondents.[11] One could speculate that Mariette originally owned the painting and bestowed it upon Penetti as a token of friendship, for it would have been an appropriate gift for an Italian who was frequently departing.

The engraving represents the moment of the posting of the King's decree to close the theater and to banish the troupe and the Comedians' response to it. The action takes place in a Parisian street formed by the Comedians' theater to the right, a building that is apparently an inn on the left, and two unidentified buildings further in the background. The corner of the theater articulates an intersection. The intersection, in the foreground, opens up a stagelike space, creating a spatial and narrative focus for the image. Scattered within this space are nine members of the Italian Comedy, recognizable by their characteristic costumes: from left to right in the foreground are Scaramouche, dressed in black with a white ruff; the masked Harlequin; and the lead *amoureuse,* with her arms open, in the center of the scene. From left to right in the mid-ground are Docteur Baloardo in his heavy academic robe and ruff; one of the troupe's *amoureux,* wearing a tricorne hat and long wig; Polichinelle, with his hunched back and overhanging belly; the maidservant Colombine, weeping into a handkerchief; Mezzetin, in his striped costume with floppy hat and ruff; and the supplicating figure of Pierrot, dressed in his traditional costume of a baggy white suit. They are reacting, with apparent emotion, to the decree of banishment that an emissary of the police on a ladder is posting high on the wall of their theater. In the right foreground with his back to the viewer, a magistrate, recognizable by his full wig and black robe, oversees the event's transaction. Three of the upper-story windows in the inn – so indicated by the projecting signboard and fir tree – across from the theater frame spectators, two couples and a single woman, who watch the events below with interest. A young tart peddler next to the magistrate observes the scene at ground level. Four figures are dressed in nontheatrical garb; three of these figures are situated toward the background, and the fourth, carrying a smoking torch, or *flambeau,* stands on the far side of the theater door. Presumably passersby, none of these figures seems concerned with the historic event that is occurring – the banishment of the Italian Comedians in 1697.

This event is the expulsion of the Italian Comedians from Paris, by order of the king, on 14 May 1697. Louis XIV had heard a rumor that the Italian Comedians were going to perform a play, *La Fausse Prude,* based on a libelous pamphlet of the same name then circulating. This tract, which had been published in Holland, was banned in France. It satirized the virtues and morals of Madame de Maintenon,[12] the king's publicly pious wife. To avoid a blot on his beloved's character and an act of the greatest disrespect, he banished the troupe.

Writings from the period contradict one another about whether this play was ever actually performed. The Duchess d'Orléans, who was no friend of Maintenon, states in her letters that the piece was played and that it earned quite a bit of money for the Comedians before they were chased from their theater. Of the performance, which she herself did not attend, she writes, "It has been said that they [the comedians] have portrayed the old trollop in the most ludicrous manner."[13] A similar account is given by Mme. Du Noyer, who states that the play was performed and that "Mme. de Maintenon was recognizable."[14] Saint-Simon, in his *Mémoires,* and Duclos, in his *Mémoires secrets,* both write that the play was performed.[15] According to other sources, however, the play was never actually performed; this is the generally accepted opinion among historians of the theater.[16] One of the most reliable of the eighteenth-century sources, T.-S. Gueullette, recounts that the Comedians asked the playwright, de Fatouville, to compose a piece in French, *La Fausse Belle Mère,* based on the Italian play *La Finta Matrigna.*[17] The piece was written, and the Italian Comedians imprudently referred to it as *La Fausse Prude* and posted bills using this title. Before *La Fausse Belle Mère,* alias *La Fausse Prude,* could be performed, the king ordered the theater closed and the theater troupe expelled. Although the theater historians the Parfaict brothers are mute on the subject of whether the play was actually performed, they do give a description of the expulsion:

> M. d'Argenson, Lieutenant-général of Police, since the 9th of the preceding January, by virtue of a *lettre de cachet* from the King, addressed to him and accompanied by a number of adjutant commissioners, and all the *Robe courte* went to the theater at the hôtel Bourgogne at eleven in the morning. They affixed the seals on all the doors of the theater, not only those on Mauconseil and Française streets, but also on those of the actors' dressing rooms, prohibiting the actors from appearing there to perform. His Majesty no longer judged it appropriate to keep them in his service.[18]

Watteau has depicted the moment when the king's orders were placed on the wall of the Italian theater. The discrepancies between the Parfaict brothers' account and the image are minor. We do not see the *robe courte* (the archers or agents of the police); moreover, at the time of the Italian Comedians' banishment, the troupe consisted of twelve members, whereas Watteau presents only nine figures who can be identified clearly as Comedians by their costume.[19] These variations are of little importance, however, and do not detract from the overall accuracy and clarity of Watteau's scene. In its clarity and accuracy, and in Watteau's use of formal elements, *Departure* belongs within the tradition of what I will term "documentary images." One can assume that Watteau consciously drew upon this tradition when he conceived of *Departure.*

By documentary images, I am referring to a particular mode of visual description intended to create the illusion of a straightforward reflection of reality. All images actively construct rather than passively reflect, yet the degree of artistic mediation that appears in an image is relative. The less mediation there seems to be, the more we read the image as truthful. Nevertheless, a truly documentary image is only a fiction. Documentary images mask power and intentions within the "truthfulness" of the image. Not surprisingly, this documentary, or even journalistic, type of image making, without recourse to allegory, makes up a whole subcategory of official art.[20]

In 1667, the Conseil du Roi undertook a vast project to have the king's properties, *chooses rare et singulières* (including his collection of art), and royal events of significance engraved. This state-supported project of propaganda, referred to as the *cabinet du roi,* had a dual function: first, to collect and classify, and second, to make the glory and wealth of the king and his

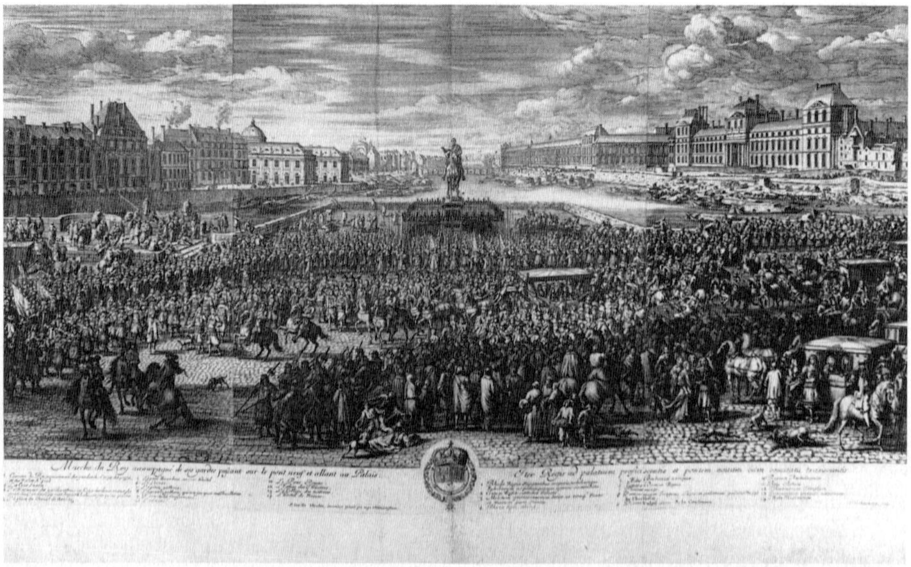

4. Johann van Huchtenburg, engraving after Van der Meulen, *Procession of the King Accompanied by the Guards Passing over the Pont Neuf on the Way to the Palace (March du roi accompagnée des gardes pasant sur le Pont Neuf et allant au Palais)*, Anne S. K. Brown Military Collection, Brown University Library, Providence, RI.

realm accessible to his subjects and to the foreign dignitaries upon whom the king bestowed the images as a magnanimous gesture.[21] The *cabinet du roi* both insured the systematic production of a visual inventory of royal riches and furthered the art of engraving. Troops of artists at the Gobelins Manufacture recorded the important people, places, and events at Louis XIV's reign and the fruits of his enlightened patronage in the arts and sciences. The prints, which were often produced in series, were offered as diplomatic gifts and also sold individually to the public through the Gobelins and various print dealers who had secured permission to sell them.

Louis XIV both publicized the royal collection of art and antiquities and demonstrated his largess by making it available to the public through engraved series of antique medals, busts and statues, paintings, and tapestries. The collection included series illustrating the natural sciences, intended, of course, to document the work of the Academy of Sciences, established in 1666. This corpus of the artistic and scientific riches of France could be seen as an encyclopedist movement that preceded Diderot.

The artists employed by the Gobelins recorded the major events that underscored the greatness and glory of the king, such as successful military campaigns (fig. 46), diplomatic coups, and the founding of major institutions, as well as events of seemingly minor importance, such as court ceremonies, processions (fig. 4), royal entertainments (fig. 5), and the arrivals and departures

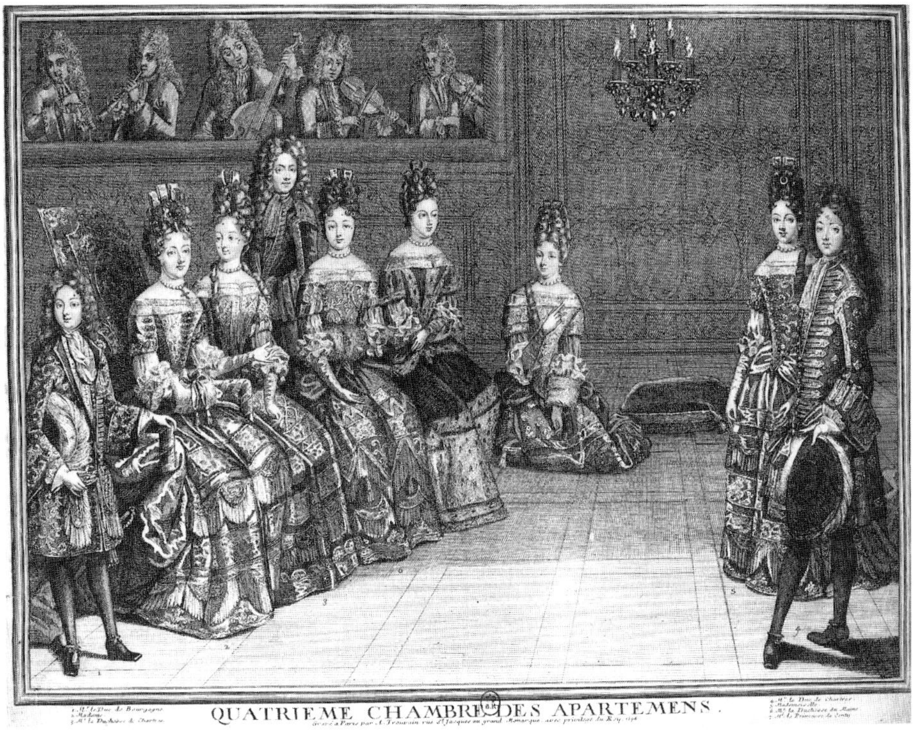

5. Antoine Trouvain, engraving, *The Fourth Chamber of the Apartments 1694 (Quatrième chambre des appartments 1694)*, 1694–98, Bibliothèque nationale de France, Paris. Cliché, Bibliothèque nationale de France, Paris.

of dignitaries, that indirectly sustained the ideological underpinnings of the Sun King. The depiction of births, deaths, and marriages elevated these normally private events and their participants to a position of public importance. In addition, topographical scenes of the royal properties, detailed delineations of interiors and exteriors, and depictions of monuments created a complete visual inventory of the vastness and richness of Louis's domain.

These images exhibit a stylistic uniformity. This is due in part to the workshop system at the Gobelins, where teams of artists worked on a single project; moreover, images were translated from one medium to another by different artists. Thus differences between particular artistic personalities were somewhat diminished, marking the productions of the Gobelins with a homogeneous, official look. In greater part, however, the visual uniformity of these documentary images is due to their descriptive function.

Certain conventions were employed because they best permitted the presentation of particular kinds of information and the suppression of other kinds. For example, as I will discuss in greater detail in the next chapter, in military scenes, such as Van der Meulen's *Marche on Courtrai* and *Dole Taken in the*

First Conquest (Figs. 27 and 46) or in scenes depicting large numbers of people and vast spaces, such as public processions (fig. 4), the artists used a bird's-eye view. This device allowed them to include all the important information pertinent to the event. Noteworthy participants who required identification could appear prominently in the foreground, and the large panorama provided adequate space for the "background information." For military scenes, this background information included the topography of conquered territories, the number of troops, and troop formations; scenes of public processions included the setting and configuration of the crowds, the notables who passed by, and the hierarchical ordering of the entourage accompanying them. Sometimes legends were included to ensure that important people and properties were correctly identified. The bird's-eye view was also employed for the views of royal chateaus, all the better to record every garden, fountain, and bit of statuary.

Artists described scenes set within a well-defined, enclosed space in a manner that is reminiscent of proscenium theatrical space. The background of these scenes appears as a backdrop with figures arranged on a stagelike area in front of it. Watteau, for example, did this in his only other historical painting, *Louis XIV Presenting the Cordon Blue to M. de Bourgogne* (fig. 3), in which one sees the major figures stiffly posed with no trace of emotion or expression.[22] It is interesting to compare the central female figure in *Louis XIV Presenting the Cordon Blue to M. de Bourgogne* with the central figure of *amoureuse* in *Departure*. Although both women have the same general pose – standing erect and facing forward with head slightly turned to the right – the subtle differences between the two are revealing. The open arms of the *amoureuse* in *Departure*, her upward gaze, and the tilt of her head mark the pose as a theatrical convention for imploring or beseeching. It is in fact a stock expression and pose found not only in the theater but also in the codes of representation followed in history painting.

The hyperlegible expressions and gestures of some figures in *Departure* call to mind Charles Le Brun's inventory of expressions explicitly described and illustrated in the *Conférence sur l'expression* – a work consulted by artists and actors alike.[23] In *Louis XIV Presenting the Cordon Blue to M. de Bourgogne* the rhetorical, expressive display of the body is limited. The king points to the infant Bourgogne, who is the focus of the ceremony; the lesser figures, who are arranged on the sidelines, show rather interchangeable poses with their arms held near their upright bodies. These inexpressive, restrained bodies seem "natural" compared to the figures in *Departure* whose bearings conform to the artifice of theatrical and aesthetic codes of expression.[24] Nevertheless, the relative naturalness of the figures in *Louis XIV Presenting the Cordon Blue to M. de Bourgogne* should also be seen as the result of artifice. The courtiers' corporeal attitudes conform to a set of conventions appropriate for court life and rituals. Their restrained postures and masklike expressions make perfect sense in this context where one did not want to draw attention to one's self. Rather, the performers in this ritual serve to focus attention on the honorific moment. In *Louis XIV Presenting the Cordon Blue to M. de Bourgogne* the male members of the royal family in the center direct their gazes at the viewer; then, through gesture and pose, they channel the viewer's attention to the awarding of the *cordon bleu.* The effect is one of a frozen tableau, staged for the benefit of the viewer. This frozen quality is appropriate, for in court ritual it was the identity of the people and their place within the social hierarchy that were essential to record. Interior scenes, such as the representation of one of Louis XIV's evening court entertainments in *The Fourth Chamber of the Apartments 1694* (fig. 5), and all scenes categorized as documentary image making are meant to be records of hierarchy, not of spontaneous or expressive behavior.

Artistic personality and compositional innovation were subjugated to a homogeneous and conventionalized mode of description. These images were intended only to "record"; in this sense, they were intended to be seen as neutral. Their meaning depended upon the larger context of the visual inventory of all great things, persons, and deeds. Merely to represent a subject elevated it, both explicitly and implicitly, to the realm of the historically significant within that context. Unlike allegorical history painting, in which contemporary events could be endowed with meaning through reference to another system of representation/signification, this documentary history painting assumed the other referent to be the truth. These images were meant to be taken as objective descriptions; but the detailed visual inventorying of people, places, and events all served a less transparent function in collectively constructing and validating an image of royal greatness and power.

We could more clearly affirm the assertion that Watteau invoked the documentary mode of history painting in *Departure* if we could determine how accurately Watteau described the setting. From maps and plans of Paris we know that the Hôtel Bourgogne, which housed the Italian Comedians' theater, was situated on the corner of rues Mauconseil and Française. The main facade faced rue Mauconseil and had a triple-portal entry. Above the central portal was a relief sculpture of scenes of the Passion. Primary access, however, was from the courtyard, which was reached through a porte cochere from the rue Française. The Hôtel underwent many alterations, and the city maps produced in the seventeenth and eighteenth centuries reflect these changes.[25] But these maps are not sufficiently detailed to provide us with a clear idea of how the building looked, let alone its setting, and no existing image is reliable enough to verify the correctness of Watteau's representation. D. V. Illingworth, who is an authority on the Hôtel Bourgogne and the theater within, suggests that Watteau could be depicting the petit corps de l'Hôtel.[26] The point of view would have been facing north, up the rue Française toward the rue Pavé. If we keep in mind that the engraving is probably the reverse of the original painting, Watteau's topographical arrangement seems accurate. However, we can never really know if Watteau's image is accurate. All we can accurately determine is that his image does not contradict the evidence we do have.

The historical nature of *Departure*'s subject, the probable accuracy of its scene, and the conventional devices that Watteau used in depicting the incident are all characteristic of official documentary image making. This suggests that Watteau drew upon the conventional mode to invoke the appearance of an objective chronicle of the event. One element, however, does not work properly within this context: the attitude of his figures. In documentary images the figures tend to be expressionless and without emotion. Their poses are rigid and reveal a minimum of action or motion. Yet in Watteau's *Departure* the figures react with an excess of emotion and motion. They do not display the attitudes proper to their situation. If we did not know from its title that the work depicts a real event, we might assume it was showing a scene from a play; in fact, the figures seem to be acting on a stage. Harlequin exhibits the conventional costume and actions that characterized his persona, as do Scaramouche, Polichinelle, Docteur Baloardo and Pierrot.[27] The central female figure follows the rules of declamation and gesture for an *amoureuse*: she avoids excessive gesticulation, leaves her hands open, and is *gracieuse* in her pose.[28] The unabashedly histrionic costumes, poses, gestures, and expressions in *Departure* undermine the historical nature and documentary function of the image. Moreover, they undermine the reading of the scene as an objective and truthful record. This incongruity becomes even more apparent if one compares Watteau's *Departure* to two other known images of this event.

The first of these images, in the Musée des Beaux-Arts, Le Havre, is an anonymous painting from the late seventeenth century entitled *The Expulsion of the Actors after the Suppression of the Commedia dell'Arte* (fig. 6). Both this work and Watteau's are set in a city street in front of a building, both depict the same moment, and both show an individual on a ladder posting a notice of the Comedians' expulsion. In the Le Havre painting, one notes a group of magistrates and officers on the left-hand side. The Comedians are depicted leaving the theater in a quiet, orderly fashion. From left to right are Octave, to whom the *greffier* hands a written order; Colombine, on her knees imploring clemency from D'Argenson; Pascariel, Mezzetin, Docteur Baloardo, Harlequin, and Pierrot. Polichinelle, whom Watteau included, is not depicted here.[29]

The most important difference, however, is one of demeanor. The Comedians depicted in the Le Havre painting are subdued, properly chastened, and resigned to their fate. They file obediently out of the theater, one by one, like sheep. The king's decree has effectively extinguished their theatrical identities; the actors and actresses have shrunk to ordinary petty offenders. From an official point of view, this is what had happened. Even Colombine's gesture of ap-

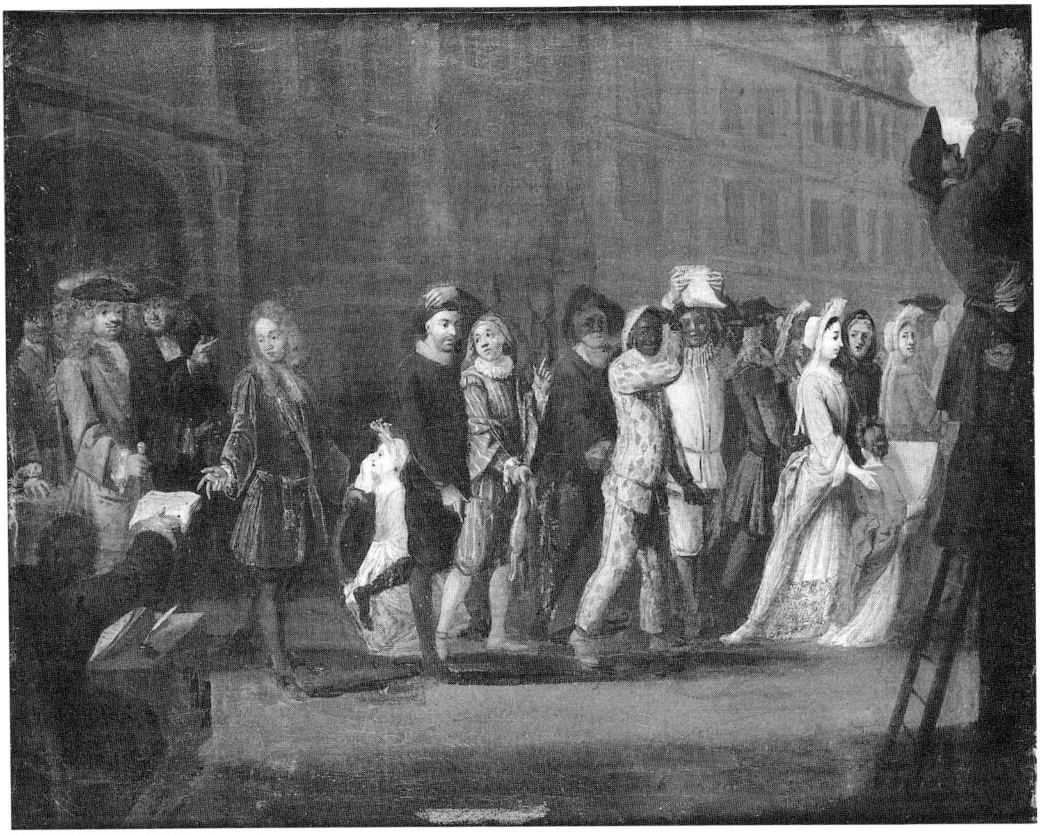

6. Anonymous, late seventeenth century, *The Expulsion of the Actors after the Suppression of the Commedia dell'Arte (Le renvoi des comédiens après la suppression de la Comédie-Italienne)*, Musée des Beaux-Arts, André Malraux, Le Havre, France. Photo, Giraudon/Art Resource, NY.

peal lacks the rhetorical flourish that would mark it as a theatrical convention. It is a nontheatrical gesture, completely appropriate and understandable within the context of the event. The posed quality of the figures and their subdued expressions remind us of the participants in the documentary scenes of court ritual. Although still in costume, the Comedians in the Le Havre painting have shed their dramatic personae and behavior; the entire scene is grounded in the realm of historical event.

Watteau's Comedians, by contrast, remain comedians and retain their theatrical identities and behavior. They employ the theatrical conventions of gesture and pose that were part of their stock characters' identity. In the Watteau painting, Harlequin, for example, is in the tightly wound, bent posture typical for Harlequin, and Mezzetin, just to the right of center behind the *amoureuse,* pulls his cap off with one hand while raising his other hand above his head – a gesture that indicates high emotion.[30] These figures respond with grief and surprise to be sure, but their responses are filtered through the hyperlegible code of a theatrical role. Their responses are clearly more appropriate to actors on the stage than to men and women who have just been excluded from Parisian society and deprived of their livelihood. Unlike the docile Comedians in the Le Havre painting, Watteau's are "acting up." They do not seem to take the event seriously, prompting the viewer also to question the gravity of the occasion.

The other version of this event is an anonymous, undated drawing that is known only through a photograph in the archives at the Bibliothèque de l'Opéra in Paris. This photograph carries, within a scrollwork frame at the bottom of the image, this title: *Burlesque of the Flight of the Italian Comedians Driven from Paris in 1697* (fig. 7). The scene is crudely rendered and was probably the work of an untrained artist, working for a popular audience. The figures are clumsy and puppetlike, and their range of scale varies.

Beyond questions of artistic merit and skill, the Opéra drawing differs in several respects from both the Le Havre painting and the Watteau engraving. The point of view is panoramic; the Opéra drawing depicts much more space and includes many more figures than the other two works. In this sense, it is closer to scenes of large-scale, outdoor processions than to interior scenes of court ceremony. One should view it as the title suggests: as a burlesque. Here we probably have a self-consciously derisive imitation of the kind of images that documented and ratified official history. In the left background, one sees a carriage approaching the central building, the Hôtel Bourgogne, accompanied by a number of dignitaries and soldiers. The Comedians, scattered throughout the mid-ground and foreground, are in costume and engaged in a variety of activities. Some are watching the events, some are helping to empty the theater, and others cry. On the far left-hand side is a group of four Harlequins who carry and play musical instruments; two of them are children. A similar group appears in the left-hand mid-ground, but this time it is a family of Polichinelles. On the far right-hand mid-ground is a cart filled with what appear to be stage sets and properties drawn by a tired-looking ass with a man on its back. In the right foreground are several theatrical characters surrounding two wigged and robed functionaries behind a desk. Upon the desk are two bags (perhaps of money), an inkwell and paper, and articles of clothing. We can assume that this had something to do with the business of closing and clearing the theater. One woman, who makes up part of this group, is wearing a stage device that makes her appear as if she is on horseback. We know that such a property did exist and was used in performances of *Arlequin Jason ou la toison d'or.*[31] An engraving, which may have publicized this piece, shows the same property with an accompanying commentary remarking on the ingenuity of the horse costumes.[32]

The Opéra drawing includes much more of this sort of detail than does either the Le Havre painting or the engraving after Watteau's painting. Whereas

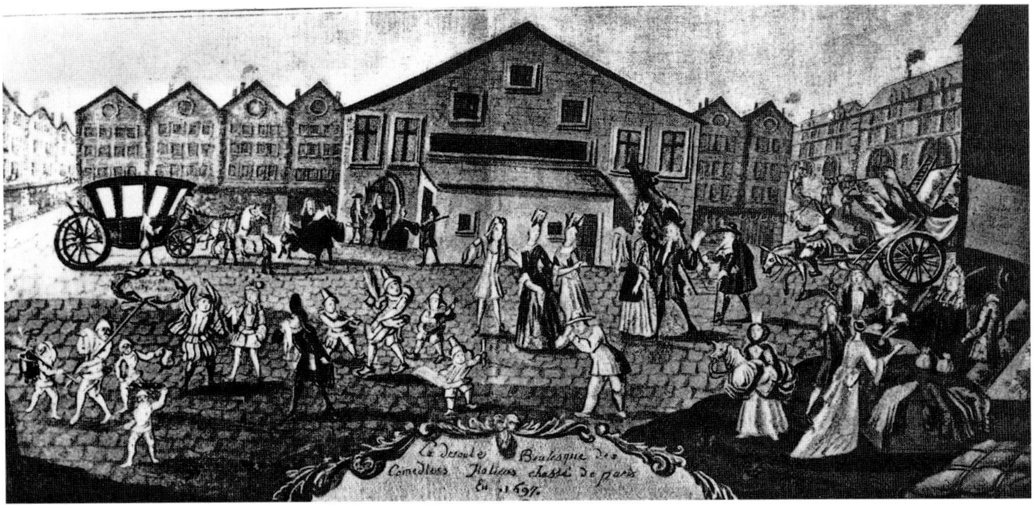

7. Anonymous, *Burlesque of the Flight of the Italian Comedians Driven from Paris in 1697 (La déroute burlesque des Comédiens italiens chassés de Paris en 1697)*, Bibliothèque nationale de France, Paris. Cliché, Bibliothèque nationale de France, Paris.

the latter two representations focus on the Comedians as they leave the theater, placing them in a closed setting, the Opéra drawing, with its more panoramic point of view, presents a variety of episodes. One can read it almost as continuous narrative: the arrival of the official entourage, the posting of the decree, the removal of stage properties and belongings, and the final accounting and administrative busywork. Here we see the whole process, the actual work, involved in effecting the banishment. By focusing on the mundane details, the Opéra drawing depicts a "behind the scenes" version of the event. It reveals the meaning of the banishment from another perspective. In so doing, this drawing raises questions about the significance of the event.

Like the Comedians in the Le Havre painting, most of those in the Opéra drawing have lost their theatrical identities, even though they remain in costume. In the Opéra drawing, we do see two groups of figures on the left side who are decidedly performing and playing musical instruments. Unlike the Comedians' behavior in Watteau's *Departure*, the histrionics of the performers in the Opéra drawing are just part of the burlesque. One reads this bit of street theater simply as an amusing aside to the main event. These are actors who are fooling around, entertaining themselves until their ordeal is over. This sort of theatricality fits into the real context of the scene without undermining it. After all, it is, as the title states, a *burlesque*.

Although different in their visual formats and conventions, the Le Havre painting and Opéra drawing more closely resemble each other than either resembles Watteau's version of the event. They both employ conventions that impart the illusion of the documentary; the Opéra burlesque, in addition, is openly satiric. While at first glance this documentary frame also seems to occur in *Departure,* Watteau's introduction of an inappropriate theatricality causes tension in the narrative structure of the work, and the viewer no longer can read the engraving with conviction as a depiction of a real event. Ultimately, this tension subverts the ideological content normally built into such documentary images.

It is my contention that Watteau consciously capitalized on the language and conventions of documentary history painting to question the implicit meaning of the genre. He did so by juxtaposing it with another genre that was equally recognizable and codified, that of the representation of theatrical performances, as practiced by his first master, Claude Gillot (1673–1722).[33]

Watteau, Gillot, and the Theater

Claude Gillot naturally drew upon the theater for subject matter for he was very much a part of its milieu. The Italian Comedians, as well as other performers and playwrights, were his friends. He designed sets and costumes, composed plays in the Italian tradition, and was probably the same Gillot who

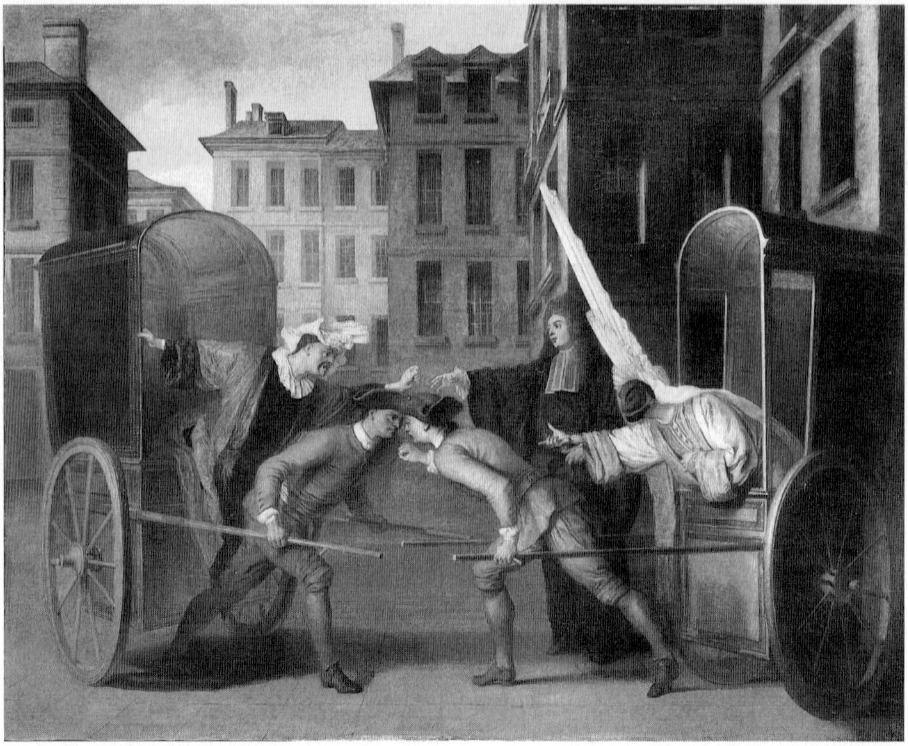

8. Claude Gillot, *The Two Carriages (Les deux carosses)*, c. 1707, Musée du Louvre, Paris. Cliché, Réunion des musées nationaux.

had a marionette theater at the Fair St. Germain.[34] Much of his oeuvre is theatrical in its subject. He produced quantities of drawings and engravings of individual actors and actresses, and his ornamental designs are peppered with characters from the theater. More important for our purposes are the representations he produced of specific scenes from pieces performed by the Italian Comedians before their banishment and by the troupes at the fairs afterward. Especially between 1703 and 1717, Gillot concentrated on this type of image. Significantly, these years include the period of Watteau's apprenticeship, from 1703–4 until 1708–9. Gillot produced numerous drawings of this type, and two series of engravings were done after his work: *Suite de quatre scènes comiques du Théâtre Italien* and *Livre de scènes comiques inventées par Gillot.* The former consists of four engravings after paintings by Gillot, and the latter of twelve images, engraved by Gabriel Huquier.[35]

The Two Carriages (figs. 8 and 9) and *Tomb of Master André: Harlequin a Glutton* (figs. 10 and 11), both of which appear in drawn, engraved, and painted versions, are good examples of this genre.[36] In both the action is

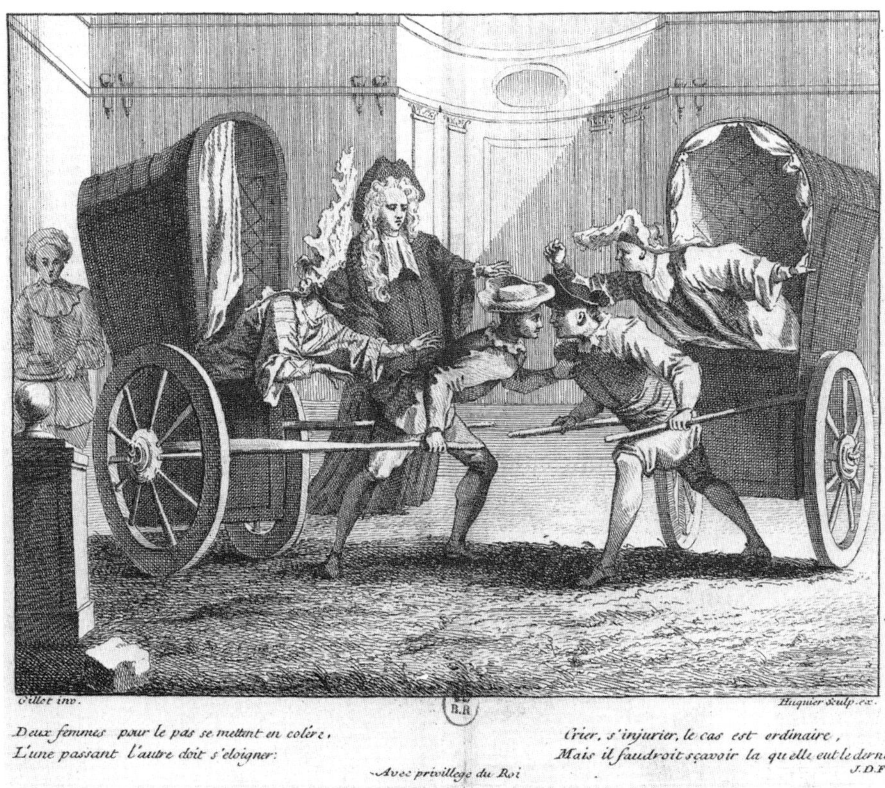

9. Gabriel Huquier, engraving after Claude Gillot, *The Two Carriages (Les deux carosses)*, Bibliothèque nationale de France, Paris. Cliché, Bibliothèque nationale de France, Paris.

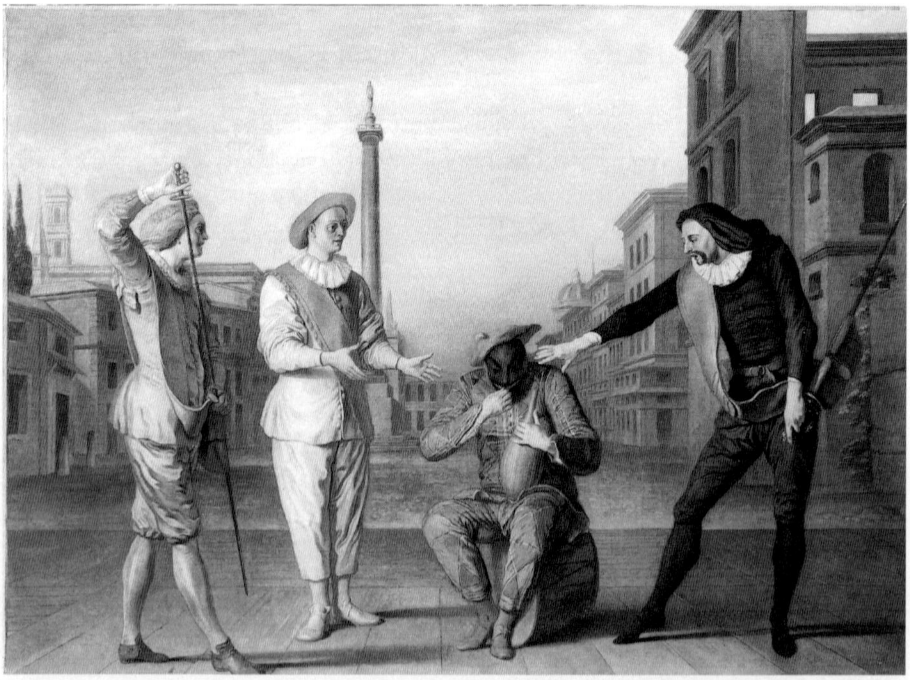

10. Claude Gillot, *The Tomb of Master André: Harlequin a Glutton (Tombeau de maître André: Arlequin gourmand)*, c. 1710, Musée du Louvre, Paris. Cliché, Réunion des musées nationaux.

clearly taking place on a stage. The actors are in costume and employ decidedly rhetorical, theatrical poses, gestures, and expressions. The background is stage scenery; no attempt has been made to suggest real, nonstage space. One can actually see the break between the vertical painted backdrop and the horizontal stage floor. What Gillot represents in these works is a performance, complete with the cues and conventions that let the viewer know that the performance is taking place on a stage and not in real life.

The Two Carriages illustrates the final scene in the play *La Foire St. Germain,* in which two carriages meet in a narrow street, resulting in a comic argument involving the carriagemen and passengers.[37] Gillot depicts an Italianate city street as the backdrop, five actors who participate in the scene, and the two carriages. There is nothing in this painting that could not have appeared in the actual performance. The engraved version by Huquier, however, is somewhat different. For example, in the engraving the Italianate city street in the painting has been replaced by a more ambiguous architectural backdrop, the costumes are not the same, and instead of the regular, smooth tiles of the painting's stage floor, the engraving shows an irregular surface, more suggestive of a "real" street than of the theater. The second example of the genre, *Harlequin a Glutton,* illustrates a scene from *The Tomb of Master André* in

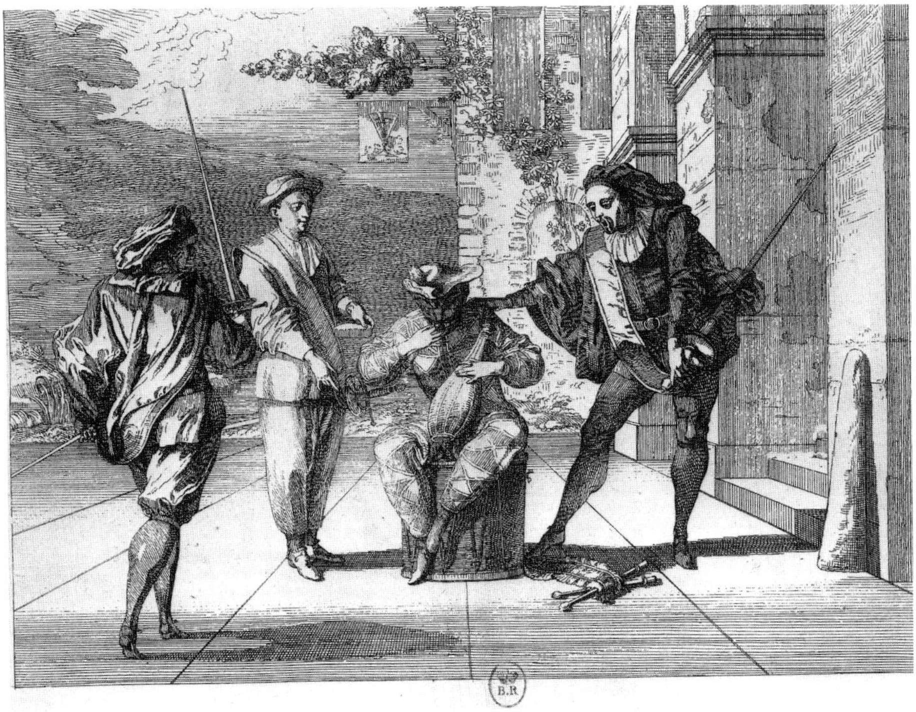

11. Gabriel Huquier, engraving after Claude Gillot, *The Tomb of Master André: Harlequin a Glutton (Tombeau de maître André: Arlequin gourmand)*, Bibliothèque nationale de France, Paris. Cliché, Bibliothèque nationale de France, Paris.

which Harlequin acts as a drunken arbiter between Scaramouche and Mezzetin.[38] Again, there is nothing depicted that does not appear in the "script." There are no incidental people, objects, descriptive bits of background, or allegorical embellishments that refer to the world outside that of the play.

Here again the painting and the engraving and drawing display some differences. Thus in the painting the backdrop represents an Italianate cityscape whereas in the engraving and drawing the backdrop is a country inn with a bit of landscape. In both images everything is understood by means of theatrical conventions and in relation to the particular script they illustrate.[39] These scenes are like enlarged book illustrations, especially the frontispieces for plays. Such frontispieces frequently depict particular scenes from the plays in the book, as in the example from *The Two Harlequins* (fig. 12), and they employ the same theatrical conventions that we see in Gillot's work. Are Gillot's images mere illustrations, reflecting how a scene looked at a particular moment on the stage? Probably not: they are most likely composite creations. The differences between the painted and engraved versions of two scenes do not necessarily mean that Gillot was recording different performances, with

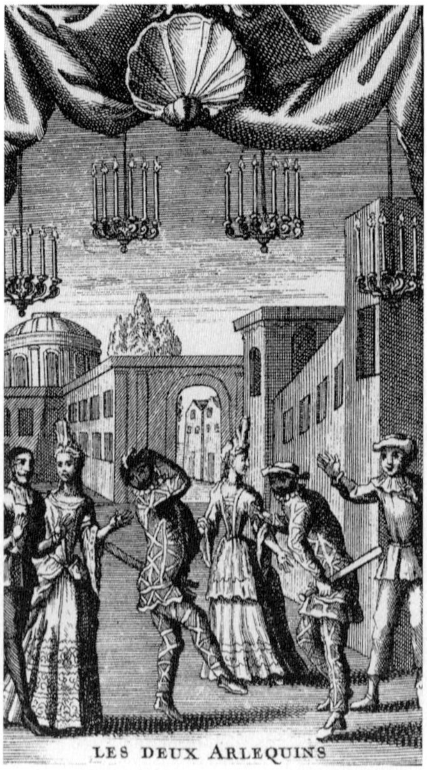

12. Anonymous, frontispiece to *The Two Harlequins (Les deux Arlequins)*, in Gherardi, *Le théâtre Italien de Gherardi*, Amsterdam, 1701. Photograph, Jennifer Laffoon.

different scenery, of these plays. The "natural" irregularity of the foreground in the engraved version of *The Two Carriages* does not reflect, at least to the best of my knowledge, a practice of piling real dirt on a theater stage. This same kind of slippage within the conventions of theatrical illustration can be seen in another engraving representing a different scene from *The Tomb of Master André* (fig. 13). On the left-hand side of the image the stage setting is clearly defined: a line separates the stage floor from the backdrop, and the wall appears to be unconnected to the setting. On the right-hand side, in contrast, there is no defining wall, and the back line of the backdrop has dissolved, disrupting an unambiguous reading of the space as theatrical.

Gillot's theatrical scenes also bear a certain resemblance to the documentary scenes of court ritual in that both are images that refer to a specific event. Moreover, both utilize similar formal conventions: an artificial posing of figures before an area that can be understood as background or backdrop. The major difference between these two categories of images is in the type of spectacle they represent and the identities of their participants. Their formal qualities are similar, but the cues, or system of signification, that allow the viewer to determine their contexts are not. A viewer in the seventeenth or eighteenth century would never mistake one type of scene for another.

Nor would a seventeenth- or eighteenth-century viewer ever confuse one theater piece for another. Contemporary viewers were very familiar with the iconography of the theater. As Marianne Roland-Michel and Daniel Rabreau have pointed out, the viewing public could immediately identify a scene from a particular play in an image where the modern viewer might recognize only a generalized theatrical scene.[40] Theatergoing was part of one's entrée into the greater social world. Learning about the theater was something of a coming-of-age ritual.[41] Many plays satirically pointed out differences between theatrical genres, giving spectators an ongoing apprenticeship about the

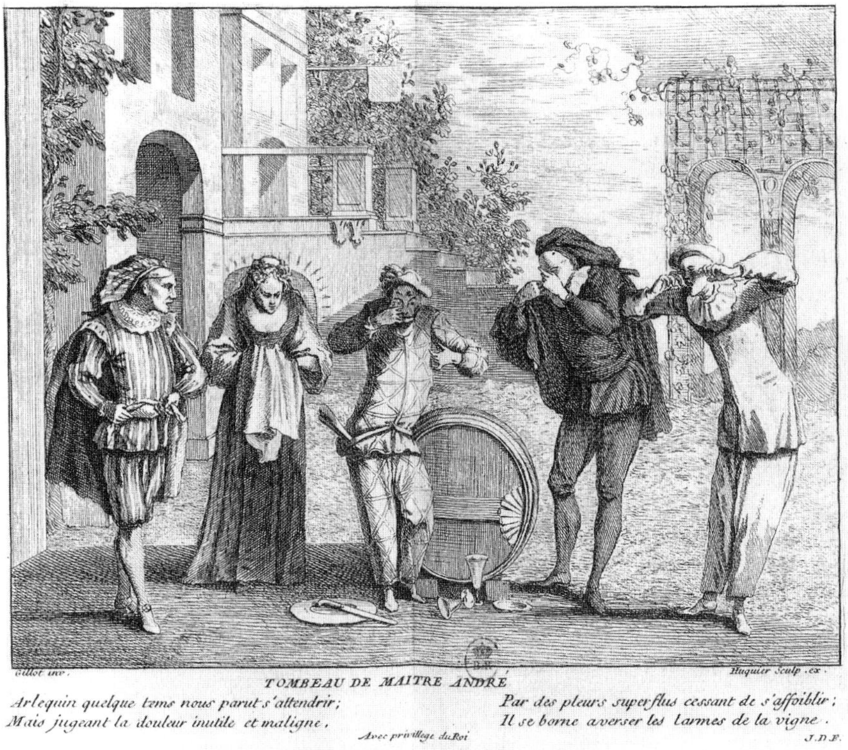

13. Gabriel Huquier, engraving after Claude Gillot, *Tomb of Master André (Tombeau de maître André)*, Bibliothèque nationale de France, Paris. Cliché, Bibliothèque nationale de France, Paris.

rules of the dramatic arts. Their participation in debates in cafés about performances and in amateur theatrics further contributed to the creation of theatrical connoisseurs. The theatergoing public of the seventeenth and eighteenth centuries was up to date on current theatrical personalities and events and would have understood allusive references to specific performers and plays.

Within the larger framework of theatre iconography was a commonly understood hierarchy of genre.[42] Even persons who never went to the theater could distinguish among the various theatrical forms practiced by the Opéra, Comédie Française, Comédie Italienne, and Opéra Comique and by the more popular theaters at fairs and identify the kinds of pieces appropriate to each. The understanding of this iconography was also reinforced by the dissemination of images. It is worth noting that in Gillot's series of individual theatrical figures, engraved by Joulain, the text below each image describes the character's "pedigree" and role. Print shops and peddlers were well supplied with images for sale of reigning theatrical personalities, stock characters, and theatrical scenes. Theatre imagery permeated popular as well as high culture.[43] The only place this imagery did not play a significant role was in the academy. One might even say that in France an unofficial national mythology of the theater coexisted with the official mythology of the Sun King and the state.

Whereas Gillot chronicled scenes drawn from the theater in the same way that official artists chronicled events from the life of the king, Watteau's *Departure* seems to do both. Watteau depicts a subject from official history – although it is a subject that is also part of theatrical history – and places it within a context that is neither entirely historical nor entirely theatrical. However, *Departure* has the look of Gillot's theatrical scenes, such as *The Two Carriages* and *The Tomb of Master André*, and we can see just how much Watteau absorbed from Gillot. Watteau's figures have overly small and dainty feet, like Gillot's. As does Gillot, Watteau shows his figures in tight, rigid poses. Watteau also learned his method of composing paintings from Gillot: he selects his figures from a preexisting stock of individual sketches and then arranges them in a setting.[44] *Departure* and *Harlequin a Glutton* were composed in this way, and the resulting effect is not so much that of a preconceived and unified composition as it is one of a collection of parts. It is not surprising that Watteau's *Departure* so clearly resembles Gillot's theatrical scenes, for most art historians agree that the work was a collaborative effort. Watteau composed and executed the work, drawing upon Gillot's stock of figure sketches.

More important than the specific stylistic similarities of *Departure* and Watteau's work in general is the theatrical context that Watteau adopted. In *Departure,* Watteau employs Gillot's theatrical framework. It would be wrong to assume, however, that he did this out of ignorance or inability or that he was so thoroughly under the influence of Gillot that he knew no other way to frame the scene. Indeed, I believe that Watteau intentionally created this dislocation between the realms of the theater and of official history.

This tension and ambiguity is most apparent in the main group of figures in *Departure,* who respond in ways that are inappropriate to the historical context of the subject. Other elements in the painting do little to clarify this ambiguity; they do not provide the clues and cues that would allow the viewer to overlook either the theatricality of the main figures or the real nature of the subject matter. Instead of tipping the balance in favor of either a purely historical or a purely theatrical reading, the other parts of the painting, I would argue, were consciously manipulated by Watteau to underscore this basic disjunctive. Thus the street scene and background, which, as far as we know, do not openly contradict a true representation of the actual place, could also be read as stage scenery.

The nontroupe figures function in a similar fashion. The boy selling tarts is reminiscent of engravings from the popular *Cris de Paris* engraved series that depicted the various *métiers* of the street.[45] He is someone we would expect to see on a real Parisian street. The man and the women who peer out from the windows are clearly not part of the spectacle they observe. As nonperformers, they subvert a completely theatrical reading. Yet at the same time they subvert a completely historical reading, for it is possible to fit them into a theatrical context. The boy is selling his wares to the viewers of this real spectacle just as vendors sold refreshments to theater audiences, and the men and women who watch from the windows above the street remind one of actual theatergoers seated in loges located above a stage.[46] These figures, although not part of the cast, can be seen as an integral part of the theater.

Watteau has consistently located everything in *Departure* in both worlds yet completely in neither. Street becomes stage, neighborhood inhabitants become audience, actors become ordinary people, history becomes theater, and back again; a stable frame of reference refuses to fix itself. Watteau structures *Departure* so that it only confounds and raises questions; it never clarifies or answers.

Because he was so thorough in his manipulation of codes and cues on every level, one must assume that Watteau had a particular reason for this manipulation. We wonder why he chose to depict this particular subject in this way; it certainly must have had some meaning for him, for Watteau was only thirteen years old in 1697, and living in Valenciennes, when the Italian Comedians were banished.

Paul Manz and Virgil Josz both offer suggestions about the importance of the subject.[47] They hypothesize that the reentry of the Italian Comedians in 1716, after the death of Louis XIV, inspired Watteau to paint the subject of their banishment. Manz goes as far as to state: "we can even consider it certain that, in order to reconstruct this well-known event, Watteau utilized the characters and costumes put before his eyes by the new troupe."[48] Although plausible, Manz and Josz's hypothesis does not work out in fact. On the basis of stylistic evidence, Watteau most likely painted *Departure* during his apprenticeship to Claude Gillot, which ended at least seven years before the New Italian troupe appeared under the auspices of the Regent in 1716. Watteau could not possibly have used the characters and costumes of this new troupe as models for his painting. More likely, Watteau's reconstruction of the event is based on Gillot's figure sketches and on verbal accounts. Nevertheless, this argument suggests that Watteau's *Departure* could be a tribute to the Italian Comedians. By depicting the Comedians' banishment, Watteau could be invoking the triumph of their return. And implicit in the triumph of their return is a critique of the Sun King. As Josz points out, the painting would have been a monument turned upside down.

Émile Dacier too intimates that *Departure* may have been conceived as a tribute to the Italian Comedians, but for different reasons.[49] He believes that both Watteau and Gillot were familiar with a painting known by its inscription *The French and Italian Comedians since 60 Years Ago and More. Painted in 1670* (fig. 14) and that Watteau drew upon its figural composition for

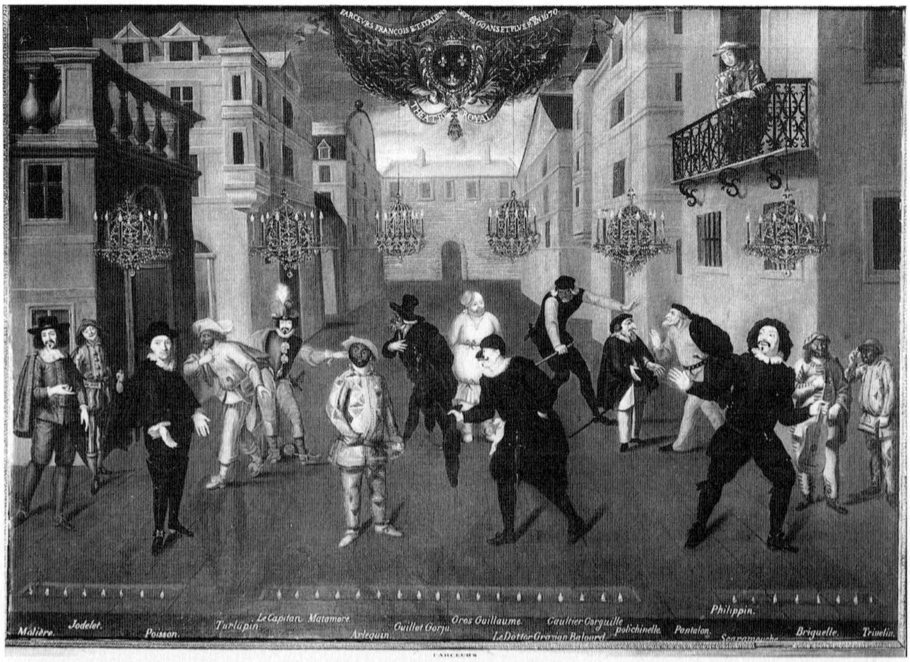

14. Attributed to Verio, *The French and Italian Comedians since 60 Years Ago and More. Painted in 1670 (Les farceurs français et italiens depuis 60 ans et plus. Peint en 1670)*, 1670, Musée et Bibliothèque de la Comédie Française, Paris. Cliché, Comédie Française, Paris.

Departure.[50] *The French and Italian Comedians* depicts fifteen actors in various costumes and poses, arranged on a stage, the set for which is a city scene. Below each figure, in a margin at the bottom of the painting, is the name of the character. A figure on the far left, designated as Molière, presents the other actors. Since eight of the actors who had made these characters famous were dead by the time the painting was done, one must conclude that the painting was meant to be a tribute to the great characters, past and present, of the royal troupes that existed up to 1670. To my mind, the figural composition of *Departure* bears only a generic resemblance to that of *The French and Italian Comedians,* in which we see the figures evenly distributed across the space of the stage. If Watteau was familiar with *The French and Italian Comedians,* one can conjecture that it was the painting's content as much as its composition that influenced him. *The French and Italian Comedians* may have provided the artist with a preexisting formula for expressing the idea of a tribute. As well as adapting the composition, Watteau may have been adopting the content.

In *The French and Italian Comedians,* the characters are clearly identified by the text at the bottom of the painting. Georges Monval has pointed out that *The French and Italian Comedians* is a pastiche of sorts.[51] It was probably produced for mass consumption (Monval cites three other existing versions of this work) by one of the hack artists working on the Pont Nôtre Dame. The artist merely lined up, like so many pots on a shelf, well-known portraits of the characters, which had been engraved between 1630 and 1670 by Huret, Faulk, Rosselet, Mariette, and Le Blonde. There are no known engraved portraits by Gillot, however, or by anyone else, that depict the particular characters in exactly the same poses in which they appear in *Departure.* There is only a single drawing by Gillot that depicts a character similar in type and pose to those in *Departure.* This drawing, in the Louvre, represents a weeping female figure such as found in the center of *Departure,* although Gillot does not provide a specific theatrical identity for her.[52]

One can easily identify the stock characters in *Departure* by their costumes and conventionalized attitudes, which appear and reappear in numerous engravings. The female figure who anchors the composition in the center is probably the leading female *amoureuse.* Behind her, two figures are positioned so as to create a frame. The figure to the left is probably the maidservant Colombine in the stock "weep of despair" pose. The costumes of the female characters were neither as distinctive nor as fixed as those of the male characters. The female costumes tended to change with fashion. The figure to the right who pulls at his floppy hat in a gesture of comic despair, is clearly identifiable as Mezzetin by his traditional costume. The supplicating figure to Mezzetin's right is Pierrot, also clearly identifiable by his costume. Slightly behind and to the left of Colombine are three other members of the troupe: from right to left there are the hunchbacked Polichinelle; one of the troupe's *amoureux,* either Octave or Leandre; and Docteur Baloardo, who, in keeping with his character as a pedant, is holding a weighty tome. In the foreground are two pairs of figures that further frame the figure of the leading *amoureuse*: to the right is the magistrate and the tart seller, and to the left is Scaramouche in the near foreground with his hands upheld in a gesture of surprise. He wears his traditional black costume with white ruff and floppy black hat. Behind him, and slightly to his left, is probably the best-known character from the Italian Comedy, Harlequin, dressed in his diamond-patch suit and black mask.

If Watteau did conceive of *Departure* as a tribute, one wonders if he was intending to honor the great characters of the Italian Comedy in general or the existing troupe at the time of their banishment. We know the names of the actors and actresses who were expelled and the roles that they played when the troupe was suppressed.[53] Of course, throughout the Italian Comedians' long career in France a number of performers may have played a single character. Engravings that specify the name of the actor or actress, however, are of little aid in pinning down identities in *Departure.* The prescribed costumes and stylized gestures effectively disguise individual likenesses. For example, an engraving of Tiberio Fiorelli in his role as Scaramouche (fig. 15) is indistinguishable from an engraving of his successor, Guiseppe Tortoriti, in the same role (fig.

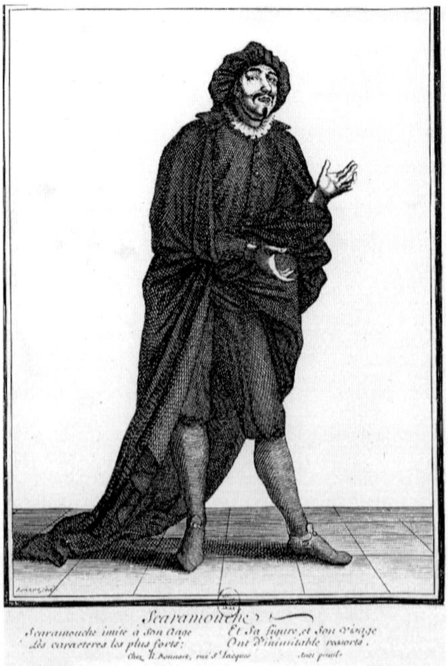

15. Nicolas Bonnart, engraving, *Tibero Fiorelli as Scaramouche*, Bibliothèque nationale de France, Paris. Cliché, Bibliothèque nationale de France, Paris.

16).[54] Likewise, images of Angelo Lolli as the Docteur and Marc Antonio Romagnesi as the Docteur are interchangeable.[55] Only the print's title lets one know who is being depicted. Thus it is impossible to determine whether *Departure* is supposed to be a generalized tribute to the great actors and actresses of the Italian Comedy or a historically accurate salute to the troupe as it existed at the moment of its suppression.

This ambiguity does not exist in *The French and Italian Comedians,* nor is it seen in the engraving that appeared as the frontispiece of the *Grand Almanach Historique de 1689,* entitled *The Royal Troupe of Comedians Performing at the Theater of the Hotel Bourgogne, all Types of Pieces . . .* (fig. 17).[56] Here we see the stage of the theater at the Hôtel Bourgogne and the troupe of Italian Comedians. It is evident that this work was intended as a specific tribute to the contemporary troupe just as *The French and Italian Comedians* was a general tribute to the great characters of the French stage. In both images the title, or text, and the image correspond. The actors are clearly on a stage, and, although they are not performing a play, they are presenting themselves to the viewer in their roles as Comedians. Both images describe characters, stage sets, and even mundane details, such as the candles at the front of the stage and the chandeliers.

In their clarity of context and intent, the *Alamanch* engraving and *The French and Italian Comedians* are far more ideologically correct than is Watteau's ambiguous *Departure.* Since its printed publication would have required the permission of the king, the *Almanach* engraving, in particular, illustrates an aspect of official documentary image making. The identities of the stock characters in this image matter little; their personal identities matter even less. What does count is their identity as a royal troupe, which exists only because of the benevolence of the king. The image of these Comedians is important in the same way that images of royal châteaux, antique medals, and conquered territories are, as objects belonging to, and under the control of, Louis XIV. Architectural views, representations of the royal collection, topographical scenes, and this image of the royal troupe are all part of the visual inventory of royal holdings. In paying tribute to the material existence, success, and well-being of the Italian Comedians, the *Almanach* engraving indirectly pays tribute to Louis XIV as well.

Departure undermines these ideological assumptions from two standpoints. First, by depicting a historical event as theatrical spectacle, its clash of contexts and genres prevents us from taking the real event seriously; it makes a mockery of the built-in ideological assumptions that documentary history painting ratified. If Watteau did intend *Departure* as a tribute to the Italian Comedians, the context of the event in which he places them denies the indirect tribute to Louis XIV and his domain. Second, the actual expulsion of the Italian Comedians added little glow to the glory of Louis XIV and his rule. It was a moment of shame rather than of celebration. The event was certainly not the high point of the Italian Comedians' career, either. If Watteau was seeking to honor the Italian Comedians, one wonders why he chose to do so in a painting that depicts the moment of their royal disinheritance.

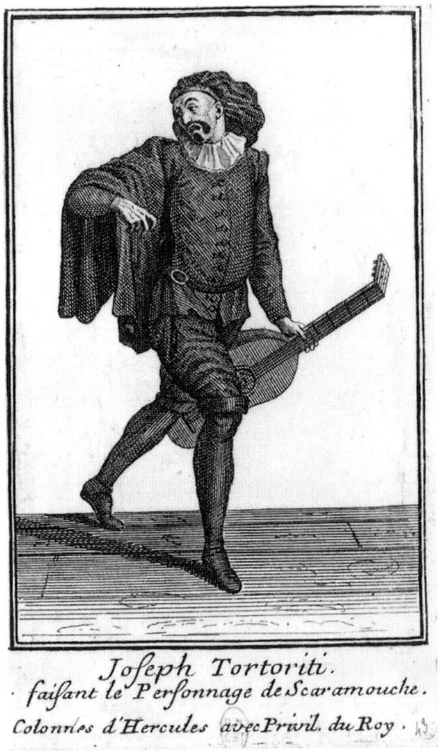

16. B. Picart, engraving, *Guiseppe Tortoriti as Scaramouche*, Bibliothèque nationale de France, Paris. Cliché, Bibliothèque nationale de France, Paris.

Watteau's *Departure* should not be seen merely as an ironic statement. If one examines the larger dimensions surrounding the expulsion of the Italians, and its later consequences, certain aspects of *Departure* begin to make perfect sense: the disjunctures and ambiguities begin to produce meaning rather than obscure it. Ultimately, *Departure* does reveal itself to be a tribute; it is a tribute, however, not only to the Italian Comedians but also to their power of subversion.

The Théâtre Italien versus the Comédie Française

The event that precipitated the king's expulsion of the Italian Comedians in 1697, the anticipated performance of *La Fausse Prude*, was really only the last straw. The Italian Comedians had become a problem and an embarrassment. They were officially objectionable on moral, financial, and political grounds. This piece from the *Mercure Historique et Politique de la Haye*, of June 1697, one month after the expulsion, speculates about the reasons for the Comedians' downfall:

The misfortune of the Italian Comedians happened so unexpectedly that there were only a few who weren't surprised. Everyone speculated about it, but those speculations varied widely. Some maintained that the principal reason for the Comedians' downfall was their refusal to suppress some foul expressions and the numerous indecent gestures which filled their performances, even though they had been ordered to do so several times. Others said that the court of France wanted to give itself completely to devoutness; that, after the publication of the Peace [of Ryswick], the court resolved to suppress all manner of entertainments, and began by banishing the Foreign Comedians. Some maintained that the Comedians had wanted to perform a new piece by Le Noble, titled *The False Prude,* which contained a most unflattering likeness of a woman highly regarded by the king. Finally, there are those who are convinced that the king banished the Comedians because they were impudents who felt no scruple at poking fun at people, going even so far as to mock members of the Royal Family, as they once did with Mme. la Dauphine. Some of these reasons could well have contributed to the Italian Comedians' banishment. But I think that the principal, or indeed, the only reason for this affair is the 18.000 livres the king would save each year; why support such an expenditure only to entertain the Parisians, at a time when the court is in dire financial straits?[57]

Other journals and gazettes published outside France speculate in the same manner as the *Mercure Historique et Politique de la Haye.* The *Gazette d'Amsterdam* of 23 May 1697 relates the event and concludes, "We have no idea of the *véritable* cause of this disgrace."[58] This can be read to mean that the publication had no idea of the "*véritable*" cause because no "official" reason was stated. Germain Brice reports the same information, or lack of it, in *Descriptions de Paris* of 1698; the expulsion occurred "for reasons which have not been published."[59]

All the reasons cited in the *Mercure Historique et Politique de la Haye* certainly played a part of the Comedians' growing disfavor with the king and their ultimate banishment. Toward the end of his reign, while under the influence of the deeply religious Madame de Maintenon, Louis turned against the theater. As did the king, so followed the court, at least in appearance. In the atmosphere of increasing piety, theatergoing was frowned upon. The Duchess d'Orléans sums up this attitude nicely: "Since the king no longer goes there [to the theater], it has become a sin."[60] Louis XIV and Boussuet, along with Madame de Maintenon and the clergy, headed an antitheater movement that gathered increasing momentum in official quarters.[61]

The Italians were particularly vulnerable to this movement, and indeed contributed to its impetus, because their pieces had traditionally been less morally uplifting and decorous than those of their officially sponsored counterparts,

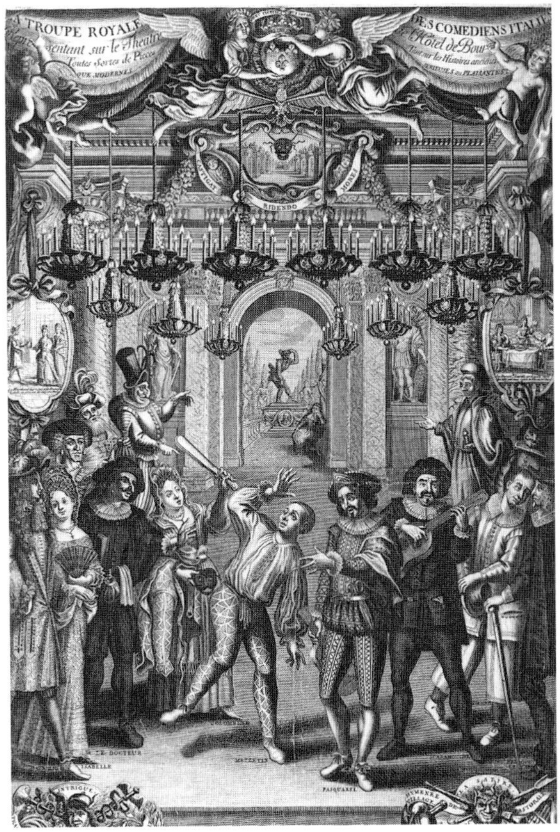

17. Nicolas Larmessin II, engraving for *Grand Almanach Historique de 1689,* entitled *The Royal Troupe of Comedians Performing at the Theater of the Hotel Bourgogne, All Types of Pieces . . . (La Troupe Royale des Comédiens représentant sur le théâtre de l'Hôtel de Bourgogne, toutes sortes de pièces . . .),* 1689, Bibliothèque nationale de France, Paris. Cliché, Bibliothèque nationale de France, Paris.

the Comédie Française and the Opéra. Slapstick, gross parody, and earthy humor had always been mainstays of the Italians' comedies; the pieces published in Gherardi's *Théâtre Italien* are full of normally unmentionable scatological and sexual references. The Italians were also very outspoken in their criticism of people and manners; they openly ridiculed values, virtues, and institutions that both the clergy and the Crown held dear.

Within the Italian tradition, lapses from conventional standards of decorum had been more readily tolerated. In fact, the Comedians' excursions into otherwise prohibited areas were their major attraction. The theatergoing public expected to see and thoroughly enjoyed the Italians' less refined, and less than innocent, humor.

Yet although the Italians generally seemed to get away with things, they could not entirely avoid official reprimands or reprisals. In 1681 and 1682 the troupe had repeated problems with the police because of the licentious nature of their satires.[62] They received a warning in 1688 to cut "all the double entendres that are too risqué."[63] The following year, there was talk of sending them away.[64] These warnings seem to have little effect because, as the *Relations Véritables* of 31 December 1694 states: "the Sorbonne, having assembled concerning the theater and the opera . . . once more demonstrated to M. l'Archevêque, that the Italian Comedians were too bold in their pieces."[65]

Many of the contemporary Dutch journals and gazettes that reported on the expulsion cite the foul expressions and indecent attitudes of the Comedians as a major cause of their demise.[66] The Italians delighted in shocking and made little attempt to curb their improprieties. Official warnings had little effect, and in a climate of increasing royal sanctimony, these offenders were an embarrassment to the Crown. That the public loved them was an even greater embarrassment. In the interests of public morality, his own reputation, and the preservation of his authority in the realm of culture, Louis XIV could ill afford to support this troupe. The *Mercure Historique* suggests, moreover, that Louis XIV could not afford the troupe financially; which element played a greater role in their banishment – money or morals – was debated in gazettes and journals published outside of France.

Certainly, there is no doubt as to the desperate state of French finances in 1697. Yet the treasury stood to gain little from the Italians' expulsion. The Comédie Française and the Opéra had much more to gain from the troupe's banishment.

The Comédie Française was founded in 1680, when, by royal order, the troupe at the Hôtel Bourgogne and the troupe at the Hôtel Guénégaud were merged to form a large, single troupe.[67] According to the *lettre de cachet* that established this institution: "His Majesty wills that only the said troupe can perform theatrical pieces in Paris, prohibiting all other Comedians performing in French from establishing themselves in the City or outskirts of Paris without his express order."[68] Thus the Comédie Française held the monopoly on theatrical performances spoken in French. Likewise, the Opéra held the monopoly on musical performances. The Opéra was under the aegis of the Académie Royale de Musique, founded by the powerful Jean-Baptiste Lully in 1672.[69] No other opera company was allowed to perform. An ordinance of 1672 indicates just how far-reaching was Lully's control. It states that because the use of musicians by other troupes would "bring about considerable detriment to the works performed in the theater of St. Jean-Baptiste Lully," no other troupe could employ more than two singers and six musicians.[70] The use of dancers or of an orchestra between acts by any other troupe was also prohibited.

The royal troupe of Italian Comedians, founded in 1653 and settling permanently in their theater at the Hôtel Bourgogne in 1680, was the third royally sponsored troupe.[71] Although all three groups received subsidies from the Crown, they relied heavily on the receipts from their performances and on private patronage. Thus they competed among themselves to attract spectators and favors. The popularity of the Italians was resented by both of the other troupes, but particularly by the Comédie Française.

In July 1687 the king ordered the Comédie Française to vacate their theater in the Hôtel Guénégaud. After much unsuccessful searching for a different theater, the troupe was obliged to build a new home. The king did not increase their subsidy and seemed indifferent to their plight. Because of this enormous expense, the troupe underwent a long period of financial difficulty. To compensate, they raised their price of admission; but it was the Italians and the Opéra who profited by increased attendance.

The Italians, who could never leave well enough alone, twisted the knife by mocking the Comédie Française's troubles in one of their plays.[72] This was nothing new, however. The Italians frequently satirized the pieces performed by the other troupes as well as their style of performing. They referred to themselves as *singes en tout* because they grotesquely imitated what was presented at the two other theaters.[73] For example, Dancourt's *Foire de Bezons* premiered at the Comédie Française in August 1695. It enjoyed a great success and was still playing in October when the Italians' "aped" version, *Retour de la Foire de Bezons,* premiered at the Hôtel Bourgogne. Corneille's *Toison d'or,* which was performed thirty-two times in 1683 and 1684 by the Comédie Française, reappeared in the Italians' repertoire as *Arlequin Jason ou la toison d'or.* The Comédie Française performed Boursault's *Fables de Ésope,* and the Italian Comedians responded with Le Noble's *Fables de Ésope,* and so on. It is characteristic that in *Departure* the players mock their own plight!

This mocking repartee was an accepted part of the Parisian theatrical scene, but it certainly did not endear the Italians to the Comédie Française, especially in light of that troupe's financial worries and the king's indifference to their plight. The Comédie Française also held another grudge against the Italians. In 1681 bits of French dialogue began creeping into the Italian Comedians' performances, and by 1682 most of the plays were either entirely in French or "frenchified" enough to be readily understood by a non-Italian audience. The Comédie Française viewed this as a violation of their monopoly on French dialogue. They complained, but no action was taken against the Italians until their expulsion. A *mémoire,* written in 1708, states:

> In the year 1689, after the Italian Comedians had disobeyed several times the king's order not to include scenes in French in their performances because the French Comedians had complained about it and because this violated the French troupe's royal privileges, His Majesty, informed of the Italians' frequent refusals to obey, dismissed them, and ordered M. le Duc de Beauvilliers to close their theater, which was done.[74]

Although it is doubtful that this was the major cause of the Italians' expulsion, their infringement on the rights of the Comédie Française did not act in their favor. Their use of French dialogue only added to an already long list of sins. *Les Nouvelles extraordinaires de Leide* reported on 6 June 1697 that the Italian Comedians hoped to reinstate themselves, and if they were allowed to continue their performances, "they could no longer speak French, but still Italian in their performances."[75] Purging their plays of French dialogue was scarcely penance enough to restore them to their stage, for the Italians were a moral outrage, a financial burden, and most important, a political threat.

The Italians were frequently imprudent and impudent in their allusions to official royal policy and important public figures. Aurelio, one of the actors, was expelled from the Italian troupe in 1689 for his remarks about Louis XIV's hostile attitude toward the pope.[76] In *Retour de la Foire de Bezons,* first performed in 1695, the Italians openly depicted a *commissaire* at Châtelet as a forger and thief.[77] This too thinly disguised portrait drew a severe reprimand from the authorities:

> [I]f it happens that they strike any indecent attitudes, use doubtful language or anything which goes against standards of respectability, his Majesty will destroy them and send them back to Italy. To this end, his Majesty would like you to send a person in whom you have confidence to the theater each day to report back what goes on there. Finally, his Majesty would like you to close their theater at the first infraction.[78]

This passage reveals the extent to which the hostilities between the Italians and the royal authorities had become a showdown and a struggle for power. Louis XIV would go to the limit to control these Comedians: he would "break" them if they did not obey. In question here is less theatrical propriety than the larger failure of Louis XIV to maintain his authority, or at least the illusion of it. Moreover, this incident illustrates the Italians' tactics in subverting the credibility of the Crown.

The Italians never named the dishonest *commissaire* in their play but, because of the scandal, the public had no trouble understanding the allusion. The royal authorities could have responded either by censoring this offensive passage or by letting it pass. If they had let it pass, the Comedians might have continued with ever greater insults. That the Comedians had dared be so insolent in the first place was an affront to the authority and benevolence of the king. If the authorities had censored the passage, it would have been virtually an admission of the *commissaire*'s true identity and his guilt. Censorship could only have drawn attention to the situation, confirming what was merely implied in the play, magnifying its importance. Suppression tended to play into the hands of the Comedians, certainly one reason that they were allowed such wide liberty. Thus in their letter of complaint the authorities never specifically mention the real source of their displeasure; they could not do so without doubly damning the *commissaire* and undermining the validity of the post. Instead, they object to the play's "indecent attitudes," and "doubtful language or anything which goes against standards of respectability."

The same evasiveness surrounds the incident that finally sent the Italians packing: the alleged performance of *La Fausse Prude.* Parisian journals and gazettes were strangely silent on the subject. No mention of this piece or of the banishment of the Italians was ever published. It was privately discussed all over town, however. In his *Mémoires,* Saint-Simon, as usual, comes straight to the point:

> The king quite precipitately banished the entire troupe of Italian Comedians, no longer wanting them or any other Italian troupe. They pushed the limits, flooding the theater with filth, and sometimes with impieties, yet nothing was done except to laugh about it: nevertheless, the Italians ventured to perform a piece entitled *La Fausse Prude,* in which Mme. de Maintenon was readily recognizable. Everyone rushed to see this piece, but after three or four successive performances, for this piece was quite profitable, they received the order to close their theater and be gone from the kingdom in a month. All this caused a great brouhaha, and if the Comedians ended up losing their establishment because of their audacity and folly, the person who banished them didn't gain anything from this action because this ridiculous event stirred up a great deal of gossip.[79]

As long as the Comedians offended only moral sensibilities they were relatively safe. But when they ventured into an arena that was politically charged, by blaspheming the woman who for all intents and purposes ruled France, they found themselves in a losing situation. Madame de Maintenon, as Saint-Simon points out, gained nothing from this affair either. Not only did her actions reveal her to be harsh and petty, characteristics for which she already held a wide reputation, but they also focused the public's attention on the very blasphemies that she wished no one to hear.

The gleeful gossip in private about Mme. de Maintenon and the affair of *La Fausse Prude* was assiduously avoided in public. After the Italian Comedians' banishment, the troupe could no longer count on influential protectors to plead their case to the king. For example, the Duchess d'Orléans refused to say a word in their behalf for fear she might be implicated in the whole affair and punished, although, in the privacy of her letters, she admits she would have liked to have seen the "old monkey" so drolly depicted.[80]

The theatergoing public regretted the loss of the troupe; Mme. de Maintenon, Louis, and his minions, the clergy and the competing troupes, did not. The incident of *La Fausse Prude* had been the last straw. By banishing the Comedians, Louis was able to rid himself of a troupe whose offensive behavior no longer pleased him or his wife and caused him nothing but embarrassment and trouble. Further, he thereby pacified the Comédie Française and drew the support and approval of the clergy. He also set an example of what would happen to any future theatrical offenders and saved the drain on his depleted treasury. Moreover, by banishing the Comedians, Louis XIV silenced their subversive insolence, which had continually threatened his image of authority and the public's faith in his rule. Their banishment allowed Louis to restore his image, at least symbolically, and to restore the illusion that all was well in his realm. This was only an official myth, however, and a weak one at that. Everyone knew the real story although no one openly acknowledged it. Instead of strengthening his credibility, Louis's actions against the Italians actually weakened it. The banishment drew attention to the gap between the official facade and a contradictory reality.

In light of the social realities surrounding the banishment, Watteau's depiction of it begins to make sense. Watteau undermines the official fiction in *Departure*; moreover, the way in which he depicts this scene underscores his intention to do so. He depicts the official history literally while figuratively alluding to another, unofficial story. All the details necessary for a narrative reading of the event appear in the engraving, but the theatrical framing of his presentation willfully disrupts the surface unity, coherence, and validity of the narrative content. By mixing up the elements of documentary history painting and the representation of theatrical performances, Watteau refuses to locate the image firmly in either genre. The ambiguities and tensions that this confusion creates are eloquent, however, for they perfectly embody both the circumstances surrounding the banishment and the unofficial narrative those circumstances produced. In *Departure*, Watteau reproduces the process by which the French public made sense of their world during this period. The imaginary, but official, version was dutifully acknowledged as true. Yet in private, people whispered about the real version while they publicly referred to it through a commonly understood language of hints, allusions, and evasions. In real life, as in *Departure*, apparent ambiguities often signaled very clear meanings.

The Comedians in Watteau's *Departure* are as subversive as the Italian Comedians were in real life. They make a "show" of an absent, imaginary official version of the banishment and in so doing reveal its illusory nature. Even the magistrate in *Departure* is "acting" like a player; his feet pointed outward like those of another character in the image, and his arm is raised, echoing the pose of Mezzetin behind him. The structure of Watteau's *Departure*, with its ambiguity of reference and juxtaposition of codes, reveals not only the larger meaning that the event held for contemporary viewers – the gap between official fiction and experienced fact – but also the way that that meaning was produced and understood at a particular moment and place in history. Watteau's *Departure* is principally an image about a crisis of authority.

The Italian Comedians and the Crisis of Authority

That Watteau chose to depict the banishment of the Italian Comedians at least six years after the fact suggests that the collective imagination had imbued this event with a meaning that resonated far beyond its actual occurrence. What happened in France between the Italian Comedians' departure in 1697 and Watteau's subsequent re-creation confirms this resonance and also focuses the meaning of *Departure* even more clearly. In this light, *Departure* is not only an image about the crisis of authority, it is also a celebration of and tribute to the resistance of the Italian Comedians to royal authority.

Although the Italians were officially out of sight after Louis XIV's decree of 1697, they were hardly out of the public's mind. Their tradition persisted and flourished "underground," in the unofficial world of the *foire* and through numerous published editions of their plays.[81] The *foires* were the temporary fairs that were held seasonally in Paris: in the spring in an area near St. Germain de Prés and in the late summer in an area near St. Laurent. Within the area of a fair, which was legally the domain of the parish church and not the city of Paris, the usual guild restrictions did not apply. The fairs could not be regulated and controlled in the same way or according to the same rules as the rest of the city.[82] Hence a certain degree of liberty could be had at a fair. The fairs offered a variety of attractions and were always the location of lively activity. The fair St. Laurent was composed of eight tent-covered markets and over a hundred boutiques arranged along intersecting alleys; an area at the east end was reserved for eating and drinking establishments and for *spectacles*. The fair St. Germain, the more elaborate and fashionable of the two, was a self-contained structure, almost a city within a city, consisting of nine major streets and a multitude of shops. Luxury items, paintings, and knickknacks were sold in these semipermanent boutiques, and objects of all sorts were peddled in the streets. Street stalls and peddlers sold a variety of special carnival treats, and cafés offered visitors a chance to eat, drink, and watch the crowds while the crowds watched them. There were also a multitude of *spectacles,* ranging from organized, legitimate troupes who performed regularly in semipermanent theaters resembling that of the Comédie Française, to crude, unsophisticated street diversions such as acrobats, high-wire acts, jugglers, trained animals, freak shows, wax works, fortune tellers, puppet shows, and the display of novel mechanical devices.[83] Even the most sophisticated entertainments at the fairs were essentially popular in nature, and it was in this marginal, outlaw milieu that the tradition of the Italian Comedians continued and thrived.

The performance style at the fair theaters had always been closer to that of the Italians – in the use of improvisation, slapstick, visual humor, and well-known stock characters – than to that of the more elevated and classical Comédie Française. When Louis banished the Italian Comedians, the fair entrepreneurs quickly filled the void left by the troupe's suppression. They viewed themselves as the Italians' heirs "*de fait de droit*" and immediately took over their repertoire and audience.[84] According to the Parfaict brothers:

> The suppression of the Italian Comedians' troupe provided fresh territory for those in the entertainment business at the fair. These entrepreneurs regarded themselves as the heirs of the Italian Comedians; they performed several fragments from the Italians' repertoire at this fair and added new actors to the troupe in order to bring off the performance. The public, which regretted the loss of the Italian Comedians, rushed in crowds to see these imitations. What they saw at the fair delighted and pleased them.[85]

In addition, members of the banished troupe, along with the more respectable playwrights who composed works for the stage at the Hôtel Bourgogne, wrote new pieces for the fair theaters. The sons, daughters, and grandchildren of the banished Italians performed with fair troupes and drew considerable crowds. With their means of livelihood cut off from above, players and playwrights sought refuge and income from below.

The crowds who attended these popular performances were not just *le peuple bas*, the common people. The audience ran the gamut from peasants and street people to the highest-ranking members of the court. In fact, contemporary accounts uniformly reiterate that the fairs' major attraction was the mingling of all sorts of people. In *Séjour de Paris* (1727), Joachim Nemeitz, a German visitor, observes about the fairs: "Everything there is pell-mell, masters with valet and swindlers with honest men. The most refined courtiers; the prettiest young women, the most subtle pickpockets are all mixed up together."[86] The temporary abandonment of conventional class behavior was liberating and exhilarating. For a few weeks each year, the traditional trappings of class and status were suspended while both the humble and the mighty participated in what Robert Isherwood has termed a popular culture of the marketplace.[87]

The *spectacles* of this marketplace culture attracted the upper classes because of their popular nature. However, watching these entertainments was more than just a fashionable form of slumming. In the physical imagery that characterized fair performances – eating, drinking, copulating, and defecating – the upper classes found a symbol for the material existence shared by all human beings and an occasion to celebrate it together. It was, moreover, a symbolic expression that had no place within the elevating, classicizing terms of what officially defined high culture. The parenthetical context of the fairs allowed, even invited, lapses from acceptable notions of propriety and *politesse*. That the upper classes could temporarily revel in the lowest common denominator of human experience is suggested in Neimetz's description of the fair: "I have observed with astonishment that even women of quality could hear and see obscenities without blushing from shame; I can only say that these women could not contain their pleasure and laughed, wholeheartedly."[88]

The fair performances also attracted the upper classes, as well as *le peuple bas* and the bourgeoisie, because they provided a vehicle not only for liberation but also for social criticism. The performances satirized and profaned officialdom and the existing social order with all of its conventionality; the audience joined in, voicing their approval of and adding to the ridicule. That everyone participated in this derision, Isherwood suggests, helped to create a sense of familiarity among disparate classes.[89] The fair performances were subversive precisely because they created a unifying, common ground of criticism. That this discourse of shared ridicule existed in the unofficial, holiday atmosphere of the fairs masked neither its real content nor its intensity.[90]

The legal no-man's-land of the fairs, their temporariness, their tumult, and their popularity made them difficult to monitor officially and excluded fairgoers from the normal constraints of the everyday world. In this confusion and temporariness the tradition of the Italian Comedians remained alive and well. In fact, fair troupes became even more outspoken and daring than the Italian Comedians had been. The short duration of the fairs made it difficult for the authorities to effect the cumbersome machinery of regulatory protocol and procedure.[91] When necessary to avoid reprimand or regulation, the fair troupes changed the location of their theaters; they disbanded from season to season and even, at times, from day to day. These heirs of the Italian Comedians not only eluded official control, but they also made of their escape a production that was as much a part of the *spectacle* as was an actual performance.[92]

The fair troupes' boastful evasions of official intervention posed a symbolic threat to royal authority. Their overwhelming success posed a real financial threat to the Comédie Française and the Opéra. During the fairs, attendance at these officially sponsored theaters dropped alarmingly. The conflict between royal authority and popular opinion manifested itself in this theatrical arena and ended in triumph for the latter. From about 1700 until the restoration of the Italian Comedians in 1716, the Comédie Française and the Opéra, backed by the weight of their official sponsorship, battled the fair troupes.[93] They tried to assert their privileges – their monopolies on dialogue and on music and dance – in an effort to restrict the fair performers and thus protect their own revenues and reputations.

In 1699, d'Argenson, the lieutenant general of police, prohibited the fair troupes from performing anything that resembled the farces and comedies performed by the Comédie Française.[94] This decree did not, however, stop the fair troupes from parodying their official counterparts just as the Italians had always done. In 1706, the police placed an even more severe restriction on the fair troupes. Comedians at the fairs were forbidden to use dialogue, which was rightfully the property of the Comédie Française.[95] This left them with monologue as the only permissible verbal mode. However, fair performers became adept at overcoming these obstacles while complying with the letter of the law, a feat that constantly exasperated both the officials and the Comédie Française. For example, since monologue was defined by law as one actor speaking alone on the stage, the fair performers employed another actor offstage to respond to the onstage actor's "monologue." Or, one actor would recite onstage and then run off the stage, and another actor would take his place onstage for the response.[96] Each victory for the fair troupes was followed by a new legal impediment; but the unofficial troupes usually had the last laugh. In 1709, for example, the fair troupes satirized their rivals by imitating the cadence and meter of the Alexandrian verse so often used by the Comédie Française.[97] They babbled lines that were in nonsense language, however, an ironical comment on the sense of the Comédie Française's pieces. In 1710 the Alard troupe introduced plays given *à la muette*: characters carried printed speeches in their pockets and held them up for the audience to read at the appropriate moment.[98] A similar device was the *toile gomme,* printed dialogue that was suspended from above the stage.[99] Sometimes the Comedians held up a large printed copy of the dialogue, and the audience sang the words at the given moment. This particular method of legally evading dialogue brought down upon the fair troupes the wrath of the Opéra, which viewed it as an infringement of their privileges.

The subversive spirit and tradition of the Italian Comedians succeeded not merely despite the restrictions placed upon them, but because of the restrictions. They succeeded by creating new forms that cleverly circumvented attempts to control them. The fair troupes thus nullified the power of these decrees and turned the whole process of circumventing them into a spectacle in its own right. Official measures intended to limit and control the fair performances and their overwhelming popular success became instead a revitalizing source of creativity, adding to the popularity of the performances. So great was the triumph of the Italian tradition at the fairs that the regent waited only one day after the death of Louis XIV to officially restore the status of the Italian Comedians. Although confined to the marginal and temporary space of the fairs, the tradition of the Italians, grounded in a shared critical discourse and liberty, persisted, resisted, and in the end, shattered the facade of royal authority.

When Watteau painted *Departure*, the battle between the fair troupes and the royal authorities was at full pitch. The Italian Comedians in general, and their banishment in 1697 more specifically, had become freighted with a multitude of meanings and associations. Theatrical iconography now generated a secondary system of signification referring to larger political and social phenomena. Italian Comedians were no longer just Italian Comedians, they were also symbols of subversion, resistance, and revitalization.

A Social Reading of *Departure*

Watteau's *Departure* pays tribute not only to the Italian Comedians but also to the persistence of their tradition and to all that the tradition had come to mean. *Departure* might best be viewed as a modern allegory celebrating resistance and subversion, for the consequences of the Italians' popular triumph broke through the marketplace culture of the fairs and were felt in the dominant official culture.

Watteau sets up a counterpoint in *Departure* between the ostensible subject of the painting, the Italians' banishment in 1697, and the triumph of their tradition at the fairs. Even though there is no overt reference to the fairs in *Departure*, the public would have easily made the connection and understood the implications. It was the banishment of the Italians that led to the triumph of their tradition at the fairs; moreover, in the nineteen years between the Italians' banishment and their reinstatement, Italian Comedy was known to the public only through the *foire* performances. Like the Comedians at the fair, the Comedians in *Departure* have not succumbed to official repression; they have made it a part of their repertoire thereby undermining the king's authority as they ostensibly comply with it.

In *Departure*, Watteau refashions existing visual structures and vocabulary to correspond to a new context and its underlying assumptions.[100] As in an official allegorical history painting, *Departure*'s meaning is revealed through the play of different discourses or vocabularies. However, Watteau's juxtapositions are unexpected, and he does not use the traditional vocabulary or follow the rules of allegorical history painting. There is no clearcut, correct solution to the puzzle created by these juxtapositions because there exists no predetermined guide to their decoding.

In addition, Watteau never seems to provide enough information for the viewer to determine a single authoritative meaning. As Bryson argues in *Word and Image,* Watteau's paintings set up a semantic vacuum; the artist supplies enough information to raise certain questions, but never enough to pin down the answers.[101] Thus Watteau's paintings are full of potential meanings. I agree that Watteau's paintings are full of potential meanings, and it is this richness of possibility that makes his works so fascinating. I differ with Bryson, however, when he asserts that the meanings in Watteau's paintings have no "signifiers" with which to pin them down.[102] Watteau always includes elements in his paintings by which one can fix meanings. These elements sometimes function connotatively, however; the associated or suggested meanings of certain objects or configurations create a secondary "text" that exists outside the painting, in history. The contemporary viewer would have understood these loaded clues and filled in the information from his or her own experience. The contradictions within the painting would make sense in relation to this outside "text," and the very lack of information would shift from incompleteness to rich suggestiveness in its ability to support several meanings at the same time.

Watteau's *Departure* produces meaning on a number of levels in just these ways. Watteau juxtaposes an official narrative, understandable in relation to documentary images, with a theatrical drama, and an unofficial narrative, understandable in relation to scenes from theatrical performances. Since both types of imagery occurred in a variety of contexts (e.g., in almanacs; in prints found in the print dealers' shops on rue St. Jacques) a rather wide range of the viewing public would have been familiar with these two types of images and, more important, would have been aware of the images' meanings and ideological assumptions. By refusing to fix the image in either one realm or the other, Watteau would have made his audience, many of whom had links to the theatre, acutely sensitive to the fundamental differences between the official and the more popular discourse. In so doing, Watteau gives form to a specific historical situation: the painting implies that everything is fiction. Viewers accustomed to the *foire* performances, where meanings were constructed in opposition to another, official discourse, would have grasped this implication without further elaboration for *Departure*'s narrative structure echoes that of the plays. The image also resembles another type of discourse or narrative structuring, namely, that of the refined modes of conversation and behavior in which one does not communicate directly, but through innuendo, indirection, and irony. The official tributes to Comedians, such as *The French and Italian Comedians* (fig. 14) and the *Almanach* engraving (fig. 17), would also have been formally evident in *Departure*, but would have suggested contradictory intentions since such tributes were supposed to celebrate official favorites, not popular subversions.

Watteau piles layer upon layer of meanings in his paintings. The result is not, as Bryson describes it, the setting in motion of a "boundless semantic expansion, a kind of rippling of meaning that knows no boundary," but a dialectical play of signification that casts out in all directions but always pulls back in, focusing on and enriching the specific.[103] Watteau sets up levels of meaning that reverberate against and intensify one another. He structures *Departure* in this fashion. All the elements of the painting refer back to, and support, a meaning that is nowhere openly stated. In turn, this larger, unarticulated meaning informs the viewer's understanding of those elements that support it. Watteau, I assert, did this quite consciously, and with great attention to detail.

By way of example, I would like to explore the meaning of one apparently innocuous detail in *Departure*, the signboard that extends out from the building on the left. I hypothesize that this signboard provides a significant clue to *Departure*'s larger meaning.

Signboards were a common sight in the Parisian cityscape; they marked commercial establishments, often illustrating their names or natures. Jutting out from the building just above the signboard in *Departure* is a fir tree, the traditional indicator of an inn or a hostel.[104] The signboard depicts a crescent with points facing upward; it probably represents the name of the establishment, for "Le Croissant" or "Au Croissant" was a common name for a cabaret in the seventeenth and eighteenth centuries. The appearance of this cabaret signboard in *Departure* seems normal and completely unremarkable, especially since the area around the Hôtel Bourgogne was well known for its cabarets and "hot spots."[105] However, this signboard may be more than just an appropriate but incidental inclusion. It may be a specific reference to the famous cabaret, the Au Croissant, which was located near the Hôtel Bourgogne.[106] (Its anonymous author mentions this cabaret in the seventeenth-century poem *Ode à la louange de tous les cabarets de Paris*.[107]) By including this landmark, Watteau could better persuade the viewer that an actual event has been depicted, as it occurred, at a specific location. The signboard is the kind of identifying detail used in documentary images, and its presence in *Departure* suggests that we should read the scene as historical fact.

Yet the signboard does not rule out a purely theatrical reading of *Departure*. We know that signboards were used as stage properties; Gillot included one in *Harlequin a Glutton* (see fig. 11), although it depicts not a crescent, but a glass of wine. Some of the plays in the Gherardi collection mention signboards as well. For example, a scene in *Arlequin Protée,* first performed by the Italian Comedians on 11 October 1683, would have required a signboard like the one in *Departure*.[108] In this scene, set on a city street, two *aubergists* try to convince Arlequin to lodge in their establishments.

> *Aubergist I:* Come, lodge here Monsieur.
> Good lodgings whether afoot or mounted.
> At the sign Au Croissant.
> *Arlequin:* Au Croissant? Now there's a sign
> that's a bad omen.[109]

This exchange has implications both general and particular. As to the general, this scene make the signboard in *Departure* recognizable as stage scenery and thus would not contradict a reading of the image as a theatrical performance. But Watteau's inclusion of this detail supplies only additional contradictory and incomplete information; it does nothing to clarify the dislocation between the theatrical and the real. It is probable that Watteau consciously included this detail because of its potential to function in either context. Its inclusion should illustrate just how carefully Watteau lodged every element in *Departure* somewhere between the theatrical and the documented. Watteau intentionally emphasized this sort of contradiction throughout the painting.

As to the particular implications of the signboard, it functions as one of those loaded clues that Watteau frequently deployed and that is rooted in one discourse but refers to another set of commonly understood practices and symbols whose meanings within the context of the painting would have been immediately available to the viewing public.

In the seventeenth and eighteenth centuries a whole language and lore of signs dating back to the Middle Ages was still familiar to the public.[110] Often witty and clever, the signs frequently presented the names of *maisons,* or public establishments, in the form of a rebus or an epigram. For example, the signboard for *St. Jean* depicted a yellow monkey, a "*singe jaune,*" and a signboard featuring a large, green letter U was a visual pun for an establishment called La Petite Vertu. This popular tendency toward visual puns probably gave rise to one form of literary satire that enjoyed a certain vogue in the seventeenth and eighteenth centuries.[111] In a Mazarinade (one of the satires against Mazarin during the Fronde) of 1649, the court is forced to search for lodgings *en ville*:

> For the King, we choose *Le Mouton* [sheep, or slang for ninny];
> *Monsieur* was lodged *Au Papillon* [butterfly, or slang for flighty],
> and the Queen
> At the *Chapeau Rouge*; but because the dwelling
> and especially their bedrooms were insufficiently
> dressed, we relocated both her servants,
> and Her Majesty: She was lodged at the *Italian Sausage*. . . .
> While the servants were lodged at *La Petite Vertu*. . . .[112]

In another of these satirical pieces, *La nouveau fourrier de la Cour* (1652), the anonymous author explains:

> Given that the court often moves from quarter to quarter and it is not a recent phenomenon that the lodgings of famous court people are marked either in the lodgings or on the hanging signs with images which designate with clarity their present station or their personal traits, it must be permitted to me to outdo the one who has whimsically assigned such lodgings to others in those places that carry disagreeable connotations for some.[113]

In this lengthy poem, the author assigns "La Boulye, *Au Croissant*." What does this reveal about the state of La Boulye's fortune or humor? One finds the answer by turning to popular jargon, where "*croissant*," according to the *Dictionnaire comique, satirique, critique, burlesque, libre et proverbiale,* first published in 1718, refers to "the horns that a man who is a cuckold wears."[114] La Boulye's wife is evidently unfaithful, and everyone knows it. The *Dictionnaire comique* further states: "to be lodged *au croissant* signifies membership in the brotherhood of Acteon, to be numbered among the cuckolds."[115] We now understand perfectly Arlequin's reluctance to lodge at Au Croissant in the play *Arlequin Protée.*

The *Dictionnaire comique* cites the first literary usage of the phrase "*loger au croissant*" to have beer in Regnard's play, *La baguette de Vulcain.*[116] The Italian Comedians first performed this piece on 10 January 1693, and it enjoyed a tremendous success. The phrase was part of a verse presented in the augmentation, an additional scene that was performed after the play proper.[117] The following verse, framed by a large crescent resembling the one from the signboard in *Departure*, appears on the engraving *Vulcan's Wand* (fig. 18).

> The vagabond Sun never rests
> ever scurries from house
> to house, as husbands would do
> if they were allowed to
> come out of their prisons,
> but of one spouse the abode is certain:

whatever path that he takes as he goes
and comes, his progress always brings him
to lodge at the sign of the crescent.[118]

Above the *croissant* and verse are the main characters, onstage, accompanied by bits of dialogue that describe the attractions of this piece.

There is no doubt that the French public understood the meaning of *loger au croissant* and that Watteau's inclusion of this imaginary inn for cuckolds would not have escaped notice. But who is the cuckold in *Departure*? Although he appears nowhere on the scene, the viewing public would have immediately inferred his identity: Louis XIV.

Louis' "secret" wife, Madame de Maintenon, had a reputation as a hypocritical and ambitious woman who was not above using people and granting sexual favors to attain a position of power.[119] Rumor had it that she was born in prison, where her parents were confined for counterfeiting. In fact, her father was probably an *avocat*, or lawyer, who had fallen on hard times. In any event, she was not, by birth, a member of the aristocracy. She was orphaned at an early age and spent much of her life in hardship, dependent upon the favor of others for survival. Eventually, she found a secure position as the wife of the playwright and poet Scarron, who had a reputation for "high living." Scarron's quarters were a popular meeting place for the literati of Paris. Gilles Boileau, in a satirical epigram, implies that it was not so much Scarron's wit that attracted crowds of visitors as it was Madame's lack of virtue.

See, upon what your error is based,
Scarron! You believe that everyone goes
to see you for your conversation, huh?
Don't you see, dim dunce, if you scratch
your head a little.
That you'll readily guess why?[120]

After Scarron's death, Madame de Maintenon used her connections to secure a widow's pension. She cultivated the friendship of the king's mistress, Madame de Montespan, and became the governess to the royal bastards. In the end, she supplanted Madame de Montespan as royal mistress and then surpassed her: she became the legal, although never publicly announced, wife of Louis XIV.

Madame de Maintenon's letters show her to have been an intensely devout and religious woman who always felt the scorn of those above her. Whether she was an ambitious hussy or a religious and noble woman who was mistreated and slandered matters less for our purposes than do her reputation and situation; as the confidante and lover of Louis XIV she was in a peculiar position for an outwardly pious woman. According to one account of her life, she justified her place on the grounds that she would make certain that the king attained salvation.[121]

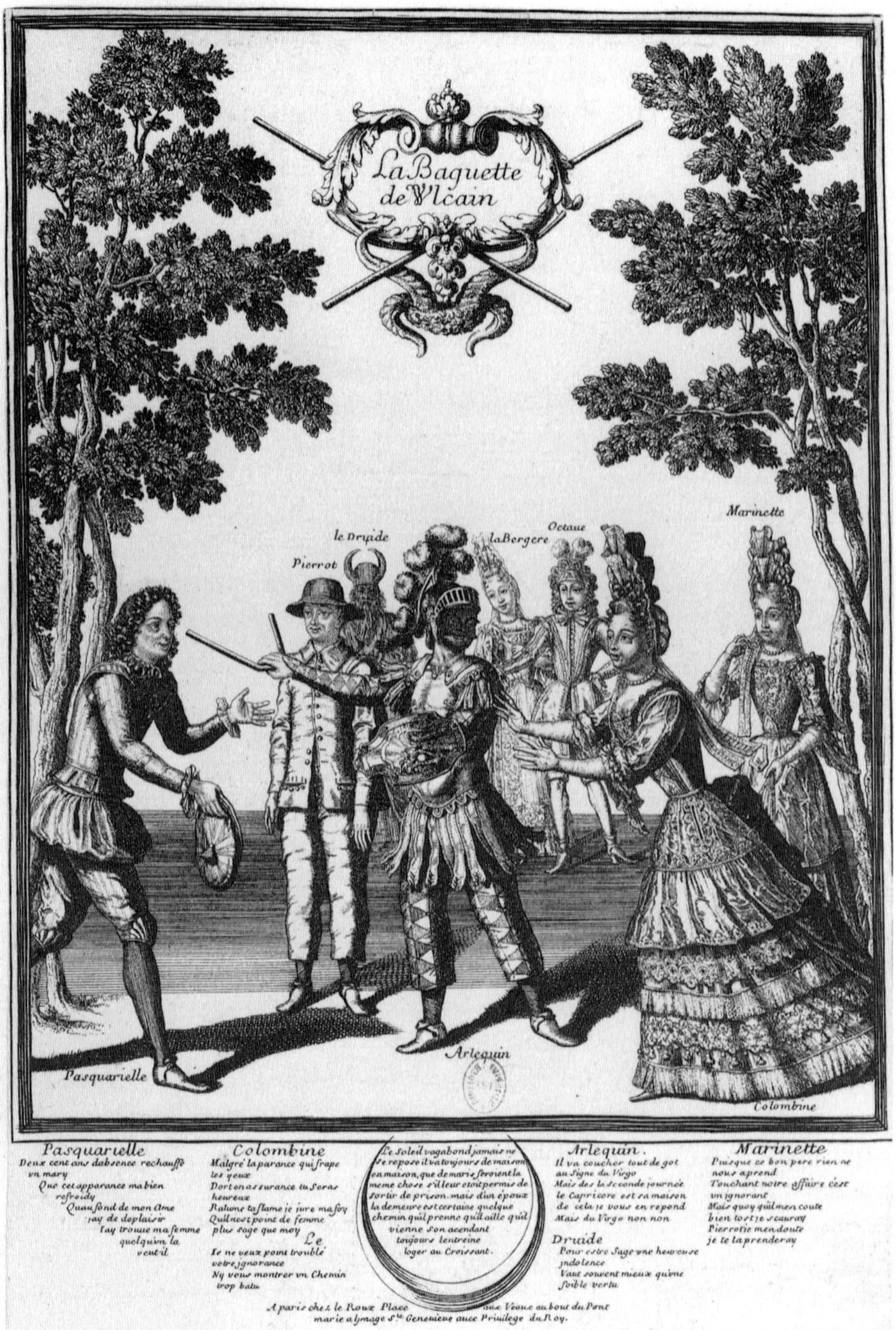

18. Anonymous, engraving, *Vulcan's Wand (La baguette de Vulcain)*, Bibliothèque nationale de France, Paris. Cliché, Bibliothèque nationale de France, Paris.

Mme. de Maintenon was also in a position of great power, which the court resented. Not only was she an upstart, a woman of low birth and the widow of a crippled writer of satirical verse, but she also instituted a policy of public piety that everyone else was expected to follow. Commonly held views were that she was responsible for the king's sudden devoutness, that she was a tyrant who dominated and took advantage of poor Louis, that she turned the court into a somber place, and that she ruined everyone's fun.

Worse, the court had to kowtow to her. The oppressiveness of her rule as royal favorite is described by Madame Du Noyer in her *Mémoires*: "I wish it were the case around here that one could enjoy a certain freedom, where one could sound off about that Maintenon and Noailles without fearing the Bastille."[122] Although members of the court curried favor from her publicly, they made her the object of great ridicule and disdain in private. She was also the subject of much satirical and malicious literature, such as *La Fausse Prude,* which circulated underground.[123] *The Secret History of the Amours of Madame de Maintenon with the French King,* which appeared in England long before it was published in France, opens with the following:

> Love and fortune produce effects so fantastik and surprizing, that a man accustoms himself to make reflections on all occurrences, cannot consider 'em without astonishment. One sees not only the vilest and most abject creatures rai'd by this means to the highest elevation of glory & grandeur; . . . Mme de Maintenon, the person whom we shall choose to be our heroine, does abundantly confirm the truth of these evident assertions; . . .[124]

The author then discusses Mme. de Maintenon's love affair with Père la Chaise, and with her servants. "For certain it is, that if she's the King's Mule, she likewise is the Mare of the Pious La Chaise and her Valet's Hackney into the bargain. Her majesties favor is more acceptable and grateful to her than his love, since she has so many servile vassals to gratify her infamous passions, and above the rest the Reverend Father Père La Chaise."[125] In *The Secret History* and in other works of the same genre, Louis XIV is clearly a cuckold.

In *Departure* too, Louis is the supreme cuckold. He is used by Madame de Maintenon, who, as Saint-Simon and Madame Du Noyer suggest, is behind the banishment of the Comedians. The cuckold's inn, signaled by the signboard on the left, becomes an ironic reply to the decree being posted on the right, which clearly bears the words, "*de par le Roi.*" In the popular imagination, it is really Madame's wishes that are satisfied at the expense of the king's reputation.

Moreover, in the context of the painting, the Italian Comedians make a cuckold of the king. They deceive him by refusing to succumb to his will; they will carry on quite well without his sanction at the fair theaters. They figuratively mock the king as well in *Departure* for the potent symbol of Louis, the Sun King, is turned on its head, and he is symbolized by the *croissant,* a waning crescent moon.

This hypothesis may help explain the appearance of theatrical subjects and motifs in paintings during the first quarter of the eighteenth century. The theatrical skirmishes at the fair were about much larger issues than providing a common ground for public enjoyment; the *spectacles* at the fairs provided the means for the expression of a collective voice of resistance – a voice that cut across the normally prescribed divisions of class and the practices and values that defined them. The theater provided an alternate iconography to the more officially acceptable iconography of heroic gods and goddesses and of ancient and biblical heroes. This substitution of one order for another in the visual arts should suggest that a larger substitution was also taking place in society.

CHAPTER TWO

Watteau's Military Paintings: Conflicts and Confluences

THE NUMBER OF COPIES of Watteau's early paintings of military subjects, the collectors of merit who owned them, their influence on subsequent painters, and the pivotal role these paintings play in the Watteau myth formulated in the eighteenth-century biographies of the artist all suggest that, at the time, viewers found the military subjects riveting. Yet most modern scholarship has found little that is notable in them and much that is derivative of Dutch prototypes. With a few exceptions, scholars of the military images address them as either an episode within Watteau's artistic development or an episode within a larger chronology of stylistic taste in France. In many ways, the military paintings resemble *Departure;* they are considered the ugly stepsisters of his late, great paintings.

What was it then about Watteau's military paintings that eighteenth-century viewers found remarkable? I would like to take another look at Watteau's military paintings with an eye to understanding why they were seen as somehow extraordinary. To do so, I will explore the historical situations that shaped the paintings' intelligibility and determined their form. I will also try to reconstruct both Watteau's own position on the subject matter and the existing codes of representation that would have informed a viewer's understanding of the images.

Rather than view the military paintings as an anomaly in Watteau's work, I assert that they demonstrate conceptual consistency with the rest of the artist's oeuvre. Watteau applied to his military paintings the same techniques he applied elsewhere. He created meaning in the military paintings by confounding, inverting, and toying ironically with preexisting painting genres, conventions, traditions, and practices, as he did in *Departure*. Moreover, as we also saw in *Departure*, this unconventional manipulation of the cultural and social codes of representation created an elliptical commentary on the construction and meaning of the codes themselves and on those who controlled them, a commentary lost on the modern audience but surely understood by the eighteenth-century viewing public.

Watteau produced his dozen or so military subjects between approximately 1709 and 1714, and from the beginning these paintings achieved a recognition that *Departure* never did. In 1744, Edme Gersaint wrote a biography of the artist that appeared in the sales catalogue he drew up to publicize the forthcoming sale of the collection of Quentin Lorengère. Gersaint, Watteau's friend and dealer, endows the production of the military paintings with a mythic resonance that he carries through the rest of the biography:

It was with him [Audran] that he [Watteau] acquired the taste for ornaments, of which we have several engravings made after examples he did. However, Watteau did not want to remain with him; nor did he want to pass his life working for someone else; feeling empowered by his imagination, Watteau created an inspired painting in his spare time that represented a departure of the troops. This painting is one of the two that M. Cochin the elder engraved. He showed the painting to Audran and asked for his advice. Audran, being both a shrewd man and an able judge of aesthetic ability, was frightened by the talent he saw in the painting. But the fear of losing a student who was useful and on whom he often depended for the disposition of decorations, and even their specific compositions, prompted Audran to disingenuously counsel Watteau not to waste his time on this kind of nonsense because it had the potential to destroy the sense of good taste he had learned. Watteau was not duped by this; his firm resolve to leave Audran, added to his desire to see his hometown of Valenciennes again, totally made up his mind. He used the pretext of visiting his parents as an honest means of leaving; but, how was he to make the trip? He needed money, and his painting became his only resource: but he didn't know how to go about marketing it. He turned to M. Spoude, currently living, who was a painter from the same region as he, and a personal friend. Chance led M. Spoude to my father-in-law, M. Sirois, to whom he showed the picture. The price was fixed at 60 livres and the sale was concluded on the spot. Watteau came and received his money. He departed cheerfully for Valenciennes, like an ancient sage from Greece; he had his fortune, and surely, he never imagined himself so rich. This sale was the origin of the liaison that my father-in-law had with Watteau until the artist's death. He was so pleased with the picture that he immediately entreated Watteau to make a pendant to it and send it to him from Valenciennes. This is the second piece that M. Cochin engraved; it represents a halt of the army done after nature. Watteau demanded 200 livres, which was given to him. These two pictures have always passed for two of the most beautiful things to come from the artist's hand.[1]

Although we can assume that Gersaint is more or less sticking to the facts as he knows them in this biography, he also follows a number of literary conventions characteristic of the biographies of artists.[2] Thus his account of the military paintings provides an episode in what is the most common trope in artists' biographies: the artist attains a place in the pantheon of creators after passing through a series of obstacles that are often created by others for less-than-honorable reasons. Watteau's sale of his military painting liberated him from an oppressive situation. That he did the painting in his spare time, without guidance from a master, is in keeping with another common literary trope, the artist as self-taught genius. It was on the strength of one of his military paintings, according to several of his biographers, that Watteau was first accepted into the Academy as a student.[3] As the works that first revealed his genius, and as the key to his overcoming a roadblock in developing that genius, the military paintings play an important role in the Watteau myth as it is repeated and elaborated by his biographers.[4] Even the Comte de Caylus, who was not always a great admirer of Watteau and often used the artist as a straw man to further the cause of neoclassicism, admitted that "these first pictures [marches and camp scenes] are perhaps the equal of his finest later works."[5] That the military paintings are singled out suggests that they gave form to something in a new and remarkable way.

The two paintings that Gersaint mentions, a departure of the troops and a halt of the army, are probably the works that we know today as *Return from the Campaign* (the "60 livre" painting) (fig. 19) and *Bivouac* (the "200 livre" painting) (fig. 20).[6] Both were engraved by Cochin in 1727 when they were in Gersaint's collection. As have many of the military paintings, the original *Return from the Campaign* has been lost; the original *Bivouac*, however, is in the Pushkin Museum, Moscow. On the surface, these two works illustrate Watteau's links with the northern tradition of military genre scenes, and as Oliver Banks and others have pointed out, they would have been popular among collectors with a taste for Dutch and Flemish genre painting.[7]

Whereas Watteau's early military paintings can be compared to northern genre paintings, his biographers consistently remark on their truth to nature. This suggests that Watteau's military subjects both conformed to and confirmed a particular "view" of military life encoded within the Dutch genre tradition. Genres in painting are in effect conventionalized forms of depicting particular subjects in order to convey certain kinds of information. Behind its conventionalized form is a commonly understood way of reading the work of art – a fixing of a point of view or an ordering of reality. On this level, conventions function as ideology. By operating on a series of assumptions about reality, conventions and genres validate the meaning and rightness of those assumptions. When conventions and/or genres change or fall out of usage, the reason is less the progress of an orderly art-historical evolution than an ideological shift, fragmentation, or reformation. Perhaps it is more appropriate to discuss conventions as ideolog*ies,* in the plural, since the multiplicity and complexity of experience cannot be neatly represented by a single corresponding visual convention. I believe that we see in Watteau's military paintings one of these moments of shift and reformation; Watteau's works articulate a changing attitude within the military and, as well, a change in military values and practices during the War of Spanish Succession.[8] This new image of

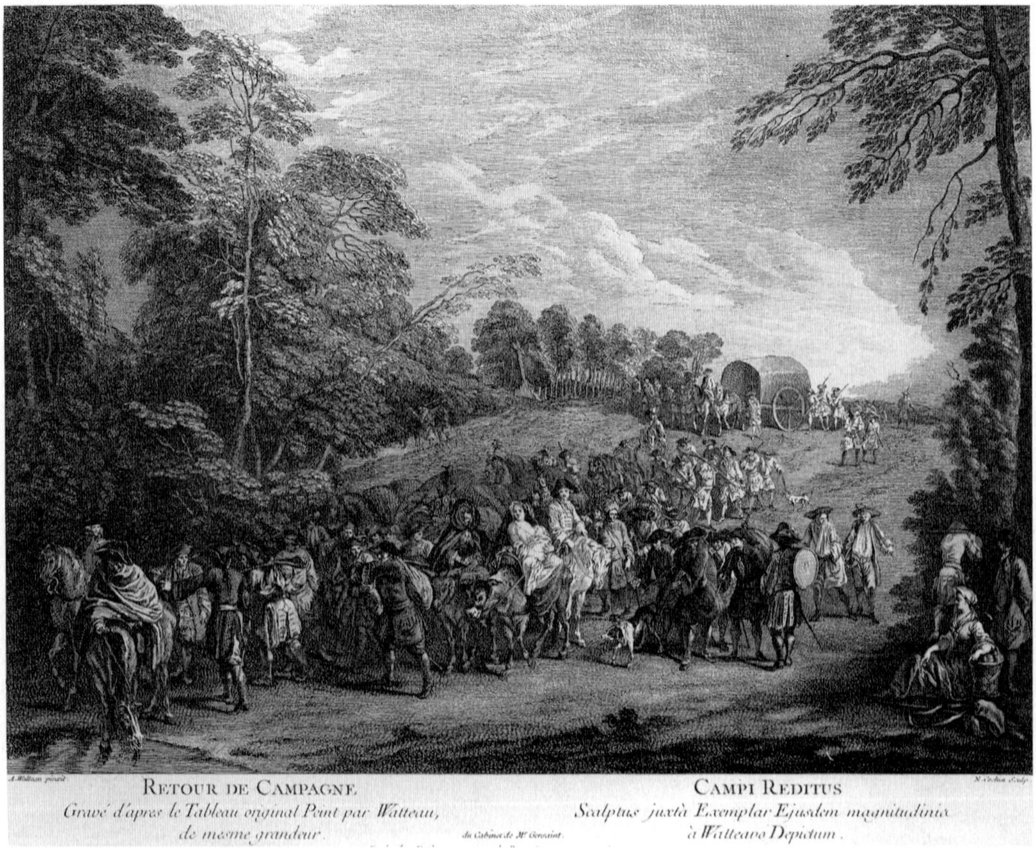

19. Charles-Nicolas Cochin, engraving, after Antoine Watteau, *Return from the Campaign (Retour de campagne)*, engraving announced 1727, painting, c. 1709, Anne S. K. Brown Military Collection, Brown University Library, Providence, RI.

the military will come into sharper focus if we look at Watteau's works in relation to existing conventional modes of military representation.

Conventions in Military Painting

A discussion of conventions in military painting should begin with an overview of those within that category of military scenes that Watteau's most closely resemble, the northern genre tradition. As the name suggests, in the northern tradition military genre scenes are characterized by their generic quality: they represent neither specific places nor specific events, and the subject types are conventional; these are not scenes of combat.[9] For example, the soldier as the merry drinker is one type of scene, or there are the tavern types made popular by Pieter Symonsz Potter (fig. 21), David Teniers, and Willem Duyster. Usually

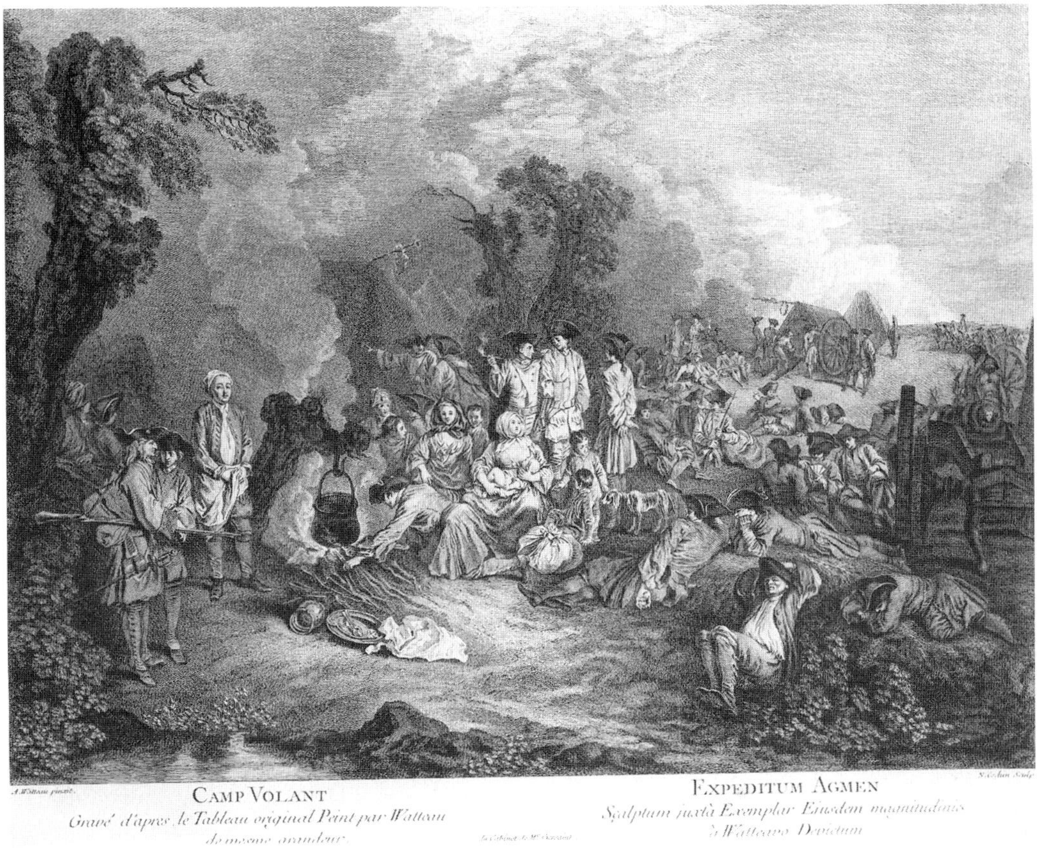

20. Charles-Nicolas Cochin, engraving, after Antoine Watteau, *Bivouac (Camp volant)*, engraving announced 1727, painting c. 1710, Anne S. K. Brown Military Collection, Brown University Library, Providence, RI.

a few soldiers are depicted as they amuse themselves by drinking and playing cards. Sometimes the soldiers are drunk and behaving badly, but this bad behavior is generally played up for its humorous and anecdotal elements. Sometimes these scenes are set outdoors, near the entry to a *buvette* – a refreshment tent indicated by a makeshift signboard of mugs and pitchers hung on a tent post. The background is neatly screened so that the overall effect is one of being indoors. Thus the outdoor space becomes interiorized both by its function, as a place of amusement, and through the visual blocking devices that exclude a background and often even a middle ground. Sometimes the soldiers depicted are more elegant, sporting fancier uniforms and displaying more refined habits, but they are still anonymous types rather than individuals. In either case, there is nothing heroic about either the soldiers or their occupations. Actual battles and the business of war remain outside the paintings. The life of the soldier is

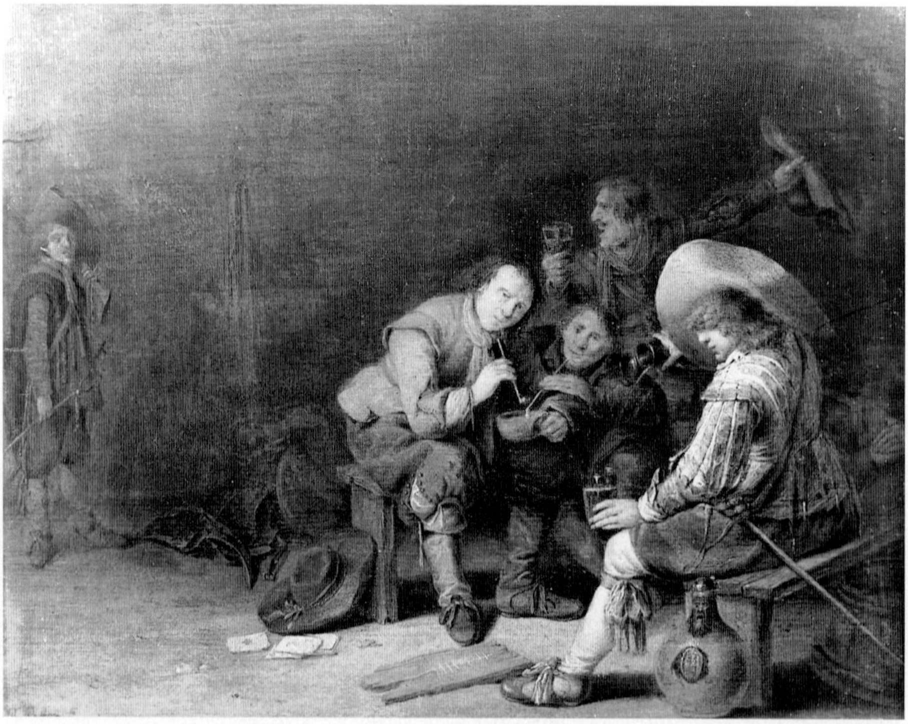

21. Pieter Potter, *Soldiers in a Guardroom*, National Gallary of Ireland, Dublin. Reproduction courtesy of the National Gallery of Ireland, Dublin.

depicted as a jolly one that takes place in a self-contained space of entertainment and that reinforces certain stereotypical ideas about soldiers.

Halts and marches comprise another stock type of military genre painting. Perhaps the most representative of this type, as well as the type that is of greatest interest in relation to Watteau's work, are those scenes produced by Philips Wouvermans (1619–68). Here, groups of soldiers are depicted in the mundane activities of moving from place to place or of relaxing in temporary camps (fig. 22). Wouvermans and the other painters who depicted this type of military scene used certain formal conventions. The foreground is on a higher elevation, affording a view of the far and middle distance. It is a bird's-eye view, but the bird never flies very high. The main action or scene on the prominence is united visually with the background and middle ground through a linking of groups of figures and the manipulation of landscape elements. Foliage, ridges, and clumps of trees lead the viewer's eye back into space; the foreground, middle ground, and background are distinct, but not disjointed. The landscape elements are as important as the figures.

The halts and marches types of military genre pictures, like the merry drinker type, do not depict combat or embody heroic ideals. The titles of some of Wouvermans's scenes of this type suggest a domestic cast – *L'Académie du*

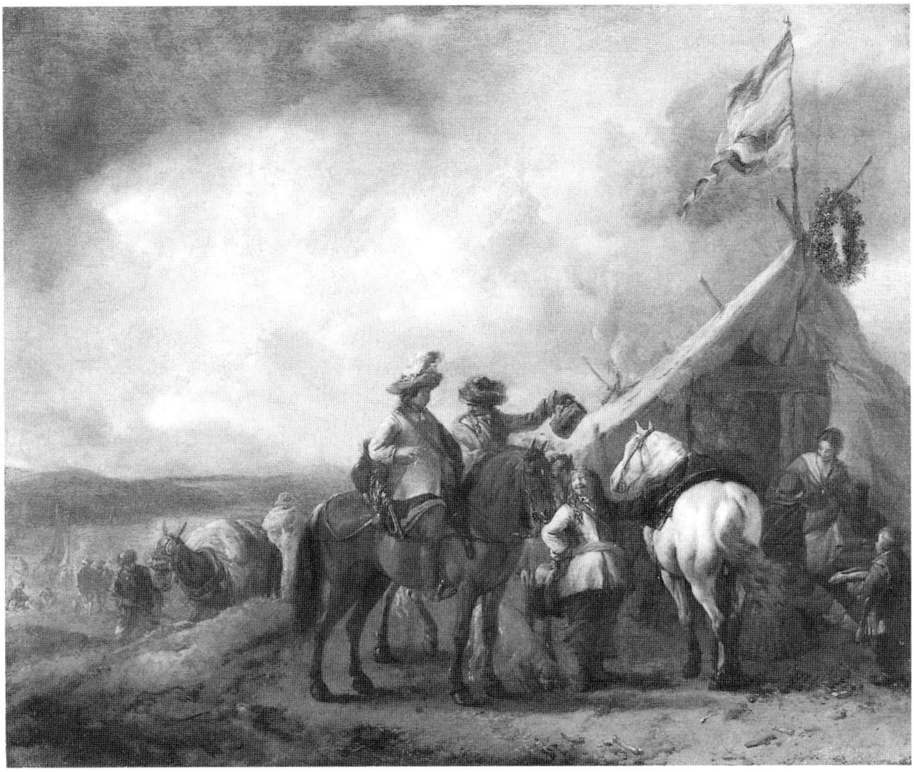

22. Philips Wouvermans, *Cavaliers in a Military Camp (Cavaliers dans un camp militaire)*, Musée du Louvre, Paris. Cliché, Réunion des musées nationaux.

Ménage, Le Quartier des Vivandiers, Reste de l'Armée. Wouvermans's soldiers are not very bellicose; when the battlefield is evoked at all, it is merely a puff of smoke in the distance. Wouvermans's camp scenes might well be termed scenes of recuperation, repair, and regeneration, for they depict mainly scenes of eating, resting, caring for animals, and tending to the material necessities of life. When his troops are in transit they are never rushing into battle or fleeing from it. They plod through the landscape, encumbered by equipment, supplies, animals, and family. Wouvermans's version of military life is appealing; there is never anything depressing or oppressive in his images.

Another type of conventional representation was a scene of a skirmish or pillaging or both. Wouvermans did numerous such scenes, including *Skirmish between Oriental and Imperial Cavaliers* (fig. 23). These scenes emphasized the drama, color, and flash of combat. The carnage we see, however, has been aestheticized and made exotic.

What war looked like in paintings obviously depended upon the points of view of artist and audience and on the assumptions they shared. F. C. Legrand has described Flemish genre as representing bourgeois wish fulfillment: the

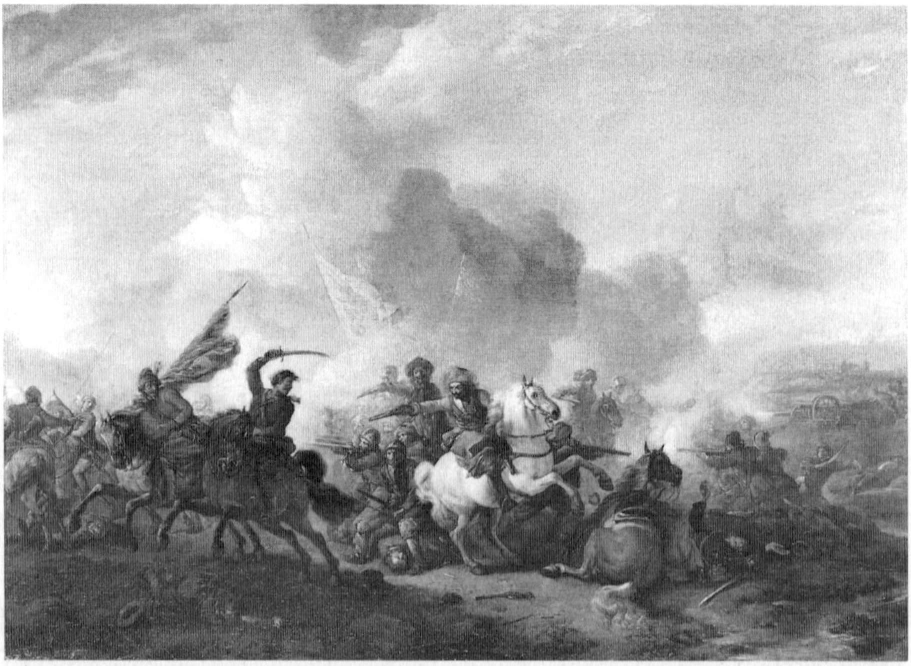

23. Philips Wouvermans, *Skirmish between Oriental and Imperial Cavaliers (Escarmouche de cavaliers entre Orientaux et Impéraux)*, Musée du Louvre, Paris. Cliché, Réunion des musées nationaux.

good life exists even in the midst of war and famine.[10] If one considers their tendency to domesticate and tame those elements of reality that are unpleasant, unruly, or beyond control, then the military subjects that were produced by northern artists were indeed bourgeois.

These paintings can also be considered bourgeois in that they were not produced for a royal patron; moreover, they demonstrate a civilian point of view. Painters sold their work on the open market, to dealers, or to private patrons; they did not have to obtain royal sponsorship to make a living. Therefore, most northern genre scenes, including those with military themes, were produced for a middle- to upper-middle-class audience. Often these paintings were exported. Northern artists produced the kinds of paintings that would sell rather than paintings that glorified the king or served a specific program. Private patrons bought these paintings either as decoration or as part of a collection; in essence, they were bought because they pleased. A military scene that emphasized death, destruction, and misery might well be appreciated by a collector for its artistic merit or because it "instructed," but it was hardly the subject to decorate the wall of a wealthy family's dining room, particularly if their wealth had been made in a war-related business.

Whereas domesticated images served bourgeois taste in a market setting, the military imagery of *Plan and Order of the Battle of Malplaquet* (fig. 24) served

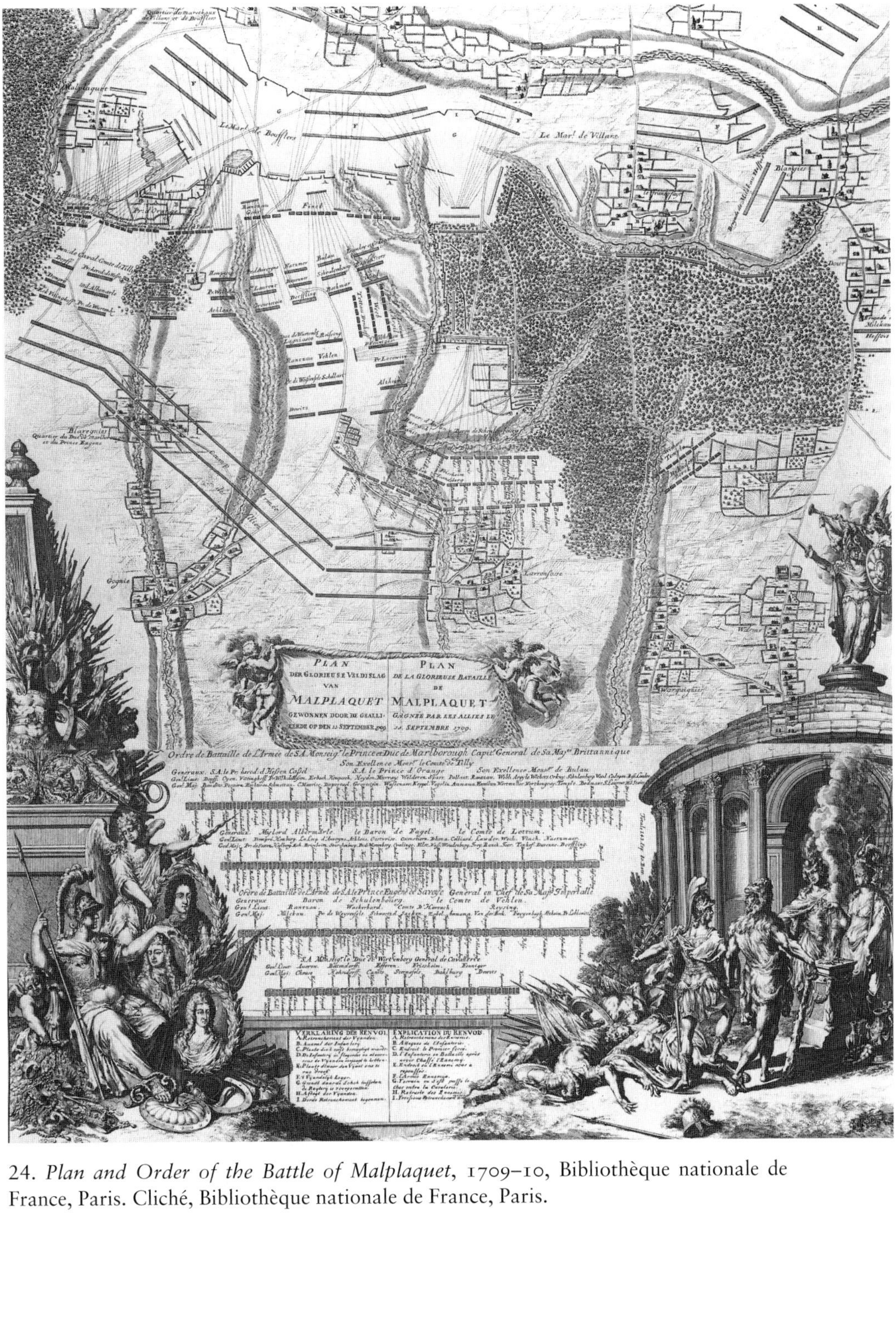

24. *Plan and Order of the Battle of Malplaquet*, 1709–10, Bibliothèque nationale de France, Paris. Cliché, Bibliothèque nationale de France, Paris.

a practical function as a widespread type of military document. This type, a plan and order of battle, is an interesting visual and verbal mapping. The formal arrangement of the names of the units and the officers corresponds to their actual places within a military hierarchy. The order of battle is just that, the ordering of the battle formation – the logistics. The order of battle and the plan above it represent two different visual conventions for conveying information. In these images it was also common to include a register of representation that conveyed yet another type of information; in this example, we see portraits of the major generals at the lower left and allegorical personifications to the right. These portraits and personifications glorify and justify military action. It was typical in this type of plan and order of battle for different registers of representation to overlap; for example, the map on the lower right extends over the classical tholos. This clash of modes seemed to cause no discomfort, and, indeed, it was a commonly understood manner of conveying diverse kinds of information.[11] This mix of representational conventions occurred more often than not in the engravings constituting the royally supported *cabi-*

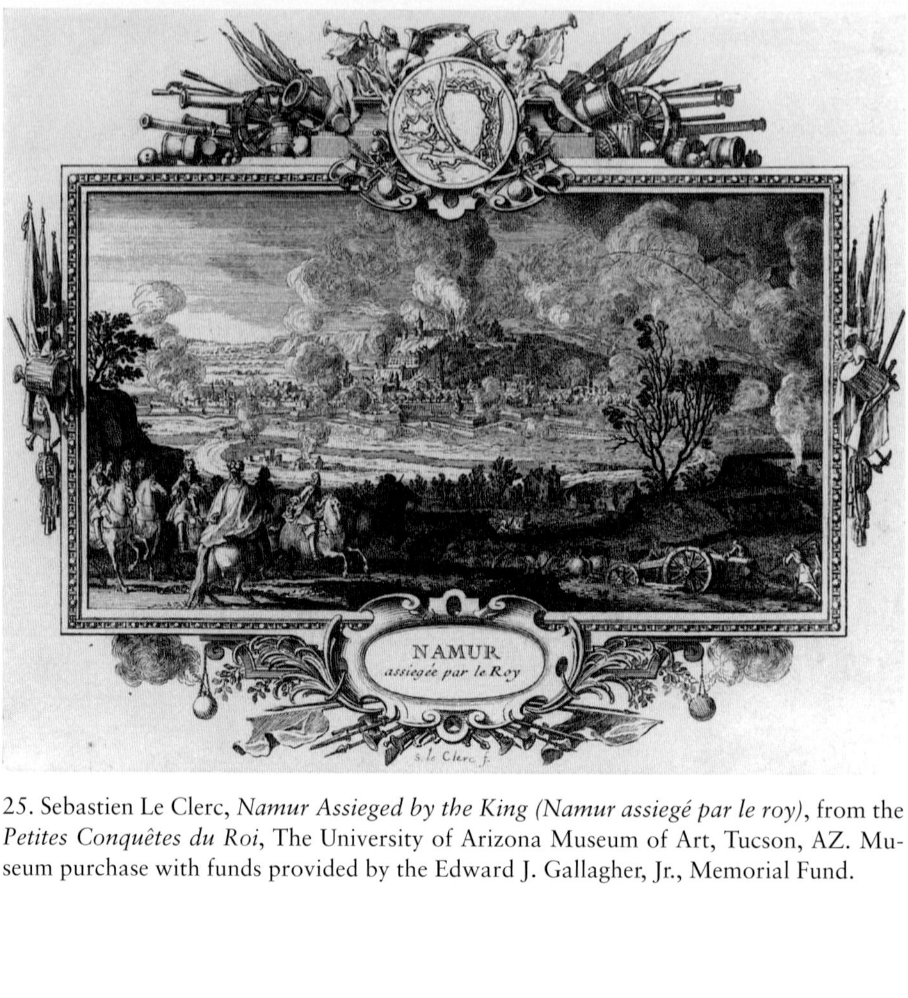

25. Sebastien Le Clerc, *Namur Assieged by the King (Namur assiegé par le roy)*, from the *Petites Conquêtes du Roi*, The University of Arizona Museum of Art, Tucson, AZ. Museum purchase with funds provided by the Edward J. Gallagher, Jr., Memorial Fund.

net du roi, especially in the series commemorating military victories called the *Petites Conquêtes du Roi* (fig. 25).[12]

This type of coding, or mapping, informs the more "naturalistic" representations of battle produced under the aegis of the Crown in seventeenth- and eighteenth-century France. The *Battle of Fleurus, 1690* (fig. 26) is a somewhat exaggerated example of this genre of painting; however, it allows us to see how the image functions in conveying the same kinds of information that we saw on the *Plan and Order of the Battle of Malplaquet.* The important generals in the foreground are like the portraits at the bottom of *Plan and Order,* and the bird's-eye view is so extreme that one reads the background literally as a map. The middle ground of the painting, which depicts soldiers in formation moving down an almost impossibly precipitous incline, recalls the area that showed the order of the battle in *Plan and Order of the Battle of Malplaquet.* Works like this naturalize certain kinds of information and an "official" point of view.

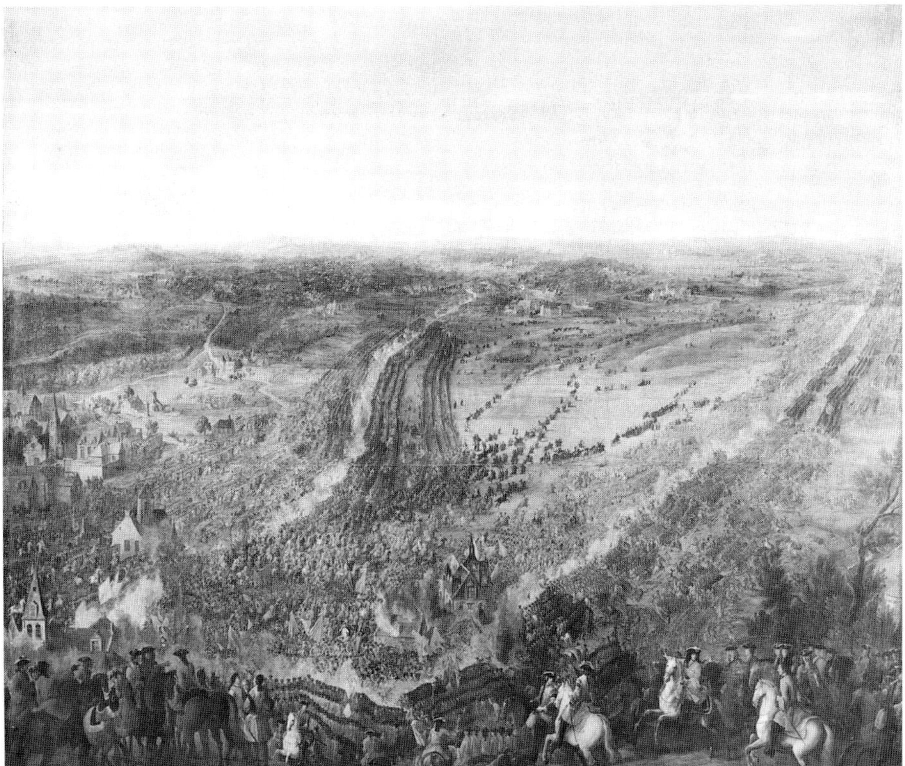

26. Anonymous, seventeenth-century French, *Battle of Fleurus, 1690 (Bataille de Fleurus, 1690),* Musée national du Château de Versailles, Versailles. Cliché, Réunion des musées nationaux.

Known as the topographical tradition, this type of military painting was institutionalized in France early in the personal reign of Louis XIV. Adam François Van der Meulen, a Flemish painter, is responsible for establishing this type of image and for fixing its conventions.[13] Le Brun installed Van der Meulen in 1664 at the Gobelins manufacture, where he soon headed a large workshop until his death in 1690. He was known as the "peintre des conquétes du Roi" and made eight trips with the army, recording the king's great deeds and the territories conquered. He later used these sketches as "notes" for the large paintings produced in the studio. These military images made up the *Conquêtes du Roi,* and some of them were included in a series that served as models for tapestries called the *histoire du roi.* Both were intended to document and validate Louis XIV as the great Warrior King.

The formal devices that Van der Meulen, and later his students, employed set the stage, so to speak, for this construction of the king's image, as illustrated in Van der Meulen's *March on Courtrai* (fig. 27).[14] Here the conventionalized form shapes the content. Among the conventions that were a staple in

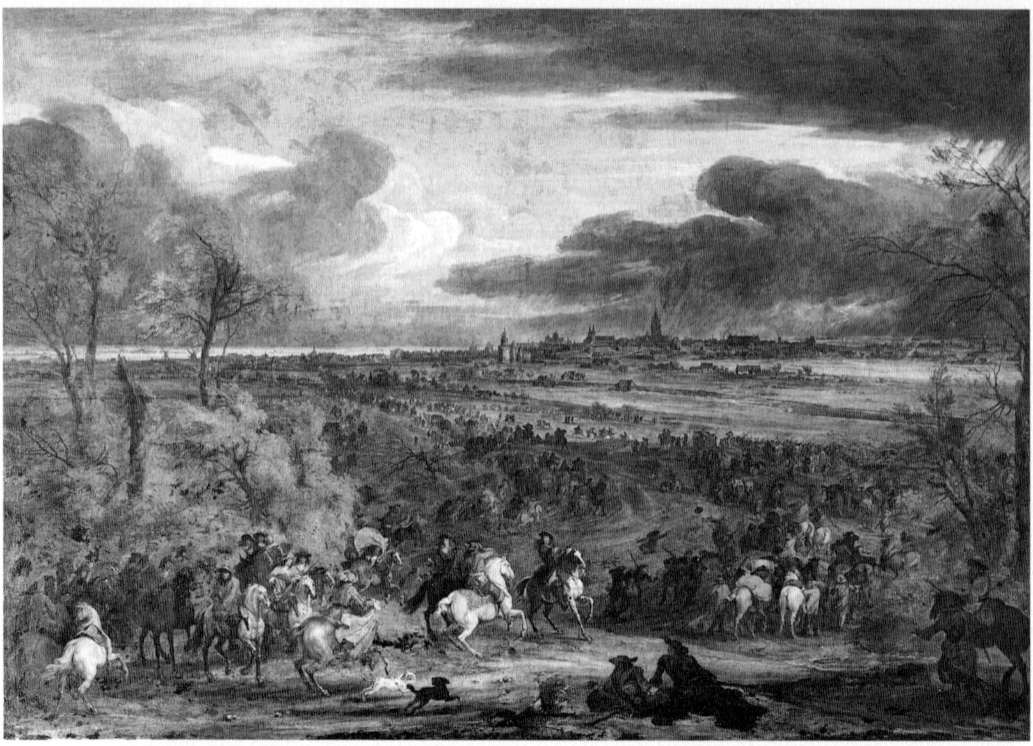

27. Adam François Van der Meulen, *March on Courtrai (Marche sur Courtrai)*, c. 1667, Musée national du Château de Versailles, Versailles. Cliché, Réunion des musées nationaux.

these images is the foreground rise, usually positioned to one side, which acts as a stage to showcase the presence of the king and other important military commanders; the rise tends to create a bowl-shaped foreground through which we see a detailed topographical rendering of the conquered territory in the distance. This dual emphasis – telescopic and microscopic – is a convention that is imposed over the natural environment, which in most cases was the flat terrain of Holland and Flanders. The transitional space between foreground and background is often "glossed over" by presenting it in the shadows or by making it indistinct. This technique formally suggests an implicit link between the king and the conquered territory. The intermediary space also provides an opportunity to present seemingly realistic and incidental activities, such as the troops practicing drills or relaxing.

The inclusion of specific details, such as the costumes and accessories worn by the figures in the foreground, the exacting topographical landscape in the background, and the seemingly candid scenes of military life, creates a documentary realism that spills over onto the image as a whole; the "realistic" detail masks the underlying conventional frame. The image is contrived to convey an illusion of transparent reality, thereby reinforcing the ideological assumptions encoded within the use of certain representational conventions.

Van der Meulen's attention to the details of military life made him a favorite of military historians, who view these paintings as historical documents.[15] Yet this exactitude should be seen as a kind of ideological shaping as much as it is factual reporting. One example of this is the avoidance of actual battle and bloodshed. It is the spectacle of a well-shod professional army that Van der Meulen represents, not the miseries of war à la Callot. Officers are competent and composed, and the army is disciplined and orderly. In Van der Meulen's paintings the army is both an instrument of a royal order that confirmed the king's power and effectiveness and a sign of economic prosperity, since war in the early modern period was a luxury linked to general economic well-being.[16] When actual combat is depicted, it is as a puff of smoke on the horizon, literally "over there."

Another example of this ideological shaping can be seen in the lack of overt emphasis on the figure of the king. Although the viewer would have no trouble identifying which figure is the king's because of his costume, recognizable physiognomy, and prominent position in the foreground, the king is not distinguished from the other commanders by traditional visual devices for denoting importance: a larger scale, a more formal pose, special framing elements, or allegorical indicators. Louis XIV is a commander whose "presence" seems to shine through naturally. The documentary aura of Van der Meulen's military images make them particularly well suited to giving form to the larger ideology of the *roi de guerre* – Louis XIV allegedly took great glee in repeating in front of a group of Van der Meulen's paintings "Here I am, I recognize myself."[17] More specifically, these images articulate official policy and diplomacy. Although it is outside the scope of this book, it is worth noting that Van der Meulen and other state-supported military painters subtly altered artistic conventions and strategies as military policy and practice changed during the four major wars of Louis XIV's reign: the War of Devolution (1667–68), the Dutch Wars (1672–79), the Nine Years' War (1688–97), and the War of Spanish Succession (1701–13).

The French topographical tradition was well established as the official mode for military painting by the early 1670s, with Van der Meulen and his atelier at the Gobelins as its foremost practitioners. The topographic tradition as a *form* came to signify "documentary truth," independent of the latent subject; its generic conventions became as much a part of the official rhetoric as were certain literary forms. These images were officially commissioned for the decoration of royal houses; they were also reproduced in paintings and engravings as gifts for important dignitaries.[18] The engravings, moreover, were made part of the *cabinet du roi,* the visual inventory of Louis XIV's vast and rich domain, of his great deeds, and of the fruits of paternal largess.[19] The public had access to these prints because Louis XIV granted reproduction privileges to Van der Meulen, who distributed them through the Gobelins and various print dealers.[20] The common appearance of these prints in eighteenth-century sales catalogues attests to their popularity among collectors and amateurs.

The conventions of the official topographical tradition also appear in the royal almanacs produced by a group of print dealers in the rue St. Jacques (fig. 28).[21] Intending the almanacs for a wide audience, the government provided subventions to their publishers and had a hand in determining which great deeds and important events of the previous year would be commemorated. The almanacs were of a relatively uniform size – around 89 cm by 55 cm – and format. At the top of the page would be a principal scene, which most likely was dictated by the state, and below this image would be the space reserved for the calendar; any number of subsidiary scenes could be added to report more fully on the year that was. Military subjects played a primary role in the almanacs; these images presented an official point of view couched within an "objective" documentary format.

Another tradition of military painting, and one with which Watteau would have been familiar, focuses on the tumult of battle. In an image of the Battle of Malplaquet by Johann van Huchtenburg (fig. 29) we can see the action of combat up close, filling the foreground. Although the work's documentary point of view is similar to that of Van der Meulen's topographical tradition, the engraving's ideological point of view is different. Such battle scenes provide another

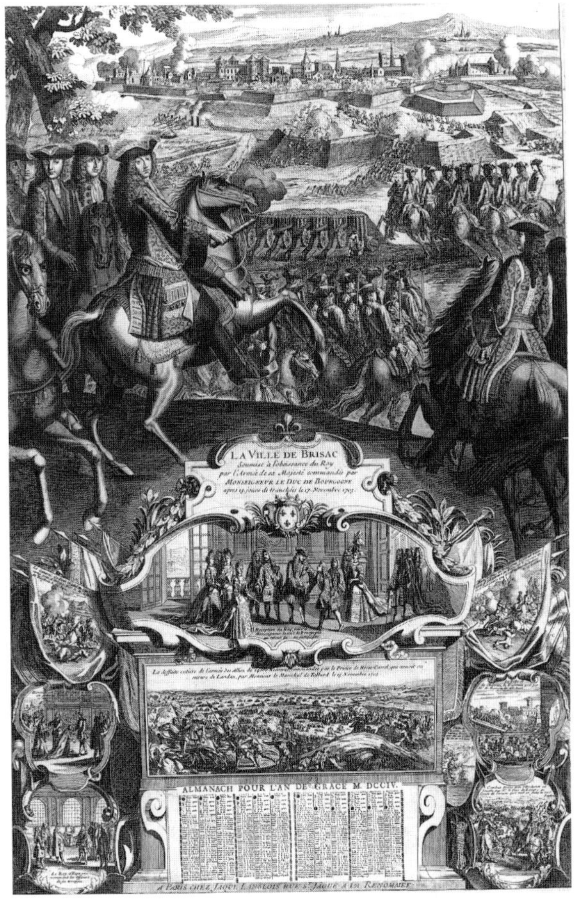

28. *Almanach Royal 1704*, Bibliothèque nationale de France, Paris. Cliché, Bibliothèque nationale de France, Paris.

kind of information and draw upon other conventions and traditions. In particular, these images reflect what is commonly referred to as the Italian tradition in battle painting, exemplified by the work of painters such as Jacques Courtois (called Bourgignon) (fig. 30) and Salvator Rosa.[22] This tradition, which was also common in the north, accentuated the commotion and drama of combat; the battles were often imaginary and admired for their "exotic" quality.

Joseph Parrocel, who had studied this genre in Italy with Bourgignon, established this kind of painting in France.[23] Parrocel was accepted into the Royal Academy of Painting and Sculpture in 1673, yet he never enjoyed the same success in official circles or the same level of state patronage as did Van der Meulen. Rather, Parrocel made his reputation through the tumultuous, imaginary battle paintings that he produced for a private clientele (fig. 31). His lack of official success is not surprising, for the generic conventions of the tumultuous mode did not meet the demands of French political culture. Whereas the topographical tradition in and of itself signified truth, the military prowess of the king, and the greatness of France's holdings, the particular meanings and associations of the tumultuous genre mitigated its success as a tool for state propaganda. First, the association of this convention with the imaginary, exotic, and fantastic was so strong that "real" battles depicted in this mode were difficult for the public to accept as "fact." Here the convention itself subverted a documentary reading of an event, especially in relation to the highly institutionalized topographical tradition. Second, Parrocel's Italian training and stylistic links with Bourgignon and Rosa provided a "foreign" counterpoint against which the idea of a natural French style (the topographical style à la Van der Meulen) was solidified.

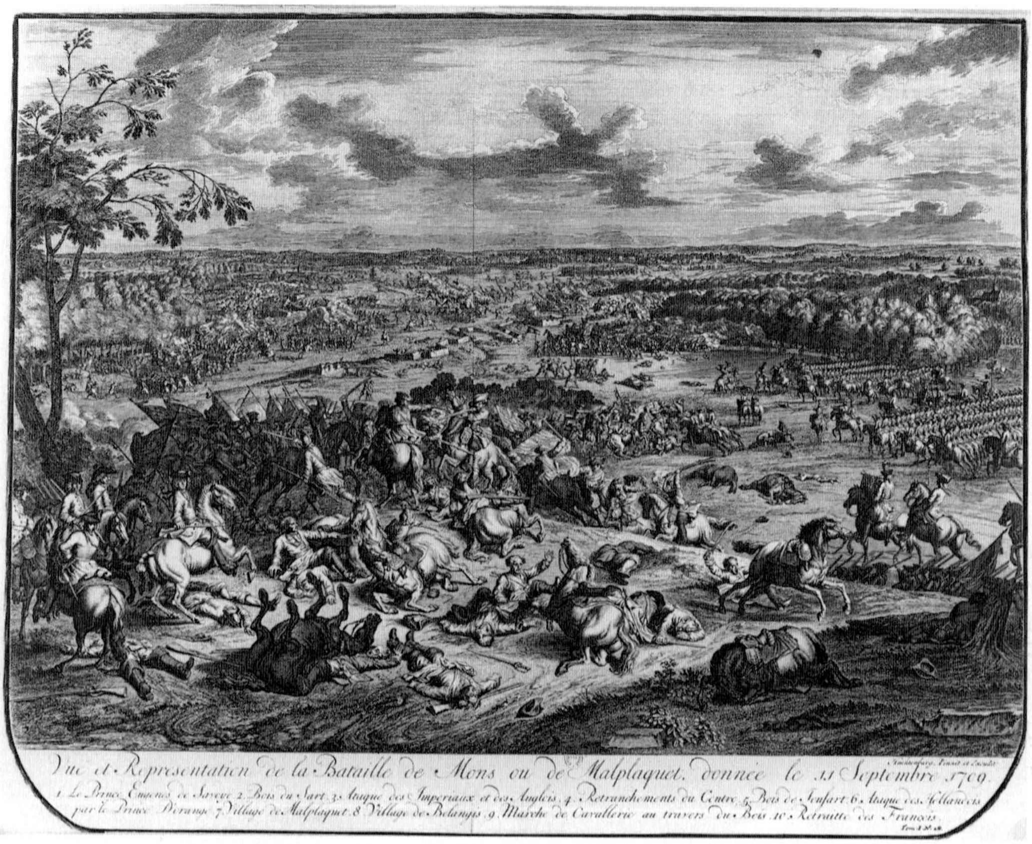

29. Johann van Huchtenburg, *View and Reconstruction of the Battle of Mons, or Malplaquet (Vue et representation de la bataille de Mons ou de Malplaquet)*, Bibliothèque nationale de France, Paris. Cliché, Bibliothèque nationale de France, Paris.

The foreignness of the tumultuous tradition also had another dimension. During the latter part of the Nine Years' War and during the War of Spanish Succession, French victories were few and far between, and the number of foreign prints representing French defeats increased greatly. The stately images emanating from the Gobelins atelier were supplanted by the more vigorous and graphic battle scenes of artists working outside France. In the *Collection Hennin* and the *Histoire de France*, two large collections of prints at the Bibliothèque Nationale concerning the history of France, the number of contemporary battle and military scenes of obviously non-French origins first shows a noticeable increase in 1690 and a marked increase again between 1700 and 1713.[24] In the absence of French military victories and conquered territories there was no longer a rationale to produce images in the topographical tradition. A more tumultuous mode was also employed in popular broadsheets reporting sensational events, including military actions and natural disasters. A good example can be seen in a

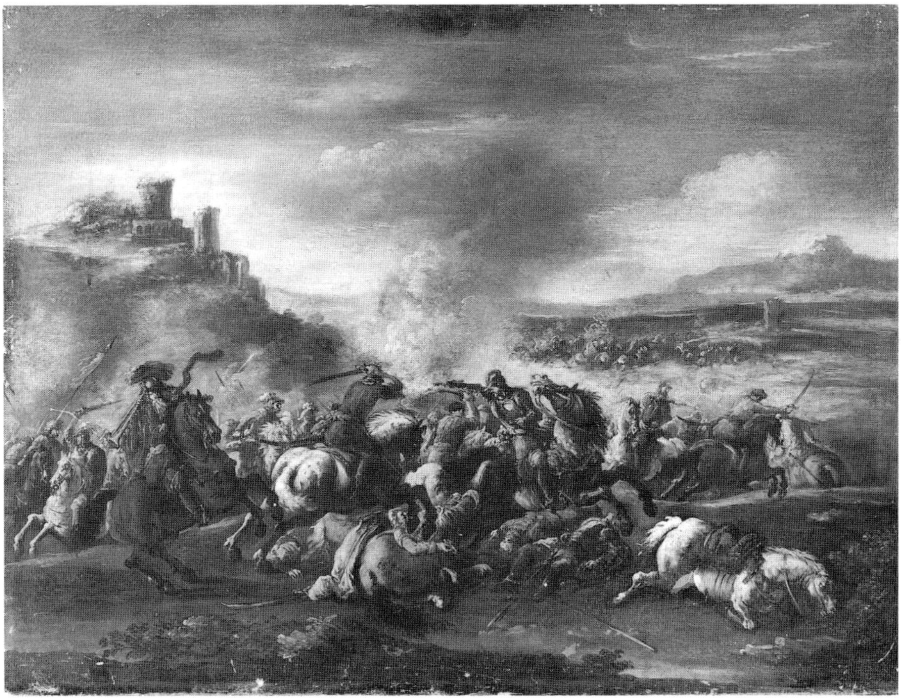

30. Jacques Courtois, called Bourgignon, *Combat*, Musée du Louvre, Paris. Cliché, Réunion des musées nationaux.

Dutch broadsheet about the Battle of Malplaquet (the same battle represented by Huchtenburg [fig. 29] and by the order and plan of battle [fig. 24]), where the tumult has become chaos and is now almost illegible visually (fig. 32). This kind of "action" imagery would have carried with it connotations of death, disaster, destruction, and defeat. The confusion and disorder that is depicted is at the expense of a visual mapping of troop formation, as can be seen in the order of battle. This near-illegibility, which is so common in these broadsheets, is a convention that conveys the melee and experience of actual combat.

I have chosen images of the Battle of Malplaquet, which took place on 11 September 1709, to illustrate some of these traditions in military painting. In this battle the French were defeated by the allied forces (England, Holland, German States, Habsburg Empire, Savoy, and Portugal), but losses on both sides were so heavy that neither side could really claim a victory.[25] The site of this battle was near Watteau's hometown of Valenciennes; in fact, in the Dutch print, Valenciennes is marked on the left horizon. When Watteau returned home in 1709 it would have been in the aftermath of this battle.[26] At this time, Valenciennes served as an administrative hub and housed a regional military hospital as well as provided lodging for soldiers. The flood of wounded into the city and the destruction of the countryside certainly would have made an

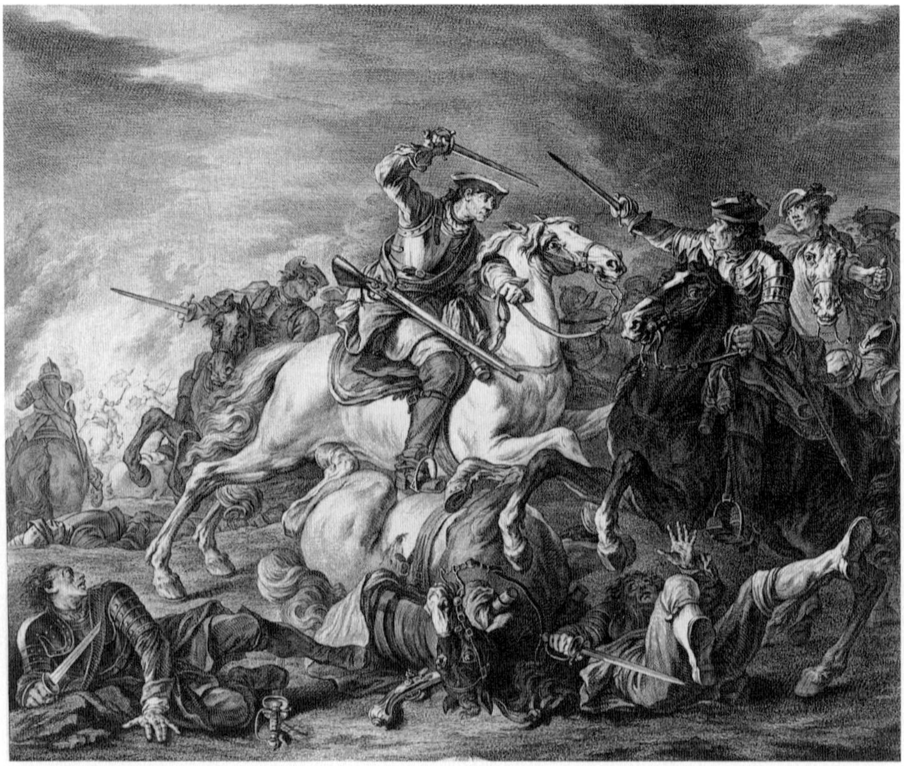

31. Engraving after Joseph Parrocel, *Battle (Bataille)*, Bibliothèque nationale de France, Paris. Cliché, Bibliothèque nationale de France, Paris.

impression on Watteau. Moreover, the region around his hometown had been contested territory and the site of military conflict since before Watteau's birth.[27] French troops took the city in 1677, after a lengthy and destructive siege. Valenciennes became part of a line of fortified cities on the northern French frontier. Vauban, Louis XIV's brilliant military engineer, oversaw the fortification of the city, and Louis XIV visited Valenciennes twice in the 1680s as part of a tour of fortified towns in the north. Just before Watteau left Valenciennes for Paris, around 1700–1701, there was an enormous buildup of troops in the region.[28] Watteau, then, was no stranger to war, to soldiers, or to military culture, and one can assume that military subjects would have had personal resonance for the artist.

In Paris, Watteau would have observed another side of military life. Some officers, both retired and active, and the members of the privileged *maison militare du Roi,* or the *Gardes du corps,* were able to enjoy the status of a military career without always having to endure the hardships of a soldier's life in the field of battle or in temporary camp. This group could live a life of ease in Paris, Versailles, or Marly (for at least much of the time) and cultivate an urbane sensibility. As well, Watteau could not have escaped exposure to the official French

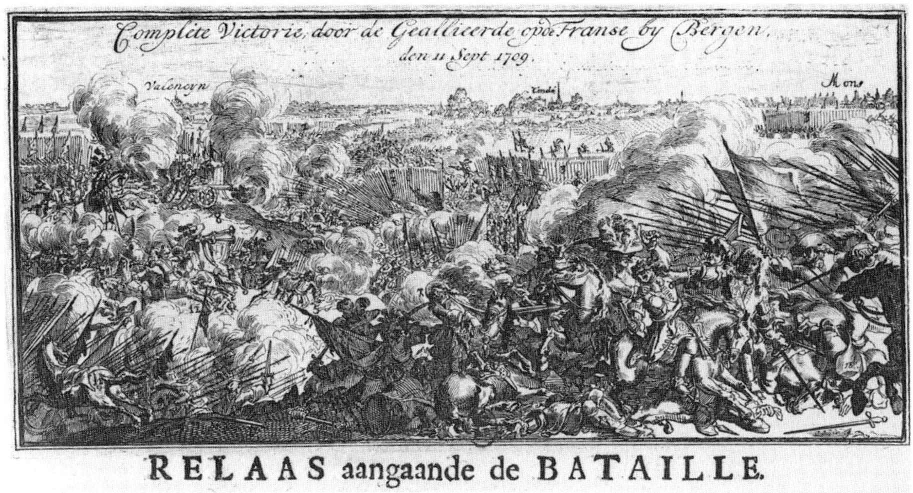

32. Dutch broadsheet, *Relaas aangaande de Bataille*, Bibliothèque nationale de France, Paris. Cliché, Bibliothèque nationale de France, Paris.

version of matters military as they were represented in images, *almanachs royaux,* and written accounts; foreign prints, gazettes, and broadsheets would have presented the "other side" of battles and military and diplomatic actions.

Watteau was thus situated at the intersection of distinct and differing experiences of military culture and war. Similarly, he was situated at an intersection in terms of his artistic training: his early training in the Flemish tradition, and his continued association with Flemish artists in Paris, provided him firm grounding in the northern tradition of genre painting. From about 1704 until about 1708, Watteau worked with Claude Gillot; he adopted and adapted elements of his master's style and, more important, was introduced by Gillot to the milieus of the *foires* and the theater. Then he worked for Claude III Audran, the concierge at the Luxembourg and one of the most fashionable decorators in Paris at the time.

There is an interpretation in Watteau scholarship to the effect that Watteau combined and recombined existing traditions to revitalize painting;[29] I am extending this interpretation to the military paintings. As I discussed earlier, Watteau's military paintings can clearly be situated within northern genre painting. *Return from the Campaign* and *Bivouac* (figs. 19 and 20) are not about actual battle or glory; rather, they depict aspects of military life that are far from heroic, which is characteristic of that northern tradition. Although the categorical similarities between Watteau and northern genre scenes cannot be denied, I do not think stopping at image matching or categorizing sufficiently explores the military paintings, given the specificity of their context. Watteau observed soldiers and military culture from a civilian's point of view at a time, during the War of Spanish Succession, when the subject of soldiers and the military surely carried its own set of meanings.

Watteau's Ironic Approach

The War of Spanish Succession (1701–13) was fought to decide the balance of power in Europe. Charles II of Spain had no direct heir, and after his death, not only Spain, but also the territories Spain controlled – the Low Countries, the Two Sicilies, Milan, and Spain's American colonies – would be vulnerable to takeover. After a series of negotiations the European powers agreed that a Bavarian prince would succeed Charles. But the prince died before Charles did, and the European heads of state then devised an elaborate plan to partition Spain's holdings. France was to receive Naples, Sicily, and Lorraine. In the meantime, however, Charles II had drawn up a new will in which he named the grandson of Louis XIV, the Duc d'Anjou, as his successor to the throne of Spain and all her vast holdings. When Charles II died in 1700, Louis XIV could not resist the temptation, and he declared his grandson to be Philip V of Spain. Immediately, England, Holland, the Habsburg Empire, and the German States allied themselves against France. By the end of the war nearly all the states of western Europe had joined in a grand alliance against France. The allies gradually wore down the French, and for much of the war the French army was sorely lacking in material and human resources. Moreover, this war was neither completely understood nor enthusiastically embraced by even the most loyal French subjects. In 1713 peace negotiations began, culminating in the Treaty of Utrecht: Philip V was accorded the crown of Spain, but only on the condition that the crowns of France and Spain would never be united.

By 1709, when Watteau was painting his military scenes, the reality of service in the military and of war no longer corresponded either to the kind of orderliness and professionalism implicit in images of the order of battle or to the spectacle of the victorious warrior king implicit in the officially sponsored images à la Van der Meulen. As Katie Scott has indicated, in the first quarter of the eighteenth-century the use of heroic themes in decorative cycles declined.[30] And Watteau's military paintings are hardly heroic; within their contemporary context, they referred to circumstances and elicited concerns from their eighteenth-century audience that were different from those that a painting on a similar subject by an artist such as Wouvermans would have produced in the preceding century. In this sense, Watteau's military paintings should be seen in opposition to the northern genre tradition they most closely resemble, while at the same time reifying certain aspects of that bourgeois wish fulfillment that was a part of the tradition.

Watteau's military works should also be viewed as constructed in opposition to the official image of war and *gloire*. Yet these are not like the blatant critiques of Louis XIV's military campaigns that we find in Dutch prints, such as in Romeyne de Hooghe's scenes of sacking and carnage, which, Scott insists, represent the "secret history," or the real carnage, that took place behind the official backdrop of Van der Meulen's paintings; nor are they like the imagery of a satirical countermythology that mocked the pretenses of official visual panegyrics.[31] Watteau's critique is more subtle. By framing them within the historical context and philosophical currents of the day, Hal Opperman has persuasively argued that these paintings are about peace rather than about war.[32] As Opperman points out, the entourage of figures in *Return from the Campaign* (fig. 19) move from the background to the foreground, a trajectory contrary to the movement of the figures in Watteau's later *fêtes galantes*. The movement toward the distance in the *fêtes galantes* suggests the normal temporal progress of love and life; in *Return from the Campaign,* the movement suggests other things. The viewer experiences "a sense not only of personal defeat but, more important, of the course of nature turned against itself."[33] This mood of reversal and abnormality, I would argue, is also produced by the inversion of the topographical formula employed by Van der Meulen and his school. The foreground rise that acts as a stage for the important commanders in the official tradition has been replaced in the Watteau painting by a depression. The elevated area in the background of *Return from the Campaign* neatly forecloses our view of what should be, in the Van der Meulen tradition, a vast panorama of conquered territory. That Watteau provides a tiny glimpse of this distant landscape only underscores that it is cut off from view. The image seems somehow wrong or unnatural because it confounds the expected conventions for military subjects of a certain type; moreover, it confounds the traditional meanings encoded within those conventions.

Similarly, *Bivouac* (fig. 20), the presumed pendant to *Return from the Campaign,* can be interpreted as subverting the message of official military imagery. The painting represents a *camp volant,* or bivouac, a subject that Van der Meulen also represented on more than one occasion (fig. 33).[34] In *Bivouac,* Watteau creates a sense of amiable disorder by crowding the image with figures: Donald Posner has counted more than fifty, engaged in activities appropriate to the situation, such as resting, conversing, card playing, and cooking.[35] Despite the overall jumble of this scene and its "realism," there is a focal point to which the informally arrayed figures respond. The nursing woman in the center of the image functions as a visual and iconographical fulcrum. Compositionally she is at the intersection of two major axes created by the seemingly random placement of the figures, and, in addition, a brighter illumination spotlights her centrality. Iconographically, this nurturing, maternal figure provides a thematic contrast to the masculine virtues of war. Themes of domesticity, rest, and retreat supplant those of the hero, heroics, and conquest traditionally associated with military painting. Mary Vidal has furthered this reading of the images, suggesting that the central position of women in both *Bivouac* and *Return from the Campaign* represents the civilizing process and social continuity within a male world of violence and social dissolution.[36] Within the context of the War of Spanish Succession Vidal's interpretation of the pointed female presence makes sense for a number of reasons.

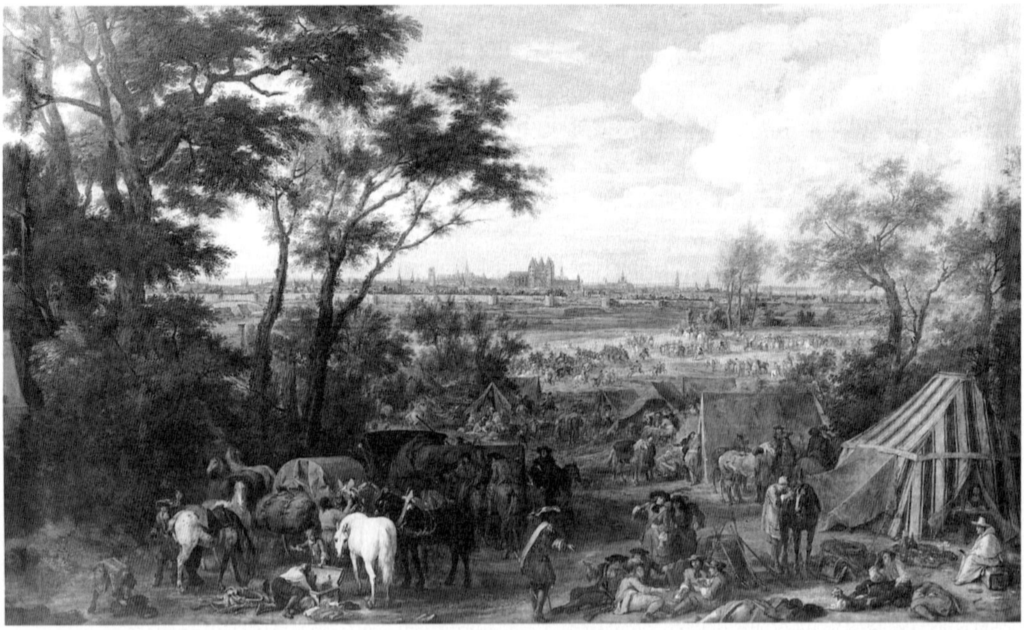

33. Adam François Van der Meulen, *The Army of Louis XIV Camped before Tournai in 1667 (L'armée du Louis XIV campant devant Tournai in 1667)*, 1668, Musée Royaux des Beaux-Arts de Belgique, Brussels.

The War of Spanish Succession was fought during the sunset years of Louis XIV, when he was no longer able to make an appearance, even symbolic, before the field of battle. Instead, Louis became an armchair commander, running the various campaigns via couriers from Versailles.[37] Military historians argue that Louis XIV, in a bid to exert his control over a war in which he could no longer effectively participate, preferred weaker commanding officers who could "take orders" to those who might assert independent action. Maréchal Villars, a competent, confident officer, was often at loggerheads with Louis XIV. This conflict crystallized around the issue of the place of Villars's wife on a military campaign. Villars had a reputation of being enormously jealous of his younger wife and wanted her to join him on campaign rather than leave her to the influences of the court. Louis XIV had a standing order that there were to be no women at the front. He wrote Villars expressing his annoyance: "How many squadrons would it take to protect her?"[38] Villars replied that he either would enjoy the company of his wife or would leave his majesty's service; eventually, she was supplied with a passport. Although I do not wish to suggest that the nursing female figure in either *Return from the Campaign* or *Bivouac* was intended to represent Madame Villars, the figure could have functioned, at the time, as an elliptical, or associative, reference to this dispute and to the general issue of women's place in the army.

Female camp followers, who were often the wives of soldiers, and children were a fact of military life, in spite of official policy.[39] Their role was always ambiguous, however; women were needed as laundresses, cooks, and camp housekeepers, and hence, their presence, in limited numbers, was welcomed. In 1706 a ruling gave children, wives, and valets some of the same privileges that the soldiers had regarding housing and food.[40] But opinion varied about what was the appropriate number of women per company: some believed that one or two women per company could be tolerated as long as they behaved correctly and contributed to the cleanliness and subsistence of the soldiers; others believed that three or four women was a more realistic figure; and some even argued that as many as eight women could be allowed as long as they were subject to military regulations. No matter how many or how few women were allowed, it was considered imperative that they be regulated and well behaved lest their unruly feminine nature disrupt and corrupt military order. Because of women's potential power to disrupt, soldiers needed permission to marry; in fact, matrimony was actively discouraged.

The women in Watteau's paintings are hardly disruptive, especially in comparison to the bawdy women in the military scenes that Watteau's student, Jean-Baptiste Pater, popularized before his death in 1736. Pater's jolly military scenes became a subgenre and were disseminated through the medium of prints (fig. 34). The spotlighted presence of the women in *Bivouac* and *Return from the Campaign* (as well as a similar presence of women in nearly all of Watteau's military paintings) would have had a particular resonance in relation to the ongoing controversy about wives and women, and their place and comportment in the army.

Watteau's women function, as Vidal suggests, as signs of domesticity and social stability, and as Opperman argues, as promoters of an ideal of peace. By all accounts, the War of Spanish Succession was not a popular war, and it helped to intensify a pacifist movement that grew around the Duke of Burgundy and his tutor, the prelate and author of progressive tracts, Fénelon.[41] Opperman finds close parallels between the attitudes of Fénelon and of Watteau, parallels that their audiences would have noted. I think Opperman very much to the point in his observation that Watteau's military paintings are not antimilitary in the sense that Callot's and Goya's works are: "Watteau gives us a more positive approach, more subtle and rarer."[42] Watteau's women provide a utopian presence; they create a "happy home" within a context not generally known for love and domesticity. They are part of an ironic critique that, I would argue, is at the heart of Watteau's military paintings. His depictions consistently draw attention to the distance during the War of Spanish Succession between the official image and ideology of war and military life and the grimy, rag-tag reality. Within the space of this distance Watteau reinscribes an alternative ideal.

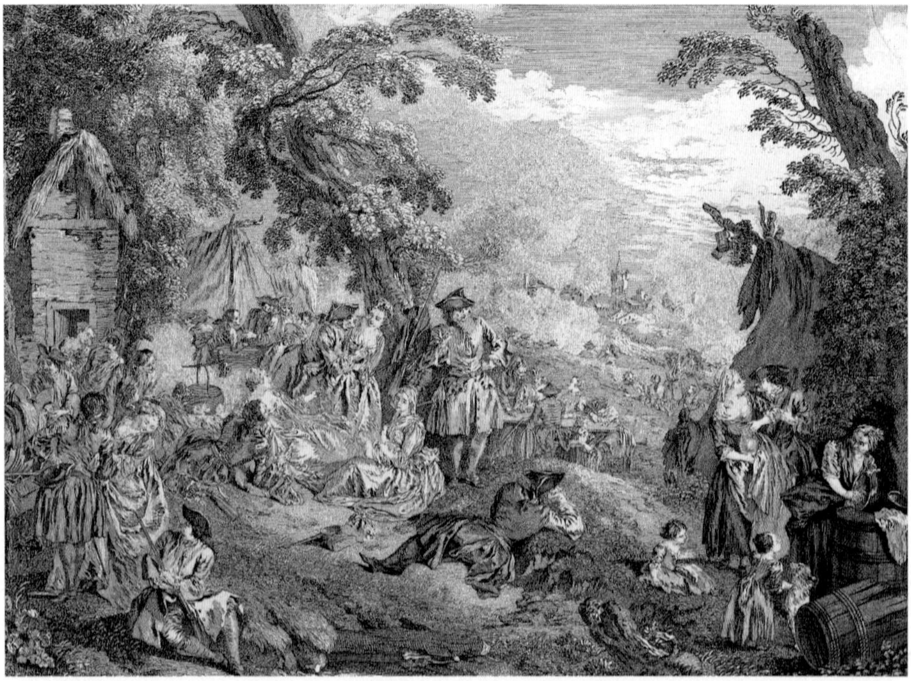

34. G. Scotin, engraving after J.-B. Pater, *The Canteen Keepers of Brest (Vivandières de Brest)*, Anne S. K. Brown Military Collection, Brown University Library, Providence, RI.

Watteau's ironic commentary can be understood only against a previously existing visual discourse, or convention, and the ideological assumptions it embodied. An image such as *Bivouac* becomes quite pointed in its message if we compare it to an official "camp scene." It is tempting to speculate that the eighteenth-century viewer would have seen in *Bivouac* a witty reply to Van der Meulen's painting *The Army of Louis XIV Camped before Tournai in 1667* (fig. 33).[43] Moreover, the number of copies of this image suggests that it was known to a fairly wide audience: Van der Meulen did two versions of this painting, and Jean-Baptiste Martin (called Martin des Batailles), who worked in Van der Meulen's workshop, made two copies after Van der Meulen's original. There was also a print that would have circulated through print dealers.

The bird's-eye point of view in *Tournai* presents a broad panorama that is quite different from the close, low perspective of Watteau's *Bivouac*. Van der Meulen's camp is an image of order. In the left foreground are a group who are unpacking trunks and caring for horses; in the center a figure wearing the uniform of the *mousquetaires* gestures to the background; and to the right a group of soldiers plays cards, converses, and sleeps. There is much activity, but its visual pace is stately; the figures are spread out and the bird's-eye view allows the viewer to "survey" the painting in a deliberate manner. A row of tents, including two gray-and-blue-striped commanders' tents, leads the viewer's attention back toward the middle ground. Soldiers can be seen around the tents, eating and drinking and preparing the table. At the end of the row of tents a pair of soldiers on horseback gallops off into the middle ground where a number of mounted soldiers appear in formation on an open, illuminated field. In the distant background on the horizon is a precise, topographical view of Tournai, the city that has just been taken. The three zones of the painting – the camp in the foreground, army in the middle ground, and captured territory in the background – are all ideologically linked. Thanks to royal riches and the administrative structure necessary to move and support the troops, the army can acquire territory and preserve civil peace. Tournai is an image about organization and about the new professionalism and regularization of the royal army.

Watteau's *Bivouac* presents a scene of irregularity and relative disorder. The viewer is mired, so to speak, in the camp, with no vista into the background. The snoozing and chatting soldiers in the right foreground create a visual chain drawing the viewer's eye to the nursing woman in the center; the cook standing on the left gazes directly out toward the viewer. Watteau has employed devices that pull the viewer into this jumbled group. Moreover, the jumble gives the group a sense of cohesion rather than the sense of isolation of the separate groups of figures in Van der Meulen's painting. In Van der Meulen's image the napping and card-playing soldiers are incidental, one group among many. The two women Van der Meulen has represented are scarcely the focal point the nursing woman is in Watteau's image; one, at the opening of a tent in the middle foreground, appears to be scrubbing a pan, and the other woman, hardly more than a speck, appears to be presenting a drink to a group of seated soldiers. Watteau's image prints an inversion of visual conventions and composition and, as well, an inversion of the built-in narrative structure. What is only incidental in the *Tournai* painting becomes the central focus of *Bivouac*.

I have argued that Watteau's painting may have constituted an ironic response to Van der Meulen's by pointing out compositional and narrative inversions. A specific detail makes this idea even more plausible. In the right-hand foreground of *Tournai* there is a figure who gestures toward one of the blue-and-gray-striped commanders' tents. Within the shadowy space of the tent we can make out a seated figure examining documents that cover the table in front of him. This figure is the secretary of war, Louvois, whose careful planning produced an exemplary and well-ordered siege, resulting in the taking of the city.[44] Louvois was crucial in helping to effect the transition of the army from a feudal to a professional organization that was ongoing from the War of Devolution (represented here) through the middle of the eighteenth century.[45] And Van der Meulen was important for visually affirming this transition. Van der Meulen's exactitude, his inclusion of details about weapons, uniforms, and so on, should be seen as ideological shaping as much as it is factual reporting. For example, regular camps replaced having townspeople board soldiers, and provisions were secured through planning and purchase rather than through local looting.[46] The introduction to M. Nodot's *Le munitionaire des armés de France* (1697) stresses the importance of the *munitionaire* (commissary) in assuring victory.[47] Nodot's work outlines the practice of the *munitionaire* in sufficient detail to make the modern reader appreciate the enormity and complexity of the task of provisioning an army. Hence, the camp and cooking scenes, I would argue, also carry meaning for the contemporary viewer familiar with military or political discourse.

Thus Van der Meulen represents the idea of the army as an instrument of royal order; even though Louis XIV is not literally present, the orderly, well-shod soldiers in the foreground and the disciplined cavalry exercises in the mid-ground confirm his power. Louvois in the tent functions as a visual "footnote," a way of crediting the war secretary's organizational skills and military acumen without directly competing with the implied presence of the king.

In Watteau's *Bivouac* a soldier standing behind and slightly to the left of the central female figure similarly gestures to an open tent. In this case, however, we know there will be no one like Louvois within the tent, engaged in the mental labor necessary for military success; this tent is a tavern, indicated by the wreath that hangs from the tent pole above the entrance.[48] Moreover, incisive and informed leadership through the secretary of war and high-ranking officers *(officiers généraux)* was not present during the War of Spanish Succession, which was notorious for its poor leadership.[49] After Louvois's death in 1691, the next three men in his position had little experience with war; they were, however, good at obeying Louis XIV.[50] The *officiers généraux*, who by tradition were appointed on the basis of birth, tended more and more to be the young, inexperienced members of noble families and to be less interested in soldiering than in adventuring. The demand for *officiers généraux* had increased dramatically; in 1702, Louis XIV created one hundred new regiments, and according to several sources, there were seven thousand officers' places to be filled in 1702.[51] The *Mémoires* of Joseph Quincy, a captain who was at the Battle of Malplaquet, are filled with complaints about these untrained, upstart officers.[52] He complains that they are officers in name only and that they lack a true military vocation; they are extravagant; they risk others' lives in search of personal glory; and they are incompetent, relying on orders from above rather than on their own good judgment. His most common refrain, however, is that they are too young and inexperienced in all aspects of military training:

> The abuse of purchasing regiments in France is the true cause of the lack of good *officiers généraux*. The consent to buy a regiment is given to a child who has just finished *college*. He tells himself: In eight years, I will be a brigadier, in fourteen

Maréchal de camp, in twenty years lieutenant général according to the table of rank. Great God, what an *officier général!* One time I overheard a young colonel: "I would rather make 100 mistakes at the head of my regiment than to consult my lieutenant-colonel." A fine attitude for becoming a great man![53]

Quincy reflects that the French army lost almost all its battles because the generals did not know the terrain; they had not spent time either with maps or reconnoitering the area. During the 1702 Italian campaign, the Marquis de Boulingneux, whom Quincy describes as an "airhead" *(d'une distraction extraordinaire),* was on horseback paying no attention to his whereabouts when he suddenly found himself in the midst of the enemy: he pretended to be one of their *officiers généraux.*[54]

The good example set by Louvois in Van der Meulen's painting was not followed by many military leaders during the War of Spanish Succession. Thus Watteau's parallel image of a tent and gesturing soldier could have functioned as an ironic reference, underscoring the gap between the past ideal of military order and the contemporary disarray. It is probable that someone like Quincy, someone who railed about the good old days – "What the devil sort of general officers do we have these days? What has happened to the lines of Turenne, Condé, Luxembourg, Catinat and Vendôme?"[55] – made this very connection, a kind of connection that may be lost on the modern viewer.

The eighteenth-century viewer may also have made a connection between Watteau's *The Defilade*[56] (fig. 35) and Le Brun's *The Canal at Bruges* (fig. 36), which was part of the *l'histoire du Roi* tapestry series.[57] This series, masterminded by Le Brun and executed with the help of the army of artists and artisans at the Gobelins, consisted of fourteen tapestries after Le Brun's designs done between 1663 and 1673. These were celebrated images that played a key role in what Peter Burke describes in the title of his book as *The Fabrication of Louis XIV. The Canal at Bruges* would have been known through the 1680 engraving by Sebastien LeClerc that was included in the *cabinet du roi* and through numerous painted copies.[58] In *The Canal at Bruges* (and also in a generically similar work from the *histoire du Roi* tapestry series, *L'Entrée à Dunkerque,* and in Van der Meulen's *Surrender of Marsal to Louis XIV*), the king and his important officers, mounted on rearing horses, pointedly dominate the image. The foreground rise from which Louis XIV clearly commands, given the position of his baton, provides a staging ground for the literal and figural display of power. The other three figures, the marquises de Condé and Créquy to the right of the king and the Marquis de Bellefonds in the center, with his back to the viewer, were the other major commanders in the 1667 French defeat of the Spanish army at the Bruges canal. In the middle ground a battle takes place.

The composition of Watteau's *The Defilade,* and of the engraving done after it, is a mirror image of *The Canal at Bruges,* a mirroring that must have in-

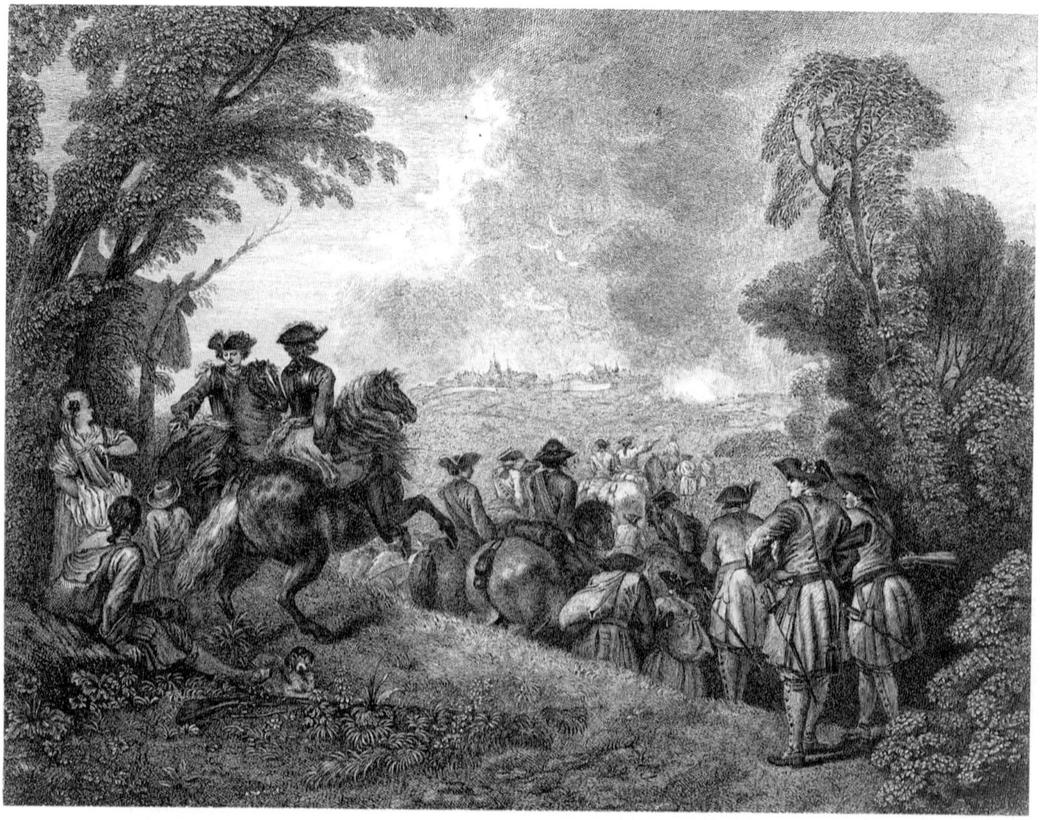

35. Jean Moyreaux, engraving after Watteau, *The Defilade (Défillé)*, engraving announced 1730, painting c. 1709, Anne S. K. Brown Military Collection, Brown University Library, Providence, RI.

vited pointed comparison. Watteau's image shows the smoke of battle in the background, soldiers moving toward the action, and a foreground rise with a few prominent figures. In *The Canal at Bruges,* Louis XIV gazes at the viewer and directs the viewer's attention toward the battle and territory in the distance through his upward gesture of command. The figure who occupies the parallel position in Watteau's image addresses his gaze and gesture downward toward the group comprising a woman polishing a tankard, a child, and a seated man to the left. The soldier's gaze and gesture suggest a reluctance to leave that domestic enclosure for battle. Moreover, his gesture and gaze, directed downward and not toward the viewer, break with the traditional visual convention that links the foreground king (or commander) and the conquered territory in the background. There is an absence of command in *The Defilade* that would have resonated with eighteenth-century viewers in light of the crisis of command and military professionalism that characterized the War of Spanish Succession. Certainly, the soldiers, both mounted and on foot, do not rush

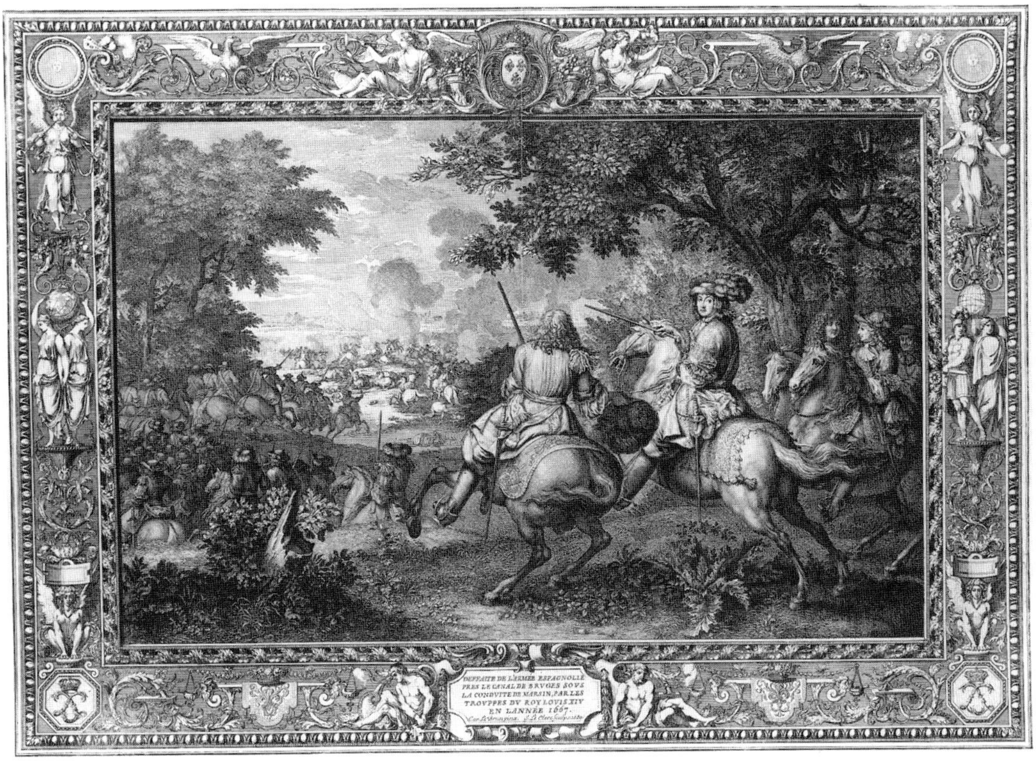

36. Sebastien Le Clerc, engraving after tapestry series *L'histoire du Roi*, *The Canal of Bruges (Le Canal de Bruges)*, 1680, Anne S. K. Brown Military Collection, Brown University Library, Providence, RI.

into battle; rather, they seem to plod along with little enthusiasm. The two figures on the right-hand side do not appear to be in any hurry to join their fellow soldiers or even to be much concerned with the event. The more prominent of these two figures has his hands on his hips; this informal, nonchalant pose is in contrast to the highly rhetorical use of body and gesture in the tradition of Le Brun and the Royal Academy of Painting and Sculpture.[59] In the didactic, propagandistic art fostered by Le Brun, the body functioned as a "legible text" that conveyed a clear, unequivocal message.

Norman Bryson has argued that the figures in Watteau's *fêtes galantes* are illegible bodies whose movements, gazes, and gestures withhold meaning in relation to the expectations presented by the larger semiotic frame of the image.[60] This aspect of his interpretation of Watteau's *fêtes galantes* applies to the military paintings as well. In *The Defilade* the stage is set for the reenactment of a particular scenario; however, the actors are not playing their appropriate roles. In a sense, Watteau presents a civilian's or foot soldier's point of view within the conventional frame of the commander's point of view. As in both *Bivouac* and *Return from the Campaign,* this opposition in *The Defilade* draws attention to the gap between official image and actual experience. This gap is perhaps even more obvious in *The Defilade* because it is the only military painting that is so clearly dependent upon the conventions of the official topographical tradition. Some scholars have suggested that this painting is a youthful experiment, and not a particularly successful one, in which Watteau is "trying on" genres and compositions.[61] I would argue that the painting should be read as an ironic commentary on the official tradition and what that tradition represented. Whether the commentary is the result of an unintentional youthful experiment or of an intentional critique is ultimately of little importance; what is important is the eighteenth-century viewer's perception of the work as well as what would have informed that perception.

The Social Context of Watteau's Irony

Watteau was often praised by his eighteenth-century biographers for his powers of observation and for the naturalness of his work. For example, Jean de Jullienne wrote in 1726 that "not only does he [Watteau] excel in *galante* and *champêtres* compositions, but also in his subjects of the army, soldiers' marches and camps, of which the simple and natural character make these kinds of pictures *très précieux*" (emphasis added).[62] One could speculate that the simplicity and naturalness Jullienne observed in Watteau's military subjects occurred in relation to official military imagery à la Le Brun, with its rhetorical gestures and poses. Naturalism, or realism, in art is always a relative designation; all art is artifice, actively constructing rather than passively reflecting the "real." The twentieth-century judgment that finds *The Defilade* to be a failed experiment is no doubt based on the fact that it is the only military image that can be so clearly "matched" to images in the official tradition. *The Defilade* does not fulfill the expectations the twentieth-century viewer has come to have regarding the official, topographical genre. This genre, so clearly invoked by Watteau's utilization of its landscape conventions in *The Defilade,* is likewise clearly contradicted by the figures within the image – hence, the work is a failure. But Watteau was addressing eighteenth-century, not twentieth-century, viewers. We must turn back to the context that would have informed the eighteenth-century viewer's mental horizon for viewing the painting: the War of Spanish Succession. In this context, the figures in *The Defilade* are realistic, and the framing landscape convention in the work – and all that they have come to represent – are in question.

The War of Spanish Succession was the last of Louis XIV's great wars, and it drained France's human and financial resources to the last drop. In 1709, in addition to other hardships, an extremely cold winter precipitated a famine. By this time, the French army was in shambles and suffering unprecedented defeats. Soldiers were recruited though conscription, always an unpopular policy, and the desertion rate was extremely high. This parody of the Lord's Prayer, which circulated in Paris, aptly reflects the prevailing mood:

> Our Father which art at Versailles, thy
> name is no longer hallowed, thy kingdom
> is no longer great! Thy will is no longer
> done on earth or on the sea!
> Give us our bread, which we lack on every side!
> Forgive our enemies who have beaten us,
> and not thy generals who have allowed them to!
> Succumb not to the temptations
> of La Maintenon, but deliver us from
> Chamillard![63]

Moreover, except for a weak Spanish force, France fought the War of Spanish Succession without allies. It was a war that seemed almost always on the verge of ending, in short, a war that did not inspire on the French side much conviction or sense of righteousness. During the summer and early autumn of 1709, when the buildup of troops in the north was at a peak before the Battle of Malplaquet, peace negotiations were taking place, and there was a strong belief that peace would soon be achieved.[64] The rumors of peace kept the dialogue going between the officers on both sides; the result was what Captain Joseph Quincy called a "droll de guerre." According to Quincy:

> The two armies were persuaded that the peace had been signed. A universal joy promptly spread in the two camps; we embraced enemy officers and our own. The enemy soldiers brought bread to our men, who were in great need of it because there had been no bread for three days. Also, as soon as a horse was killed, they sliced the meat, roasted it and then ate it. The French soldiers gave them brandy.
>
> What a surprise for the Maréchal Villars when he returned to the army. He demanded the reason for such a suspension of arms. He was no sooner informed than he gave orders to the enemy high officers to withdraw immediately; if they didn't he was going to fire upon them. . . . Thus our joy didn't last long.[65]

Thus in *The Defilade,* the reluctant soldiers, the absence of clear military leadership, and the more relaxed demeanor of the figures in the foreground give form to this "droll de guerre."

The Defilade's presumed pendant, *The Halt,* similarly presents a scene where war and peace, soldiers and civilians, are mixed (fig. 37).[66] The large tree in the center divides the image into two parts. On the left, in the engraving, there is a group of four resting soldiers, one of whom is wounded. A woman dressed in peasant garb with a baby is also a part of this visual unit. The placement of these figures below the horizon and in a row creates a horizontal emphasis, especially in comparison with the group on the right. The

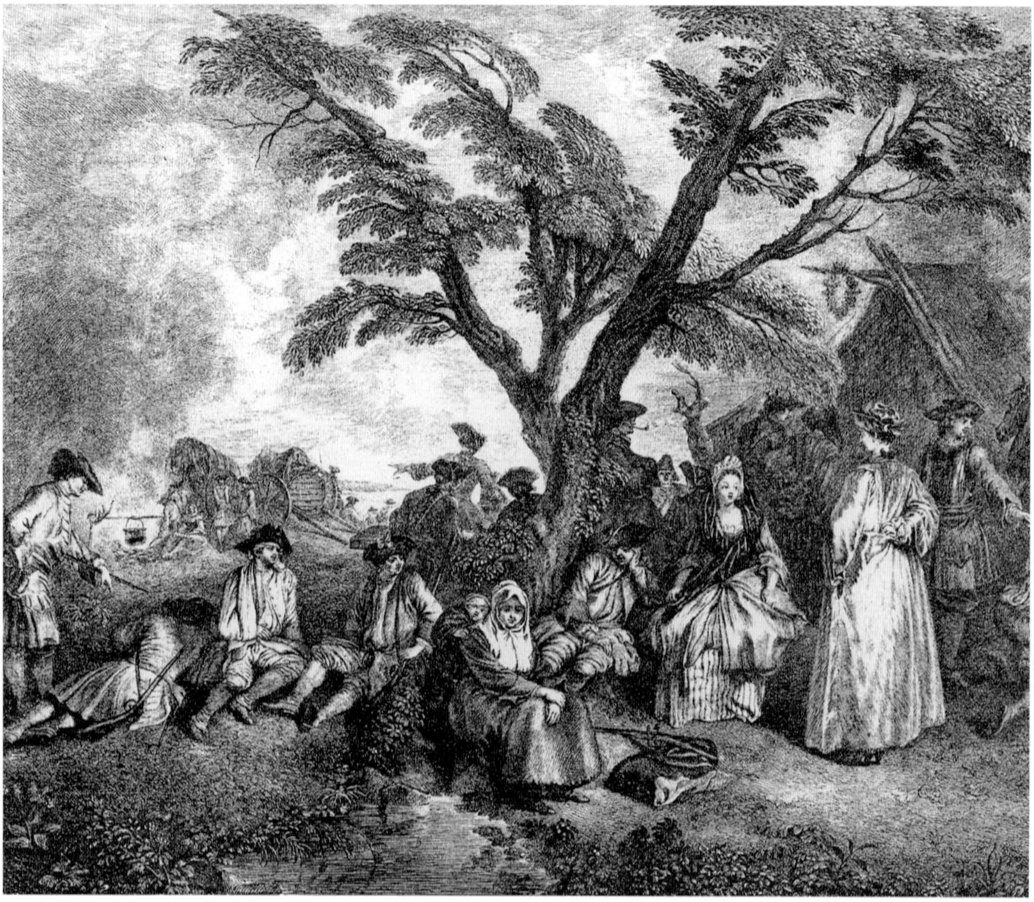

37. Jean Moyreau, engraving after Antoine Watteau, *The Halt (Alte)*, engraving announced 1729, painting 1709, author's collection.

right-hand-side scene is dominated by two women in elegant clothing; next to them a finely uniformed soldier (in red in the painting), probably belonging to the king's guard, gives orders to his servant.[67] The tavern tent, marked by the sign of the wreath, creates a unifying frame for this side, which has a more pronounced vertical emphasis than the left.

The division created by the tree sets up several potential comparisons. For one, on the left are the hardships of war, and on the right, the more pleasurable moments of military life. This division is consistent with Watteau's treatment of military subjects in general in that he frequently juxtaposes contrasting aspects of military life. For example, Watteau contrasts the harsh tedium of troop movements in *Return from the Campaign,* with the rest and sociability associated with camp life in its pendant, *Bivouac.* Similar thematics appear in the pendants *The Burdens of War* (fig. 38) and *The Respite from War* (fig. 39).

These works belonged to Antoine de la Roque – a friend of Watteau's and a retired officer in the king's guard.

This thematic play is congruent with the structuring of decorative painting that Watteau learned and practiced during his tenure (1708–9) with one of the foremost decorative painters in Paris, Claude III Audran. This kind of decorative painting required an often vague but all-encompassing "master theme" that could accommodate a variety of individual subjects, such as the seasons, the elements, the senses, or any number of mythological motifs.[68] Watteau painted a number of these decorative suites that we know today only through engravings. This mode of painting and its structuring of subject matter should not be overlooked in considering *The Halt* or Watteau's military painting in general. The conventions of decorative painting likely provided Watteau with a way to articulate and to comment upon the War of Spanish Succession that circumvented the conventions of official military imagery or the northern tradition.

The compositional divide in *The Halt* also presents the viewer with another comparison – one based on class distinctions: the left side of the engraving represents the lowly, and the right represents the high. The women are the key figures here, and their costumes and placement indicate a world of difference. Mary Vidal's description of these women in her discussion of Watteau's military paintings is quite telling: the women on the right are "aristocratic," and the seated woman is "humble."[69] The "aristocratic" women are neither servants nor the soldiers' wives who took care of the troops' domestic needs – their costumes convey as much.

Aristocratic women, especially members of the court, did visit the army in the field, viewing the troops and camps as a privileged spectacle. This practice was more common, however, during Louis XIV's earlier wars, such as the War of Devolution or the Dutch Wars, than it was during the War of Spanish Succession. Moreover, in *The Halt,* the finely dressed women are in the camp, not viewing it from a safe distance. The implausible presence of women from a class not normally part of military life raises questions and invites speculation. Vidal contends that these women represent the continuity and accomplishments of civilized society – ideas that were articulated in the pro-feminine literature of the period and with which the viewers of Watteau's paintings were presumably familiar.[70] The women's presence in the painting serves as a counterpoint to a masculine heroic ideal. "The bravery of the soldier is still honored here, but it is second in importance to the image of what bravery claims to protect: the continued performance of the rituals of civilization."[71]

In Vidal's interpretation, only women of a certain class could function as the purveyors of *civilité,* and in turn the expression of the rules of *civilité* was what marked one as a member of this elevated class. The seated peasant woman and child do not belong on the same visual, symbolic, or societal level as the other women; her seemingly normal, or natural, presence further height-

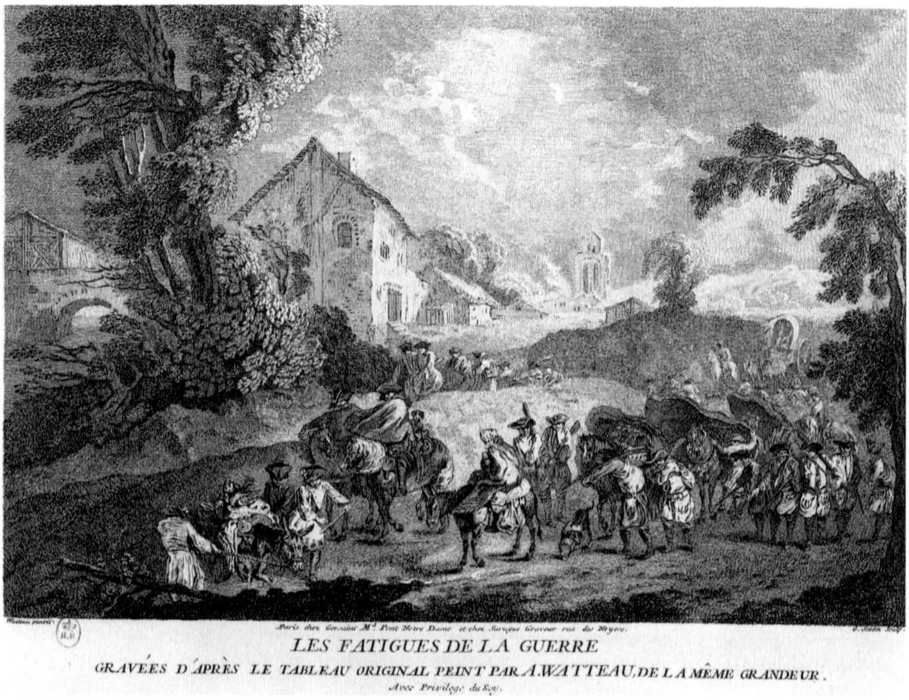

38. G. Scotin, engraving after Antoine Watteau, *The Burdens of War (Les fatigues de la guerre)*, engraving announced 1731, painting c. 1712, Bibliothèque nationale de France, Paris. Cliché, Bibliothèque nationale de France, Paris.

ens the "unnaturalness" of the well-dressed, aristocratic women within the scene. Whereas Vidal convincingly argues that these two women represented a civilizing force to a public familiar with both contemporary feminist writings and the pacifist movement, there are other events and currents that we should consider in reconstructing the eighteenth-century viewer's reading of these elegant women.

It is instructive to recall the case of Mme. Villars in relation to *The Halt*'s overdressed and "out-of-place" women. Mme. Villars was allowed on the field of battle in spite of Louis XIV's objection ("How many squadrons would it take to protect her?"). It is easy to imagine that the viewing public, too, would remember the story of Mme. Villars and its implications as a symbolic assault on the authority of Louis XIV as "chief commander." Despite the disruption of military order – especially given the king's prohibition of women at the front – Villars succeeded in having his wife present. Moreover, even though Mme. Villars probably did not require squadrons to protect her, her presence in the field would have necessitated special arrangements. Mme. Villars represented a disruptive element that would have resonated with a general sense of decline and dissolution within the military.

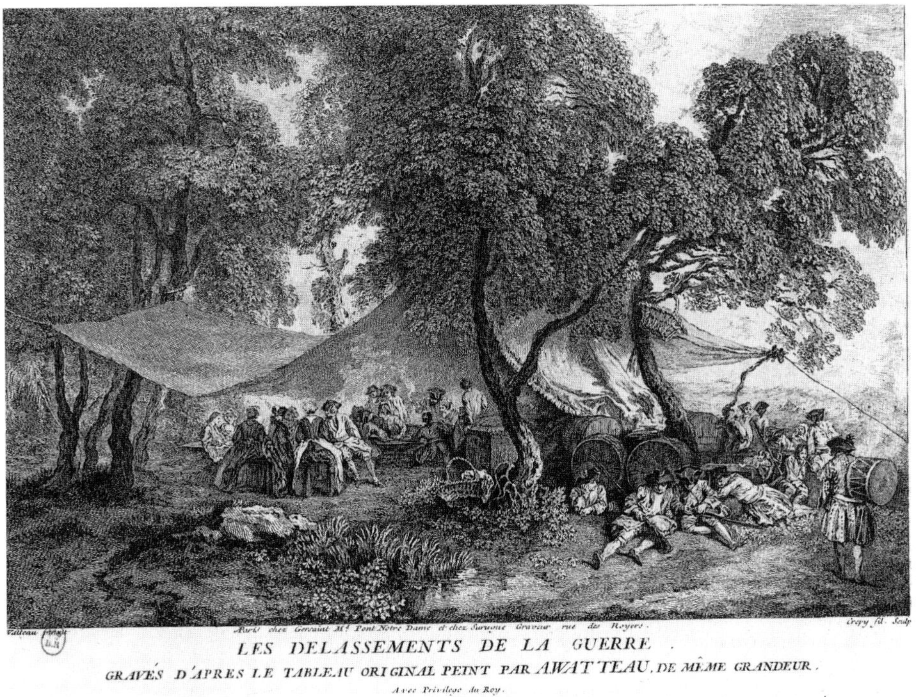

39. Louis Crépy, engraving after Antoine Watteau, *The Respite from War (Les délassements de la guerre)*, engraving announced 1731, painting c. 1712, Bibliothèque nationale de France, Paris. Cliché, Bibliothèque nationale de France, Paris.

Perceived as both contributing to and symptomatic of the decline of *l'esprit militaire* in the army was an ostentatious display of luxury.[72] Quincy draws attention to the excessive luxury exhibited by some of the *officiers généraux* and members of the king's guards.[73] For example, Quincy recounts meeting M. de la Feuillade at the Battle of Turin in 1706. This gentleman was "adorned as if he were going to a ball: he had a uniform of scarlet trimmed with gold embroidery, his hair was perfectly powdered, and he mounted a handsome gray horse."[74] The French lost Italy at the Battle of Turin. Quincy claimed that there was really no reason for the French army to have lost the Italian campaign except that the *officiers généraux* were too busy hiding all the money they had stolen from Italy. Implicit in his statement is the notion that the officers had stolen to support their taste for luxury and luxurious objects.[75] A display of *luxe* by the *officiers généraux* was nothing new, however; it was expected that high-ranking officers would flaunt the signs of their privileged position. Indeed, evidence of "living nobly" was proof of one's nobility. Moreover, high-ranking military positions were generally reserved for members of the nobility; it was only natural that these officers should live according to their station.[76] In comparison to the spectacle of luxury displayed during earlier wars (the War of Devolution, the Dutch Wars, and even the Nine Years' War), when Louis XIV and his entourage still visited the front, the War of Spanish Succession was a modest affair.

Whether or not Quincy's concerns about luxury in the army were well founded is not the issue here. What is important is the *perception* of excessive luxury – of luxury to an extent that overstepped the bounds of propriety and disrupted the natural order. Saint-Simon viewed such an excess as symptomatic of a wider decline in values and morals, in both the army and the nation.[77] Writing in 1747, three decades after the War of Spanish Succession, Brucourt warns the young aristocrat in *Essai sur l'education de la noblesse* of the dangers of the profession of "armes" (interestingly, the dangers he warns of do not include death or dismemberment):

> Luxury, indolence and voluptuousness should never accompany officers in the army. The King has already provided sage rules regarding this. Wouldn't it be shameful to treat warriors as voluptuous *femmellettes* [a derogatory term for a silly woman or an effeminate man]? There have been companies where the officers only pursued the best wines and the finest cuisine. We have seen mules loaded with cooking utensils in greater quantity than we have seen supplies on the mules supporting the artillery. A magnificent display of equipage, gear of such an opulence and voluptuousness that it excites the desire [greed] of the enemy and which, often, becomes their sought-after prize. A multitude of useless valets and superfluous animals which bloats the army without increasing its force.[78]

Brucourt expresses the same fears as do Quincy and others writing earlier in the century: a fear that luxury, vanity, and sensual excesses will corrupt and feminize the *homme de guerre*. That this corruption takes on gendered terms in Brucourt's essay is hardly surprising since a tendency toward excess, dissoluteness, and deviation from the "natural" has traditionally been represented in Western culture in feminine terms.[79]

The ability to tempt, seduce and corrupt has long been associated with women. For examples one need only think of Eve or of the personification in the Middle Ages of *luxuria* as a woman. In her study of Artemesia Gentileschi's paintings *Susanah and the Elders* and *Judith and the Head of Holofernes*, Mary Garrard has shown how female heroes who are self-sacrificing and virtuous can also represent qualities that are quite the opposite – seductiveness, duplicity, and indulgence in unnatural excess.[80] A rhetorical tradition, established in antiquity, represented excess, unnaturalness, and dissoluteness through metaphors of femininity.[81]

Viewed from this gendered perspective, the elegantly dressed women in *The Halt* could be interpreted simultaneously as civilizing and corrupting. These women could even be seen as prostitutes.[82] Prostitutes as well as soldiers were a staple of northern military genre painting in the sixteenth and seventeenth centuries.[83] Watteau's student Jean-Baptiste Pater specialized in scenes of military bordellos, such as *Vivandières de Brest* (fig. 34).[84] The subject of prostitutes in the army might even recall the case of a specific camp follower who was enamored of an officer and followed him during the northern campaign of 1709. In his memoirs, Quincy pays tribute to this beautiful and famous courtesan, Mlle. Chevalier.[85] She bravely nursed the wounded on the field during the Battle of Malplaquet, saving many of them from death. According to official policy, camp followers such as Mlle. Chevalier were sources of corruption in the army; the actual behavior of Mlle. Chevalier was heroic and exemplary. Whether the eighteenth-century viewer read *The Halt*'s female figures as a civilizing force or a corrupting force is not the point here, because one could make convincing arguments for either interpretation. What is important is the multivalency of these figures; they can be read simultaneously as corrupting and civilizing.

In the military paintings as in *Departure,* this kind of multivalency, this ironic toying with conventions and codes, also functions to reveal the disjunctures between the official fiction and the actual state of affairs and nature of the experience. It is precisely in this nexus of contradiction that meanings are produced. As Opperman and Vidal argue, Watteau's military paintings are not simple pieces of counterpropaganda visually shouting against the war and the military; instead, they represent the unheroic, unofficial, human experience of war. This experience encompasses not only the negative aspects of war for the ordinary soldier – the pain, the suffering, the discomfort, and the seemingly endless boredom – but also some of war's positive aspects, such as camaraderie and the cultivation of social relations and civility under duress.

Watteau's military paintings are about the distance between a set of outmoded military ideals, encoded in the conventions of the official topographical tradition, and the contemporary experience of war. They are also about the crystallization of a new set of military ideals and values. Watteau's military paintings deconstruct official fiction and, simultaneously, construct another, new fiction.

By transforming liabilities into ideological assets, this new fiction preserved a national sense of military pride during a war in which France had little of which to be proud. The humiliating defeats suffered by the French army provided opportunities for officers to exhibit their tactical acumen, and a new kind of valor, by knowing when to surrender and how to negotiate the terms of capitulation. Similarly, officers and soldiers could display their honor by retreating with good manners and grace. With the loss of an effective officer corps, of willing troops, and of the *esprit de combat,* the *belle retraite,* perhaps inevitably, became the new ideal of military honor.[86] Moreover, the values of the *belle retraite* would have appealed to the new breed of officers described and decried by Quincy.

A dedicated career soldier, Quincy resented that he was consistently passed over for promotion while young, inexperienced officers were placed in charge of regiments. Yet even Quincy, who could hardly be considered one of these new, ornamental officers, included glowing accounts of the French army's orderly and pretty retreats. About the Battle of Malplaquet, Quincy wrote: "If our infantry made a *belle retraite*, you have to admit as well, that our cavalry, that I saw to our right in a fine field, carried out the retreat with the most beautiful order in the world."[87] The nineteenth-century military historian Louis Pelet provides a similar account in *Mémoires militaires relatifs à la succession d'Espagne sous Louis XIV*. He notes that all the *rélations* (official reports) comment upon the order and dignity of the retreat: "The retreat took place with an order that one wouldn't have ventured possible for the defeated, and with a calmness that one wouldn't expect in front of the victorious army."[88] Likewise, disorderly retreats or troop movements were derided, especially if *officiers généraux* were involved. "We admired the valor of this respectable corps [of carabiniers]; but, the precipitous retreat of the *troupe dorée* [officers of the king's guard] in our retrenchments made us burst with laughter."[89]

The *belle retraite* and revision of the meaning of "honor" is understandable as last-ditch efforts to compensate for defeats and for an army that was in a deplorable state.[90] The *belle retraite*, in which appearance counts for so much, also reflects a tendency to consider war increasingly as a spectacle. This tendency, according to military historians, is an indicator of the decline of a more traditional military conviction, *l'esprit militaire*.[91] A lack in leadership and enthusiasm facilitated the habit of viewing war as spectacle and judging military achievement by the aestheticizing and distancing standards of appearance and performance. Even the dedicated Quincy suggests this habit of perception: "You can speak all you want to me about spectacles, about *comédies*, about *opéras*, about *carrousels*, of all the most beautiful spectacles in the world; there is nothing which is more striking to the sight than an army awaiting the enemy in battle, or an army marching into battle."[92] The art theorist Abbé J.-B. Du Bos shared Quincy's aesthetic appreciation of the dangers of battle. In his *Réflexions critiques sur la poésie et la peinture*, first published in 1719, Du Bos argues that one function of art is to provide the experience of strong emotions without the attendant dangers; he specifically cites Lucretius, who states that it is pleasant to be a spectator of a battle from an eminence where there is no apprehension of danger.[93] No doubt the staging of real military exhibitions contributed to the spectacular view of war.

The most common *divertissements militaires* included *carrousels, grands et petites maneouvres* (displays of military exercises and the review of troops), and *petites guerres* (mock battles). The royal review of troops and military exercises were most commonly held at the Champ de Mars and at Marly. The sheer numbers of handsome soldiers (there are accounts of officers temporarily replacing the less attractive members of their regiments for these reviews), armed and dressed to kill in dazzling uniforms, and moving with military precision provided a display of power, pride, and prosperity that attracted enormous crowds.[94] This was theater – the theater of the military state and the *roi de guerre*. Beyond the ornamental reviews at the Champ de Mars, the review of troops in the field presented an intimidating display of might.

The largest, costliest, and most sumptuous of these *divertissements militaires* was the *revue général* that took place at Compiègne in 1698. Lasting twenty days, from 31 August to 21 September, it included the participation of seventy thousand men (not including invited companions and guests). Ostensibly, the review performed a didactic function: to instruct the Duc de Bourgogne and his princely brothers on the tactics of war and to illustrate the correct manner of holding a siege. There was another, equally important motive, as Quincy points out:

> The king wanted to show all of Europe that in spite of the war that he had been forced to support against nearly all the great powers in this part of the world, France was in no way diminished – neither in terms of manpower nor of money. He assembled a considerable army in the area of Compiègne; all the troops were of an extraordinary magnificence. . . . The Duke of Bourgogne was named the general in chief and the Maréchal de Boufflers was named général.[95]

This event was indeed a display of great magnificence; uniforms were decorated by miles of silver and gold, saddle clothes and pistol cases were embroidered, and all the uniforms appeared new and clean.[96] Saint-Simon remarks that many of the officers were ruined by the expense of outfitting their regiments for such a display.[97] The Marquis de Grignan expressed similar sentiments: "This was a ruinous magnificence from the moment the king arrived at Compiègne on 31 August, until [21 September when] he left; it is difficult to estimate what this *fête militaire* must have cost France and all those who by their occupation were obliged to take part in it."[98] A great village with wooden houses was built to house the members of the court who came to observe. The vast and elegant tents for officers and their regiments were dressed of satin from India.[99] From all accounts, the magnificence of the camp of Maréchal Boufflers was without equal; it contained beautiful furnishings including paintings of the king and other members of the royal family, tapestries, and elaborate clocks. The maréchal kept an open table with a great feast from morning until evening. His staff included between 60 and 72 cooks (depending upon who is describing the event) and 340 servants. The table settings and linens were beyond belief.[100] In general, all descriptions of this event emphasize the spectacle of *luxe* displayed by both the military and the invited spectators. François Nodot wrote a *nouvel galant* about this event – *La rivale travestie ou les avantures galantes arivées au camp de Compiègne avec tous les mouvemens de l'armée.*[101] He based this novel on a real incident, but he changed some names and diminished or augmented certain situations for the sake of the story. Interspersed within a series of romantic intrigues, complete with disguises and mistaken identities, are descriptions of the military enactments and maneuvers. Nodot (who was the author of *Le munitionaire des armés de France* mentioned earlier) makes a point in the preface of informing the reader that his military descriptions are real and that he has a trained eye for detail since he spent so much time on various campaigns. Despite his claim to documentary fidelity, Nodot's passages describing the camps have the air of the fantastic and remind one of the descriptive and narrative conventions employed in *contes de fées* and in real and fictive accounts of *fêtes*.[102]

The featured spectacles at Compiègne, however, were the enactments of battles. For the benefit of those who were there to learn the art of war, history came alive through the re-creation of great combats and sieges of the past, such as the Battle of Rocroy, and demonstrations of different tactics and weaponry. These demonstrations were designed not only to educate but also to delight and entertain. It was not every day that one could watch "real" combat without the attending fear and worry. Nodot described one mock siege as though he were reporting on a display of fireworks: "You couldn't see a more beautiful display of firepower than the volley between the two sides. The cannon was used as quickly as the muskets. The grenades, launched from both sides, made thousands and thousands of circles in the air; they were repeated endlessly, creating a bower of fire from the little river up to the Chapelle gate."[103]

This *fête militaire,* this spectacular display of national wealth and military power in a time of peace, was reproduced on a smaller scale and for a smaller, "private" audience during the War of Spanish Succession – a time of national impoverishment and military weakness. "*La petite guerre*" was the term that referred to the practice of staging mock combats during the long periods of inactivity that characterized camp life. *Petites guerres* kept the soldiers in form and productively occupied them when they might otherwise be bored. In many ways *petites guerres* were like sporting events, with one team pitted against another; and, like a sporting event, *la petite guerre* often had an audience. Sometimes *petites guerres* were staged to honor the presence in the camp of visiting or local notables; sometimes those same notables would request a *petite guerre* as a form of entertainment. At the camp of Parma, for example, it was reported that "the *petite guerre* attracted not only the noble women of the neighboring area, but even the *belles dames* of the court."[104] Quincy reports that a *petite guerre* was expressly staged for the Marquise d'Havrincourt, the Comtesse d'Oisy, and her daughter.[105]

Sometimes these *petites guerres* pushed the game to its limits by involving the enemy. In 1710 lieutenants from several infantry regiments embarked upon a *petite guerre* disguised as hussars. They approached the enemy's camp, and the enemy responded. This little combat lasted several days, but the general, who feared what might follow, ordered his officers to abandon this game under penalty of prison.[106]

Quincy recounts yet another incident that supports this taste for the spectacle of war. In 1710 one of Quincy's civilian friends, M. Du Cheray, a counselor in the Paris Parlement, came to his camp during the northern campaign in Flanders. M. Cheray was curious: he wanted to experience life in the field firsthand and to see the king's enemies. Quincy accompanied him to a position very near an enemy post; however, Quincy knew full well that the post was under order not to fire.[107]

This desire to experience strong emotions, to acquire memories of the heroic from a safe distance, would have been appealing to the members of the *Maison militaire,* or the *Gardes du corps de Louis XIV.* In 1664, Louis XIV created this elite, personal army as a body distinct from the rest of the army.[108] One of its functions was to be the king's bodyguard; however, this task was actually accomplished by a rather small number of faithful comrades. The *Gardes du corps,* as they were also called, provided Louis XIV with a personal army; they were called upon for military exercises, they were sent on campaigns, as were the companies in the "regular" army, and they provided a pool of men from which officers were often elected. Members of the *Gardes du corps* were principally gentlemen who were selected by the king. However, according to an ordinance in 1702, if there were not enough gentlemen to fill the corps, the sons of the high bourgeoisie who "lived nobly" would be accepted. In actual fact, the makeup of the *Gardes du corps* was often more "plebeian" than their reputation would suggest.[109] Nevertheless, they enjoyed a privileged position and the reputation of an elite force. Part of their reputation derived from their splendid appearance. The king provided their uniforms, their horses, and their accouterments, and he provided the best. Appearance counted for much in the *Gardes du corps.* Later in the eighteenth century, the *Gardes du corps* would be known for their extraordinary *raffinement* – the embodiment of the character Tulip la fan fan – and, beginning with the War of Austrian Succession, they rarely appeared on the battlefield.

During the War of Spanish Succession the *Gardes du corps* were called into combat, although not nearly as often as were nonroyal regiments. In part, this was because they did not have the same combat skills or experience (recall Quincy's and his companions bursting into laughter at the "precipitous retreat of the *troupe dorée*") as did the regular troops. Compared to the other regiments, they were pampered, especially when in their lodgings and the type and amount of food they consumed. The *Gardes du corps* were simply not accustomed to privation and hardships; when not in the field, most of the officers had their permanent domicile in Paris, St. Germain en Laye, Marly, or Versailles. Many members of the *Gardes du corps* enjoyed a life of a certain luxury and occupied themselves with nonmilitary pursuits.

For the *Gardes du corps,* the military ideal of honor translated into *honnêteté.* The values of the *belle retraite,* the artifice – as opposed to art – of war, and the search for strong emotions and memories of the heroic – to be experi-

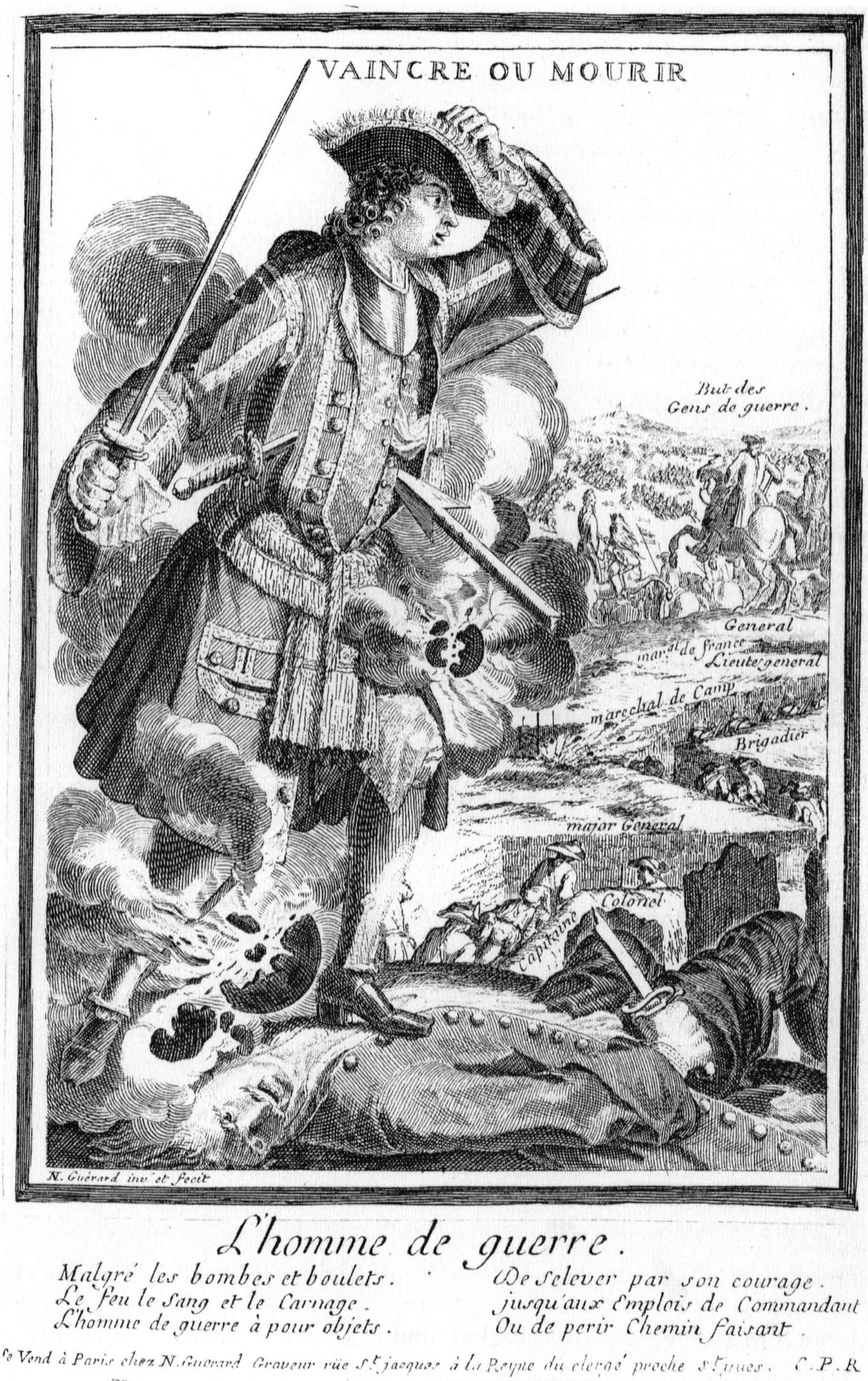

40. Nicolas Guérard, engraving, *The Man of War: Vanquish or Die (L'homme de guerre: Vaincre ou mourir)*, Bibliothèque nationale de France, Paris. Cliché, Bibliothèque nationale de France, Paris.

enced at a safe distance – all helped shape a new image of the *homme de guerre*. It was not a bad image, given the alternatives of clinging blindly to a bankrupt and unattainable image of the *homme de guerre* as a man of honor willing to sacrifice his life for the larger good of God, country, and king (although the reverse order might be more to the point here), or of acknowledging war's destructive reality and the hopelessness of receiving compensation or redemption for possible death or disfigurement. In this context, it is interesting to compare two images of the soldiers: *The Man of War: Vanquish or Die*, c. 1700, by Nicolas Guérard (fig. 40), *Standing Pikeman* from Charles Parrocel's *Different Poses of the Cavalry and the Infantry Drawn and Partially Engraved by Parrocel, Gentleman Painter of the King*, c. 1720 (fig. 41). In *The Man of War* we see a representation of the *l'homme de guerre* such as was elaborated in seventeenth-century instructional manuals for the nobility, including *La parfait homme de guerre ou l'idée d'un heros* (1699).[110] The anonymous author of this book describes a heroic, masculine ideal characterized by self-sacrifice, courage, loyalty, mental and physical forcefulness, self-control, and virtue. In Guérard's *Man of War* a soldier in the foreground steps on the body of a dead and vanquished enemy. He seems oblivious (and impervious) to the exploding bombs and cannonballs before him and to the sword and lance that penetrate his body; his attention is directed at the mounted figure in the background, who is identified as a general and as the "goal for the *gens de guerre*." Connecting the soldier in the foreground to the "goal" in the background is a "path to glory" – a zig-zagging trench with soldiers who represent the ascending ranks in the military hierarchy. This image resembles the conventions used in representations of the choice of Hercules, with its high rocky road leading to virtue. In this case,

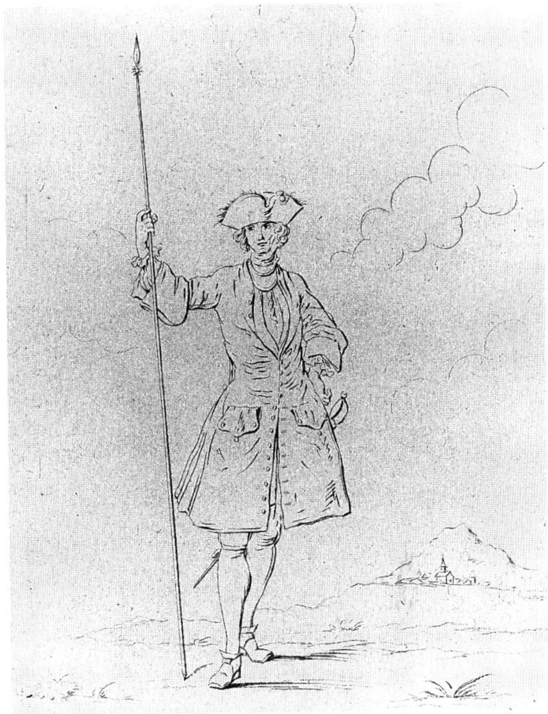

41. Charles Parrocel, engraving, *Standing Pikeman (Piquier debout)*, from *Different Poses of the Cavalry and the Infantry Drawn and Partially Engraved by Parrocel, Gentleman Painter of the King (Differentes attitudes de la cavalerie et de l'infanterie dessinée et partie gravée par Parrocel, peintre ordinaire du Roi)*, Anne S. K. Brown Military Collection, Brown University Library, Providence, RI.

however, the low road of vice is not even a choice; for this *Man of War* there is only one clear path. This idea is affirmed by the engraving's legend:

> Despite the bombs and cannon balls
> The fire, blood and carnage
> *L'homme de guerre* has as his quest
> To attain by courage
> The position of Commander
> Or perish along the way.[111]

By contrast, *Standing Pikeman* depicts a single figure in a minimally defined landscape with no trace of any battle or reference to his place within the military hierarchy. What is most apparent in this image is the gracefulness of the figure's pose; the figure resembles a mannequin more than it does a soldier. Figures such as this one, and the numerous military fashion plates that were available, articulated the new image of the *homme de guerre.* The gentleman officers of the *Gardes du corps* would have found their own likeness in Parrocel's engraving – whether real or desired. Likewise, it is possible that they would have found in Guérard's outdated image of the military man a parody of those ideals – this soldier has suffered too much to be alive, let alone believable.

Watteau's military paintings would have appealed to the gentleman officers of the *Gardes du corps.* Indeed, we know of several officers who acquired military paintings by Watteau. The Comte de Caylus, who housed Watteau in Paris and who wrote a biography of the artist, began his own military career at a very young age and fought at the Battle of Malplaquet.[112] Although not a member of the *Gardes du corps,* Caylus did head his own regiment. He abandoned a military profession after the Peace of Rastadt in 1714 and devoted his energies (and independent fortune) to travel and to literary, artistic, and archaeological pursuits. It is tempting to speculate that Caylus's military experience fostered his appreciation of Watteau's military paintings, which he described as the equal of the artist's finest later works. Caylus's cousin, the Comte de Murcé, is another example of a military man who enjoyed Watteau's paintings.[113]

The most interesting example of officer gentlemen as patrons of Watteau is Antoine de La Roque (1672–1744), who acquired a pair of the artist's military paintings. La Roque had been in the military since 1684 and had worked his way up to the rank of captain.[114] We know that he was a member of the *Gardes du corps,* in the division of the *gendarmes de la garde ordinaire du Roi.* He had seen action in 1684 when he participated in the Siege of Valance in Italy; he also participated in the Battle of Audenarde in 1708. In 1709 he was wounded at the Battle of Malplaquet.[115] According to all accounts, the *Gardes du corps* performed less than brilliantly during the Battle of Malplaquet; many attributed the French defeat to their poor judgment. One officer, who signed his letter of complaint to Voysin, the secretary of war, "a longtime officer in the army," wrote: "We lost the field of battle because cowardice has reigned for such a long time in the *Gardes du corps*. They dropped the ball in this last affair."[116] There were so many complaints about the dishonorable performance of the *Gardes du corps* at Malplaquet that an inquest was held; ultimately, no sanction was recommended. We know nothing of La Roque's comportment at Malplaquet, only that he lost his leg in the battle and convalesced at the military hospital at Valenciennes until April 1710.

Watteau would have been in Valenciennes at the same time as La Roque, and it is quite likely that they met at this time.[117] Quincy was in Valenciennes until May as well, and one wonders if he knew either La Roque or Watteau.[118] In *Mémoires,* Quincy writes that he attended several *fêtes* and participated in concerts and theatrical performances given by the Elector of Bavaria while he was garrisoned in Valenciennes.[119] Quincy played the *basse-viole,* and his musical abilities made him an attractive guest for musical evenings. He describes his *basse-viole* as his *passe-partout* because whenever he was stationed for any periods of time in or near a town, he would be frequently included in the local social scene. Although he does not mention attending a specific concert or *souper* in Valenciennes, apart from those given by the Elector of Bavaria, it is very possible that Quincy, La Roque, and Watteau crossed paths while they were there. Nothing is known of Watteau's trip to Valenciennes, but one can speculate that the artist was viewed in his hometown as a local boy who had succeeded in the big city; when Watteau returned to Valenciennes he had just finished an apprenticeship with one of the most fashionable decorators in Paris, he had worked on the decor for the royal château de La Muette, and he had widely expanded his circle of influential contacts. Perhaps he was viewed as a guest who could add a certain "prestige by association" to a social gathering. Although we can never know for sure if any of these three men met while in Valenciennes, we can hypothesize a horizon of possible social networks within which they might have met.

We do know that Watteau and La Roque became friends in Paris, probably through their common social circle. Other members of this group included Edme Gersaint, one of Watteau's dealers as well as a friend, and Pierre Crozat, one of the artist's most important patrons. Both La Roque and Gersaint wrote biographies of Watteau in tribute to their friend.[120] When La Roque returned to Paris, he abandoned his military career and devoted his life (thanks to his royal pensions) to literary pursuits, making a sort of personal *"belle retraite."* He associated with artists and men of letters; he wrote two *opéras,* and he embarked upon a number of literary projects, including a *histoire des peintres* and a *histoire du théatre françois,* neither of which he ever finished.[121] La Roque probably had little time to spend on these ambitious, long-term projects after he took possession of the *Mercure de France* in 1721. In his hands, the *Mercure de France* became the most important journal in the eighteenth century for reporting on literary, artistic, and intellectual currents, as well as on noteworthy events of the day. La Roque was representative of the officer gentleman; the pensions he received from his military career allowed him to cultivate his interests and his new career in literature and journalism.

La Roque's interest in the arts was, according to Gersaint, "his dominating passion," and his collection of works of art and other precious objects was very considerable for an individual of his standing.[122] The collection contained "choice paintings, drawings, prints, bronzes and other works of sculpture, porcelains, lacquers of all kinds, diamonds and other fine stones with perfect color, worked stones, both engraved and in relief, and shells."[123] The sales catalogue that Gersaint drew up after La Roque's death in 1744, lists more than 240 paintings, including three Watteaus: *The Burdens of War* (fig. 38), *The Respite from War* (fig. 39), and *St. François.*[124]

Not appearing in the sales catalogue was the portrait of La Roque that Watteau painted for his friend sometime between 1715 and 1718 (fig. 42). This

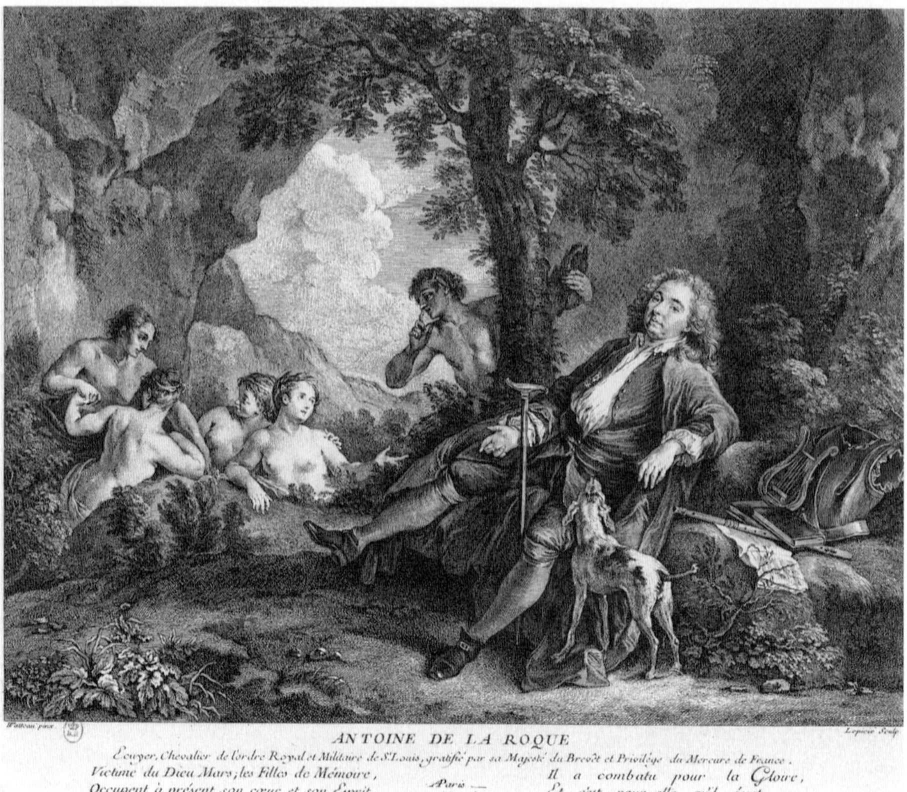

42. Bernard Lépicié, engraving after Antoine Watteau, *Portrait of Antoine de La Roque*, engraving announced 1734, painting c. 1715, Bibliothèque nationale de France, Paris. Cliché, Bibliothèque nationale de France, Paris.

portrait historié must have been kept in the family.[125] Watteau depicts a graceful La Roque relaxing in a sylvan setting with his dog at his side. His pose, gesture, and prominently placed walking stick call attention to his wooden leg, the result of his injury at the Battle of Malplaquet. Allegorical embellishments allude to his retirement from the military and to his life as a man of letters; to the right is a cuirass, against which have been placed a lyre, two books, and a flute. The books and musical instruments most likely refer to the two *opéras comiques* that he wrote. To the left are a group of assorted muses and, perhaps, the god Apollo; a satyr in the center of the composition shushes the group.

La Roque is representative of a cultivated, theatergoing public that would have savored Watteau's clever manipulation of conventions, his allusions, and his appealing scenes of noncombative military life and nostalgic evocation of aspects of military culture. The kinds of private patrons for whom Watteau worked were not interested in the heroic gesture, particularly if, like La Roque, they had experienced the horrors of war firsthand. As Norma Betten notes, these patrons would have preferred images that functioned as souvenirs, evoking the more pleasurable moments of camp life.[126]

The compositionally rich *Halt of a Detachment* (fig. 43) would have appealed to this taste. A group of tired soldiers are at rest in a vaguely defined setting. In much the same way as he did in *Return from the Campaign* and

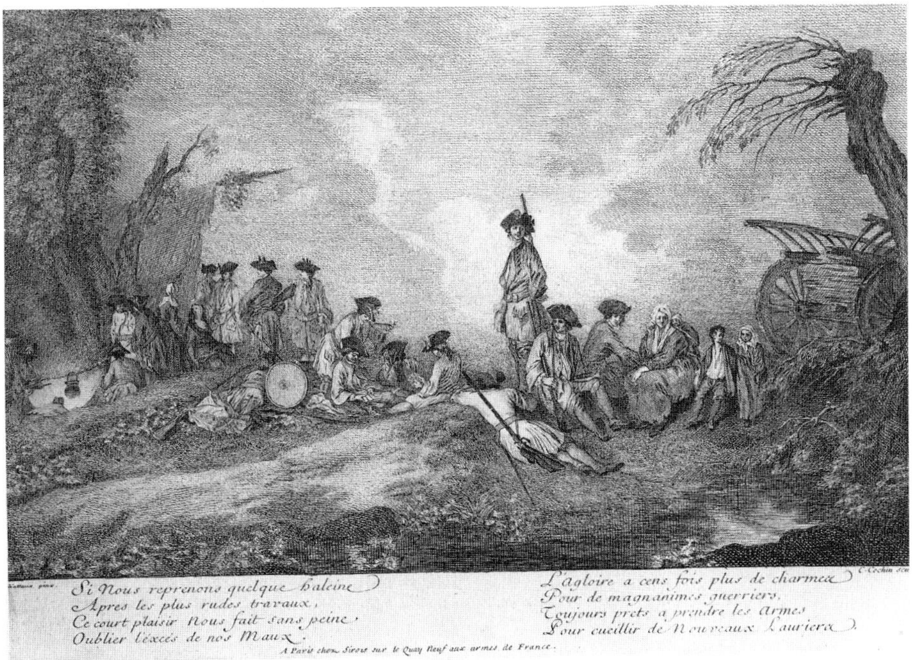

43. Charles-Nicholas Cochin, engraving after Antoine Watteau, *Halt of a Detachment (Détachement faisant alte)*, engraving announced 1729, painting c. 1710, Anne S. K. Brown Military Collection, Brown University Library, Providence, RI.

Bivouac, Watteau inverts the landscape conventions of the topographical tradition in *Halt of a Detachment.* Mary Vidal has pointed out that Watteau's military scenes are drained of tension, and indeed, the figures in *Halt of a Detachment* seem to be devoid of strength, mired on the ground as if the force of gravity has suddenly increased.[127] This "weariness" is further enhanced by the bowl-shaped curve created by the heads of the soldiers and framing devices on either side of the image. A graceful, attractive soldier stands in the center of the image, silhouetted against a bright sky. This figure (who seems more appropriate to a *fête galante*) and the peaceable figures around him call to mind the values of the *belle retraite* rather than the glory of the siege, or the *prise.*

I think that viewers such as La Roque, in addition to savoring the nostalgic, would have understood and appreciated the potential for ironic commentary of Watteau's military paintings. A good example of this potential can be found in Watteau's *Portal of Valenciennes* (fig. 44). The painting presents a group of soldiers under an arch, with fortifications in the distance. The fortifications and arch appear to be in ruins – possibly a reference to the *ceinture de fer,* or

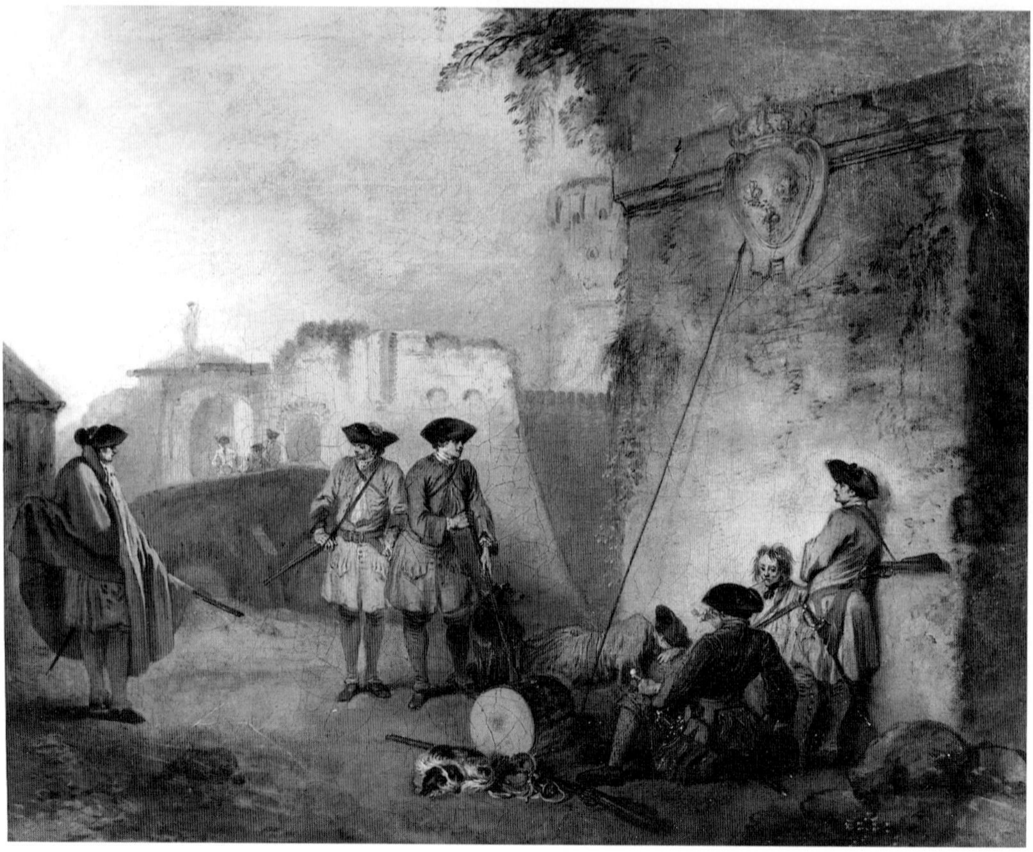

44. Antoine Watteau, *Portal of Valenciennes (Portail de Valenciennes),* c. 1710, The Frick Collection, New York. Copyright The Frick Collection, New York.

the great ring of fortifications, that Vauban constructed on the northern frontier, including some in Valenciennes. Van der Meulen frequently included careful renderings of these fortifications in his military images during the victorious days of the Dutch Wars. The ruined fortifications resonate with allusive possibilities: perhaps they are meant to suggest the expense of warfare, which had brought France to financial ruin, or perhaps they are meant to evoke the *vanitas* theme that time destroys all things. It might be useful to think in terms of an overlapping of these two possibilities. To the right, we see a group of four soldiers: two are smoking, one is sleeping, and the other is standing. The bareheaded soldier is unkempt and wears an expression that could be described as stupefied. The motif of smoking harks back to the northern tradition, in which it was associated with idleness, with the passing of one's time in vain pursuits.[128] This *vanitas* theme would have struck a resonant chord with viewers in the context of the War of Spanish Succession. Edgar Munhall offers this compelling interpretation in *Little Notes Concerning Watteau's "Portal of Valenciennes"*:

> Looking at the dreamy figures assembled in Watteau's picture, the same question might well be asked about them [Is it necessary to send the best men to death?], and that may be precisely what Watteau had in mind. Could his picture not be a depiction of young men likely soon to die, and specifically to die at the behest of their aged monarch, so obviously alluded to by the pike pointing at the royal arms?[129]

Munhall suggests that the pike pointing up to the royal arms on the portal may have had another meaning as well.[130] Aux Armes de France was the name of Pierre Sirois's shop, and Sirois was the buyer of Watteau's first military paintings. The prominent position of the coat of arms with the pike "pointing it out" may have been the artist's tribute to Sirois. Munhall also notes the similarity between the rococo escutcheon surrounding the arms and an escutcheon and arms in *The Sparrows' Nester* (fig. 58): This painting, done by Watteau around the same time as *Portal of Valenciennes,* was likely used as a signboard for the dealer's shop. The original painting has been reduced, and it is easier to see the escutcheon and arms in Boucher's print of the related arabesque (fig. 57). Who would have understood this pointed reference? Certainly the dealer Sirois, who sold Watteau's first two military paintings, and probably the network of dealers, collectors, and artists at the time. I would argue that this detail would have delighted that group, whose members could take pleasure in their inside knowledge. Moreover, this kind of playful visual punning and multivalency was typical of Watteau. Nowhere is this narrative tactic better demonstrated than in another military painting by Watteau, *Recruits on the Way to Join the Regiment* (fig. 45).

Recruits was done sometime between 1709 and 1712; there are four painted versions of this image, and there has been much debate over which of these, if

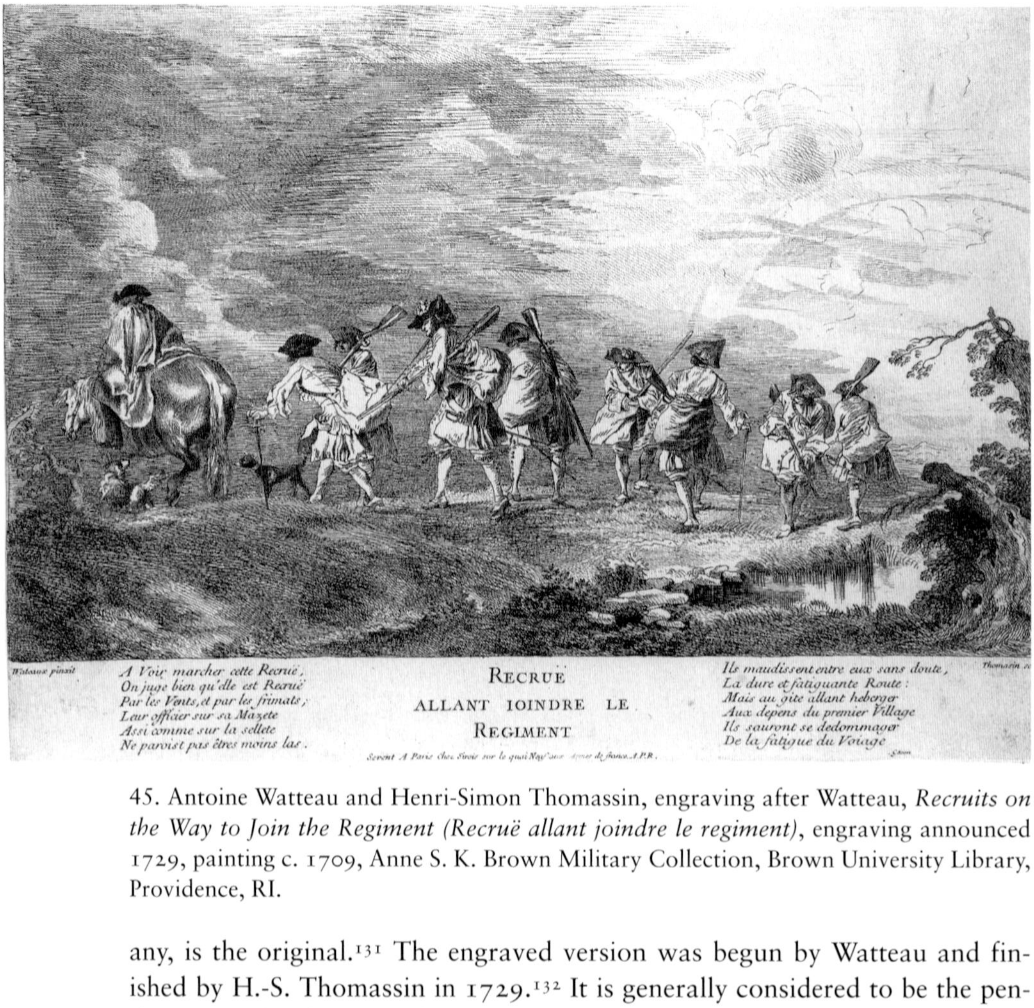

45. Antoine Watteau and Henri-Simon Thomassin, engraving after Watteau, *Recruits on the Way to Join the Regiment (Recruë allant joindre le regiment)*, engraving announced 1729, painting c. 1709, Anne S. K. Brown Military Collection, Brown University Library, Providence, RI.

any, is the original.[131] The engraved version was begun by Watteau and finished by H.-S. Thomassin in 1729.[132] It is generally considered to be the pendant to *Halt of a Detachment,* and, as such, it would have created another pairing of contrasting states: movement and rest. The painting depicts an officer on horseback leading eight recruits through a landscape devoid of identifying details. A scene like this would have been typical during the War of Spanish Succession because it was, above all, a war of movement, with regiments moving on the average of every two to three months. More to the point for this image, however, was the army's desperate need for fresh soldiers. It was not uncommon during the war to see small groups of newly recruited soldiers being taken to their regiments. France's need for soldiers (and for officers too, for that matter) was so acute during the War of Spanish Succession that the use of less-than-honorable recruiting practices was tolerated.[133] Recruiters were sometimes devious and would promise potential recruits rewards that they could never furnish. Minimum age requirements were disregarded, and often men were enrolled, not for life or for six years, as was the standard enlistment,

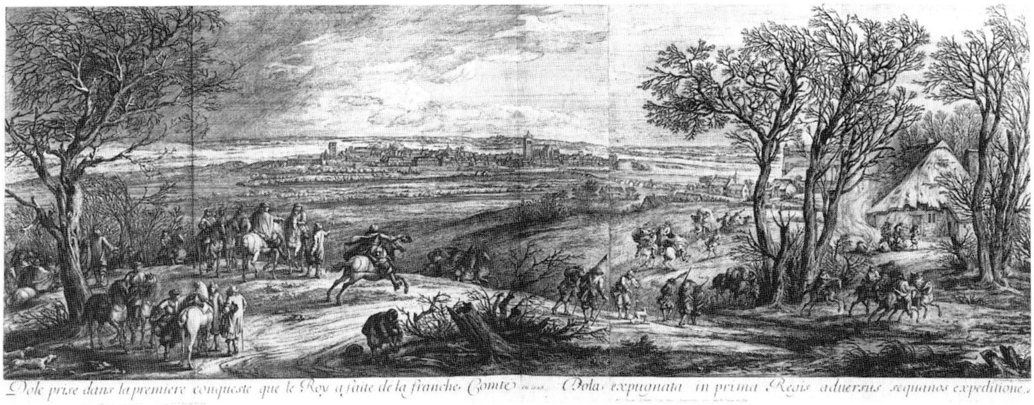

46. Adriaen-Frans Baudouins and Johann van Huchtenburg, engraving after Adam-François Van der Meulen, *Dole Taken in the First Conquest that the King Made of Franche Comté in 1668 (Dole prise dans la première conqueste que le Roy a fait de la Franche Comté en 1668)*, engraving 1685, painting 1668, Anne S. K. Brown Military Collection, Brown University Library, Providence, RI.

but for only the duration of a battle. In addition, toward the end of the war, prisoners became a source of recruits. Conscription was instituted as well as towns were required to form local *milice* (militia groups). But instead of functioning as a local national guard, *miliciens* were sent directly to the regiments and companies that needed men. Abuses in forced recruitment abounded, and under the pretext of raising men, local authorities could dispose of vagabonds, thieves, and general undesirables as recruits. This policy of conscription obviously made for uncooperative, ill-prepared troops; it also resulted in very high desertion rates. The figures in *Recruits* are obviously unschooled in the military movements appropriate for long marches – as prescribed in the handbooks of military exercises.[134] Everyone seems to be going in a different direction. This image of an undisciplined, rag-tag army of newly recruited soldiers was a realistic one. Within the context of the War of Spanish Succession and its often controversial recruitment and conscription practices it is likely that eighteenth-century viewers would have perceived a charged meaning in *Recruits* that viewers would not have seen in a march by Wouvermans or by another northern artist of the previous century.

Another context that would have shaped the intelligibility of *Recruits* for the eighteenth-century viewer was that of the official topographical tradition of military painting, which I discussed earlier. I would argue that viewers would have seen this work in opposition to the topographical tradition in general, and to Van der Meulen's *Dole Taken in the First Conquest . . .* (fig. 46) in particular. A number of art historians have asserted that the composition for *Recruits* was taken from the group of straggling figures in the mid-ground of

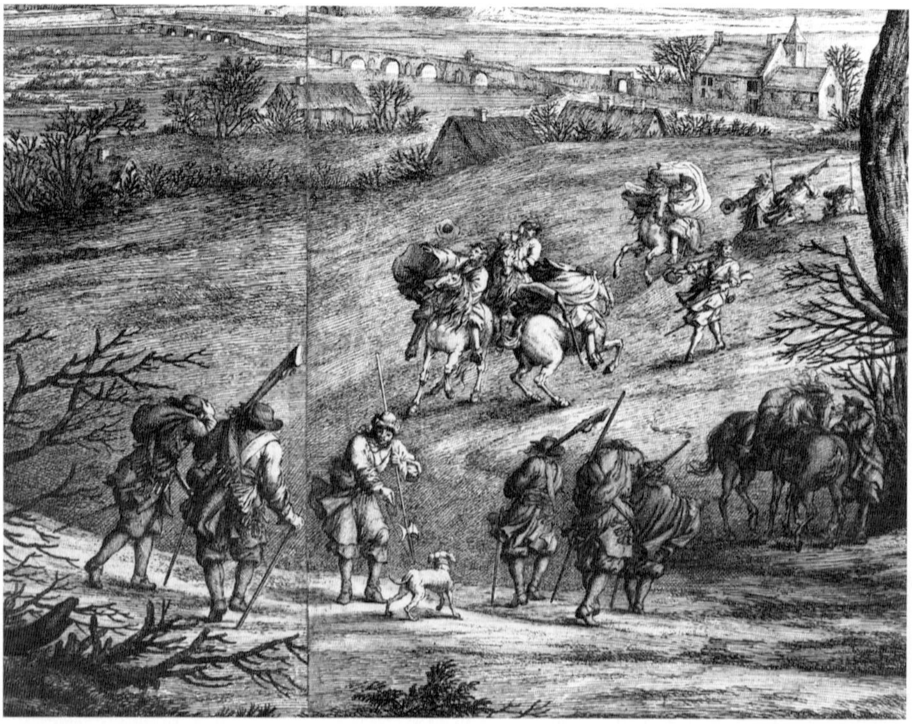

47. Detail of *Dole Taken in the First Conquest . . .* , Anne S. K. Brown Military Collection, Brown University Library, Providence, RI.

this painting (fig. 47).[135] This image, like many others by Van der Meulen, was reproduced in numerous painted copies and in prints that were sold to the public at the Gobelins.[136] Moreover, these "straggling soldiers" were something of a generic motif that frequently appears in the topographical tradition, such as in Van der Meulen's *March on Courtrai* (fig. 27). We can never know if Watteau did take his composition from the *Dole Taken,* but in light of Watteau's practices, it is tempting to speculate that he did, and that in *Recruits* he wittily and pointedly subverted the conventions and meanings of Van der Meulen's painting. According to the convention in the official tradition of military painting of using placement to indicate importance, these soldiers are clearly staffage behind and below the officers on the prominence in the foreground. But in *Recruits* the staffage have become the stars. They are the only figures situated on a slight prominence in the foreground; in short, they have taken the officers' place. Other conventions of official military painting are inverted as well; the near worm's-eye point of view does not allow the viewer to see the territory beyond. The express topographical exactness of official imagery is formally foreclosed in *Recruits.* Apparently, the officer is leading his recruits into an unseen and hence unknown territory.

Lacking the identifying, "factual," frame of reference in official painting, *Recruits* has made the soldiers seem like lost souls. In fact, their configuration in pairs, moving toward an unseen destination, suggests that Watteau may be toying with another conventionalized type of image – the danse macabre – as an ironic commentary on *gloire* and the heroic soldier. (On a similar note, Opperman suggests that *Recruits* may have informed Goya's *No saben el camino [They Don't Know the Way],* which shows a group of prisoners being led away from war.[137])

Nevertheless, there is something that is quite pretty and graceful about this image, something that is not entirely in keeping with the ostensible subject of tired, unwilling troops marching off to war. These figures seem almost to be couples; they seem almost like figures from a *fête galante.* In fact, there is a similarity between the arrangement of the coupled figures who progress diagonally from the foreground to the background in *Recruits* and in *Pilgrimage to Cythera* (see fig. 48). Men such as Antoine de La Roque would have savored the multiple references and playful contradictions that Watteau deployed in the earlier as well as in the later painting.

The double rainbows in the sky of *Recruits* also belong to this category of multivalency. They function much as the signboard does in *Departure* – as a loaded cue in which are crystallized a number of intersecting discourses and overlapping systems of meaning. For example, the rainbows would have been understood as a symbol of hope; this reference would have made sense within the context of the specific subject and of widely held pacifist sentiments abroad during the War of Spanish Succession. However, the cultivated, theatergoing audience would also have understood another set of references that Watteau deftly wove into the ironic commentary in *Recruits:* that of the Italian Comedy. As we have seen in *Departure,* Watteau often alludes to theatrical subjects that would have carried a specific set of associations for the eighteenth-century viewer.

The rainbows in *Recruits* may also allude to the *régiment de l'arc-en-ciel* – a fictive regiment made up of lackeys who took on the aspect of a rainbow because of the various colors of their livery. According to the *Dictionnaire comique, satirique, critique, burlesque, libre et proverbial:* "To be in or of the Régiment de l'Arc en Ciel. Is to be a lackey, to wear the colors."[138] This colorful regiment made its first literary appearance in the plays of the Italian Comedy. In Regnard's *Foire St. Germain,* Arlequin explains this regiment to Colombine:

> *Arlequin:* [At Paris] I have been a *cuissier de guet* [patrol] for three years, after having served as a volunteer in the regiment of the rainbow.
>
> *Colombine:* I've never heard of this regiment.
>
> *Arlequin:* It is nevertheless one of the largest regiments in the kingdom; the soldiers in it are sometimes footmen, sometimes

coachmen, and they are dressed in green, in red, and in yellow, according to the whims of their captains.

Colombine: I am just now beginning to see several shades of your regiment.

Arlequin: What the devil! It is the most necessary *milice* to the state, and it is the regiment that makes its way the fastest; it is from there the officers are selected to fill the most lucrative posts. I know twenty commissioned officers who have never done their exercises except in that corps.[139]

The Italian Comedians never minced words, and the institutional policies of war and the military were the target of their derisive humor on more than one occasion. In the "Scene des Adieux" from the play *Le Phénix*, Arlequin and Colombine mock the traditional ideals of glory and the heroic in a lengthy dialogue.[140]

The *régiment de l'arc-en-ciel* and the Italian Comedy's critique of war and *gloire* would have conjured up other related events for our eighteenth-century viewer. In particular, a regiment of lackeys would have brought to mind a variety of shady recruitment practices, such as employing lackeys as substitutes for conscripted masters or drawing upon lackeys when officers needed to inflate their men's numbers on the regiment's roll. Hence, the rainbow above in conjunction with the recruits below would have generated a chain of intertextual associations for the Parisian viewer that ultimately forged the larger critical commentary of *Recruits*.

The engraving's legend and title would have contributed to this commentary as well:

They complain to each other no doubt
About the hard and exhausting route:
But at the camp where they will rest
At the expense of the first village
They will know how to make up for
The fatigue of the trip[141]

Opperman has pointed out that the word "recruits" in the title has a double meaning, referring both to the recruits themselves and to a state of tiredness or jadedness.[142] The legend suggests that the recruits' fatigue owes more to boredom than to real action and that their "fatigue" will be compensated for at the expense of the next village in which they will make their camp. This is one of the few cases where we know with certainty that the title and the legend were most likely to have been selected or approved by Watteau.[143] Again, *Recruits* ironically draws attention to the distance between a past, official image of war and war's contemporary, unheroic reality in a way that the Parisian public would have appreciated.

Re-creating the "mental horizon" of the eighteenth-century viewer is necessary if we are to restore rich, nuanced meaning to the images. Yet it is impossible to completely reconstruct that horizon because of historical distance; we can know the past only incompletely, through representations (both visual and textual). Nevertheless, we can interrogate the conventions and codes of representation that appear to have been understood by a particular eighteenth-century public. The play of conventions and codes that we find in the military paintings means something, even if we have to seek that meaning in indirect and often unlikely quarters. Watteau's work in the military paintings is both deconstructive – in that he comments upon and critiques certain past traditions – and constructive. His military images embody the larger substitutions and displacements that were occurring in the first part of the eighteenth century. More specifically, Watteau's military paintings articulate a new model for the *homme de guerre*, in a period when older defining discourses no longer held.

CHAPTER THREE

The *Fête Galante* and the Cult of *Honnêteté*

IN EDME GERSAINT'S BIOGRAPHY of Watteau the author recounts the charming if dubious story of how Watteau first entered the Academy. Watteau wanted to go to Rome to study the old masters but did not have the money for such a trip. He decided to solicit a royal pension – these were generally granted to members and students of the Royal Academy of Painting and Sculpture. Watteau was neither associated with this institution nor connected with an Academy member who could sponsor him for admission, and he set out to remedy this situation. He exhibited the two military paintings that he had earlier sold to Sirois, *Departure of the Troops* and *Halt of the Army,* in a room through which the Academy members had to pass. The Academicians all admired the paintings by this young, unknown artist. Antoine de La Fosse, who was at this time at the height of his fame, was so impressed by the work that he interceded on Watteau's behalf, demanding that Watteau be allowed to enter the Academy.[1] Thus his military paintings provided Watteau's entrée into the Academy at a time when he had stopped painting that subject. What he did paint during his years of association with the Academy were in the genre for which he is today best known – the *fête galante.* Although we can trace narrative, formal, and thematic progressions linking the military paintings to the *fêtes galantes,* works in the two genres would have been received in significantly different ways by the Academy. The military paintings would have been viewed as mere genre painting within the Academy's hierarchy of genre, whereas the *fêtes galantes* would constitute a new and unprecedented form of painting that demanded a redefinition of categories.

In 1717, Watteau submitted a painting to the Royal Academy as a reception piece for his entry into that august institution. The piece was titled, and the secretary of the Academy first recorded it as, *Pilgrimage to Cythera;* since its execution, it has also been referred to as *Embarkation for the Island of Cythera* (fig. 48). The work was categorized as a history painting, for when a work was accepted as such, it was Academy practice to enter the title

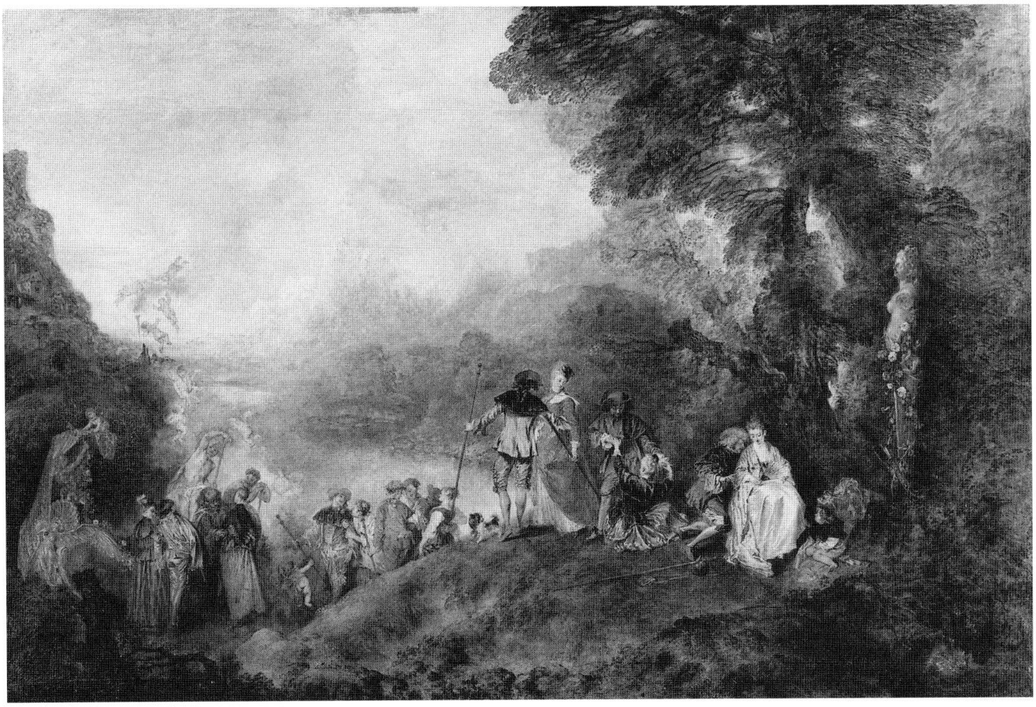

48. Antoine Watteau, *Pilgrimage to Cythera (Pèlerinage à Cythère)*, 1717, Musée du Louvre, Paris. Cliché, Réunion des musées nationaux.

of the work; for works accepted in one of the minor genres, only the name of the genre was generally recorded – for example, a landscape or a still life. The ostensible status of Watteau's work as a history painting was changed, however, when the title *Pilgrimage to Cythera* was crossed out and replaced with the appellation *une feste galante*. This marked the first time the term "*fête galante*" was formally used to designate a genre of painting.[2] The formulation of a new category of subject suggests that a form of social practice had crystallized to the point that it could be conceived of as such; at the same time, this new category helped to articulate the social form. The christening of *Pilgrimage to Cythera* as a *fête galante* was singularly appropriate, for the genre of paintings known as *fêtes galantes* recapitulated neatly, in form and content, the social practice known as the *fête galante;* both the social ritual and its visual counterpart tested the limits of authority and official culture.

If one asserts that social practice generated the content and form of *Pilgrimage to Cythera* in particular, and of Watteau's prodigious output of *fêtes galantes* in general, several questions immediately arise: What was the *fête galante* as an actual social event? What went on at *fêtes galantes*, or at least, what can we glean from existing descriptions and literary representations about what went on? Both in reality and in the collective imagination, what did the *fête galante* signify and why? And why was Watteau the person who was able to articulate this vision in a meaningful way?

The *Fête Galante* in Practice

Before examining the images, therefore, we must consider the meaning of the kind of *fêtes* that relate to the images. What, as a significant and signifying entertainment, could be considered a *fête galante?* The following accounts of actual *fêtes* should provide a general idea.

On 21 May 1713, Joachim C. Nemeitz attended a *bal, petite comédie et souper:*

All of the spacious garden was illuminated by an infinite number of lamps and candles, either suspended between the trees, or placed on the ground. The theater, for the comedy written by Dancourt and titled *L'Impromptu de Suréne,* was constructed at the rear of the garden. Everybody was allowed to enter, especially those in masquerade, and in the garden there were four different areas. The number of people there in masquerade was beyond words: in addition, since it was the most beautiful time of the year, this ball lasted until six o'clock in the morning.[3]

Madame Du Noyer's description of "the most original" *fête,* given by the Ambassador of Venice, is even more fantastic: the ambassador created an enchanted indoor garden. "There were several *allées* of orange trees and four fountains of orange-flower water. The scent filled the entire room, which agreeably surprised everyone there."[4] The women were all chosen as queens, which was seen as an admirably gallant gesture.

From these accounts, it appears that the creation of an enchanted, irreal atmosphere was necessary to a setting for the enactment of a *galante* species of make-believe, often played out in masquerade. Balls and theatrical performances provided both a diversion and a fitting parallel to the intrigues of the participants. The spectacle of intrigue, especially of the amorous sort, was the centerpiece of any *fête galante.* At a ball, Mme. Du Noyer reported:

During the height of the dancing, a woman I knew noticed something white on the ground, which from the look of it, appeared to be a letter. Letting her handkerchief fall on it, she gathered them both so as not to draw attention to her find, which was, it turns out, a letter, or at least a note, containing nothing but the following four lines:

Since my heart is charmed
How do you find the pleasure of being loved?
Ah! if you are equal to it
You are rather a lover than a friend.[5]

The sender's identity was never discovered; Mme. Du Noyer concludes her story by commenting that this kind of gallant "special delivery" was quite common at *fêtes.*[6]

That skill in *galantrie* was requisite for success at *fêtes,* whether the *fêtes* were impromptu or of the more ostentatious sort offered by the Ambassador of Venice, is underscored by Nemeitz. He advises the foreign, upper-class visitor to Paris that when sharing the pleasures of the summer at a *maison de plaisance* (second, "vacation," homes that appeared in great numbers on the outskirts of Paris during the early years of the eighteenth century):

> To be a misanthrope is out of the question. You must be witty, winsome, and laugh readily; you must be willing to play cards, to hunt and do such things in the same manner as your company. A man who is either ordinary or bizarre is quickly judged as having a peculiar nature, which is not at all in keeping with that of the French, much less with those Frenchmen accustomed to living in the midst of pleasures and mirthfulness, and who always behave with a similar *bonne humeur.*[7]

In other words, a certain charming gaiety was the only acceptable public persona for those who participated in *fêtes.*

The *fête galante* was a form of elite behavior, enacted and perpetuated for specific reasons. Beyond the activity of men and women entertaining themselves in pursuit of love and music, *fêtes* signified social identity. The *fête galante* was perfect for the conspicuous display of two fundamentally aristocratic conditions: leisure and exclusivity. Not only did *fêtes galantes* define and codify the behavior appropriate for aristocratic leisure, but they were also opportunities for displaying elite behavior. *Fêtes* were occasions that endowed total idleness with a recognizable form and purpose. In turn, participation in and performance at *fêtes* signified an individual's membership in an exclusive circle. One might view the *fête galante* as a ritualistic proving ground for the elite.

Elite behavior at *fêtes* was marked by a refusal to succumb to the liberating nature of a *fête.* An escape from the mundane concerns of ordinary life, the *fête galante* offered participants unusual experiences and the opportunity to indulge in passions and desires that they normally restrained. These passions and surprises could be dangerous, however; a reveler might be overcome by them, subjugated, rather than stimulated. As Terry Castle has discussed them, masquerades reveal the untrustworthiness of social appearances, such as the sartorial conventions.[8] They show that the categories by which we make sense of the world are arbitrary and constructed rather than natural or divine. The resulting sense of disorientation could be both compelling and deeply disturbing. At a masquerade, the line between chaos and the liberation that comes from leisure was a thin one, and the line between boredom and leisure even thinner. Lending interest and diversion to life, and giving it form, demanded the "dangers" of a *fête*. Yet to succumb to one's impulses or to be taken unaware was a sign of rude inferiority. The aristocrat, or anyone who aspired to aristocratic status, could not be the pawn of his senses or of his heart; nevertheless, he would like to be titillated and partake of pleasure. What distinguished the elite from the common folk was the ability to control these liberating forces in a way that allowed the individual to profit from them: to test their limits. To do this required a distancing from and mediation of experiences that were raw and erotic. This mediation was accomplished through a highly ritualized and artificial mode of behavior, one that masked sexual tactics. Under the guise of an artificial second self, the individual was free to enjoy the erotic pleasures and dangers of a *fête* indirectly, filtered through an aestheticizing refinement and distancing.

That one understood the nuances of this complex and self-deceiving game, that one could practice the correct rituals of speech, comportment, manners, dress, and, especially, seduction, and was able to display this knowledge without affectation or sign of effort, marked one as superior. In theory, the undefinable *je ne sais quoi*, the elevated *esprit* that allowed one to carry off the act, was the sign of true "inner" nobility. In practice, however, it was less inner nobility than familiarity with one's company – knowledge of their strengths and weaknesses, likes and dislikes, and experience with the forms and rules of the game – that permitted one to master the unexpected and to respond artfully to it. This noble comportment, and the transformation of the self into a work of art, is part of the cult of *honnêteté*.

The *Honnête Homme* at Court

The concept of the *honnête homme* has been well charted by scholars.[9] As with any projected social ideal, the *honnête homme* was always in the process of formation through a dialectical exchange with agencies of power.[10] As political and economic realities change, so, too, do the construction and constitution of *honnêteté*. The concept of the *honnête homme* in France dates back to the beginning of the seventeenth century and was a response by the seigneurial class seeking to protect their interests in the face of increasing monarchical absolutism. If this class were to retain their offices and any real power, they had to insinuate themselves around the source of that power, the king, by accommodating themselves to the demands of the court and by projecting an image of worldly capability and selfless service. In short, they had to adopt the persona of the ideal courtier, as articulated in Castiglione's *Il Cortegiano*, whose goals in life were to please others and to serve his prince.[11]

These ideals and precepts were rearticulated by Nicolas Faret in his handbook for the courtier, *L'honneste homme ou l'art de plaire à la cour*, of 1630.[12]

In fact, in many places, Faret copied Castiglione word for word. Like Castiglione, Faret viewed the aristocratic courtier as the king's virtuous counselor. This courtier shines at court and wins the king's confidence through his good behavior, through his exemplary appearance, manners, dress, skill in conversation, and noble activities, and above all, through his cultivation of a pleasing and polished nonchalance. Faret's nonchalance echoes Castiglione's ideal of *sprezzatura* – where all effort and artistry is made to seem effortless and natural. The courtier's outward signs of perfection reveal his inner perfection and nobility. Faret, however, placed no emphasis on scholarly pursuits, although Castiglione had emphasized them.[13] This is not surprising since the seigneurial class in France had traditionally been more interested in matters military than in matters of the mind. Moreover, literary and scholarly pursuits were eschewed as a tedious form of labor, more appropriate for the bourgeoisie than for the nobility. Faret reduced the scope of the courtier's knowledge to stylish subjects that could further his social ambitions. Thus from the very beginning the French *honnête homme* focused on manners, fashion, and ornamental skills.

This tendency to cultivate fashionable forms of *politesse* and social protocol intensified when the high aristocracy realized that selfless service to the state and pleasing the king and his court brought them no closer to retaining power and never would. Under Louis XIV, the cult of *honnêteté* was employed as a form of political and social control, whereby members of the high nobility were transformed into ornaments and awarded household offices of only symbolic worth. It must be added, however, that these offices carried with them generous stipends. Offices of real power and importance were no longer granted to the *noblesse de race* and long-established ennobled *officiers* – in short, to the *honnête homme* – but could be bought by those of lower rank. This rendered the old aristocracy useless, and Faret's version of the *honnête homme* obsolete, even self-defeating.

More than ever, the aristocrat needed to distinguish himself from his inferiors, especially from the new service class surrounding Louis XIV. In what Domna Stanton has described as a reaction formation, the new aristocracy capitalized on the very object of their degradation, their uselessness, and cultivated it as a sign of their distinction.[14] By a mental sleight-of-hand, the "true" aristocrat saw himself as both above needing to be of practical service to the king and independent of the king's power to signify or confer status. Indeed, for an aristocrat to show an interest in worldly affairs would have been interpreted as a sign of inferiority. The high aristocracy, cut off from access to real power, displaced their ambitions to the one arena that was rightfully theirs, and that served to distinguish them from others: conspicuous forms of leisure and a hyperrefined *politesse*. The cultivation of pleasure and *politesse* provided the noble men and women who were at the court, dependent on the favor of the king, with a mode of operation that allowed them simultaneously to succeed at court and to set themselves apart from it. They thereby preserved at least the illusion of their importance and superiority.

By 1660 the *honnête homme,* as defined by Faret, had become a myth, useless as an ideal of behavior after the high aristocracy's failure to secure its power under the Sun King. The cult of *honnêteté* was not obsolete, however; it persisted and was transformed to accommodate the demands of a different situation. Another image of *honnêteté,* steeped in cynicism, was formulated as early as 1630 and appears in the writings of the Chevalier de Méré, which were not completely published until 1677.[15] Through Méré, one can see the thwarted social ambitions of Faret's courtier turned inward. Méré's *honnête homme* was no longer really a man of honor. He sought to please others not because of a desire to render selfless service, but as the means to his own pleasure and financial gain. He accommodated himself to the needs and desires of others in anticipation of eventually seducing them, having power over them, and thereby demonstrating his own superiority. Much of Méré's argument revolves around maintaining the illusion of the high aristocracy's "inner" superiority to and independence from the king's court and from the service class. And indeed, Méré distinguishes, by virtue of an indefinable "spiritual quality," between a man who is an *honnête homme* and a pretender at court. "We must consider the court and the *grand monde* separately," he writes, "and remember that the court, out of habit or out of whim sometimes approves things that the *grand monde* would not tolerate."[16] For Méré, the king's courtiers were "irritating negotiators rather than people of good company."[17] Being "good company" was what counted for Méré: increasingly, that good company was not found at court.

The *Honnête Homme* at "Countercourt"

The good company of those who possessed the undefinable *esprit* that marked the *honnête homme* was located in exclusive coteries: the private "countercourts" where one was at liberty to pursue single-mindedly the noble aims of sociability and the cultivation of useless aesthetic pleasures and conspicuous leisure. The prototype was the Hôtel Rambouillet (1615–1640s) and the *chambre bleue.*[18] Méré was a habitué of this "secret society," where the company and pastimes were thought to be far superior to those of the royal court. After the demise of Rambouillet during the Fronde, others, including the princes of Condé and Conti, tried to recapture the brilliance of the "secret society" in the *salons* that they formed. Méré's formulation of *honnêteté* is directed to the goals of this new *salon* society, to an aristocracy in nostalgic retreat, cultivating the one activity that marked them as superior: the way they employed their leisure.

Aristocrats now directed their resources toward transforming themselves and their leisure activities into consummate works of art. As Stanton has written, *honnêteté* was an amalgam of artistry and aristocracy.[19] It was also a means of staving off boredom, the perpetual enemy of the useless aristocrat; to be manifestly bored revealed one's lack of inner superiority and *esprit*. An *honnête homme* never actually revealed his boredom. By playing the game of masking desire and by cultivating highly complex and oblique modes of behavior and expression to achieve an aesthetic distance from direct experience or expression, one could dissimulate, having created a superior self and a fictive realm richer and more brilliant than real life. As Routrou wrote, "This game is no longer a game, but truth in which by my actions I am represented . . . I, the object and actor of myself."[20] The process and product are conflated in a game of displacement and indirection. Body and behavior no longer reflect a corresponding inner self, as described by Faret; rather, they create an armor of artifice that protects the individual from being directly apprehended and manipulated by others, while better positioning that person for the selective presentation of a self that will please others, will captivate them, and, ultimately, will seduce them.

To be a victor in this war of wittiness, *politesse,* and pursuit of love marked one as superior. Indeed, Méré's language recalls military terminology. And for good reason, for, in Warren Roberts's words, "Beneath the cultivated language and refined manners of the aristocrat was a destructive need to dominate."[21] The elite enclosures of *salon* society were a displaced battleground upon which participants could honorably recapture their collective past glory and maintain an illusion of their superiority in the present, even if only through symbolic and ritualized modes of behavior.

The necessity for displacement through symbol and ritual grew more acute even within the royal court at Versailles as the century progressed and Louis XIV's taste for elaborate entertainments diminished. From 1686 until 1697, the number of *fêtes* and royally sponsored entertainments – apart from the weekly *appartements* and public ceremonials – declined, and from 1697 until Louis's death in 1715, the number decreased dramatically.[22] Louis XIV was growing old and was no longer interested in these sorts of pastimes. Moreover, with the advent of Mme. de Maintenon as the king's favorite and the arbiter of court conduct, an attitude of piety and devoutness, not *galantrie,* was required if one was to please and be successful at court. Even the Duchess d'Orléans, who was neither frivolous nor *galante,* wrote in 1687: "Court life is becoming so dull that one can hardly stand it any longer, for the king imagines he is pious when he sees to it that everyone is properly bored and bothered."[23] Military reverses, and an ever-depleted treasury as well, made conspicuous and costly forms of entertainments inappropriate.

This decline in the number of festive occasions suggests that even the symbolic function and status of the aristocracy at Versailles was being foreclosed. Official culture could no longer accommodate or use the ornamental aristocrat; moreover, the court could no longer provide the means for the public display of one's elevated status in relation to the service class. An aristocrat's success at court now entailed a denial of those signs of privilege and a descent into a boring existence. Mme. de La Fayette wrote in 1689 that "the Balls given at the court were so sad that they didn't begin until midnight and were always finished before 2 A.M."[24] She added that at these balls, nothing of interest ever happened and everyone avoided having a good time for fear of having a scene with the king the next day.[25] Louis XIV cut off access to those pleasures that signified and were fundamental to aristocratic existence at Versailles. Mme. de La Fayette wrote that the Princess de Conti had planned on attending a ball given by M. de la Feuillade, but: "The King did not approve, saying that one never went to these sorts of affairs without some disagreeable *conte,* and that women of a certain standing should not go to these balls. That meant that the Princess who so loved her pleasure was deprived of it, much to her great regret."[26] With the expulsion of the Italian Comedians in 1697, Louis XIV eliminated another real source of aristocratic pleasure, as Mme. Du Noyer, for one, lamented.

Although they are not a completely reliable source, Mme. Du Noyer's letters reflect the sentiments engendered by the increasing distance between official culture and an aristocratic culture that was already marginal. In a letter to a provincial friend, Mme. Du Noyer complained, "We had a different sort of *fête* here than you do. It was nothing more than a pompous procession, given by the order of the King for the public entry of the *Grande-Maître* of Malta."[27] These disparaging remarks about the procession – which was a *fête* in name only – contrasts with her lengthy and lavish descriptions of *fêtes* held elsewhere, outside the king's jurisdiction, such as the "most original" *fête* given by the Ambassador of Venice, described earlier. Another *fête,* which she describes at extraordinary length, was held in Utrecht. It lasted three days and included a masquerade. According to Mme. Du Noyer, this masquerade was far more interesting than any of those given at the court because the participants had to invent their own costumes, thereby testing their ingenuity.[28]

Mme. Du Noyer's *Lettres galantes et historiques* were first published in 1704, eleven years before the dissolution of the court at Versailles. Yet one can already see from her letters, as well as from the writings of others, that the royal court no longer stood at the center of society and that official culture was losing its authority. As the decline of this centralized and official culture continued, the aristocracy and the upwardly mobile bourgeoisie sought cultural means to revitalize their social status; consequently, *salon* society became even more important than it had been. However, it was no longer a *salon* society that functioned entirely in opposition to the court, for Paris had become the new locus of cultural production.

Paris, Culture, and the *Honnête Homme*

If Paris had become the center of cultural production, it was also a place where the traditional indicators of social difference could not be trusted: wealth, a bourgeois criterion, not rank, was most manifest in the Parisian world. The Chevalier de Mailly wrote, "One has to admit that Paris is a *petit monde;* it is the place where luxury reigns more and more. It has spread even to the common people; it is difficult to recognize men of quality at first sight."[29] A Sicilian visitor of 1710, Jean Paul Marana, elaborated on this observation.

> Gold and silver have become so common, as I have already said, that it sparkles on the costumes of all types of people, and this immoderate luxury confuses the master with the valet, and low people with the most elevated. Everyone carries a sword, and Paris resembles the Utopia of Thomas More, where none can be distinguished.[30]

The true status of those with whom one had contact was increasingly difficult to determine. In addition, what determined status was in the process of changing, especially during the regency and the boom-and-bust years of John Law's *système,* when vast fortunes were made and lost overnight.[31] Within the stream of undifferentiated strangers in early-eighteenth-century Paris, individuals had to make great efforts to color and to define their social place and relation to others.

Appearance and dress consequently took on an intensified importance, and the cycle of *modes* – first set by the court, then appropriated by the bourgeoisie, finally trickling down to the common people – quickened. Of interest, the consistent and sustained production of *gravure de mode,* or fashion plates, coincided with this new emphasis on dress during the last decades of the seventeenth century.[32] This suggests, of course, that there was a market for this type of instructional fashion image. Writing later in the century, J. H. Marchand revealed the importance of dress as an outward sign of place and rank and the difficulties that often arose in interpreting these wearable signs. He likened the material objects of luxury to a hieroglyphic language. "I see equally that the alphabetical characters of this language are multiplied in each piece of our dress, or each instrument of our mores: these symbolic characters change even more rapidly in their form than do those of ordinary languages."[33] Such confusion surrounding the outward markers of appearance suggests a breakdown in commonly understood sartorial and social codes, as does the explosion of sumptuary laws (generally ineffectual) appearing around 1700.[34] Yet despite the infinite variety of fashionable signifiers, the signification of *bon ton* remained perfectly stable; it was the property and instrument of the elite.

In this system, the body was a mannequin, theatrically dressed, and was not an expressive, living being. This sort of masquerade of everyday life was employed as much to disguise as to define, and it recalls the ideas Méré elaborated in his prescriptions for the *honnête homme*. Paint and large wigs obscured the face; masks were frequently worn in public.[35] The mask itself had become a mark of elite status. In speaking of aristocratic women, one visitor to Paris wrote, "They have the privilege to go masked at any time, to hide and show themselves when it pleases them; and with a mask of black velvet, they sometimes enter the churches as one would the ball or the comedy, unknown to God and to their husbands."[36] The mask and masquerade left the preserve of exclusive aristocratic entertainments; in the public context of the city, the mask became a portable and easily recognizable mark of superior status. Yet it was a treacherous mark, for one was never certain if the wearer's true identity corresponded to the outward meaning of the mask. A 1737 ordinance against masks attempted to regulate this situation and to prevent masked party crashers "who entered *maisons* and took their place at a banquet without being invited."[37]

The city, unlike the royal court or the "secret" seventeenth-century *salon* societies, was an unknown entity. It was not so much the rules of the game that had changed, but the game itself. The elite now had to recover and reinvent those forms of behavior that had traditionally differentiated them from their lessers. On the one hand, the exclusive elite *salons* and the *fêtes* they sponsored were more important than ever for preserving and producing signs of distinction. On the other hand, without a strong and viable royal court, the cult of *honnêteté* – and the complex modes of leisure and behavior it fostered – had lost much of its former rationale and significance. The act of withdrawing from the royal court had to be recast and recontextualized if it was to maintain its signifying power and independence from the absolutist state. And this recasting took a plurality of forms.

One such effort lay in a last-ditch attempt to preserve the outward trappings of the cult of *honnêteté*. Witness to this are the activities at the Château de Sceaux.[38] Mme. du Maine, who was the daughter of the Grande Condé and the wife of the king's illegitimate son, the Duc du Maine, presided over Sceaux.[39] One might view Mme. du Maine as one of the last *frondeurs*. There was a hope that the Duc du Maine would be legitimized, placing the heir of the Grand Condé on the throne as queen. The playful fantasy court created by Mme. du Maine at Sceaux recalled the tradition of her father's brilliant countercourt at Chantilly and his hopes for a return to power. The cabal to legitimize the Duc du Maine, which divided the court during the reign of Mme. de Maintenon, ultimately failed; after the accession of the regent in 1715, the duke and duchess were imprisoned until 1720.

From 1703 until 1717, Sceaux was the meeting place for the nobility and the bright lights of Parisian society. In an atmosphere *"mi-feerique, mi-medieval,"* the romanesque tradition of the ancient aristocracy was preserved in fantasy form. Mme. du Maine instituted an imaginary chivalric order that mimicked the chivalric orders in the king's court. The group was called the *mouche de miel,* or order of the honeybee, and its insignia was an image of a honeybee with the legend: "they are little but have a big sting." This was a reference to Mme. du Maine, who was extremely tiny but filled with boundless energy. The Queen Bee, Mme. du Maine, presided as *grande chancelière* over the thirty-nine "chevaliers." The *mouche de miel's* activities reproduced the rituals and ceremonies of the court, but playfully, without the court's heaviness and seriousness. Mme. du Maine drew up a set of rules (they included dancing at all times, even during the dog days of summer), which she then had read and sanctioned in a brilliant ceremony. After this, the chevaliers were invested with an appropriately precious pomp.

In addition to the order of the *mouche de miel,* other entertainments at Sceaux also drew upon older practices. A good example is the most spectacular of the *fêtes* staged at Sceaux, the fifteen *Nuits de Sceaux,* presented in 1714. These elaborate displays of luxury and conspicuous leisure, organized around a different theme each night, were widely discussed. Saint-Simon, exasperated with the Maines' aggrandizement, wrote: "Sceaux was more than ever the scene of the follies of the Duchess du Maine, . . . all-night parties passed in lotteries, games, *fêtes,* illuminations, fireworks, in a word, *fêtes* and fantasies of every kind, every day."[40] Much expense and energy went into these *fêtes,* a fact that Saint-Simon found ridiculous. He was particularly critical of the passion for the theater that ruled at Sceaux. "But others [certainly including himself] could not understand why people should be mad enough to tire themselves out dressing up as actresses, learning and declaiming the longest parts, and making a public spectacle of themselves on the stage. . . . Besides the absurdity, these pleasures were never cheap."[41]

Although the *Nuits de Sceaux* were certainly less restrained than royal court entertainments, they preserved and pointedly parodied the formal structure of royal court entertainments. Like the *Nuits de Sceaux,* royal entertainments often took place over a number of days. The *Divertissements de Versailles* of 1664 presented on its first day a ballet entitled *Plaisirs de l'Isle Enchanté;* the next day, *La Princesse d'Élide* was performed, and on the next, the *Palais d'Alcine.*[42] At Sceaux, one could again find the opulent entertainments of Condé and his circle, and of the early royal court at Versailles before they disappeared in the growing atmosphere of austerity that marked the end of Louis XIV's reign.

Chief among the lost pleasures one could find at Sceaux was the theater. After Louis XIV lost his taste for the theater, the courtiers were deprived of a form of entertainment they believed was rightfully theirs.[43] As Saint-Simon disparagingly pointed out, the staging of theatrical productions was a mania at Sceaux. The meaning of these productions went beyond the pleasure one derived from watching or performing: amateur theatrics were traditionally a sign of aristocratic status. The sort of performances that were staged at Sceaux generally drew upon the classical repertoire of official culture but transformed it to fit a fantasy court and to please a patroness devoted to play.

Mme. de Stael's description of a ballet she composed for one of the *Nuits de Sceaux* is very interesting in this regard:

> The subject was Taste taking refuge at Sceaux and presiding over the diverse occupations of the Princess. First Taste brought on the Graces who prepared a robe while they danced, while others sang airs provided with suitable words. This made up the first *intermède.* The second consisted of personified card games who brought in card-tables and set out everything that was necessary for play. . . . Finally the last *intermède* consisted of figures of laughter who came and set up a theater in which was given a comedy of one act.[44]

This ballet recalls many of the royal ballets, such as the *Ballet des Arts,* performed in 1663, with the king dancing a major role. It had seven *entrées:* agriculture, navigation, *orfévrerie,* painting, the hunt, surgery, and war.[45] The entertainment at Sceaux retained the traditional allegorical framework of the royal ballet but stripped it of all pretensions to seriousness. The result is less a satire on the almost extinct royal entertainments than it is an appropriation, transformation, and preservation of them by removing them from the confines of official culture and its categories.

In the preface to Abbé Genest's *Divertissements de Sceaux,* a compendium of poems, playlets, imaginary letters, and literary games, the reader is clearly warned that nothing in the text is the product of serious effort or work.[46] "These are pure amusements, impromptu games, and not mediated compositions; even the performances which seem the most professional, are truly only a kind of spontaneous game, appropriate only for the occasion which gave birth to them."[47] At the very moment that the official court was on the verge of dissolution, Mme. du Maine and her *habitués* "played" furiously at preserving its outward forms. René Démoris has suggested that the *fêtes* at Sceaux acted as substitutes for the former *fêtes* at Versailles and were an attempt to recapture the signifying power of those elite rituals.[48]

However, neither the substitute rituals nor the cult of *honnêteté* and its complicated literary games and forms of comportment had any real meaning without the legitimacy of the court. The participants at Sceaux therefore had not only to create and perpetuate the traditional forms of aristocratic comportment, but they also had to create a fictional framework to give them meaning. The *fêtes* at Sceaux tried to reaffirm the boundaries in which and against which the cult of *honnêteté* could still function and continue to signify elite status. Old court forms were prolonged at Sceaux.[49] Yet, this sort of retrenchment, this perpetuation of outmoded forms and rituals, did little to create the forms and signs that would effectively function in a new situation.

At the other end of this fictional fixing of the boundaries was an attempt to relocate and redefine them. As this description of a *fête* by Mme. Du Noyer suggests, popular culture and the marginal but very public world of the fair provided a means through which and against which the signs of elite status could be preserved:

> he [Comte de Taroucu] presented diverse areas; in one, was *la Bassette* [a card game], the *théâtre du bal* was in another, in another one sat eight boutiques which made up a sort of fair St. Germain and which was filled with everything one could desire of the most exquisite sort. . . . The so-called merchants cried and called to the passersby as one is accustomed to doing at the fairs, and to make sure their stock was inexhaustible, there was a central *magasin* in one of the other areas from which they took, at any moment, whatever they needed to restock their boutiques and replace what had been consumed. Thus, no matter how great the crowd was at this fair, because all the masks were allowed to enter, and although it lasted until six in the morning, the boutiques were always well furnished.[50]

The fair at this *fête* was as much a fantasy as the "court" at Sceaux; what differed was the kind of reality that was fictionalized. The ability to live one's life as a fiction, and bring that artifice to life, the hallmark of the cult of *honnêteté,* was transferred to a new context. In a double turn of self-definition, the elite proved themselves superior to what they imitated by their ability to make the imitation better than the original. In appropriating the lower-class culture of the fair, members of the elite could demonstrate their superiority to that culture by their ability to recreate it convincingly in an elevated and alien context. In short, they could transmute the base into the gold by the distancing effect of artifice.

The vogue for *contes de fées,* which flourished from 1690 until around 1730, is part of this same phenomenon.[51] The oral tradition of folklore and the recounting of fairy tales to quiet children and to make drudgery more pleasant were transformed into a literary game of the elite. In her *Epître aux fées modernes,* Mme. Murat distinguishes between the *contes de fées* of popular tradition, which "amused only servants and nursemaids," and the *contes de fées* produced by her refined and exclusive company. These men and women, by reason of their "brilliance and refined sensibilities," had the ability to endow these "poor stories with wit, beauty, eloquence and sparkle."[52] Most collections of *contes de fées,* such as Mme. Murat's *Le voyage de campagne,* or Mlle. Durand's *Les petits soupers de l'été de l'anneé 1699,* frame the text of the *contes de fées* with a *fête galante.*[53]

The description of these *fêtes* and their participants are lavishly detailed and replete with incidents that underscore the elite nature of the occasion. Once the superiority of the setting and participants was safely established, license could prevail. The skill in conversation necessary to the appropriate recounting of *contes de fées* was an attribute of the group's elite status. In Mme. Murat's *Voyage de campagne,* a group of *mondains* leaves Paris for a visit to a country house. In a trope that was surely old when Bocaccio used it, while staying at the house, they occupy themselves by telling tales to one another. They receive a visit from some of the neighboring inhabitants, *"moitié-ville, moitié-compagne,"* who join in the activity. However, the local narrators reveal their inferiority by the way in which they "throw" themselves into the conversation, telling their fairy tales with "shocking pedantry and affected grimaces." The host concludes by affirming that one must have elevated taste to appreciate and tell these low stories correctly.[54]

One can attribute the elite's appropriation of popular culture to the desire to find a new framework in which they could prove their difference and carve out a new ground on which to apply the practice of the traditions prescribed by the cult of *honnêteté*.[55] The pleasures that the *mondains* sought – as opposed to those sought by the older *honnête homme* – when they mingled with the populace (either in fact or in writing) were in the finding and the savoring of the contrast between their habitual discourse and the one that they mimicked, as well as in seeing how far they could push the limits of this irony. This testing of the limits had a liberating dimension. Under the guise of playing at marginal cultural forms one could express and experience those things that either were normally prohibited or had no acceptable outlet within the constraints of traditional cultural forms. Another example of this kind of testing was *mignardaise,* a way of speaking of bodily functions, especially of the sexual sort, in a disguised, precious way.[56]

The *mondains* enjoyed dabbling with impunity in the "forbidden." The attraction for them of mingling anonymously with the populace is well documented. Mme. de La Fayette wrote, "The pattern that Monseigneur follows at balls is to change his costume frequently for the simple pleasure of not being recognized and of speaking to people indiscriminately."[57] Beneath the disguise of a mask, or behind literary games such as telling *contes de fées,* there was freedom and an outlet for the cultivation of complex and convoluted modes of leisure and comportment. The extent to which elite behavior was focused on disguise is attested to by Saint-Simon's account of the vogue for wax portrait masks: "During the preceding winter, several wax masks of court personalities, very lifelike, were worn under other masks in such a way that at the moment of unmasking one was tricked, and took the second mask for the true face, and truly, it was someone quite different who was underneath; everyone was very amused by this silliness."[58]

This precious punning and playing with identities took on an even greater allure when the people who were masked were totally unknown to one another. It was fashionable for members of the court and the high aristocracy to frequent public places, such as gardens or promenades, that were the scenes of lively masked balls and *fêtes,* especially during carnival. This prevailing taste intensified during the later years of Louis XIV's reign, when, as Mme. de La Fayette characterized them, the officially sponsored balls were "sad."

People could test their skills at disguise and dissimulation at public balls and *fêtes;* moreover, they could temporarily live out their fantasies without consequences.[59] These events offered the chance for unexpected adventures and amorous intrigues. The author of *Le voyageur fidèle ou le guide des étrangers dans la ville de Paris* describes a ball at the Champs-Elysées, a popular promenade, for the newcomer to Paris:

> Balls are given here which attract a huge crowd of all states, ages, and sexes, and they enjoy the masked parties and taste this sort of entertainment with more liberty, because here, one takes *grisettes* for women of quality, and the bourgeois for seigneurs. . . . Having nothing for a seat except the lawn, one sits without ceremony and, as chance presides at these meetings more than anything else, I was thrown in with a young woman, . . . we continued our conversation and she played her role in the pleasantries, *mots d'esprit* and the double entendre soon came to be mixed with them. Finally love, which is always the hero of the piece, appeared.[60]

This account of the ball at the Champs-Elysées is theatrical; indeed, participants presented themselves theatrically and performed in a mutually acknowledged spectacle. From this passage, it would seem that everyone benefited from the deception, and the "piece" ends happily. The accounts of these balls are highly conventional; intrigue, mistaken identities, chance encounters, and sparkling conversation are the mainstays.

However, from Nemeitz's description of Parisian balls during carnival, the reader comes away with the sense that these pleasures were perverse at heart and could be dangerous, especially for those who, like our author, were not intimately familiar with the ins and outs of the social scene.[61] "One here has the liberty to appear in all sorts of disguises, men dressed as women, women dressed as men, costumes from all different countries, all ages and all fashions however strange and droll they might be. Everything here is permitted and the more bizarre a disguise, the more one admires it."[62]

Nemeitz's warning of the dangers of balls has a decidedly tongue-in-cheek quality: the reveler might get lost in the crowds, be robbed, or get overheated and faint, especially if he or she has drunk too much alcohol. Frenchwomen at the balls may be dangerous too; they might humiliate their suitors by making them fetch and carry all night. Nemeitz further recounts that at the previous year's ball "around twenty people perished in violent deaths, occasioned by these entertainments."[63] Yet despite these dangers, Nemeitz eagerly attended the balls; furthermore, he makes helpful suggestions for others who attend, such as that buying a suitable disguise at the beginning of the season is more economical than renting one. His advice that the fewer masquerades one attends, the better, rings hollow in light of his apparent definition of "fewer" as not four or five nights in a row.[64] The balls were attractive; certainly, the potential dangers and the disguises associated with balls added luster to the lure. At the public balls and masquerades, one's anonymity meant the liberty to be perverse.

The public balls and masquerades were similar to the *fêtes* at Sceaux in that they were a continuation and preservation of an already established mode of elite entertainment. Unlike the entertainments held at Sceaux, however, where the boundaries between the elite inner circle and the outside world were clearly drawn, the public balls, where men and women of all classes appeared in disguise, blurred the boundaries between the select and the others. These public balls and *fêtes* might best be seen as a sort of metaphor for everyday life in the city, where appearances were deceiving, and social position was no longer easy to represent or to decipher. The *fêtes* reproduced and fictionalized in play a situation that was disturbing in real life. Much of the power of masquerade as a sign of aristocratic status was diluted in this public sphere. To recapture the signifying power of masquerade, without giving up any of the "adventure," liberties, or pleasures that it offered, the elite had to reestablish clear boundaries between the high and the not-so-high that were muddled at these public *fêtes*. This need brings us back to Mme. Du Noyer's description of the fantasy fair at the *fête;* for the fair provided the means to redraw the lines.

The fair became important in the collective imagination because of its marginality. What most captured the public's attention were not a fair's boutiques selling luxury items, but its theatrical performances. Fair theaters were attractive to the elite and others, not just because their productions were entertaining but also because they had come to represent resistance to authority. As was discussed earlier, despite attempts from above to delegitimize them, the fair actors continued the tradition of the banished Italian Comedians. Certainly, the displaced elite found satisfaction in retrieving the pleasure of their beloved Italians' performances, not just as a nostalgic remembrance but also as an occasion for complicity in something now illicit and subversive. They must also have taken great satisfaction in the fact that the fair comedians consistently made monkeys of the authorities: the audience could savor this mockery of those powers that had marginalized both the Italians and the elite.

What especially intrigued the elite spectators was the lowest form of fair theater, the *parade. Parades* were the short, unpolished pieces performed *en treteaux* (literally, "on sawhorses," because a stage was created by placing lumber across sawhorses) in front of the theaters to attract customers. They were artless and rude, combining street entertainments, such as tightrope walking and acrobatics, with bits of theater. Often bawdy and scatological (certainly much more so than the Italian Comedians were before their banishment), the actors exhibited the grossest sorts of physical humor. What the elite enjoyed at these performances were their imperfections and lack of polish. They were entertainments that were outside the bounds of a traditional hierarchy of literary genres and, as such, were not to be taken seriously. Beyond literary constraint and within the liberating context of the fair, spectators could experience the thrills of physical and earthy humor.

One might say that the Italians' ultimate triumph at the fair theaters provided the scenario and the masks that enabled the revitalization of the *fête galante, à la* Sceaux, changing it from a bankrupt ritual to a rich and expressive symbol of cultural resistance.[65] The *parades* were appropriated by the elite and transposed to private drawing rooms and country residences. The originator of this theatrical craze was Thomas-Simon Gueullette, a magistrate from a noble family.[66] Around 1707, he and his friends, as a respite from their studies, began composing their own *parades* in Paris. These were later performed onstage at an inn just outside Paris, at Auteuil. Eventually, these amateur *parades* were incorporated into the framework of large elegant *fêtes* held at Gueullette's property at Charenton and, after 1718, at Choisy. Here we see how the thrills of public masquerades and balls and of the resistant, renegade fair *parades* could be meaningfully appropriated by the elite with loss of neither esteem nor status. Gueullette wrote of these affairs:

> Our diversions, always new and varied, attracted, apart from our invited friends, an astonishing gathering of spectators of the highest rank. Since we did not begin the performance until eleven o'clock in the evening, a number of gentlemen and ladies left Versailles *en poste,* after the King's supper, to participate in our amusements. Following the example of what goes on in Venice, we admitted those in masquerade to our entertainments. We gave a ball afterwards: all this made for a night-long revelry which seemed to please everyone.[67]

Unlike the theatrical performances at Sceaux, which, according to Abbé Genest, were "1,000 times more agreeable than anything in the public theaters because there are none of the defects one finds there," the *parades* at Charenton, Auteuil, and Choisy attracted through their defects, which freed the performances from the need for bourgeois professionalism and from the confines of official hierarchies.[68] The amateur *parades* were as simple as the entertainments at Sceaux were complex. Gueullette recounts that the costumes, sets, and props were minimal; the plots could be learned quickly; and the dialogue was improvised. Although the fair *parades* were appropriated by Gueullette as a form of elite entertainment, they were not transformed into something more refined or spiritual.

This was the point: by including the rough-and-tumble unprofessional *parades* within the framework of elite *fêtes,* the participants preserved the necessary contrast between what one was, and what one was not. As Démoris has pointed out: "As soon as the Italians' costumes no longer appeared on the stage, they became less the mark of a profession than the mark of noble divertissement, a sign of a being capable of giving a dimension of fiction to one's life."[69] Without the stable point of reference provided by the marginal world of the fair, *fêtes* like those at Sceaux would have been meaningless. At Sceaux, the elite could play at being elite; the "nobleness" of life as fiction had itself become a fiction.

The cult of *honnêteté,* as a form of behavior cultivated to resist official consolidation and to distinguish one's status in opposition, found both a new costume and a renewed rationale in the public and popular arena of the fair. In the end, the elite gained more than they had lost when the Italians were banished. The passage of the Italian tradition through the marginal and unmanageable space of the fair provided an easily imitatable spectacle of cultural resistance; moreover, it legitimized contact with an exciting, direct, and physical kind of experience without undermining the ideological assumptions of the cult of *honnêteté.* The breakdown of the cultural hierarchy that was so much the point in the battle between fair theaters and officials was put into the service of the upper classes to enable them to redefine and reaffirm their own status; the cult of *honnêteté* was transformed in the amateur *parades* into a cult of masquerade. Within the boundaries of these exclusive *fêtes,* where everything that occurred was intentionally muddled and juxtaposed, testing the limits of how far playing with identities could be carried became itself a sign of status.

Watteau and the *Fête Galante*

Watteau's *fêtes galantes* – in both what they represent and how – are part of the recasting and recontextualization of the cult of *honnetêté.* Once we realize that Watteau's *fêtes galantes* depict the sort of elite entertainments in which theatrical costume and masquerade were so important, the costumed characters of the Italian theater, such as the Pierrot, Harlequin, and Mezzetin in *The Pleasures of the Ball* (fig. 49), are not out of place. They are models of the new *honnête homme* in action, dabbling in a play of identities. The mixing up of the real, the theatrical, and the fantastic in Watteau's paintings is perfectly representative of experience at a *fête galante.*

Thus Watteau's *fêtes* are not his personal visions or dreams. When Donald Posner writes about *The Shepherds* (fig. 50), "It is an unlikely assembly he shows, mixing rude peasants with elegant people playing '*pastorale*,' " he is overlooking the fundamental importance of masquerade in elite self-definition.[70]

Gueullette's account of the antics of one of his fellow actors, Pierre Pasquereau, belies Posner's assertion and helps us to see *The Shepherds* in its proper perspective:

> Using the name Bertrand and in the dress of a true peasant, he imitated people of this sort with such naturalness and accuracy in speech, song and dance that when, after changing his make-up and costume, he came to sup with people meeting him for the first time, they never recognized him. And when we unmasked him, they would never believe that it was the same man they had seen that afternoon.[71]

Moreover, Gueullette mentions that the peasants and bourgeoisie of the village at Charenton joined with the more exclusive company at his outdoor impromptus.[72] Even at Sceaux, the peasants, unknowingly, became part of the *spectacle*'s decor. Abbé Genest commented that the fireworks had an effect on the villagers who watched the *spectacle;* in the pyrotechnic light they appeared transformed – clean and proper.[73]

Whether pretend or real, peasants and shepherds did form a part of the *fête galante*'s, landscape, and their appearance in Watteau's images should not be seen as completely imaginary. Watteau would have had access to this sort of high life through one of his patrons, Pierre Crozat. Crozat (1665–1740) was a wealthy *financier*, an avid collector of art and curiosities, and a bright light in Parisian society.[74] Watteau met Crozat sometime after 1712 and lived with him in Paris for at least one period, and probably several. Watteau also made retreats to Crozat's country house, Montmorency; the gardens of this residence appear in *The Prospect (La Perspective),* at the Boston Museum of Fine Arts. At Montmorency, Watteau would have witnessed the sort of outdoor elite entertainments and *promenades* he pictures in his *fêtes.*

It would be misleading, however, to suppose that Watteau's *fêtes galantes* are faithful renderings of actual events. Rather than reproductions of reality, the *fêtes* are artful re-creations that focus on certain aspects of this particular kind of sociability. That Watteau "invented" the costumed figures he used in his *fêtes* and did not always derive them from firsthand observation is attested to by the Comte de Caylus. In his biography of the artist, Caylus mentions that Watteau kept a collection of *galant* and comic costumes in which he

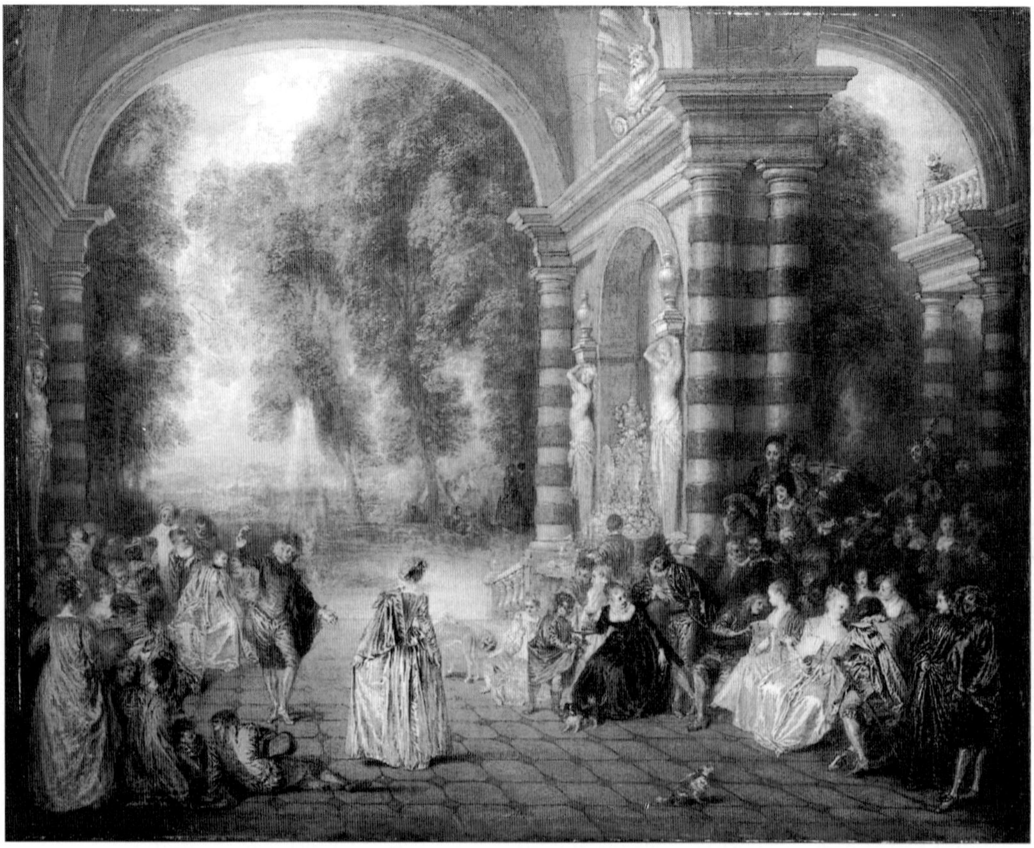

49. Antoine Watteau, *The Pleasures of the Ball (Les plaisirs du bal)*, c. 1717, Dulwich Collection, London. By Permission of the Trustees of Dulwich Picture Gallery.

would dress up persons willing to model and then sketch them in natural and simple poses.[75] Evidence suggests that Watteau drew upon such sketches for his *fêtes* and enjoyed himself in the process, for the contrast between subject and costume is often witty and humorous. For example, the portly and phlegmatic figure on the left side of *Venetian Entertainments* (fig. 51), commonly held to be Watteau's friend Vleughels, seems comically miscast as a dainty, mincing dancer in an elaborate and exotic oriental costume complete with turban.

Watteau consciously manipulates the contradiction between theatrical costume and an "other" identity. Framed within the larger social function of masquerade and disguise at *fêtes,* and primed with the assumptions of the cult of *honnêteté* that underlie the act of masquerade, these contradictions clarify rather than confuse. At a *fête,* by donning a costume of what one was not, whether it be an Italian Comedian or a shepherd, one defined one's status. The very act of disguising oneself had a meaning independent of what the costume

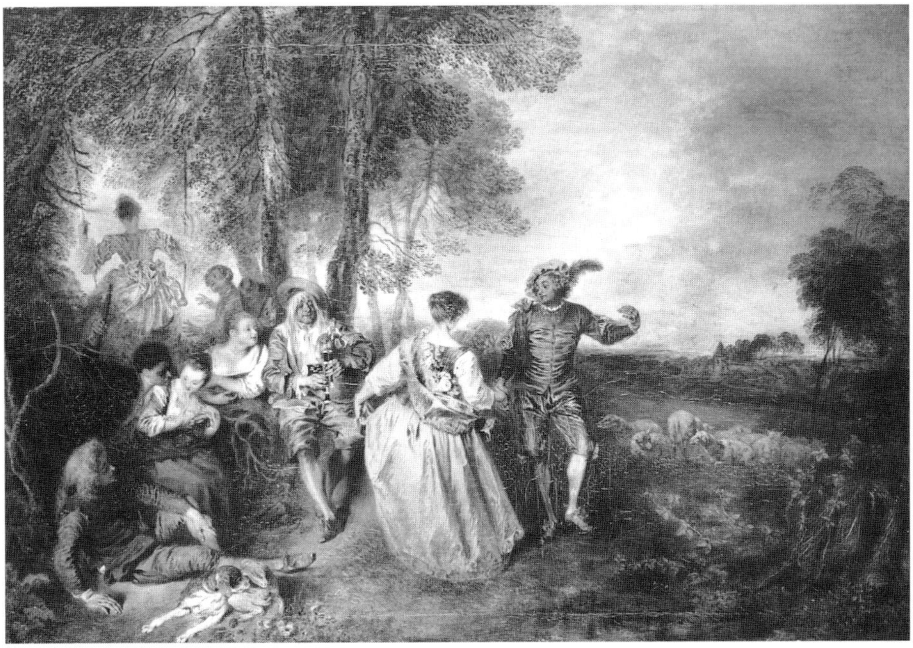

50. Antoine Watteau, *The Shepherds (Les bergers)*, c. 1716, Charlottenbourg Castle, Staatliche Schloesser und Gaerten, Berlin, Germany. Photo, Giraudon/Art Resource, NY.

represented. Bryson overlooks this dimension of the masquerade when he writes:

> Watteau's figures are not wearing their customary social clothing, but theatrical disguise, and though the disguises emit clear messages, we cannot then re-attach the messages to the bearer. In masquerade, the pleasure comes precisely from re-joining the message of the costume to the person beneath the disguise: here the messages fit, there they do not. But in a Watteau masquerade, only the participants can do this – all we have is one side of the equation.[76]

Watteau's figures in theatrical costumes do emit clear messages, but of a different sort than those Bryson suggests; the masquerade is a sign of a status, not of a role. Viewed from this perspective, the message of the costume does not actually need to be rejoined to the person beneath it; a certain correspondence is already assumed. The wearing of a theatrical disguise implied a reverse identification: I am not what I am dressed up as. In a milieu where "customary social clothing" could be misleading and where the mode was in constant flux, theatrical disguise was a clear and legible statement of one's position: as a privileged individual capable of living life as fiction.

What Watteau manages to capture so well in his *fêtes* is the paradoxical role of masquerade in the economy of elite self-definition. The costume was a sign of what one was not; yet, at the same time, one's ability to play that role, to

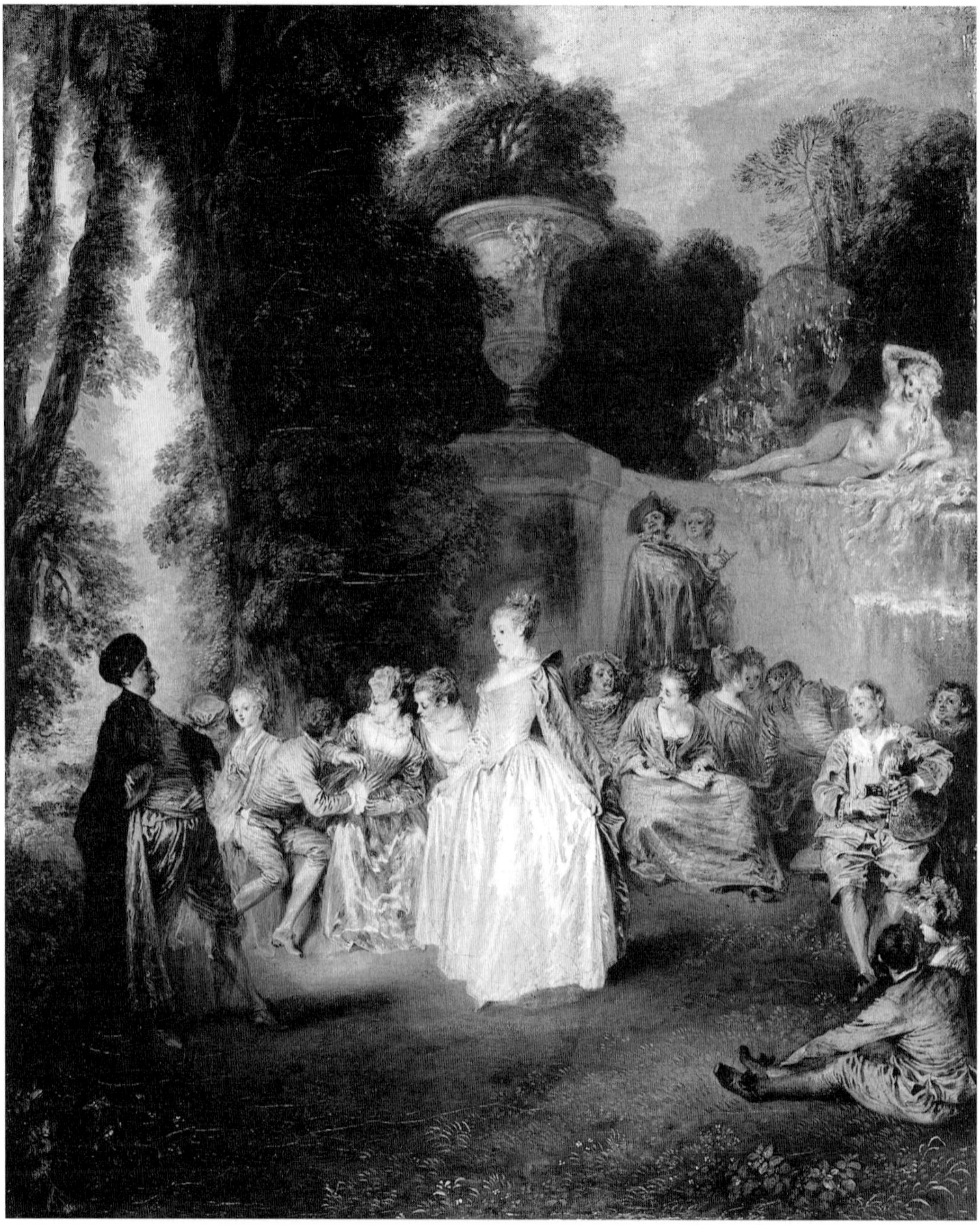

51. Antoine Watteau, *Venetian Entertainments (Fêtes vénitiennes)*, c. 1717, National Gallery of Scotland, Edinburgh.

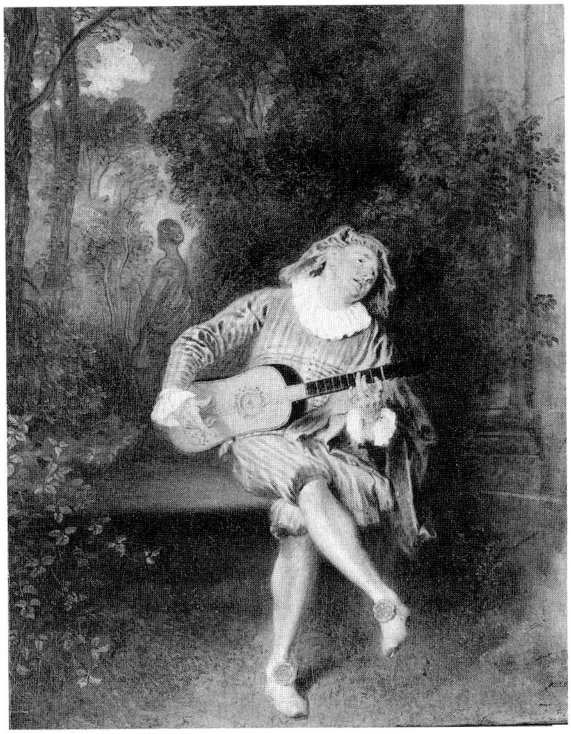

52. Antoine Watteau, *Mezzetin (Le Mezetin)*, c. 1717–18, New York, Metropolitan Museum of Art, Munsey Fund, 1934 (34.138).

bring it to life, was important. Watteau articulates the fit or lack of fit between the disguise and the wearer. Predominating in his *fêtes* are Italian Comedians and seventeenth-century troubadours who are pointedly not what they appear to be. Watteau's Harlequins, Mezzetins, and Pierrots rarely match the physical types or the stylized postures and movements belonging to the characters that their costumes represent. The elegant and delicate Mezzetin who is the focal point of the painting *Mezzetin* (fig. 52) has nothing in common with the coarse, clever servant of the same name in the Italian theater. Even within the setting of the painting, which could easily be understood as the theatrical space of the stage, it would be difficult to reconcile the costume and its wearer. Sometimes, by contrast, the fit is all too close. The Harlequin in *Do You Want to Succeed with the Ladies . . .* (fig. 53) looks like a conventional Harlequin and acts like one too. His salacious gesture frightens Colombine. Yet we know that this is a *fête*, and we might assume that Harlequin, in Ronald Paulson's words, "may be trying to trick, frighten or seduce Isabelle precisely because he is a noble lover disguised as Harlequin."[77] What is always in question in Watteau's *fêtes* is just how far the fiction has gone, how well the player has succeeded. The artist pushes this ambiguity to the limits, just as participants did at actual *fêtes*.

On another level, Watteau implicitly marks the elemental defining difference between acting as a profession and acting as a mark of elite status: Watteau's bodies do not register or emit any clear signs of emotion or feeling in contrast to the way in which actors use their bodies on the stage. The physicality of expression that was so much the trademark of the Italians' brand of humor is absent from Watteau's *masques*. Here Bryson is to the point when he states that we have only one side of the equation in a Watteau masquerade.

Watteau was the master of the evasive gesture: backs are turned, heads are tilted away, and eyes are downcast in his work. The face, that principal agent

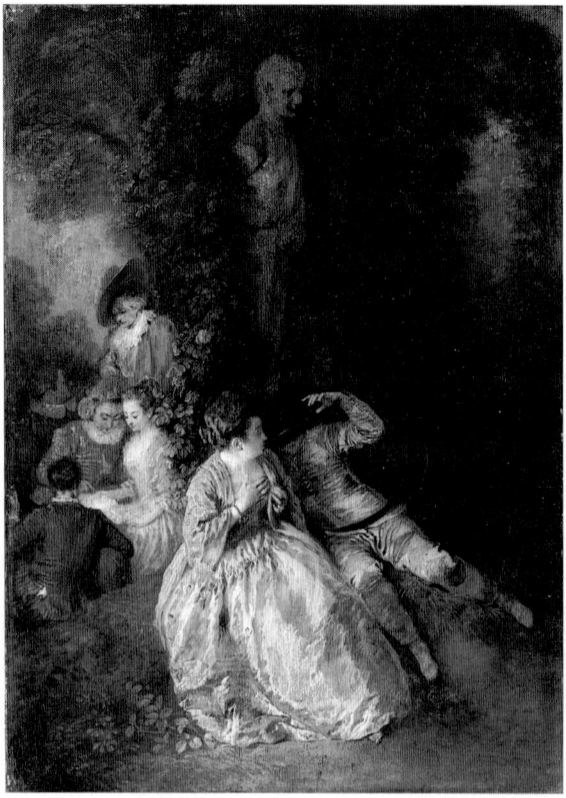

53. Antoine Watteau, *Do You Want to Succeed with the Ladies . . . (Voulez-vous triompher les belles . . .)*, c. 1716, Wallace Collection, London. Reproduced by permission of the Trustees of the Wallace Collection, London.

of expression, is often hidden from view, or only partially revealed. In the exquisite, almost miniature, *Gathering in a Park (Assemblée dans un Parc)* in the Louvre, the faces of only four of the ten figures can be seen, and even those four are only partially revealed. We have the feeling that if Watteau had slightly shifted the tilt of a head, or adjusted the angle of a hat, we could read the expression on the faces. When we do see faces, however, they are usually impassive; the figures seem to be absorbed in something inaccessible to the viewer. For example, the Pierrot in the left mid-ground of *The Pleasures of the Ball* (fig. 49) stares blankly out at the viewer, and the expression of the doll-like woman in the foreground of *Les Champs-Elysées* (fig. 54) could be read in a number of ways.

Watteau's poses and gestures, too, tend to conceal rather than convey emotion. His figures are frozen in transitional poses and unfinished gestures; frequently, they are depicted as in the middle of some action. This incompleteness makes it difficult to determine exactly what is going on: Watteau hints at an outcome or starts an action, but he represents neither and resolves nothing, leaving it to the viewer to do both. As well as creating expectations, the ambiguity of pose and gesture focuses attention on the smallest details and nuances.[78] Confounded by ellipsis, the viewer searches for potential meaning in the crook of a finger, the position of a foot, the tilt of a head, or the way a figure holds a rose or a fan.

Watteau's unresolved gestures and poses also give rise to a sense of instability. The artist has a knack for freezing gestures at their most ungainly. We know that the suitor who is in the process of kneeling beside the *belle* on the right side in *Pilgrimage to Cythera* (fig. 48) will eventually rest his knees on the ground. But caught in mid-action, regardless of his place within the larger, compositional progress, he appears clumsy and about to tumble from the exertion of holding the pose. Similarly, both the figure of Harlequin in *Do You Want to Succeed with the Ladies. . . .* (fig. 53) and that of the man who is mak-

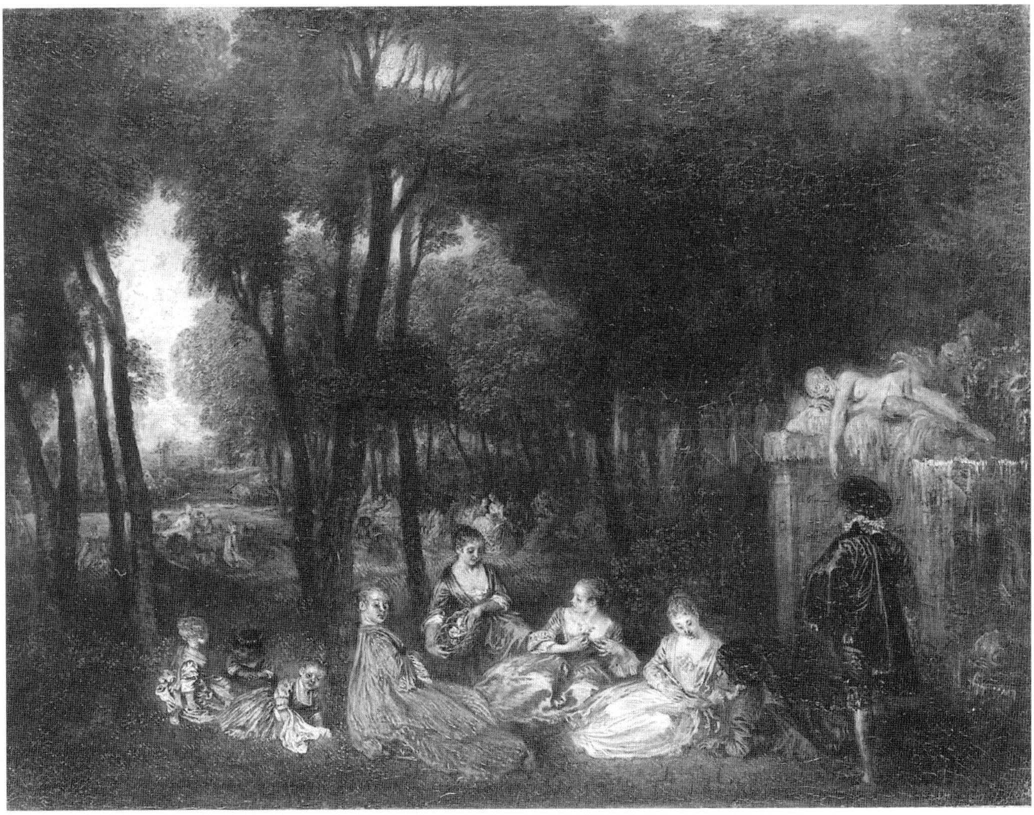

54. Antoine Watteau, *Les Champs-Elysées*, c. 1716, Wallace Collection, London. Reproduced by permission of the Trustees of the Wallace Collection, London.

ing advances toward a young lady on the left side of *Venetian Entertainments* (fig. 51) appear to be off balance. Their positions seem precarious, and we mentally carry through the motion, lest they topple from their seats. This lack of clarity of expression must have been infuriating to someone such as Caylus, who expected the body to register and convey the "passions" that would inform the subject's narrative. We can understand why Caylus complained that Watteau's figures express no passion and that his paintings have no focus.

What must have been further exasperating for Caylus, and for the viewer seeking a clear rhetoric of the passions codified in Le Brun's *Traité des Passions,* are the intense yet unobjectifiable gazes of Watteau's figures. The crowded company on the right-hand side of *The Pleasures of the Ball* presents a crisscross of absorbed gazes. Everyone is looking intently. *The Music Lesson,* at the Wallace Collection, London, presents five three-quarter-length figures, set against a background of sky and clouds that fills the canvas. A figure in the costume of Mezzetin, standing to the right, plays a lute which he rests on one upraised knee. To the left, a seated woman holds a book of music. Directly behind her a man, wrapped in a cloak and wearing a floppy hat reminiscent of the costume of Scaramouche, leans over the shoulder of the seated woman. Tucked into the space between the lute-playing man on the right and the seated woman and man on the left, are two young girls, one who looks toward the man and woman, and the other toward the lute player. In the absence of a developed setting the five figures become the sole object of the viewer's attention. These figures' absorbed looks create narrative tension and pique the viewer's interest, just as their gestures and poses do. Is the man on the far left looking at the woman's neck or, more suggestively, at her bosom? Is the book that the woman is concentrating on also the focus of his attention? What is in that book that could be so interesting? One little girl appears to be looking up at the woman. The other has an animated, almost coquettish expression. Has she seen something just outside the range of the canvas, or has the lute player gotten his fingers tangled up in the strings, making her smile? Watteau often does not let us see the object of the gaze; he cuts the object off or makes it uncertain. Watteau's gazes exclude the viewer from what is happening on the canvas. The faces of his figures are like masks that reveal no expression but that of "attention." From the intensity of the attention portrayed, however, we can assume that something important is going on, but we are given few clues as to what is happening.

In theatrical manuals of the period the gaze from one actor to another is usually reserved for scenes of high passion. As Bryson has pointed out:

> In Watteau the eyes behave as though in this theatrical representation of "high passion." . . . But the body does not support this passion. . . . What emerges is a disparity between the nonsignaling bodies engaged in their physical activity, and the eyes, which, within the theatrical convention, signify intense feeling through the attentive inter-crossing. The two sets of signals are contradictory, and to reconcile their opposition the viewer creates an array of meanings which are not in themselves directly represented.[79]

What Watteau does represent through these contradictory signals is a painterly embodiment of the mode of behavior prescribed by the cult of *honnêté*. Watteau's disguised nonsignaling bodies create a visual counterpart to the armor of artifice, which both hides and dissimulates. Directness, clarity, and even unguarded communication rarely appear in Watteau's works. His figures act out a complex ritual of seduction in which the more primitive and physical emotions are displaced onto a set of idealized signs. Glances are charged with erotic meaning, and the smallest gestures are loaded with possible significance. For example, in *Les Champs-Elysées* would the seemingly innocent gesture of stepping on or near someone's cloak have been understood as a veiled act of aggression, a ritualized invasion of another's amorous territory within the system of elite comportment? To answer would require insider's knowledge of the signs and codes. Watteau's pointed hints and suggestions both give form to and play off of the exclusivity and secretiveness that endowed aristocratic self-definition with meaning. A true aristocrat would understand the complex code governing gallantry and would recognize when others were adhering to it. Similarly, Watteau's *fêtes* challenge the viewer to recognize and understand the hints and suggestions he deploys: they demand, Are you one of the elect, or are you one of those who has to be told things directly?

Yet in their gallant game of love, Watteau's actors do let real signs of desire slip through. All passion is not repressed in the service of aesthetic seduction. One device Watteau exploits is the inclusion of a couple engaged in obvious amorous combat, in contrast to the more refined and controlled love play represented by other figures. For example, in *Venetian Entertainments* (fig. 51) and *The Pleasures of the Ball* (fig. 49), among others, a woman pushes away an overly eager suitor who grabs at her unceremoniously. Another "slip" may arguably be the engorged, red hands of many of Watteau's male figures. Although it may simply be that Watteau had difficulty rendering hands, especially those in complex positions, the consistency with which he displays these swollen hands suggests that they may be meant to signify displaced erotic desire. The swollen hands of the central male figure in *The Shepherds* (fig. 50), for example, inform the nature of his dance of desire; likewise, the hands of the man in the background who is swinging a woman transform innocent child's play into a frankly erotic adult game.[80] In two other works, the hands of the guitar player in *Mezzetin* (fig. 52) and of the lute player in *The Charms of Life* (fig. 55) seem to stumble, as if the men's desire has made it impossible for them to pursue the sort of controlled amorous ritual implied by the playing of a stringed instrument, a symbol for elevated, ideal love. This displaced symbolism adds erotic intensity and urgency to the often staid and ritualized activities in which the men and women are engaged. These excursions into the physical representation of desire within the frame of the ideal love of a *fête galante* might be seen as analogous to Méré's injunction to add a touch of true sentiment to one's performance. This touch of truth will prevent both Méré's courtiers and Watteau's *fêtes* from having "a vain appearance like the action of the theater" and will lend credibility to the fiction.[81]

Watteau's figures send out contradictory signals and provide incomplete information in a way that visually articulates the underlying assumptions and outward forms of elite social practice. How else could Watteau give form to the values of the cult of *honnêté* – so steeped in the indirectness, disguise, and dissimulation, the poeticization of the erotic, the exclusivity, and the carefully included "genuine sentiments" that persisted in these elite *fêtes* – except through representations in which meaning depends upon indirectness, implication, and juxtaposition? We have seen this mode of representation in his figures, but, perhaps of greater importance, it extends beyond the separate figures to condition the entire structuring of his images. What we have in Watteau's *fêtes* are images of a particular kind of elite play. The artist's visual

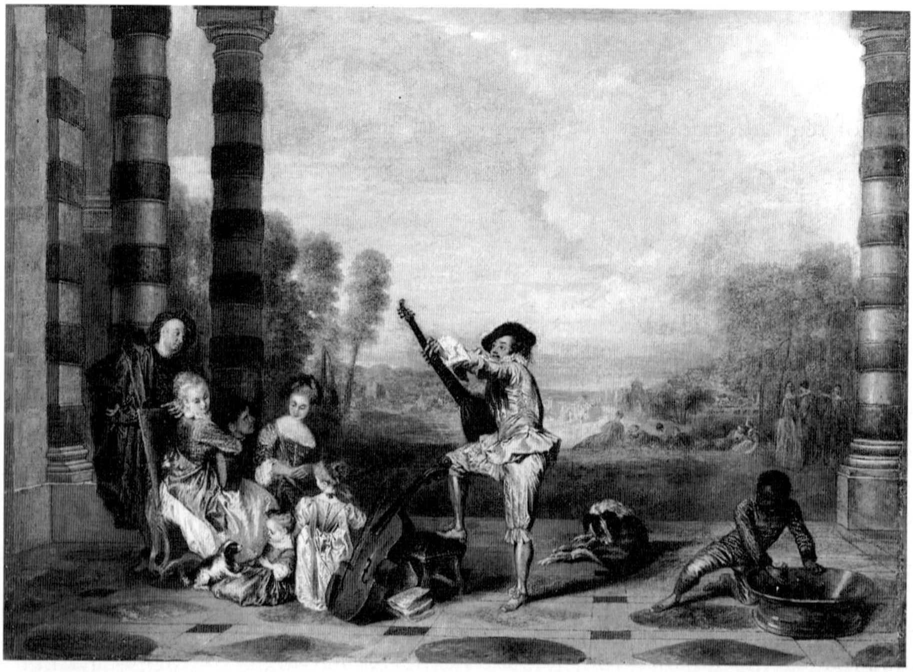

55. Antoine Watteau, *The Charms of Life (Les charmes de la vie)*, c. 1718, Wallace Collection, London. Reproduced by permission of the Trustees of the Wallace Collection, London.

economy and structuring of the scene reproduces in many ways the processes by which the elite play operates and produces larger meanings in real life. For example, Nicholas Mirzoeff has proposed that Watteau's paintings embody a changing discourse about seduction that challenged traditional assumptions about gender, visual pleasure, and performativity.[82]

Watteau's paintings are transgressive; like masquerade, they call attention to the arbitrariness of cultural and social categories. On every level in his *fêtes,* Watteau sustains a productive play of contradictions, indirections, and ruptures. Watteau's facture is no exception. His painted surfaces are deliberately inconsistent; some parts of a painting have a highly realistic "Dutch" finish, while other parts have a sketchy, unfinished quality.[83] This disjuncture is particularly apparent in his larger paintings, such as *Les Champs-Elysées* (fig. 54) and *Halt During the Hunt (Rendez-Vous de Chasse)* at the Wallace Collection, London. The seated figures in the foreground of *Les Champs-Elysées* are highly finished and worked. The detailed and carefully rendered textures of their garments are in sharp contrast to the sketchy, shorthand notations he uses to indicate grass and vegetation. The effect is a bit disturbing, for the female figures appear almost to be mired and sinking into the ground on which they sit. Watteau's dabs and traces are less the mark of a work of the painterly profession than they are reminders that what we see is not "serious" painting, but a form of spontaneous, frivolous aesthetic play. The presence of marks of facture in some places and their concealment in other places create a dual register of realities: the work declares itself to be a fiction, an aesthetic production. The dual register of techniques constantly reminds us that the pleasure we take from the painting is the result of artifice and rests as much in the independent play of paint as in the finished product of a representational image. At the same time, the rough, sketchy, and sloppy portions have the effect of making the more polished and finished parts seem all the more amazing and beautiful. This echoes the *honnête homme,* who adds a bit of sincere sentiment or reveals an imperfection here and there in order to make the creation and deployment of his artful second self seem that much more dazzling, convincing, and natural. Mary Sheriff has discussed how certain ideas that developed in eighteenth-century French art theory correspond to ideas about the ideal courtier formulated by Castiglione in *Il Cortegiano.*[84] Among these ideas are *facilité* and *négligence. Facilité* refers to the appearance of a certain practiced ease in painting, to artistry that can make the most difficult painterly techniques look natural and easy. *Négligence* refers to the artful arrangement of imperfections to create effects that seem to have happened by chance. *Facilité* and *négligence* are aligned with the aristocratic ideal of *sprezzatura.*

The perhaps unwitting mixture of professional polish and unprofessional roughness in the paintings might be seen as a parallel to the role of masquerade and of the amateur *parade* in the social economy of a *fête.* In *The Charms of Life* (fig. 55), the cello, lute, and copper bowl that are depicted, as well as some of the figures, exhibit a highly realistic technique. The terrace upon which the figures are arranged appears solid and substantial. The tiled floor recedes according to the rules of perspective and creates a convincing illusion of three-dimensional space. Yet where the terrace ends, the image becomes indistinct and slightly vaporous.[85] We see the marks of scumbling and the evidence of a quickly painted unfinished surface. The illusion of three-dimensional space also vanishes; we tend to read the background as the vertical, two-dimensional surface of a theatrical backdrop. This theatrical representation of space suggested by the "fake" painted background promotes an understanding of the terrace as a stage and of the costumed figures as actors. Watteau never resolves these contradictions.

The same dislocating spatial ambiguities in *The Charms of Life* appear throughout Watteau's *fêtes.* In *The Pleasures of the Ball* (fig. 49) we also tend to read the landscape background that we see through the large arch as a theatrical backdrop. Despite the balustrade that appears beside the supporting column, the figures on the terrace have no means of entering the background: Watteau does not depict the stairs that normally accompany a balustrade; there is no transition, no real middle ground. This is true as well for his *fêtes* set entirely out-of-doors. In *Country Amusements (Divertissements Champêtres)*, in the Wallace Collection, London, in *Mezzetin* (fig. 52), and in *Les Champs-Elysées* (fig. 54) the transition between foreground and background is abrupt. The middle distance is masked by a row of trees and darker vegetation. The figures in the background of *Les Champs-Elysées* seem too small, as if they were separated from the foreground by a large, unseen gulf. The figures on the left, in particular, seem to hover above the foreground in some imaginary, unlocatable space. In *Halt During the Hunt* this effect is heightened, and the small area of illuminated background appears almost as a separate and independent scene. This area is "dream space"; in its position above the heads of the woman and her suitor, it has the quality of a visualization of her idealized, secret desires.

The contrast between the crowded merrymakers in the foreground of *The Pleasures of the Ball* and the painting's quiet pastoral background might be interpreted as a visual representation of the larger social and cultural desires that were expressed in elite entertainments. These desires were aimed at preserving the illusion of an ideal aristocratic past, such as was illustrated in romances, including Honoré d'Urfé's *L'Astrée*. The ideological assumptions of innate aristocratic superiority manifested in the cult of *honnêteté* in the pastoral romances persist in the *fête galante* as background. In the foreground, as in the present, we see the persistence of this myth in new costumes: those of Italian Comedians. By donning a costume appropriated from the popular theater, the aristocrat preserves his distinction; he pulls the past into the present. Although the outward cultural forms have changed, the function of social definition has not. Nowhere is this more clearly displayed than in Watteau's *Do You Want to Succeed with the Ladies . . .* (fig. 53), where Harlequin and Colombine in the foreground are juxtaposed against the group of gallants in archaic seventeenth-century costume in the left background.[86] The former group has replaced the latter in signifying social status. The Italian costume conjures up and symbolizes the ideological content represented by the *honnête homme* of pastoral romances.

As well as giving form to some collective social desires, the spatial disjunctures also represent individual erotic desires. Like the eroticization of Watteau's glances, his eroticized spatial arrangements hint at a narrative that is never anywhere openly depicted. Posner has iconographically explicated the figural group in the foreground of both *Les Champs-Elysées* and *Country Amusements* as the entry into the initial stages of love and courtship.[87] The rose is the flower of Venus and a symbol for love; consequently, the woman who holds the basket of roses has not yet chosen her love. The woman next to her, who is fastening a rose to her bosom, is in the process of selecting her suitor; one assumes that the man opposite her will soon move closer. The third woman with the rose already in place has chosen her suitor, and indeed, she is glancing at the young man at her side. This initial stage in the ritual of courtship is contrasted with the activities of the figures in the background, who, according to Posner, have symbolically moved into a second, more intimate stage of love play: a couple dances the *branle,* a lively peasant dance, which in eighteenth-century jargon was a euphemism for sexual excitement. We see the fulfillment of the expectations of the foreground figures in the background. The viewer mentally carries this game through to its conclusion.

Moreover, Watteau peppers his *fêtes* with symbolic markers of desire that make explicit the erotic intentions and activities at the *fête galante.* The rose and the *branle* are two examples of this, but also, the dog in the foreground, whom the little girls coax on, is a visual reference to animal, or physical, desire.[88] In *The Shepherds* (fig. 50), the somewhat comical juxtaposition of the dog licking his genitals and the reclining man whose pose mirrors that of the dog, save for the telling gesture, is transformed into an emblem of human desire. Mirimonde has convincingly demonstrated Watteau's indebtedness to the emblematic tradition of employing musical instruments to create a lexicon of love.[89] The lute, with its complicated tuning system, represents an idealized love whose harmonies are equally difficult to realize. The bagpipe, with its suggestive form and inharmonious squawking sound, alludes to a base, physical love.

Many Watteau scholars have commented upon the suggestive use of statuary in the *fêtes.*[90] Statues, too, connote the nature of love play. Plump, voluptuous nudes, which seem more of flesh than of stone, are strategically placed. In *Les Champs-Elysées,* the reclining nude female statue directly above the solitary figure glancing over at the seated women is a visualization of his erotic fantasies. The viewer cannot help but make the connection between the man, his gaze, and the statue to create a meaning that is nowhere explicitly represented. In a similar configuration, the reclining sleeping nude statue above another solitary gazer in *Country Amusements* is an embodiment of desire. The same type of reclining nude appears, but in flesh and blood, in the Louvre's *Jupiter and Antiope;* the satyr who voyeuristically leers at Antiope represents the erotic content only alluded to through juxtaposition and displacement in *Les Champs-Elysées.* Lack of fulfillment and unrequited love are also the implied messages of *Mezzetin.* Here, the musical message of love suggested by the lute player will never be heard by the stone deaf statue of Venus with her back turned to the mournful musician.

This sort of *galante* iconographical system owes less to the grand and ultimately propagandistic schemes of allegorical history painting than it does to the decorative schemes of the arabesque.[91] Within the format of the arabesque, Watteau fused the vocabulary of the pastoral, the rustic, and the lively world of the fairs as well as "low density mythology and minor league deities."[92] Moreover, we see the imagery of the fair *parades* clearly placed within an aristocratic context.

In an arabesque dating from around 1708, entitled *The Children of Momus* (fig. 56), we see five putti arranged on a stagelike platform. Two of these are dressed in costumes from the Italian theater, those of Mezzetin and Pierrot, a third wears a very theatrical shepherd's costume, another wears a vaguely arca-

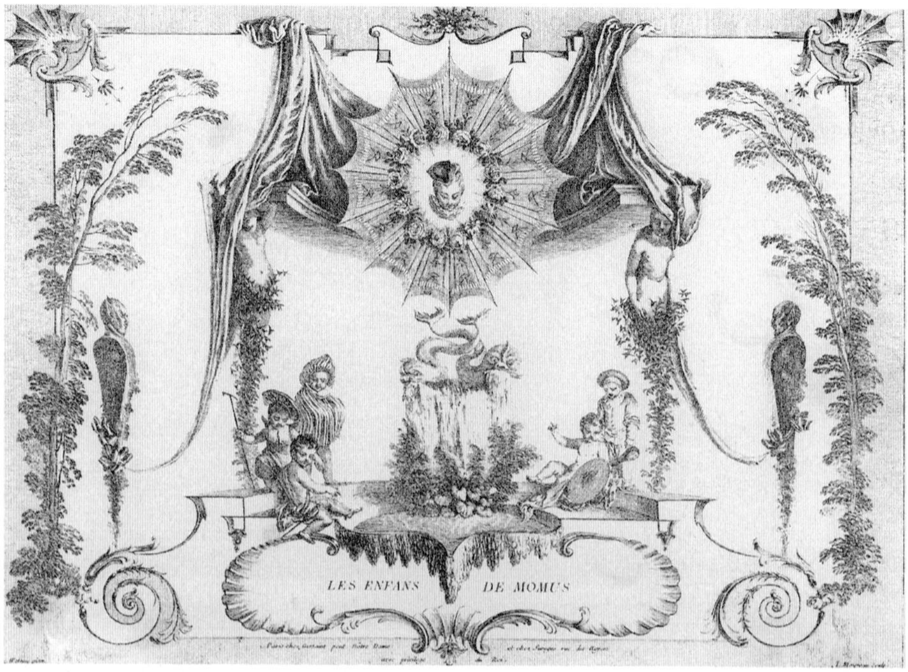

56. Jean Moyreau, engraving after Antoine Watteau, *The Children of Momus (Les enfans de Momus)*, engraving announced 1729, author's collection.

dian drape, and the last wears nothing, but is surrounded by the paraphernalia of a jester. From the center of this platform rises a fountain with two dolphins, the traditional messengers of love in classical mythology. Beaming down on the scene from above, is an out-of-scale head of Colombine, surrounded by a radiating circle of roses. Behind her, and extending out on either side, is a curtain that rests partially on a platform and is held back by two half-length nude female figures. The bottom part of these seemingly "real" women have their male counterparts in two stone hermes with the heads of sileni, which, along with a gracefully bowing branch, flank and frame the central portion. The stone men and flesh women are literally connected by a bit of curtain that trails down from the women to a suggestive spot on the satyr's plinth.

On a formal level, we have a fantastic aesthetic game in which substance dissolves into pure ornament; the pleasure of viewing arabesques consists in charting these effortless, seemingly magical shifts from one dimension to another. On an iconographic level, we see a mix of symbolic vocabularies. Here, meaning is suggested by juxtaposition. *The Children of Momus* is a rich and playful exposition of love: the bonds of love, the folly of love, the bawdy love of the Italian theater, and the ideal love of the pastoral romance.

In a later arabesque, *The Sparrows' Nester* (fig. 57), the central scene has been expanded and elaborated; it no longer fits within its ornamental frame.

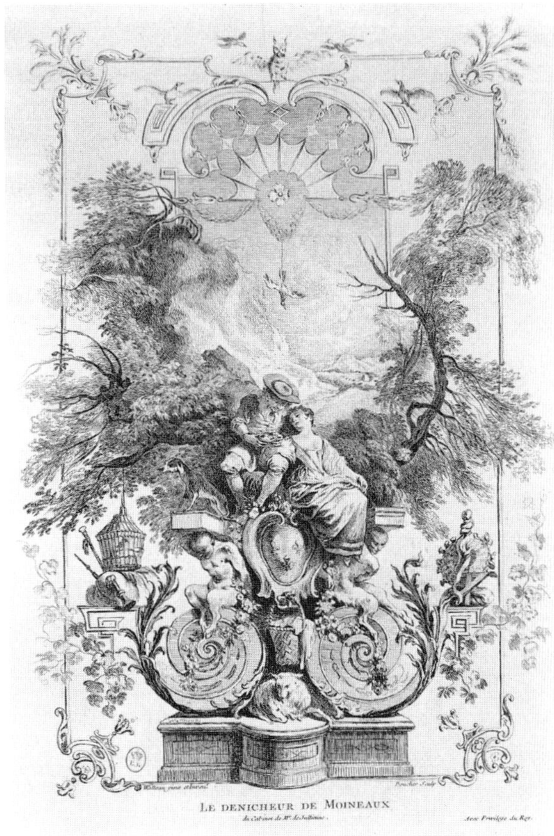

57. François Boucher, engraving after Antoine Watteau, *The Sparrows' Nester (Le dénicheur de moineaux)*, engraving announced 1727, Bibliothèque nationale de France, Paris. Cliché, Bibliothèque nationale de France, Paris.

The tender couple in the center of the arabesque, precariously perched on a pedestal supported by satyrs, is surrounded by emblematic accessories. This ensemble suggests that things are not, or will not be, as tender as they appear. Above the erotically suggestive bagpipes, supported on another ornamental shelf, hangs a caged bird, a traditional Dutch symbol for the conquest of love and the loss of virginity.[93] A basket of eggs, another symbol for the fragility of virginity, sits atop a ram, itself a symbol of animal lust. Hanging from an ornamental cartouche above the couple's head is a dead mother bird; the man holds the empty nest, and other birds "shriek in alarm to the proverbial owl about imminent disaster."[94]

Although, save the bird's nest and the dog to the left of the man, these various emblematic elements are outside the central illusionistic scene, they supply a textual gloss to its content. The result of this interchange is the possibility of a dense and multilayered allegory of desire that could accommodate even its more disorienting and darker aspects without directly representing them. We can see how much is lost without the bawdy subtext of symbols in the painting *The Sparrows' Nester* (fig. 58), which is an expanded version of the central scene in the arabesque placed in a landscape setting.

The painting of *The Sparrows' Nester* and the arabesque date to around 1710, and they indicate the direction Watteau would take in his later work. In his mature *fêtes,* Watteau succeeds in transposing intact the structure, syntax, and mixed vocabulary of the arabesque to a single unified image.[95] The spatial disjunctures seen in *Les Champs-Elysées,* where parts of the painting seem to be framed by vegetation and not completely integrated with the rest of the scene, reveal Watteau's indebtedness to the decorative arabesque, as well as expose some of the compositional and technical problems he never completely

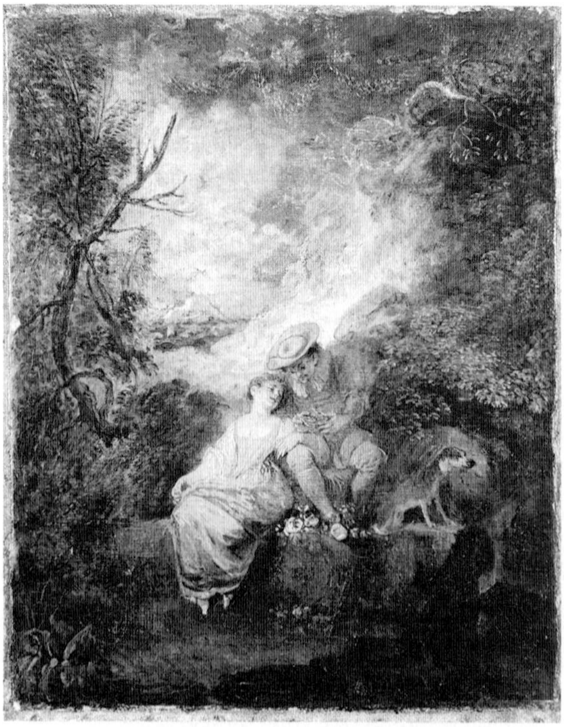

58. Antoine Watteau, *The Sparrows' Nester (Le dénicheur de moineaux)*, c. 1710, National Gallery of Scotland, Edinburgh.

overcame.[96] It is tempting to speculate that Watteau consciously capitalized on these painterly problems because of their potential appeal to a certain audience: the same audience who would have appreciated the unpolished, unprofessional quality of Gueullette's amateur *parades* would have recognized and appreciated similar qualities in Watteau's works.

Thomas Crow has argued that Watteau's *fêtes galantes* were a kind of painting distinguished by a self-conscious artificiality and that it was this artificiality that allowed a "realistic" depiction of its subject without aligning itself with the lower genres.[97] "Rather than some kind of realist grounding of the genre, we are dealing here with two related and artificial systems of representation being maneuvered into productive contact."[98] These two systems are the popular (and politicized) theatrical representations at the fairs, and their progeny, and an aristocratic and highly irrealistic form of decoration, the arabesque. As I have discussed earlier, Watteau was at a confluence of the practice of these forms: his training was in the tradition of Netherlandish genre scenes; from Gillot, he learned the conventions of theatrical images; from Claude III Audran, he learned the art of the arabesque; and through his association with the society of the Crozat circle he gained access to the world of elite entertainments. In his *fêtes galantes,* as Crow argues, Watteau legitimized a type of experience that expressed ideological assumptions associated with neither the elevating official culture nor the low culture. Likewise, as a genre in painting, with particular formal conventions and subject matter, the *fête galante* was associated with neither the didactic function and classical foundation of history painting nor the already existing lower genres. And this brings us back to Watteau's *Pilgrimage to Cythera.*

Pilgrimage to Cythera Redux

How do we account for why *Pilgrimage to Cythera* was first recorded as a history painting? The kind of playful symbolic subtext in Watteau's *fêtes,* which also permeates *Pilgrimage to Cythera,* can be seen as a visual counterpart to *mignardaise;* beneath the surface of outward refinement, those who understand the game will find another, more direct and less innocent meaning. Perhaps the Academicians who made decisions about classification were able to perceive a message and a moral. On second thought, however, the Academicians may have found that the erotic nature of the message and the unconventional means by which it was conveyed did not jibe with traditionally accepted ideas of what constituted history painting: *Pilgrimage to Cythera* did not depict a scene from either ancient, or biblical, or officially sanctioned contemporary history. Although the painting did refer to classical mythology, it lacked an appropriately elevating textual pedigree. Indeed, the content of *Pilgrimage to Cythera* was ultimately neither moralizing nor elevating, and the narrative structure by which *Pilgrimage to Cythera* produced its meaning was neither transparent nor rhetorical. There are some questions to be posed here: did the eighteenth-century viewer perceive *Pilgrimage to Cythera* as having a larger, allegorical meaning? And if so, what was that meaning?

The answer to whether the eighteenth-century viewer perceived larger meanings in *Pilgrimage to Cythera* is given by two contemporary sources. According to the announcement for the print after the second version of *Pilgrimage to Cythera* (now in Berlin and hereafter referred to as the Berlin version) that appeared in the *Mercure de France* in 1733: "The subject, as much gallant as allegorical, represents the embarkation of pilgrims for the island of Cythera."[99] In addition, the Comte de Caylus, who was not one of Watteau's admirers, grudgingly approved of *Pilgrimage to Cythera* in 1748 because:

> To put it briefly, with the exception of certain pictures, such as *The Village Bride* or *Wedding,* the *Ball,* the sign done for Monsieur Gersaint, and the *Embarkation for the Isle of Love* which he painted for his Academy reception piece and which he repeated, his compositions have no focus, they do not express any passion, and therefore lack one of the most exciting elements in painting, namely, action.[100]

The answer to what was the meaning of *Pilgrimage to Cythera* has been the object of much art historical discussion. Much of the debate concerns the question: Are the pilgrims setting forth on their journey to Cythera, or are they departing from the island of love, at the end of the pilgrimage?[101] For reasons that will become clear, I am convinced that *Pilgrimage to Cythera* represents a departure from, rather than an embarkation to, the Island of Cythera. But to focus on the question of comings and goings overlooks the larger point, namely, the appeal that the subject – a pilgrimage to the Island of Love – would have had for an eighteenth-century viewing public steeped in the traditions of the cult of *honnêteté.*

The idea of a pilgrimage of love, a voyage from the real world to an enchanted, mythical island of Cythera, would have been very familiar to the eighteenth-century public. It was a subject that had enjoyed a literary and theatrical vogue since the end of the seventeenth century.[102] Louis de Fourcard hypothesized that the last scene of Dancourt's *Les trois cousines,* performed first in 1700 and again in 1709, provided the inspiration for Watteau's *Pilgrimage to Cythera.*[103] Although Watteau could have seen the play performed in 1709, it would be presumptuous to suppose that *Les trois cousines* was his specific source, especially since there were so many other theatrical pieces that included a pilgrimage to Cythera. Among these possible theatrical sources were Corneille's *Psyche,* La Fontaine's *Amours de Psyche et de Cupidon,* Fuzelier and Le Sage's *L'École des Amans,* and Fuzelier's ballet, *Les Amours déguisé,* to name just a few.[104] Literary works about Cythera were equally common; the most popular of these was Paul Tallemant's *Voyage de l'Isle de Cythère,* first published in 1633, with a new edition appearing in 1713 under the title *Les avantures de Mlle. de Meyrac: Histoire véritable.*[105]

Literary and theatrical sources apart, a "pilgrimage to Cythera" would have had a particular resonance in relation to contemporary language and social activities, which the public would have understood immediately. As Robert Tomlinson has pointed out, many of the pilgrimage plays are grounded in reality, making reference to the contemporary Parisian practice of taking a day trip to the nearby suburb of St. Cloud.[106] A "pilgrimage to Cythera" was an eighteenth-century turn of phrase for an excursion to St. Cloud and, by extension, a commonly understood reference to a voyage into the world of illicit sexuality. Nemeitz remarked, "Especially on Sunday, many people go there [St. Cloud] for diversion."[107] As well as being a pretty, pleasant place to enjoy the country air and a popular place to imbibe at one of the numerous *guingettes,* St. Cloud also had a notorious reputation as a *rendez-vous* for illicit trysts and for *noble débauche.* Hence a "pilgrimage" to St. Cloud carried certain implications.

The implication that erotic liberation reigned at St. Cloud appears in Furetière's poem, first published in 1659, *Voyage de Mercure,* in which a deceived husband questions his unfaithful wife:

> Quand il lui dit: D'où venez-vous?
> Aussi, sans scruple et sans hônte,
> Sans congé, ni sans rendre compte
> Elles vont de nuit et de jour
> Avec des plumets de la cour
> En des bals, en des promenades,
> Où se dressent des embuscades
> Si puissantes contre l'honneur,
> Qu'il n'en revient que par bonheur.
> C'est par ces licences publiques
> Que Mercure perd son pratique.
> Car dès qu'on fit ces rendez-vous.
> Ces Bagnolets et ces Saints Clouds
> Qu'on fit des courses, des Voyages,
> Des voeux et des Pèlerinages . . .[108]

Indeed, there was a "love boat," which left from a point near the present location of Samaritaine, that took "pilgrims" to St. Cloud. Tomlinson describes these pilgrimages as having a form that wittily and irreverently paralleled the Christian pilgrimage ritual. Pilgrims stopped at an *auberge* placed in the garden and then went through the maze up to the fountain where a statue of Venus could be seen in her "temple of love."[109] The darker connotations of Cythera are illuminated in Marchand's reference to a fellow who sold pornographic images as an *"espion de Cythère"*; this spy, or voyeur, as the case might be, can be seen as representative of the kind of double entendre fostered by the cult of *honnêteté*.[110] This example suggests that "a voyage to Cythera" also represented the meeting ground of the high and the low in expressing the carnal and corporeal that official high culture sought to deny and proscribe. The Comte de Caylus illustrates this public denial when he decried Watteau's paintings for not meeting the officially accepted criterion for significant works of art – that they express elevated passions or actions – Caylus's private literary production was at odds with his public pronouncements. In private, Caylus was the author of erotica. The title and "publication information" of one of these works should suggest the extent to which Cythera, Venus, and so on had become incorporated into the language of *mignardaise: Le volupteux hors de combat, ou le défi amoureux de Lygdame et de Chloris* [A Cythétheropolis, chez Pierre J'Arrétin, imprimeur de l'Académie des Dames à Vénus de Grèce].

Given this broad literary and theatrical treatment of pilgrimages of love as well as the numerous slang references to pilgrimages and Cythera, it is not a surprise that Watteau had addressed the subject before he painted his reception piece. There are studies of gallant pilgrims, at least one of which was incorporated into the engraved series *Figures de Modes* and *Figures Françoises & Comiques*. Two other paintings are *The Island of Cythera (L'ile de Cythère)*, of 1706, in the Städelsches Kunstinstitut, Frankfurt, and *Bon Voyage* (c. 1713–17), known only through the engraving *Pilgrimage to Cythera*. Thus Watteau's reception piece was not without antecedents; rather, it was the continuation and development of an already established subject and theme, part of a modernized, modish mythology understood by those both of the street and of the elite. Given the elliptical and ironic perspective intrinsic to the cult of *honnêteté* and inherent in the treatment of the pilgrimage of love, we ought not to be astonished that Watteau should have painted his reception piece in such a way as to exploit allegory but deploying a whole new set of references. For in *Pilgrimage to Cythera* Watteau gave form not only to the ritualistic qualities of a *fête* but also to the idea of pushing the limits, to the idea of dangers existing beneath the illusions of life as fiction. *Pilgrimage to Cythera* tests and redefines the limits of allegorical painting as well as other cultural and social limits.

In *Pilgrimage to Cythera* we see a group of men and women in a woodland setting, at the edge of a body of water. Mountains appear indistinctly in the mist of the far background. In the center of the foreground, a little hillock creates a compositional and narrative division. The three couples on the hillock to the right create a progression, suggestive of motion in time.[111] The couple the farthest to the right, and the closest to the statue of Venus, are seated. The couple in the middle are in the process of rising: the man is helping the woman up. The third couple, to the left, are already standing. On the other side of the hillock, in a spatially ambiguous mid-ground, are five more couples. They appear to be moving toward a rather ornamental boat, tended by two seminude figures. Above this vessel, a group of putti caper about.

As Michael Levey has convincingly argued in "The Real Theme of Watteau's *Embarkation for Cythera*," the setting and the iconographic cues justify reading *Pilgrimage to Cythera* as a departure from the Island of Cythera.[112] Levey has pointed out the significance of the term, or herm, of Venus, which indicates that the setting is Venus's sacred isle – not the ordinary world. The pilgrims have already arrived at their destination. Moreover, the term of Venus is garlanded with roses, the flower of Venus and an age-old symbol of love. This suggests that the pilgrims have already made their offerings, that their ritual has been completed. Cupid, too, has completed his task, for he has set down his quiver and bow at the plinth of the statue. One of the putti who flutter over the ship carries a flaming torch, a traditional, well-established device for symbolizing the "flames of love" in emblem literature (fig. 59).[113] The presence of this *feu d'amour* would, thus, emblematically denote an island of love and not the ordinary world.

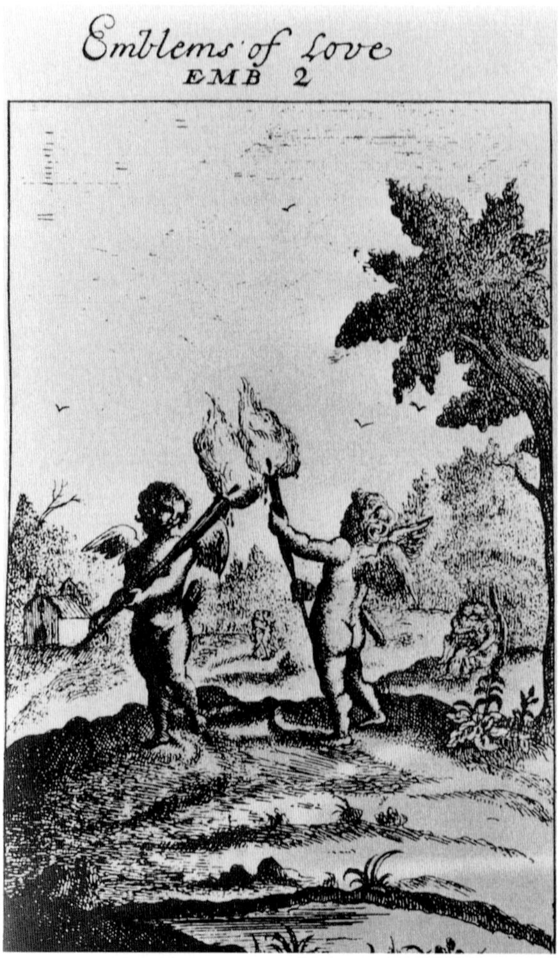

59. Emblem, *Mutual Love*, from Philip Ayres, *Emblemata Amatoria*, 1683. Photograph, Jennifer Laffoon.

The arrangement of the statue of Venus in relation to the three couples on the hillock in the foreground suggests a narrative progression that also justifies, according to Levey, the reading of the painting as a departure. Watteau similarly uses this device in the Wallace Collection's *Country Amusements* and in *Les Champs-Elysées* (fig. 54) to indicate a progression through the stages of love. In *Pil-*

grimage to Cythera, the seated man and woman nearest the term of Venus are the couple most clearly under love's spell. They are fully absorbed with each other. A small cupid tugs at the woman's skirts, as if to remind her that it is almost time to leave. The next couple are preparing to leave. They are further removed from the statue, hence less bewitched by Venus's power. The third couple stand at a pivotal point in the composition and in the narrative. They are the furthest removed from the statue and its spell of love. Completing this progression, they are in the process of leaving, about to cross the threshold created by the hillock. The woman gazes back at what has been – the spell of love – while the man, with his back to the viewer, urges her away.

The diagonal line of the hillock formally and physically separates one group of lovers from another. On the far side of the hillock are a group of pilgrims who have left that "hot zone" of love behind. Their placement and gestures lack the slow, graceful rhythms of those of the three couples clearly on Venus's turf. Moreover, this group are no longer obviously paired off as couples: the six figures create a single visual unit. These figures have merged back into the larger social unit – the company of gallants – from which the original pairings came. I would assert that Watteau is hinting at the inevitable dissolution of all the couples back into that social group. Yet the desires – both social and sexual – that sent them on their quest have not been forgotten. Two of these women address their attention to each other, not to their partners. One can imagine the women comparing notes on their amatory experiences or perhaps planning the next adventure. In fact, the whole configuration of gazes and the objects of those gazes suggests a reshuffling of interests. Here, the memory of desire fuels desire. Each can fall in love all over again with someone else, on another pilgrimage, or at another *fête galante.*

Two other details in *Pilgrimage to Cythera* lend support to the interpretation of the scene as a departure. One of these details is what appears to be an erect phallus, uncannily illuminated, in a woody recess just to the left and behind the statue of Venus.[114] Scrutiny (extremely close scrutiny, I might add) proves this image to be illusory, and it dissolves into an innocent configuration of vegetation. But from the normal viewing distance of two or three feet, and even from the close proximity of a *curieux,* the image could certainly be construed as a phallus. In fact, it is easy to perceive the entire configuration as the lower part of a large pale term, or herm, in the distance. The juxtaposition of the lower part of a male statue with the upper part of the statue of Venus creates a surprising effect. If these two statues could merge, they would create a herm-aphrodite, or a witty image of coupling. Although we bridge this gap in our imagination, these stone statues can never merge. These frozen, incomplete statues illustrate the inherent incompleteness of desire: the lack that fuels desire.

The other detail is on the same order of visual punning. In the lower-left-hand corner is a portion of a dead and gnarled tree. Painted in dark tones, these clawlike branches would seem more an apparition from a Friedrich painting than part of a landscape in a *fête galante.* The trunk of this tree – suggestively phallic in shape – is superimposed over the boat in which the pilgrims have already traveled and will again. This "vessel" is more a luxurious symbol of the transports of desire than it is a functional boat. It is too small actually to accommodate all the pilgrims in the painting. Moreover, as Charles de Tolnay has observed, the boat resembles a bed, a *lit de parade,* complete with canopy.[115] On the prow of this boat/bed is, according to de Tolnay, a siren, the mythical creature whose song proved fatally attractive to Odysseus's sailors.[116] In *The Odyssey,* seduction leads to destruction. In the painting, behind the siren's head is a shell, a common symbol of feminine seduction, and in the eighteenth century, a slang reference to female genitalia.[117] The satyr, who holds up the canopy, and who has just been garlanded with roses, is a symbol of masculine powers. The juxtaposition of the boat/bed, with its symbolic ornament, and the dead tree produces an ominous warning: desire ends in its own destruction.

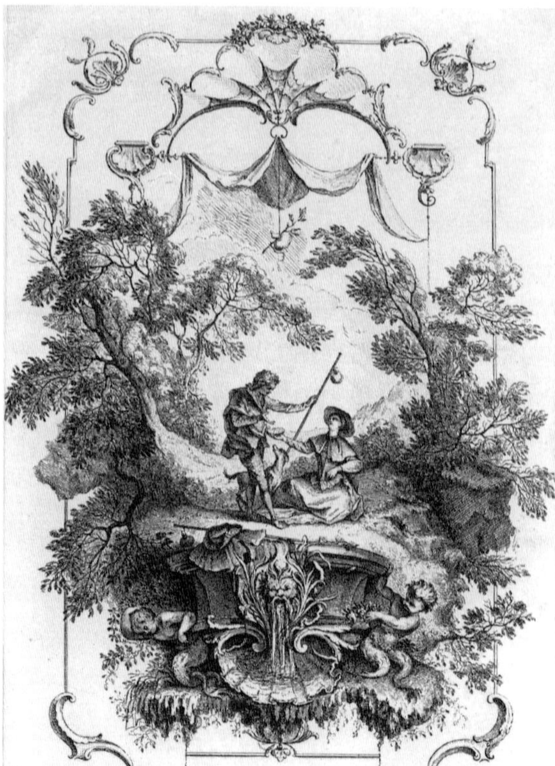

60. Gabriel Huquier, engraving after Antoine Watteau, *The Corrupted Pilgrim (La pèlerine altérée)*, Bibliothèque nationale de France, Paris. Cliché, Bibliothèque nationale de France, Paris.

The putti, too, as well as being appropriate accouterments on Venus's island, play into the topoi of love and loss. Watteau's putti are less mythological beings than purely physical ones; they are bundles of animated flesh and fleshy desire. In fact, two putti, just above an oarsman's head, act out this desire in an extremely adult fashion. As we have seen in Watteau's arabesques and his other *fêtes galantes,* this type of erotic displacement is very common and certainly must have been savored by sophisticated viewers. Along the same lines are the sexual double entendres to be found in the traditional accessories associated with pilgrims and pilgrimages; the scallop shell, which was the badge of a pilgrim making his or her way to Santiago da Compostello, could be understood in this context as a badge of a less spiritual order. Whereas this shell's connotation in street language was decidedly female, the pilgrim's staff, with its attached gourd, made a parallel reference to the male genitalia.[118] Tomlinson has found several passages from pieces performed at the fair theaters that demonstrate that the sexual connotations of shell, gourd, and staff would have been commonly understood by the eighteenth-century audience. The following passage, from Charpentier's *Les Avantures de Cythère,* provides a good example:

> My gourd will always be full
> of a juice divine,
> I can easily refresh you morning and evening,
> And during the course of our route,
> Obliging maiden,
> When I pour you wine,
> present your shell.[119]

An arabesque by Watteau, *The Corrupted Pilgrim* (fig. 60), can be seen as a visual translation of this verse. The male pilgrim is holding the pilgrim's gourd, while the female figure offers up her shell to him. Below this couple, water passing through a narrow channel falls into a shell-shaped basin. On the same level of double entendre is this passage from Antoine Fuzelier's *Pèlerins de Cythère,* in which Pierrot teases a man who has been fooled by a woman of easy virtue:

> Really, poor pilgrim
> You are going to lose your shells,
> And you will be most fortunate
> If you save your pilgrim's staff.[120]

The symbolic implications of the four putti above the oarsman's head in *Pilgrimage to Cythera,* who cluster around the flame of love, are more ominous. They call to mind the numerous emblems that illustrate mottoes such as "thus a lively pleasure leads to death" and whose overall message warns of the potentially destructive powers of love (fig. 61).[121] In these images, moths or butterflies are attracted to the flames of love, only to be consumed and destroyed by them.

That Watteau was attempting to convey the dangers inherent in desire and the ultimate loss of love in *Pilgrimage to Cythera* is given even greater credibility if we compare the first version to the second version, which he painted in 1718 (fig. 62). Although the second version is generally

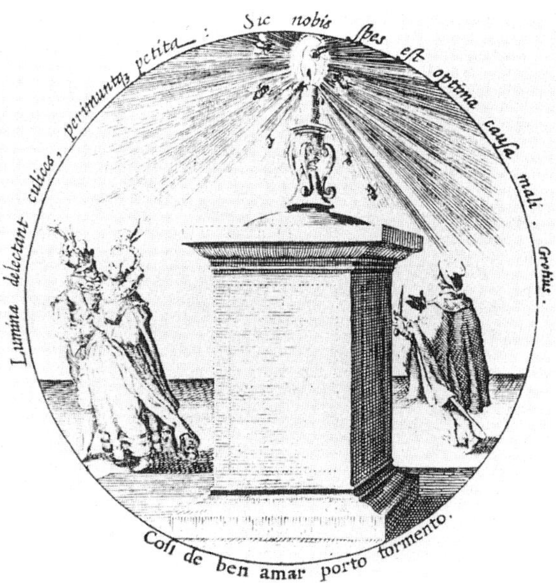

61. Emblem, *Love Bears Torment (Cosi de ben amar porto tormento),* from Daniel Heinsius, *Emblemata Amatoria,* 1607. Photograph, Jennifer Laffoon.

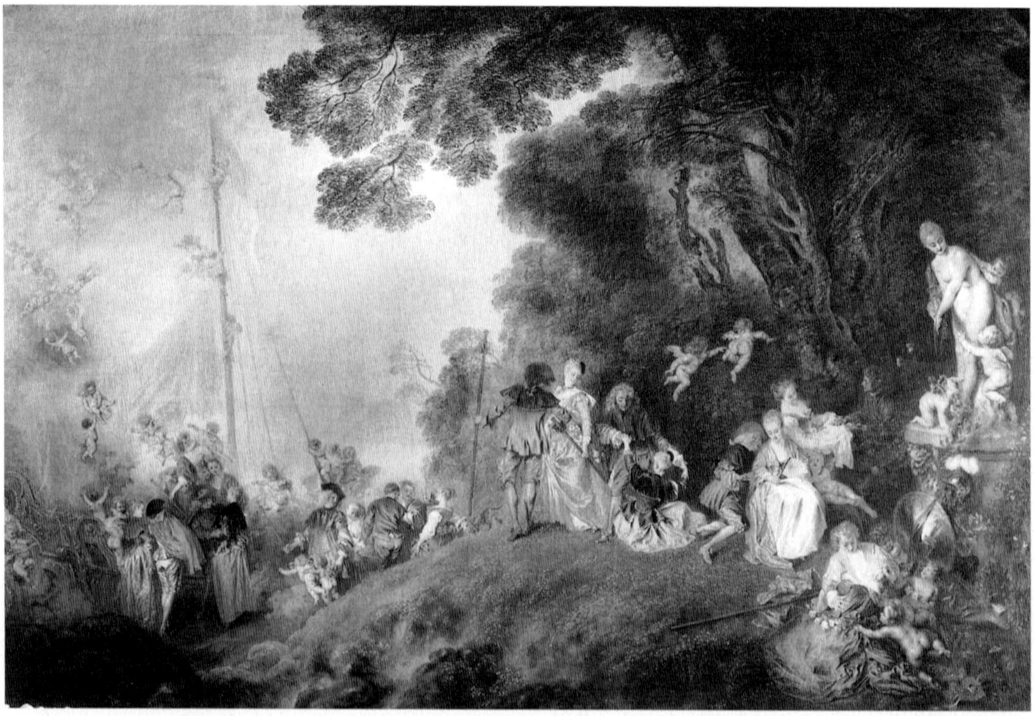

62. Antoine Watteau, *Embarkation for the Island of Cythera (L'embarquement pour l'île de Cythère)*, 1718, Charlottenbourg Castle, Staatliche Schloesser und Gaerten, Berlin, Germany. Photo, Erich Lessing/Art Resource, NY.

considered to be more optimistic in its mood, a wholehearted affirmation of love and its powers, the symbolic subtext, I would argue, remains consistent with the message of the first version.[122] In the second version, the cast of characters has grown; two additional couples appear near the statue of Venus and two other pairs are now on the pilgrimage boat. The statue of Venus, which in the first version was an image of incompleteness, has been transformed into an image of fullness and voluptuousness, one of those typical Watteau statues that seem made more of flesh than of stone. The boat, too, has also become more substantial, and even functional; it now supports a mast and sail. The putti have also solidified; they are explicitly corporeal, exhibiting clear proof of gender. They are so fleshy that one wonders how they can even leave the ground. Moreover, the putti have multiplied. They grab at one another and pose in suggestive positions, gleefully sliding up and down the ship's mast in erotic abandon. In the midst of all this flesh and abundance, however, is a small but significant detail. In the lower-left-hand corner – the same place that in the earlier version we saw that ominous juxtaposition of the dead tree and the boatlike bed – a cupid shoots a reversed arrow, feather end first, toward a couple. We can see this image in the detail in Tardieu's engraving after the Berlin version of

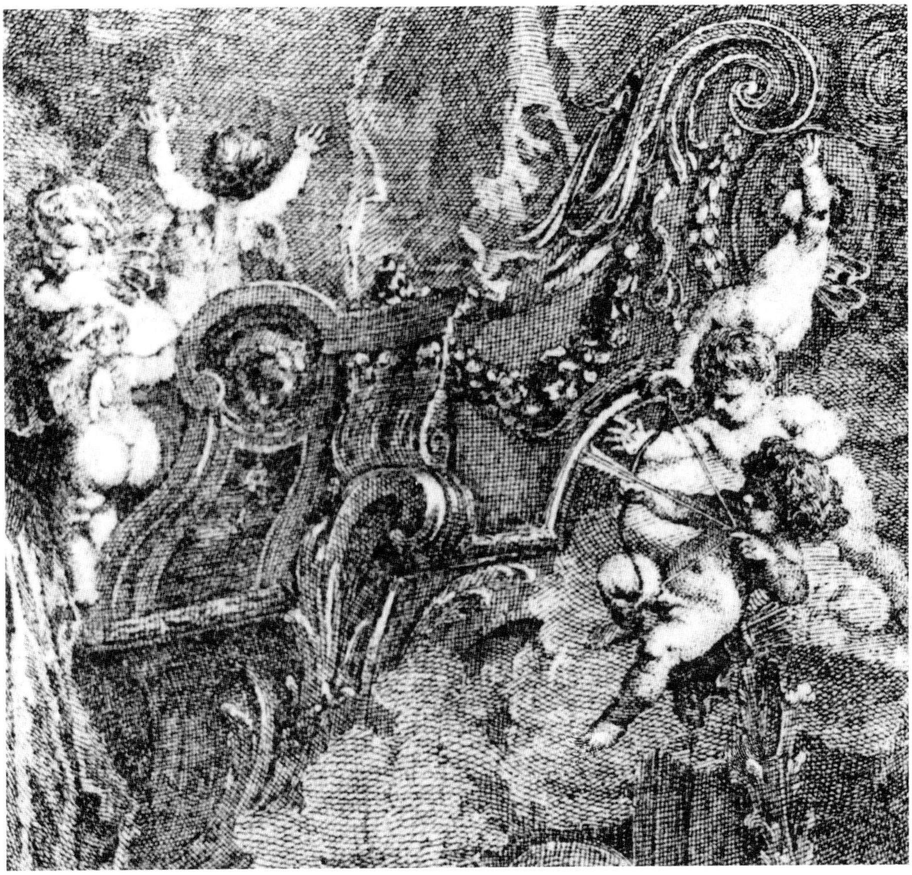

63. Detail of engraving by Nicolas-Henri Tardieu after Antoine Watteau, *Embarkation for the Island of Cythera (L'embarquement pour l'île de Cythère)*, from P. L. Jacob, *XVIIIe siècle: Institutions, usages et costumes, France, 1700–1789*, 1875. Photograph, Jennifer Laffoon.

Pilgrimage (fig. 63). Michael Levey, who first drew attention to this detail, has suggested that this represents a threat to the couple's unity.[123] According to Levey's interpretation, this cupid's action cancels the original sting of love's arrow; once the lovers return to the real world, they will no longer be in love. Although I have yet to find a specific example of this "suicidal" putto in emblem books, other inversions of the same order are abundant. One example is the numerous images of the flame of love held upside down to illustrate a motto such as "what ignites me extinguishes me" (fig. 64). Moreover, this kind of inversion, playing on traditional devices to produce unexpected meanings, is a tactic very much a part of Watteau's pictorial strategy, one that he employed in *Departure* and in his military paintings as well.

Watteau's constant references to endings, departures, desire, and death do not merely evoke a mood: they set up a very real and profound resonance be-

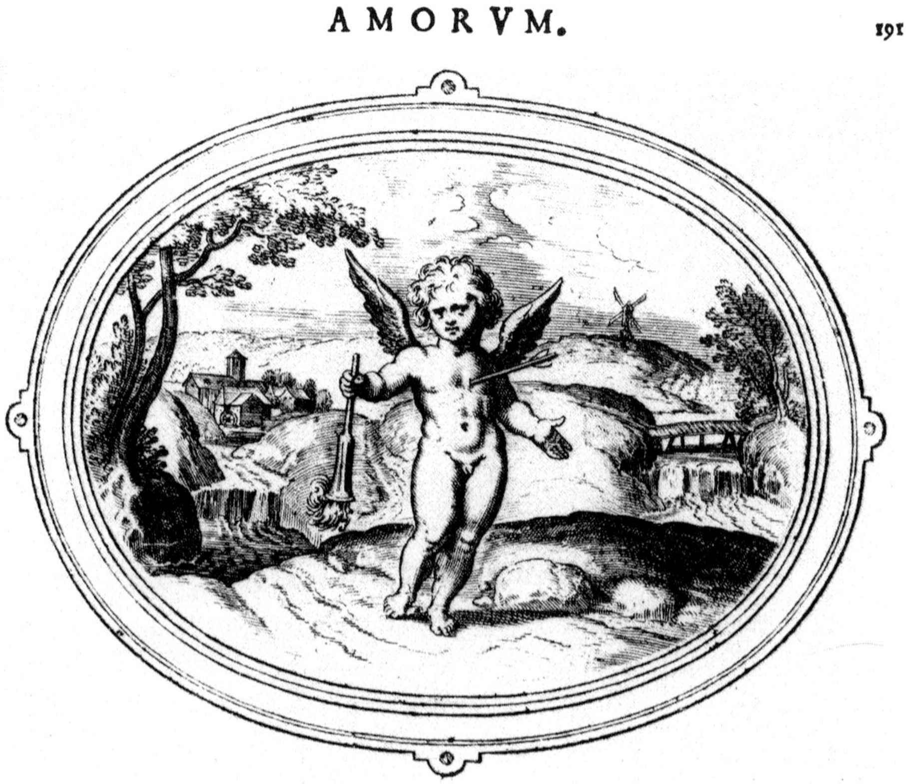

64. Emblem, *Love Killed by His Own Nouriture,* from Otto van Veen, *Amorum Emblemata,* 1608. Photograph, Jennifer Laffoon.

tween the image of a mythical *fête galante* and the reality of human experience at a *fête galante.* A *fête galante* is an activity, a lived fiction involved with pushing the limits between fact and fantasy. At a masquerade, there is always a difference between the masked and unmasked identities. In the liberating space created by the fiction of the mask, anything goes, but there are also implicit dangers. The game may become all too real, with consequences that extend beyond the realm of play. Like the double-edged meaning that the phrase "pilgrimage to Cythera" had in the eighteenth century, Watteau's image also alludes to darker possibilities. The evocative theme of *Pilgrimage to Cythera* and its dense and complicated allegorical subtext refer to things that could not be directly represented, especially within the context of elite behavior, with its insistence on life as fiction. For example, nowhere in the painting do we see the pilgrims actually engaged in erotic activities; what we do see is a ritualized form of love play enacted within the context of commonly understood contemporary theatrical references. Watteau's fruitful juxtapositions, his substitutions, and his free appropriation of divergent cultural discourses structurally reproduce and document the very process by which cultural transformations and social redefinitions occurred within early-eighteenth-century France. The secretary of the Academy who originally received *Pilgrimage to Cythera* was therefore correct in spirit when he recorded it as a history painting; history, however, demanded the *fête galante*.

CHAPTER FOUR

The Meeting of High and Low Culture in Watteau's *Gersaint's Signboard*

IT MUST BE REMEMBERED that Watteau worked in eighteenth-century Paris. Despite the widening circles of those who participated in the art world of producers, patrons, and dealers, the vast majority of Parisians remained beyond the compass of aesthetic cultivation or even of letters. Yet Parisians, whether cultured or common, daily encountered in the shared public space of the city a Rabelaisan profusion of images that stimulated, amused, and informed through an iconography complex enough to satisfy an Academician: signboards. In his *Tableaux de Paris* (1781–88), Louis-Sébastian Mercier commented on this welter of fantastic yet mundane images that assailed every passerby: "The signboard offered an image of a race of giants to the most stunted people in Europe: a sword-guard six feet high, a boot as big as a hogshead, a spur as broad as a carriage wheel, and a glove which could have housed a three-year-old child in every finger."[1] Watteau's last painting, a gift to his friend, the picture dealer Edme Gersaint, was a signboard.

That Watteau's final and largest work was a signboard is not surprising, for casting a major work in a minor form is in keeping with the subversive strategies the artist employed in *Departure*, in the military paintings, and in his *fêtes galantes*. In all these genres Watteau stretched, juxtaposed, and jostled the conventions to reveal, whether intentionally or not, the arbitrary and ideological nature of representation. In *Gersaint's Signboard*, Watteau, near the end of his life, takes this play with the conventions of signification to a logical, and, one could even say, dramatic, conclusion.

Gersaint's Signboard (fig. 65) was one of Watteau's most fully realized works: ambitious and sophisticated in size and execution, in visual economy, and in content. His contemporaries immediately declared it a success; their assessment remains unchallenged. Scholars have praised the signboard as a summation of Watteau's artistic career, as a visual explication of his artistic theory, and as an application of his talent to the elevation of commerce by masterfully depicting a pedestrian subject – in short, a celebration of the transforming power of art. Few scholars have investigated the reason for the success of the

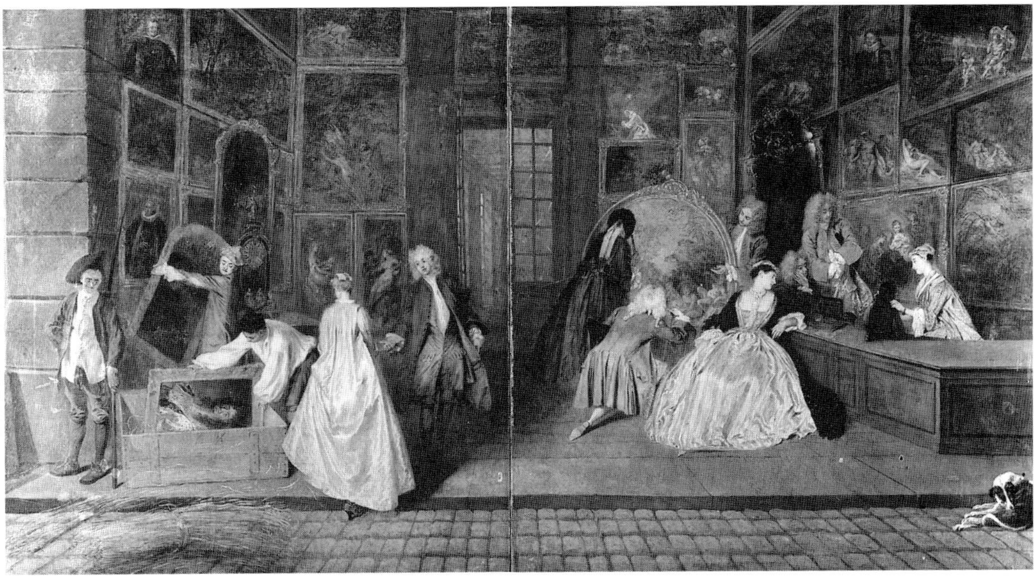

65. Antoine Watteau, *Gersaint's Signboard (L'enseigne de Gersaint)*, 1720–21, Charlottenbourg Castle, Staatliche Schloesser und Gaerten, Berlin, Germany. Photo, Foto Marburg/Art Resource, NY.

signboard among Watteau's contemporaries, and none has explained what is apparent to all: *Gersaint's Signboard* was a signboard as well as a painting.

Masquerading under the guise of a signboard, categorically a lowly craft product not worthy of the appellation art, the acknowledged masterpiece *Gersaint's Signboard* is the most striking example not only of Watteau's transformation and transcendence of the traditionally accepted boundaries of genre but also of what his breaking of those boundaries meant in relation to the production and consumption of art within existing social practice. In the *Signboard,* as in *Departure* and his *fêtes galantes,* Watteau brings together conflicting cultural codes and practices and breaks the traditional boundaries that distinguished high art and popular culture. Watteau pushes his earlier tactics even further in the *Signboard:* the playing of one painterly and cultural discourse against another in a visual dialogue that could more fully articulate the complex relationships that existed among culture, power, and class during the early eighteenth century. By confounding the boundaries between high and low art and between traditional genres, Watteau demonstrates their inadequacies in representing a whole range of lived experience, social practice, and shared aspirations. Watteau's *Signboard* gives, for the first time, monumental form to a new class of collectors and dealers and to a system of artistic production and consumption that existed outside the authority of official, state-controlled culture.

The work itself, measuring 166 cm × 306 cm (5 ft. 3 3/4 in. × 10 ft. 1 in.), is large, either as a signboard or as a painting; it stands out as the largest work

Watteau ever produced. Originally, the upper portion of the *Signboard* was curved to conform to the arched shape of the overdoor at Gersaint's shop. Alterations to the signboard probably occurred shortly after its completion when canvas was removed from the sides and transferred to the top to create the rectangular form we know today.[2] Other changes occurred subsequently: the pile of hay and the standing figure replaced a hand cart filled with hay, and paintings were added to fill in the new space in the upper corners. It has been hypothesized that Watteau's student, Jean-Baptiste-Joseph Pater, may have made these changes under the direction of Watteau himself.[3] The *Signboard* is made up of two independent canvases that were attached when the work hung as a shop sign.[4]

Represented in the *Signboard* is a new form of sociability, involving the collecting and savoring of artworks and luxury objects. The front wall of Gersaint's shop, Au Grand Monarque, has been painted away, as was the convention in signboards of this sort, to reveal the interior and all the sumptuous objects offered for sale. Clients enter from the cobbled street in front of the shop to browse and scrutinize the objects on display. The shop walls are covered with paintings varying in size, subject, and style. On the far back wall, at the point where the two canvases are joined, is an open door, offering a glimpse into another room beyond. This door creates a compositional and narrative division within the signboard. In effect, this division results in two independent scenarios within the unified space of the shop.

In the scenario on the left-hand side of the painting, two men, dressed in obviously workday clothing, are crating up a portrait of Louis XIV and a large mirror. One worker has already placed the king's portrait in the crate, while the other, behind him, holds the large, cumbersome mirror. A third man, in equally workmanlike garb and holding a pitchfork, leans against the exterior corner of the shop and watches the packing. A bundle of hay, presumably packing material, rests on the street in front of the crate. In contrast to these workers is the couple, to their right, who are entering the shop. They give this packing activity only a passing glance. The man, who is already in the shop, turns, facing the viewer, to offer his hand to the woman, who is dressed in a glowing, pink satin gown. With her back to the viewer, she is caught, midmotion, as she takes her last step from the street into the shop. The graceful, effortless gestures, dancer-like poses, and fashionable clothes of this couple have become something of a visual cliché; the couple are the embodiment of refined society, and this scene marks the difference between the realm of leisure and the realm of work.

On the right-hand side of the painting, clients are absorbed in an examination of objects offered for purchase by two shopkeepers. A man and a woman, who appears to be dressed in widow's weeds, examine a large, oval painting, surrounded by a gilt frame, of nude females in a frothy outdoor setting. A shopkeeper holds up this painting for their inspection with a proffering gesture. And inspect the painting they do. The bewigged man, dressed in an elegant gray satin jacket, supports himself with his walking stick as he kneels on the floor, his bent back to the viewer, to look carefully at the nude figures. He is as close to the painting as he can get without touching it. The woman regards the landscape portion of the painting at close range through a lorgnette. To their right is a group of three figures, equally absorbed in looking. A seated woman in a sumptuous pink-and-blue-striped satin dress leans upon the display counter with one elbow. Her pose wittily mimics that of the nude in the painting that the gentleman in gray inspects. Across the shop counter are two men, bewigged and in fashionable dress. One of them leans languidly upon the counter, his head in his hand; the other stands, inclined slightly to the left. The object of their gazes is held up by a female shopkeeper behind the counter. Presumably it is a mirror, part of the vanity set prominently displayed on the counter and slightly tilted up so that its contents are visible to the on-canvas clients but tantalizingly withheld from the off-canvas viewer. In the street below, a dog – a quotation from Rubens's *Coronation of Marie de Medici* – hunts for fleas. The perspective of the viewer would be that of a person standing in the middle of the street, looking in on the activity within the shop. This nicely rounds off the structure of the painting, for, since virtually every figure is engaged in the act of looking, it is fitting that the viewer is pointedly placed in the position of looking at people who are themselves looking.

The questions scholars most frequently address concerning the *Signboard* are what is the nature of the subject and did Watteau intend a larger meaning. Two schools of thought have emerged: one views the *Signboard* as a genre painting, a simple slice of life with little or no ulterior meaning; the other views the work as an allegory, with a coherent, programmatic meaning.

The school of thought that holds the slice-of-life view of the painting may be taking its cue from Gersaint's account of the creation of the sign. According to Gersaint, "It was done from life; the attitudes were so varied and graceful, the composition so natural and the groups so thoughtfully done that it attracted the attention of passersby."[5]

The school of thought that attributes a coherent meaning to the painting, may be taking its cue from the Comte de Caylus, who wrote that the *Signboard* was an exception to the typical Watteau painting, which lacked focus, emotion, and action.[6] That Caylus viewed the *Signboard* as an exception suggests he saw an object or purpose to the work; in short, it expressed something. However, Caylus gives no further indication as to what he may have thought that object or purpose might be. Modern scholars have suggested some possibilities.

One explanation is that the *Signboard* represents Watteau's artistic testament; the paintings displayed on the shop wall represent the works of artists who had influenced him and whom he admired. The *Signboard* is, according to this explanation, a personal allegory, a final summing up of Watteau's position within the world of art in the form of an imaginary picture gallery.[7] Another, related, interpretation also focuses on the selection of paintings depicted on the shop walls as a clue to the *Signboard*'s meaning. In 1946, L. Aragon observed that the paintings displayed on the left-hand side of the *Signboard* seemed to represent works of the old masters, while those on the right-hand side seemed to represent modern works. This contrast, according to Aragon, is the key to interpreting the work: the *Signboard* is a visual defense of modern painting and a critique of the old.[8]

That Watteau intended the viewer to arrive at some sort of comparison between the old and the new cannot be overlooked in light of his care in selecting and arranging the paintings within the image. This interpretation is strengthened by the painting of Louis XIV – certainly a symbol of that older taste – that is being crated. This detail not only supports the previous interpretation but also has led to the reading of the *Signboard* as a complex *vanitas* allegory, commenting on the transience of life and art. Oliver Banks develops this argument, suggesting that the crating of the portrait is a reference to mortality and has an emblematic significance.[9] Part of Banks's project is to relate these objects to the existing northern baroque emblematic tradition with which Watteau would have been familiar. He identifies other objects in the shop that carried well-established symbolic meanings associated with the *vanitas* theme. I want to mention just a few of Banks's examples. The clock, strategically placed above and behind the portrait of Louis XIV, was commonly understood to symbolize the devouring nature of time. A gilt figure representing fame surmounts the clock, while at its base are two statuettes of lovers: fame and love are not exempt from the ravages of time. Within the overall economy of the *Signboard,* this emblematic touch lends poignancy to the woman's passing glance at the portrait of Louis XIV. It becomes a personal reminder of the fleetingness of life's pleasures. Similarly, the mirror functions as a symbol and enhances the narrative. In the eighteenth century, the mirror (especially a woman admiring herself in a mirror) was a common emblem of vanity, referring both to the passing of a woman's beauty and to the passing of passion. Gérard Le Coat carries the idea of a *vanitas* theme elaborated by Banks even further.[10] He proposes that the *Signboard* is quite specifically an allegory of the journey of life. In his accounting of the image, nearly everything (including the use of color) plays a role in articulating this allegory; for Le Coat the painting has a fixed program and a fixed meaning.

The question always arises, to what extent should we impose an intended, programmatic meaning on the *Signboard* or on any of Watteau's works? Are the realism and genre elements at odds with a specifically allegorical and emblematic program? Must we choose between one or the other? Or, is it precisely the overlapping of these two systems of meaning that matters in the *Signboard* and Watteau's works in general? It is accepted that Watteau was familiar with the traditional emblematic and allegorical vocabulary and that he employed it in new and surprising ways; certainly, the *Signboard* was no exception to this practice. By means of the symbolic subtext that he similarly employed in *Departure* and in his *fêtes galantes,* Watteau introduces another level of meaning into the *Signboard.* Thus it was no accident that Watteau included these allegorical references into his depiction of modern life. As Le Coat suggestively remarks, "modern enchantment and traditional didacticism were not mutually exclusive during the *Régence.*"[11]

The idea of contemporaneity is important to making sense of the *Signboard;* in a series of deft substitutions, Watteau creates a contemporary allegory by including within his painting nontraditional iconographical material derived from contemporary popular culture and social practices. The meaning of such material would have been commonly understood by contemporary viewers. Robert Neuman fruitfully explores these possibilities in his 1984 article, "Watteau's *Gersaint's Signboard* and Baroque Emblematic Tradition."[12] Neuman examines the *Signboard*'s relationship to the iconography of popular contemporary images of commerce and fashion as well as to the iconography of official imagery. By restoring the painting to its eighteenth-century French context, Neuman, as it were, brings the painting home.

Rather than merely match images to establish iconography, Neuman establishes the meaning of the images by rooting them in contemporary social, economic, and artistic fields, thereby providing the larger context from which the *Signboard* grew. One illustration of Neuman's meaningful connections is his discussion of the portrait of Louis XIV that is shown being crated in the *Signboard.* Neuman's argument, here greatly condensed and simplified, finds the pictorial sources supporting the reading of this detail as an entombment, not in Flemish baroque *vanitas* images, but in the well-established iconographic tradition of including a bust-length portrait of a sovereign in an image as a symbol for the authority of that individual's office. This use of portraiture within images was not uncommon in the abundant entombment and funerary imagery produced in the years following Louis XIV's death in 1715.[13] Neuman states that this body of entombment images and funerary literature ranged "from literal depictions of the obsequies to a group of schematic popular images celebrating the succession of Louis XIV."[14] We can infer from this statement that much of the popular imagery had an implicit message: the office of the king and its authority, ensured by the rights of succession, were immortal. We can further infer that popular artists underscored this message at a critical moment in France's history by employing the device of portraits within an image. Neuman contends that Watteau used these established iconographic devices and their meanings in the *Signboard* to suggest, ironically, the idea of succession, for dealers and collectors were the true successors to Louis XIV as patrons and protectors of the arts.

The portrait of Louis XIV being packed away is an image that plays several roles in the painting: a symbolic, or allegorical, role within a *vanitas* theme and a narrative role within a scene of everyday life. It has also been recognized as playing another role: the portrait functions as a signboard within a signboard, alluding to the name of Gersaint's shop, Au Grand Monarque. This should remind us of the reference to Sirois's shop, Aux Armes, in *Portal of Valenciennes* (fig. 44) that also functioned as an allusion to a more contemporary kind of *vanitas* theme during the War of Spanish Succession.[15] Watteau's use of a signboard within a signboard is in keeping with his frequent strategic use of a symbolic subtext as a commentary upon the activities depicted in his paintings. Moreover, it was also in keeping with the visual and verbal wit often displayed in signboards of the seventeenth and eighteenth centuries. Although the *Signboard* hung outside Gersaint's shop for only fifteen days before it was taken inside, thus raising its status from sign to art, its original function as a signboard should not be forgotten.[16]

Indeed, it can be argued that to overlook the original status of the painting is to overlook a significant reading of it, for signboards were an integral part of the urban landscape, rich in meaning. Watteau had devoted part of his early career to sign painting; moreover, the practice of sign painting served as a line of demarcation between commerce and officially recognized culture. Since Watteau customarily utilized popular culture both to comment upon and to enrich high culture, it is important to explore the realm of meaning that signboards represented, as well as Watteau's intentions, for the *Signboard* was a signboard.

Signboards and the Visual Culture of Paris

Before street numbering became widespread enough in the 1780s to be practical as a system for finding places, signboards were the means by which one navigated Paris. To find one's way around the city, one either had to be familiar with the signboards that acted as landmarks in the city's geography, or, as in the case of a visitor to the city, had to pay close attention to them. Complaining about the slowness of street numbering, Louis Sébastian Mercier reveals the practical problems inherent in negotiating the city by its signs. "It would be more advantageous and easy to go straight off to the abode of Mr. So-and-So, number 87, than to find Mr. So-and-So at the Sign *Au Cordon Bleu,* or *A la Barbe d'Argent,* fifth door to the right after such and such a street."[17] Obviously, visual awareness was of the essence in finding one's way about, especially since the welter of signboards was subject to constant change. New signboards went up when businesses were established, and old signboards moved along with a business when it changed locale. This engendered a particular way of reading space based on kinesthetic sensation and familiar perception.[18] The Parisian public made sense of the city, and located themselves within it, through the visual subtext of signboards. The reading of signs was a habit of thought and perception ingrained in urban consciousness.

In addition, signboards lent tangible character to places, sometimes creating a rich urban mythology based on long-standing associations between a signboard and any number of meaningful events that occurred within the defining limits of the sign, whether past or present. A good example of the signboard's role in perpetuating and disseminating shared urban lore is the metamorphosis of the rue de la Petite Truanderie (little vagrancy) into the rue du Puits d'Amour (well of love), which occurred sometime during the middle of the seventeenth century.[19] According to legend, during the reign of Philippe-Auguste, a woman named Agnès Hellebic threw herself down a well out of despair over an ill-fated love. From that time on, the well, known as *puits-d'amour,* was a celebrated *rendez-vous* for lovers. Sauval, writing in 1724, informs us how the legend of this place name was kept alive through a signboard and how, in turn, the signboard prompted a spate of imitations, becoming a recognized iconographical motif within the lexicon of signboards.

> With time, the name ("well of love") had become associated with a nearby building. And as this name seemed *galant* to the merchant who rented the building, he had his signboard repainted, heightening its effect with vivid colors. In order better to represent this fable, he had depicted a well, surrounded by pretty girls and young men, with a little Cupid shooting arrows at them, and these words below: At the Well of Love. Now, as other merchants found this sign much to their liking, and so many more found the sign comical, or upon being noticed, attracted customers, some copied it entirely, others contented themselves with imitating it.[20]

Moreover, the popularity of *Puits-d'Amour* as a signboard certainly benefited from the meaning this term carried in street language: everyone would remember a shop that publicly bore an allusion to the private parts of female anatomy.[21]

Signboards not only marked location and lent character, they also announced vocation: they indicated specific commercial establishments and provided information about the nature of the goods and services to be found within. Obviously, if both shopkeeper and client were to benefit, it was important that a signboard convey the proper message – and that this message be widely understood. The commercial messages of signboards were conveyed through a commonly understood language of imagery, predicated upon years of established usage. For the eighteenth-century Parisian, an understanding of the iconography of signs would have been as much "second nature" as the perception of signs as geographical landmarks would have been.[22]

The "sign language" of commerce ranged from the simplistic to the arcane. Signs that presented an image of the object or a symbol of the service to be found within the shop appealed to common sense and drew upon time-honored tradition. For example, a bunch of grapes or a barrel of wine on a signboard would clearly indicate the location of a wine-merchant's shop. But the obvious one-to-one correspondence between the object or the service depicted on a sign and its being provided within the shop was often mediated by long-standing cultural conventions, resulting in a more complex level of symbolism. For example, gold workers' signboards did not depict a lump of metal or a piece of jewelry; traditionally, they carried an image of St. Eloi, the patron saint of the goldsmiths' guild. A hatmaker's establishment would be marked by the image of St. Jacques. A sign bearing an image of a *pomme de pin* (pine cone) would have informed the passerby that a drink could be had within. Dating back to antiquity, and established through years of usage, the *pomme de pin* was a popular emblem for taverns because of its original reference to the pine resin used to protect the interiors of wine barrels.[23]

Certain names characterized certain kinds of establishments; common, almost generic, names for cabarets included Au Croissant, discussed earlier, and Au Bon Soleil (at the good sun). The makers of signboards reworked familiar formulae; this had to be the case if the public were to make the appropriate connections. Yet proprietors also wanted a signboard that would distinguish their establishment from others in the memory of passersby. After all, signboards were an early form of advertising meant to attract attention, establish a mental-visual association between sign and place, and seduce customers.

The sheer visual impact and physical presence of this welter of signs must have been tremendous. Signboards were everywhere in Paris. Fournier has estimated that between fifteen hundred and two thousand signboards were produced in the city each year.[24] Prominently displayed, signboards were principally of two types: *plafond* (ceiling) and *potence* (bracket). Watteau's *Signboard* is of the former type. Signboards *plafond* were mounted on a shop flush with the facade, generally placed over the door and, if there was one, under the awning. The top of the signboard was often tilted at an angle to provide better viewing. The signboard *plafond* was less popular among merchants than was the sign *potence*. The signboard *potence* projected out over the street, perpendicular to the shop's facade. It was suspended from a metal frame, the *potence*, hence the appellation. These projecting signboards were more popular for the simple reason that they offered greater visibility and would attract more attention. Moreover, the signboard *potence* was well established through centuries of usage. The signboard *plafond*, which was a relative newcomer as a common type of commercial sign, in part was instituted for very practical reasons.

The signboards *potence,* which often projected well into the middle of the street, could be a real nuisance. Mercier gives us this description of the difficulties they caused. "When the wind blew all these signs creaked, knocked and clattered against one another, making a discordant and plaintive racket, absolutely unbelievable to anyone who has never heard it."[25] When the wind blew, there was also the danger that the signs might fall, harming passersby. When they projected too far into the street, or were hung too low, the signs impeded both pedestrian and carriage traffic. By day they blocked light and prevented fresh air from circulating through windows, and at night they cast large shadows, dimming the light of lanterns and making the streets unsafe.

These dangers and inconveniences prompted the police to limit the size of signs and awnings in 1666. But it was difficult to alter practices dating back several centuries and to limit the prerogatives of the *corps de métiers* to display their signs. That tradition prevailed; that the *corps de métiers* had enough power to maintain their signs is clear from another ordinance, passed in 1669 by La Reynie, the lieutenant general of police, to control the excessive size and show of signboards. This ordinance stated: "The reduction of signs to a uniform width, height and extension over the streets is desired for the embellishment of the city and to prevent the abuse of some merchants and artisans, who affix to their establishments, signs of an excessive cost and size."[26] La Reynie even instituted a standardized model for the *potence* of the sign.

The vision of the authorities was of a regularized city, one controlled from above. This official meddling in affairs that previously had been left in the hands of the *corps de métiers* was part of a larger struggle for power that dated from the time of the Fronde. But proprietors could get around these regulations by paying a fee to the *bureau de la voirie,* a subdivision of the police charged with the maintenance and safety of the city's streets. The merchants, who were attached to their signs for their practical, sentimental, and symbolic value, generally preferred to pay the fee rather than give up the signboards. By 1679 signs were again as large as they had been before the 1669 ordinance. In 1688, La Reynie noted that he had never seen a greater number of oversized signs.[27] Throughout the last decades of the seventeenth century and until 1761, when projecting signboards were legally prohibited altogether, there were repeated efforts to regulate and control the size and display of signboards. The *bureau de la voirie,* according to Fournier, "exerted every type of vexation against the proprietors of these signs," while the *syndicats* of the *corporations* resisted and protested.[28] One of the "vexations" was a system of yearly taxation, covering not only projecting signboards but also signs *plafond* and sculptural ornaments that might function as signs.[29] Taxes were levied for the display of new signs or for changes of location, and permission was needed before any alteration or addition could be made.

These byzantine tax laws and regulations were meant, of course, to control the appearance of the public face of the city, to ensure public safety, and to curb the *corporations'* political power and the public's power of expression. The intended regulation of signboards did not, however, follow; instead, increased funds for the *bureau de la voirie,* additional fuel to the fire of corporational resentment, and endless legal battles worthy of those waged between the foire comedians and the authorities were the results. This "battle of the signboards" has remarkable parallels with the "battle of the theaters"; in both cases, we see an attempt to control officially an arena that offered a potential threat to established power. Public safety and convenience were certainly justifiable reasons for regulating signboards, but the ongoing struggle for power between the *corps de métiers* and the state probably played a role at least as important. Moreover, the effort to regulate might be interpreted as an attempt by the authorities – whether conscious or not – to rationalize patterns of perception and to suppress the mixed messages that could be conveyed by signs in the public space of the streets.

Signboards not only supplied information, they also created new and surprising messages and ways of reading those messages; above all, signboards provided the public with a spectacle that was at the same time familiar, funny, and exotic. One has only to recall Sebastian Mercier's declaration, "The signboard offered an image of a race of giants to the most stunted people in Europe."[30] In their forms, and in their often fantastic juxtapositions on a street, signboards played upon the public's imagination, expanding the boundaries of ordinary experience. Daniel Roche has expressed this quite nicely: "To the elite, the sign was a mutilator of language, but to the popular classes it was a spectacle and a simple stimulant with an inexhaustible potential for dreams and creativity."[31] Many signs were creative mutilators, or multipliers, of language, drawing upon visual/verbal puns for their effect. This type of sign must have been very popular, if their numbers are any indication, and they certainly must have delighted the public.[32] I have previously mentioned several examples of this type of sign, but I cannot resist citing just a few more: an establishment called *Vin sans Eau* (a comment, obviously, on the quality of the wine sold there) depicted, in three tiers, the numbers 20, 100, and 0. The *Signe de la Croix* was represented by a *cygne* with a cross entwined around its neck. Such irreverence toward sacred subjects sometimes provoked the intervention of the police.[33]

Besides this kind of playful punning, signs could also satirize or comment upon contemporary figures and events. A case of signboard vengeance is recounted in *Les Historiettes de Tallement des Réaux:*

A one-eyed clerk having made claims to which he was not entitled upon a tavern-keeper, the latter, in revenge, had depicted upon his sign a portrait of the clerk in the form of a thief, with this inscription: At the One-Eye Who Takes *[Au*

> *Borgne qui prend].* The clerk, finding himself insulted, went to find the tavern-keeper and repaid him the money from the claims in question, on the condition that he would alter his sign. The tavern-keeper, to satisfy the clerk, removed but the *p* so that it read: At the One-Eye Who Repays *[Au Borgne qui rend]*, instead of At the One-Eye Who Takes *[prend]*.[34]

Explicitly political signboards were far less common. Fournier, however, does cite two very interesting examples. During Louis XIV's war against Holland, a Dutch merchant took *"A la Paix perpétuelle"* as his signboard.[35] In the period of the Fronde, during the siege of Paris, a fearful merchant had on one side of his signboard *"Vive le Roi!"* and on the other side "Vive la Ligue!" As circumstances changed, so did the side of the signboard he displayed.[36] Although overtly transparent references to politically charged topics would have brought police intervention, there must have been many other signboards with oblique references and veiled allusions to the political scene.

Along with the intentional semantic play inherent in a signboard, the random juxtaposition of several signboards within a field of vision must also have generated unintentional meanings, creating humorous or ironic "dialogues" between signs. Mercier provides a concrete example of the creative possibilities of these juxtapositions as he muses over the old signboards for sale at the *Quai de la Mégisserie,* the location of commerce in used signboards later in the eighteenth century.

> There, all the kings of the earth lie together: Louis XIV and George III kiss each other fraternally, the king of Prussia sleeps next to the empress of Russia, the Emperor is ranged among the Electors; there, finally, the tiara and the turban mingle. A cabaret owner arrives, pokes about all the crowned heads with his foot, examines them, randomly selects an image of the king of Poland, takes it away, hangs it up and writes at the bottom of the sign: *Au Grand Vainqueur.*[37]

In *Departure of the Italian Comedians in 1697,* I have argued earlier, Watteau may have been employing a similar juxtaposition of signs – the *croissant* that hangs out over the street and, being pasted on the wall, the decree that reads *"De par le Roi"* – to create a dialectical commentary on the scene. Moreover, Watteau's habitual use of a symbolic subtext and his semantic play of one symbol off another probably reflect the larger mental and perceptual patterns engendered by the reading of signboards, with their multiple functions and associations.

Signboard Painting in Social Practice

Because of the importance and omnipresence of signboards, the Parisian public must have had a certain degree of visual awareness. Yet looking at signboards and looking at art constituted two very different activities; similarly, fabricating images for signboards and fabricating them for paintings constituted two very different kinds of artistic practice. Signboards were part of commercial culture, not of high culture. The painting of signboards was generally done by unskilled hacks, and, indeed, most signboards were rather crudely done. Signboard makers had a bad reputation within the painterly profession. In the eighteenth century, one of the cruelest epithets that one could hurl at an artist was "sign painter." Sign painters were ridiculed in the theater, in pamphlets, and in songs.[38] One example is the proverbial insult "We say of a bad portrait, of a bad painting, that it is only fit to be a signboard."[39] A similar proverbial entry appears under the word "*Enseigne*" in Le Roux's *Dictionnaire comique, satirique, critique, burlesque libre et proverbial:* "One also says of a bad portrait or of a bad painting, that it would make a good beer sign. This is because these sorts of signs are always very poorly done."[40] Under the word "*Peintre,*" we find this entry: "Formerly, one said, Pathetic as a painter. But in more recent days, when painting has become a cultured and ennobled art, this proverb has proven false. One ought rather to say Glorious as a painter."[41] Clearly, a distinction was made between a painter of signs and a painter who practiced a more cultivated, noble pursuit. The distinction between painter and hack was quite real; it was a distinction, moreover, that was institutionally determined and supported.

Prior to the founding of the Royal Academy of Painting and Sculpture in 1648, any painter, whether a house painter, a sign painter, a decorator of objects, or a painter of serious and ambitious *tableaux,* had to belong to the *maîtrise des peintres, sculpteurs, doreurs et vitriers,* which was part of the *communauté des ouvriers.*[42] Court artists or *brevetaires,* were an exception who enjoyed special protection and privileges and were exempted from the normal restrictions imposed by the *maîtrise.* With the founding of the Royal Academy a division between art as a learned, elevated pursuit, practiced by Academy members, and art as manual labor, practiced by members of the *maîtrise,* was created. According to the *Lettres Patente* of 1648, Louis XIV founded the Academy "only to elevate the most beautiful of all the arts, with no intended prejudicial treatment, whatsoever, to the *corps de la maistrise.*"[43] But prejudice against the corporation of painters – an institutional distinction between the practitioner of the most beautiful of all the arts and the painter of houses and signs – was just what the founding members of the Royal Academy wanted. The Royal Academy, after it was firmly on its feet in 1663, was a privileged, royally sponsored institution, whereas the *maîtrise,* under the appellation of the Academy of St. Luke, remained bound legally, institutionally, and by class to the *communauté des ouvriers.* The social distinction between Academician and signboard painter was a clear one in the late seventeenth and early eighteenth centuries, as was the distinction between a painting, belonging to the realm of culture, and a signboard, belonging to the realm of commerce, at least in theory.

In actual practice, these distinctions were not so clear cut. It was not unusual for an artist to paint an occasional signboard. In fact, it was quite common for aspiring artists to paint signboards at the beginning of their careers, or for established artists to paint them when times were hard. François Le Moyne, who became First Painter to the King in 1736, painted at least two signboards.[44] According to D'Argenville's *Abrégé de la vie des plus fameux peintres:* "During his stay at Amiens, he [Le Moyne] made *another* signboard for a hairdresser, which is no longer exposed to the ravages of the weather, since the hairdresser has placed it inside his shop" (emphasis added).[45] Le Moyne's trip to Amiens took place in 1718, at which time he was not well known; supposedly, the signboard was one of his first works to attract attention.

Similarly, Chardin first received artistic recognition for a signboard he painted for a surgeon's shop. This "discovery" has become one of the great art-historical myths, canonized by the Goncourt brothers, who connect Chardin's signboard with Watteau's *Signboard* and its legendary status in the history of art. "A surgeon, a friend of his father's, asked him to do a signboard *à plafond* as it was then called, for his shop, and Chardin, who may have seen the picture Watteau painted for Gersaint's signboard, attempted a similar work."[46] Like Watteau's *Signboard,* Chardin's signboard transcended the boundaries of the commercial genre and was recognized as a work of art. The Goncourt brothers describe the painting in dramatic and narrative terms, as if it were a history painting. The subject is a duel; amid a great deal of motion and emotion, a dying dueler is being tended by a surgeon and a sister of mercy. According to the Goncourt brothers, this signboard was more than the surgeon had bargained for:

> The surgeon, to whom Chardin gave no warning, asked what was happening and why there were all those people. He was taken to look at the sign and searched it for the subjects he had commissioned: trepans, bistouris, a parade of all the instruments of his profession. He was on the point of anger, but was disarmed by public admiration. Gradually, the success of the picture gathered strength, and it was through this signboard that the Academy discovered the name and the ability of the painter.[47]

How much credit should be given to these accounts of signboards functioning as a *deus ex machina* in the lives of artists is open to question. The important point is that the lowest, most despised kind of painting could, and did, serve as an entrée into the world of high art. In the accounts of Le Moyne's and Chardin's discoveries we see a new venue for displaying and viewing paintings,

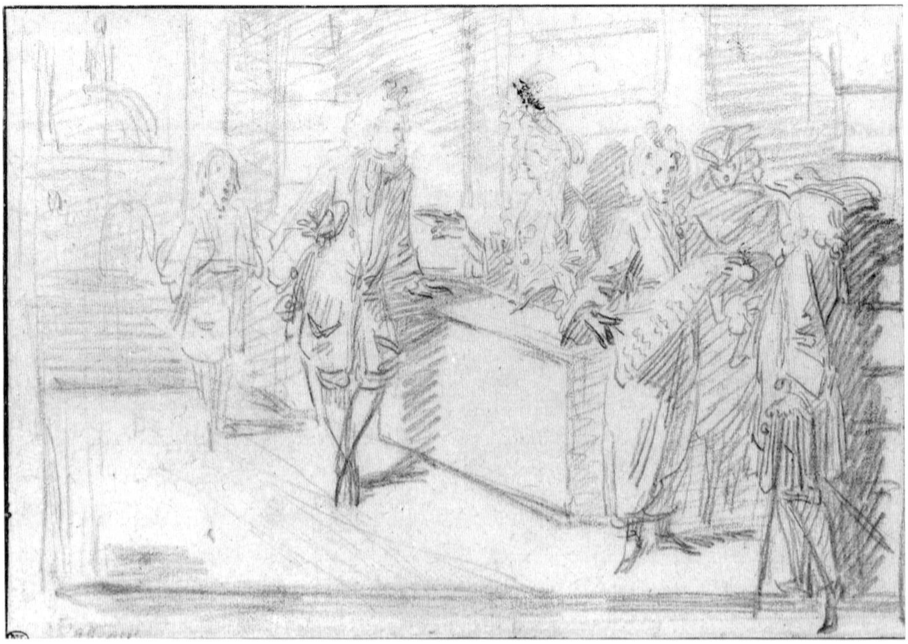

66. Antoine Watteau, sketch, *A Draper's Shop (La boutique d'un marchand d'étoffes)*, Musée du Louvre, Paris. Cliché, Réunion des musées nationaux.

even if those paintings are categorized as mere signs. Watteau's *Signboard* and its reception, it would seem, served as the model for this myth of metamorphosis and discovery.

Watteau painted an indeterminate number of signboards besides the celebrated one for Gersaint. On the basis of his early experience as a hack painter in Paris, we can assume that he probably did more than those known today. One work of his that is presumed to have been a signboard is *Vertumne et Pomone,* dated between 1714 and 1716, in the Wildenstein Collection, Paris. According to the manuscript notes in Pierre-Jean Mariette's *Abecedario,* this work "was used for some time as the show piece of a painter's shop on the Pont Nôtre Dame in Paris."[48] *Vertumne et Pomone* is certainly of a different artistic order than *Gersaint's Signboard;* it lacks the sophistication of conception, is rather poorly executed, and is small in scale (40 cm × 30 cm). Because of the size of *Vertumne et Pomone,* Roland-Michel finds it unlikely that work was a signboard; rather she translates Mariette's use of the word "*montre*" literally, suggesting that the work was merely shown at the picture dealer's shop.[49] Another work that may have served as a signboard is *The Sparrows' Nester* (fig. 58), which is approximately the same size as *Vertumne et Pomone.* In the engraving done by Boucher in 1727 (fig. 57) there is an escutcheon bearing three *fleur de lys,* flanked by fauns. This detail has led Fourcaud to hypothesize that *The Sparrows' Nester* originally served as the sign for Sirois's

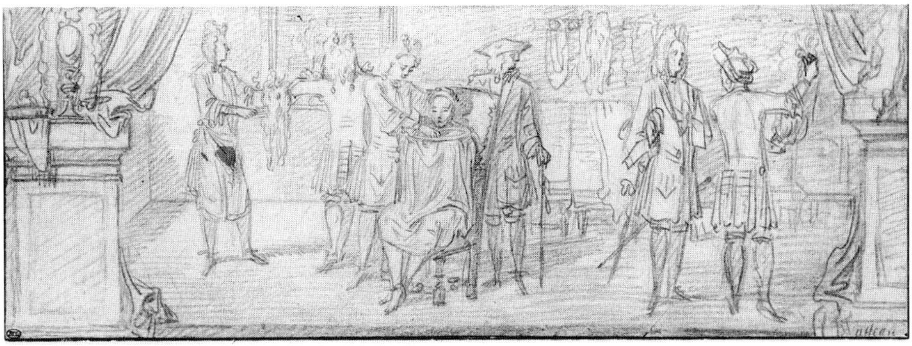

67. Antoine Watteau, sketch, *A Barber's Shop (Une boutique de barbier)*, Musée du Louvre, Paris. Cliché Réunion des musées nationaux.

picture-dealing shop, Aux Armes de France.[50] Fourcard has also hypothesized that Watteau's *The Alliance of Music and Comedy,* in a private collection, was to have served as a signboard for a shop selling musical instruments.[51]

Although the identification of these three works as signboards is only tentative, there is evidence that Watteau worked on other signboards before he worked on the one for Gersaint. Two drawings at the Louvre are clearly sketches for signboards. One is of a draper's shop, dated to 1705–6 (fig. 66), and the other is of a barber's shop (fig. 67), dated to 1709–10.[52] Both works depict the interior of a shop in a manner similar to the way in which Gersaint's shop is shown in the *Signboard.* In the drawing of the haberdasher's shop, the configuration of the space and the diagonally placed counter are remarkably similar to the right-hand portion of the *Signboard.* Because of these similarities, it is generally thought that Watteau may have later recalled this drawing for the composition of the *Signboard.*[53] In the drawing of the barber's shop, six standing figures and a seated figure, are engaged in appropriate activities: examining wigs and being shaved. The motif of a man closely examining a painting appears in the drawing, and again, it may have been later reworked by Watteau in the *Signboard.* Although these two drawings are similar in their general format to the *Signboard,* they exhibit none of that work's sophisticated and complex treatment of its subject. The drawings fall well within the conventions for depicting scenes of commercial activity, rather than manipulating those conventions and transforming them. Scenes of commercial activity, which began to appear in greater numbers between 1680 and 1700 as signboards, engraved series of *métiers,* and illustrations for almanacs and Bureaus d'Adresse, generally followed a common formula.[54] The interior of a shop and its goods are shown; to one side is a counter, behind which a salesperson proffers objects to a client. What Watteau's drawings do confirm is his early practice as a painter of lowly signboards and his long-standing familiarity with the conventions for depicting commercial activity.

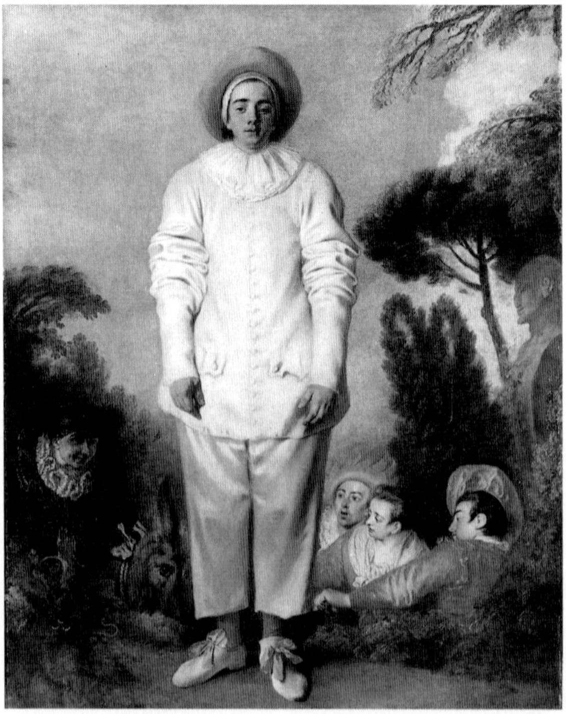

68. Antoine Watteau, *Gilles*, c. 1719, Musée du Louvre, Paris. Cliché, Réunion des musées nationaux.

It would be incorrect to say that Watteau "reverted" to signboard painting at the end of his life since the *Signboard* is so much more than a simple signboard. Watteau pointedly explored and exploited the lowly genre of signboard painting as an alternative arena for serious artistic expression. That Watteau was up to something with the *Signboard,* that he had specific intentions when he painted a "masterpiece" under the guise of a signboard, is given further credence if we accept the hypothesis that another of his most monumental, enigmatic, and sophisticated works – *Gilles* – was originally created as a signboard (fig. 68). This painting, the controversy surrounding the identity of its main figure – Pierrot or Gilles – and its unusual provenance are well known.[55] Hélène Adhémar first noted the similarity between the painting and a description of a signboard for a café run by the retired actor Belloni.[56] According to this description, written by the Parfaict brothers in 1743, Belloni "had as his signboard a portrait of himself dressed in the costume of Pierrot."[57] The signboard would have been painted between 1718, when Belloni quit his theater, and 1719, when the café went out of business. The identification of Watteau's *Gilles* with this signboard resolves several enigmas surrounding the painting. It was never engraved in the eighteenth century, and there is no known mention of it in eighteenth-century art literature. No one seemed aware of the work's existence until Baron Vivant Denon discovered it in 1805 as an advertising come-on in a picture dealer's shop. That it was originally a signboard would help to explain its unusual imagery, why such an extraordinary work escaped the notice of collectors and amateurs, and its large size (184.5 cm × 149.5 cm). Although large in relation to the rest of Watteau's work, its size would not have been unusual for a signboard. Moreover, it would explain why Watteau painted his last major work as a signboard; he had already been experimenting with the signboard as an alternative avenue of artistic expression.

Jeannine Batice, however, in "Pierrot, Gilles et les autres," argues that this work probably was not a signboard, since it was painted on fine canvas, perhaps from the same bolt as that Watteau used for *Pilgrimage to Cythera*. In addition, X rays reveal neither accidents nor repainting, indicating that the painting probably had not been used as a signboard, since it is perfectly intact.[58] But Baticle's argument is not conclusive. It is plausible that what happened to the *Signboard* also happened to *Gilles:* the short duration of Belloni's café's existence may have protected *Gilles* from long-term outdoor exposure. Moreover, the two paintings may have been produced under similar circumstances; just as Watteau painted a signboard for his friend, Gersaint, so too may he have known Belloni and presented him with a gift of a signboard.[59] Finally, the painting's temporary descent into obscurity may be attributed to the audience that viewed it; café clientele may have been indifferent to the quality of *Gilles,* whereas the patrons of an art dealer immediately recognized the *Signboard* as something of special artistic worth. Accepting *Gilles* as a signboard would provide a certain continuity in Watteau's artistic practice near the end of his life and would make his decision to paint the *Signboard* less anomalous.

Gersaint's Signboard as Representation of Social Practice

Whether or not the *Signboard* represents the continuation of a trend in Watteau's artistic practice, it was incontestably painted as a signboard. Thus far, I have treated the significance of the *Signboard* exclusively as a by-product of its place in the work of Watteau; of equal importance is recognizing the significance of the painting as a signboard in and of itself. This recognition, however, requires an understanding of the artist's intentions. To reach such an understanding, it is important not only to interrogate Watteau's work but also to raise the questions of who would have appreciated Watteau's intentions and why they would have done so.

I have argued earlier that Watteau frequently played one cultural and painterly discourse against another in order to articulate more fully the complex relationships between culture, power, and class in eighteenth-century France; Watteau is working in the same mode in the *Signboard.* By 1721 those relationships had changed, in practice, if not in theory. The "captains of culture" were no longer the king and the state, but a group of collectors, dealers, and connoisseurs. The arbiters of taste and recognized authorities on art were no longer the august body of the Academy, but men like the wealthy banker Pierre Crozat and his circle of friends with a like-minded interest in art. This circle, including the dealer Pierre-Jean Marriette, Jean de Jullienne, the Comte de Caylus, and an international cast of visiting artists, entrepreneurs, and dignitaries, formed what might be considered an alternate "academy."[60] This unofficial academy exerted a greater influence on the production and consumption of art than did the official Academy and state patronage. These were the men to whom culture mattered most and who stood to gain the most from the promotion of the arts. For many, especially the dealers and artists, this gain was economic, but there was more than money to be made in interest in and cultivation of the arts.

Collecting, appreciating, and knowing how to talk about art had become a sign of social status reflecting an elevated and noble taste. That many of the dealers and collectors had risen, or were in the process of rising, from the ranks of the upper bourgeoisie suggests just how much status was at stake in the creation of *cabinets*.[61] Witness to the entrenchment of this emergent alliance between culture, commerce, and class is the proliferation of "advice" literature about the "art" of collecting, which appeared around mid-century. Gersaint and others began publishing annotated sales catalogues that provided the would-be collector with general information about artists and the various schools of art, as well as with information about the provenance, market value, and aesthetic merit of the particular works offered up for sale.[62] The *contes de fées*, too, reflect this vogue for collecting. Replete with elaborate and detailed descriptions, the fairy palaces become huge *cabinets de curiosités*.[63]

In short, a number of groups used art to "pull themselves up by the bootstraps" because of art's power to confer upon its owner a certain nobility of *esprit*. This process is clearly evident in the introduction to the *Catalogue raisonné des diverses curiosités du cabinet de feu M. Quentin de Lorangère*, drawn up and written by Gersaint in 1744, only twenty-three years after Watteau painted his signboard.

> What advantages can a *Curieux* customarily derive from his curiosity? . . . His title of *Curieux* gives him access to the most famous collections and he can go to divert himself there; in the capacity of *Curieux* he becomes equal to those same people given over to this noble passion whose rank or condition is beyond his: as such he is invited to and received with pleasure at their gatherings established for the purpose of communicating to one another their discoveries or their acquisitions; he benefits from and rejoices with them over these novelties and he acquires daily some information and knowledge thus enlightening himself in the course of entertaining himself.[64]

Watteau had addressed the *Signboard* to the same audience for whom Gersaint wrote.

Watteau's *Signboard* both reflects and legitimizes this new state of affairs in artistic practice and the new position of the dealer and collector. It gives monumental form to the substitutions that were occurring in who controlled and who consumed culture. Moreover, Watteau's *Signboard* articulates a new system of signifying status within the social order, one based less on traditional markers of class than on the display of one's appreciation of art. Watteau's *Signboard* represents art's powers of transformation within actual social practice. In this context, we should view the *Signboard* as a modern history painting, documenting a contemporary activity that carried a larger associated meaning.

The Rise of the Art Dealer: The Example of Gersaint

Gersaint's own account of the circumstances surrounding the production and reception of the *Signboard* is a useful starting point for exploring some associated meanings. This account was part of the biographical notice on Watteau prefacing the announcement of a group of Watteau's engravings in the sales catalogue Gersaint drew up in 1744 for Quentin de Lorangère's collection of art, the same catalogue in which appeared the passage cited earlier on the advantages of collecting. The implicit content of this passage about collecting, I would argue, provides a telling background for a critical reading of Gersaint on the *Signboard*.

> On his return to Paris in 1721, when my business was still in its early stages, Watteau came and asked me if I would receive him and allow him, in order to keep his finger supple – those were his very words – if I would allow him, as I was saying, to paint a sign to be exhibited outside the shop. I was not in favor of the idea because I would have preferred him to work on something more substantial; but seeing that it would give him pleasure, I consented. The success of this picture is well known; it was done from life; the attitudes were so varied and so graceful, the composition so natural, and the groups so well thought out that it attracted the attention of passersby: even highly skilled painters came several times to admire it. It was done in eight days, and even then he only worked in the mornings; his delicate health, or, to be more accurate, his weakness, prevented him from working on it any longer. This was the only work in which he ever took the slightest pride; he told me this quite frankly.[65]

Gersaint then goes on to recount Watteau's death in an equally dramatic tone: "From day to day he hoped to gather sufficient strength to make the journey [to the country where he thought he might be better] on which I was to accompany him; but his weakness increased and, giving way suddenly, he died in my arms at the said Nogent a little after July 18th, 1721, aged 37 years."[66] Here Watteau has come down to us as a romantic hero, languishing and sickly, yet so committed to his art that he rose from his sickbed to create a masterpiece.

Gersaint's description of Watteau's heroic efforts during his last days, and of the dramatic death scene, must be viewed with more than a little skepticism. Gersaint, writing twenty-three years after Watteau's death, evidently depends upon his memory, which cannot be taken as a completely reliable source. Moreover, Gersaint's biography of Watteau is part of a larger literary tradition, one going back to antiquity and probably best known through Vasari's

Le vite de' più eccellenti architetti, pittori, et scultori Italiani: the artist's biography. Artists' biographies are notoriously inaccurate; they are filled with literary tropes rather than facts, and, more often than not, they situate the artist within a preexisting mythic legacy of creative genius rather than carefully document a particular life lived at a particular time.[67] Gersaint's biography of Watteau is no exception. Therein Antoine Watteau triumphantly takes his place in the pantheon of great creators after dutifully passing through a series of predictable episodes bearing a sometimes tenuous relationship to events. It is not only Watteau who attains mythic proportions in the biography, however, but also the biographer. If Gersaint strewed the painter's triumphal path with rose petals, he did not hesitate to tread upon them himself as well. The biography of Watteau provided Gersaint with the medium through which he could construct his own myth.

Although Gersaint's account cannot be accepted as a factual record of Watteau's life, I disagree with the conclusions drawn by Oliver Banks concerning the usefulness of this biography for understanding the *Signboard*: "Thus it would perhaps be best to forget Gersaint's document entirely, and to depend largely, if not exclusively, on the internal evidence of the work itself for an understanding of the picture's meaning."[68] How, then, do we fruitfully approach the reading of Gersaint's text?

One approach to Gersaint's biography of Watteau is to draw upon the premises of psychoanalytic techniques. We can view the inaccuracies, contradictions, and ambiguities within the text as red flags signaling a meaning to be found in some other discourse. Moreover, in reading any artist's biography we must keep the conventional quality of this genre in mind and be on the lookout for those conventions, or tropes, that have typically been employed. It is important that we note whether these tropes have been refashioned and, if they have been, that we ask why. In some cases, the alterations are merely a matter of updating, of recasting a long-standing formula to make it more relevant to contemporary experience. In other cases, however, the changes can and should be viewed as clues to other meanings. If Gersaint is falsifying or faltering, there must be reasons other than simply a faulty memory. Only the premises of psychoanalysis can offer us today a suggestive means for thinking about possible explanations: after all, Gersaint is not around to be consulted. To arrive at an account of Gersaint's work that neither denies plausible psychological resonances nor depends too heavily upon them, and that acknowledges the larger arena in which the biography *and the painting* were formed, we must interrogate the context to which we do have access.[69]

This context might best be thought of as a complex web both actively forming and passively formed by artists, viewers, collectors, dealers, journalists, writers, and readers – the world in which Gersaint and Watteau were enmeshed and that I have been trying to evoke. This web's strands included discourses that Gersaint might manipulate for reasons unconscious as well as conscious, personal as well as social: he projected fantasies onto the preexisting framework of artists' biographies in a way that served his own psychic and social interests.

As I suggested earlier, in his biography of Watteau, Gersaint mythologized not only Watteau's success and genius but also his own. Gersaint could rewrite history, from a comfortable position in 1744 when he wrote the biography. Much had changed in this picture dealer's life and business, and in the business of selling paintings and luxury objects in general, between 1721 – Gersaint's date for the *Signboard* – and 1744. These changes obviously influenced the narrative, tone, and covert message of Gersaint's account. In 1721, Gersaint's shop on the Pont Nôtre Dame, under the sign "Au Grande Monarque," was little more than two years old and still a fledgling operation. Established in October 1718, Au Grande Monarque had been built literally upon the ashes of an earlier venture: a fire in April of the same year had destroyed a picture-and-frame-dealing business in which Gersaint had invested a sizable sum only thirteen days earlier.[70] By 1744, however, Gersaint's business was thriving, and he had become a dealer of international repute. From announcements in the *Mercure de France* we learn that Gersaint made frequent buying trips to Holland between 1734 and 1744 and that his stock-in-trade had expanded to include not only works of art but also a wide variety of the luxury items and *nouvelles curiosités* much sought by fashionable Parisian collectors.[71] To better indicate the new range of his merchandise, and his merchandising of collectibles in the *goût chinois* – which he actively promoted – Gersaint changed the name of his shop. In 1740 Au Grande Monarque became A La Pagode.[72] His new business card, drawn by Boucher and engraved by the Comte de Caylus, clearly illustrated in the image and described in the text the *nouveautés* he now offered:

> Gersaint, Merchant and Jeweller on the Pont Nôtre Dame, Sells every sort of Wares, Novel and of Taste, Jewels, Mirrors, Small Paintings, Pagodas, Lacquer and Porcelains from Japan, Shells and other specimens of Natural History, Stones, Agates, and generally all sorts of Unusual and Exotic merchandise.[73]

The success of Gersaint's business venture and of his expanded line of merchandise is not surprising; it can be seen as the logical outcome of Colbert's economic policies and their impact on social, cultural, and commercial practice. What began as a state-sponsored effort to foster commerce in luxury items in order to increase a favorable balance of trade ended by engendering a system of consumption and production that remained outside the bounds of state control.[74] Effectively, what began as the state's exertion of its power over the economic realm resulted in a diffusion of that power. It follows, then, that Gersaint's shop in 1744 was not what it had been when Watteau painted his signboard; the trade in pictures had been subsumed by a larger trade in luxury items and fashionable collectibles. Written more than two decades after the event, replete with factual inconsistencies, Gersaint's account suggests not merely a faulty memory, but a rewriting of history meant both to conform to and to confirm his new position. By treating this text as a rewriting of history, that is, by examining its inconsistencies and reading between and beyond its lines, we can use Gersaint's account to explore these changes.

We should begin this task by setting the record straight: what facts are questionable, or completely discountable, in light of recent research and documentary evidence? The first factual error appears in the opening sentence, when Gersaint places Watteau's return to Paris from England in 1721. It has long been established that Watteau returned from England in 1720.[75] In all likelihood, this error can be explained by the vagaries of memory. Another contradiction, although one whose resolution is dependent upon interpretation as much as on documentation, can be found in Gersaint's assertion that the *Signboard* was done from life. Taken literally, this statement would lead us to believe that the *Signboard* is an accurate representation of Gersaint's shop. However, Paul Alfassa has determined, on the basis of contemporary engravings and archival material, including ground plans, that the dimensions of the shop depicted in the *Signboard* are pure fabrication. In fact, according to Alfassa's findings, Gersaint's shop on the Pont Nôtre Dame was much smaller – slightly more than ten feet in width and slightly less than that in depth – than the space represented by the painting.[76] Hence, Gersaint could not possibly have displayed the number of paintings Watteau depicted in the *Signboard*. Moreover, it is unlikely that Gersaint, at this stage of his career, could have afforded or obtained that array of prestigious paintings by old and new masters. Attempts to identify these paintings have been inconclusive.[77] It is generally agreed that the paintings are pastiches, meant to represent certain artists and schools of painting generically rather than reproduce any particular work. These findings suggest that Watteau did not faithfully transcribe Gersaint's shop and its contents, but Gersaint's statement that "it was done from life" should not be understood as willful misrepresentation. Rather, it should be taken figuratively and most likely refers to Watteau's method of composition, in which figures he had sketched from life were later arranged within a larger setting. Further, Pierre Rosenberg has suggested that Gersaint meant that the work was a completely new composition and not a copy.[78]

Perhaps the least plausible of Gersaint's assertions is that Watteau completed the *Signboard* in a mere eight days, working only during the mornings. Although there is no evidence either to confirm or to refute Gersaint's account, common sense forecloses the possibility of such a feat. Technically, the *Signboard* is far from polished, and most scholars agree that it was probably done in some haste. Yet given the magnitude of the work (approximately five feet by ten feet), eight consecutive mornings would not have provided enough time for its preparation, much less for its execution.[79] Even supposing that these eight mornings were spread out over a period of weeks, as some scholars have projected, Watteau would still have had to work incessantly to finish the *Signboard,* a proposition that his poor health makes even more unlikely.

Why would Gersaint wish the reader to believe that a work as ambitious as the *Signboard* was only an artistic exercise – something dashed off in a brief period to keep Watteau in practice? Banks has hypothesized that Gersaint might have been trying to defend himself against those who thought Watteau's efforts on this gift had contributed to his death.[80] Banks and others have noted that in this account of Watteau's production of the *Signboard* Gersaint is deliberately playing up his role as the artist's friend and completely circumventing his role as a dealer. Gersaint wants the reader to believe that Watteau's herculean effort was a labor of love. This intention is underscored when Gersaint tells us that Watteau "died in my arms."

Gersaint exploits this relationship throughout the biography, in which he asserts his insider's connections to Watteau. From the outset, and in a very forthright manner, Gersaint lets the reader know that he was on intimate terms with Watteau; in the second paragraph of the biography, Gersaint writes: "I lived with Watteau for long enough and we were close enough friends to have learned certain *particularités,* which I will happily share with the public."[81] Gersaint also uses more subtle means to reinforce readers' awareness of the privileged nature of his relationship with Watteau; for example, while recounting an anecdote from Watteau's life, Gersaint includes this parenthetical aside: "he told me this one day."[82] Gersaint consistently inflates his role in facilitating the naive Watteau's success and in developing his talents, while he downplays the contribution of others, including Watteau's father and his two masters, Claude Gillot and Claude III Audran. (Recall Gersaint's statement that Audran tried to discourage Watteau from painting military scenes, those very scenes that led to Watteau's being discovered by the picture dealer Sirois.) Whether intended or not, Gersaint has woven into the biography a subtext: with the aid of Gersaint in the role of a substitute father figure, Watteau managed to overcome the roadblocks these other "friends and teachers" had created.

The motif of the substitute father and the overcoming of obstacles created by those closest to the artist are standard fare in artists' biographies.[83] In Vasari's life of Giotto, considered the prototype of this trope in subsequent artists' biographies, Cimabue discovers the rustic shepherd boy and becomes his teacher and father figure.[84] The desire to substitute a more exalted parent for the real one is a common childhood and adolescent fantasy, which Freud termed "family romance." This fantasy is recast in artists' biographies as the myth of the discovery of unrecognized genius. Whereas in Gersaint's biography Watteau is the discovered genius, Gersaint unabashedly casts himself in the role of the exalted discoverer. Even if he did not directly discover Watteau, he did so indirectly, through a member of his family, his father-in-law, Sirois. According to Gersaint, "This sale was the origin of the liaison that my father-in-law had with Watteau until the artist's death," and, of course, it was in Gersaint's arms that Watteau died. Gersaint, I would speculate, is inserting his own fantasy into the preexisting framework found in artists' biographies.

It is interesting to note that Gersaint is given short shrift as an influential figure in the artist's life, and the *Signboard* is all but ignored, in other French eighteenth-century biographies of Watteau.[85] These lacunae in the biographical literature support the idea of a self-serving subtext in Gersaint's accounts. In this light, one may safely assume that Gersaint used his description of the *Signboard*'s production and the dramatic deathbed scene to establish further the importance of his friendship with Watteau. The *Signboard* was a priceless gift to Gersaint that cost Watteau much effort in his weakened state at the end of his life and was a tribute to their friendship. Moreover, according to Gersaint, it was the only work of which Watteau was proud. Gersaint writes that "even highly skilled artists came several times to admire it."[86] Watteau's *Signboard* was more than just a parting gift to a beloved friend, it was also a masterpiece! In his account of the *Signboard*, Gersaint acknowledges this tribute in an appropriately self-deprecating manner, while simultaneously glorying in its reflected (and retrospective) glow of greatness.

At the same time, however, Gersaint derides the importance of this painting, writing it off as a mere trifle that was dashed off in a few mornings' work. Gersaint's account reveals a certain ambivalence toward this painting. This ambivalence, moreover, is only compounded by the subsequent fate of the work. If it was the labor of love that Gersaint makes it out to be, why did he sell it? When Gersaint wrote his biography in 1744, he had not owned the painting for at least twelve years. At an unknown date, Gersaint sold the painting to Claude Glucq, *conseiller au parlement*, and then, at some point before 1732, the painting passed into the collection of Glucq's cousin, Jean de Jullienne.[87] Jullienne had the work engraved in 1732, and the announcement of this engraving in the *Mercure de France* supplies the following information:

> This piece, which measures 9 feet long and 5 feet high, *has always been regarded as the masterpiece of this excellent painter.* It depicts the shop of a merchant that is filled with a variety of paintings done by the most famous masters; one can recognize the hand and the taste of each of these particular great painters.
>
> This famous signboard was displayed outside the shop for only fifteen days; its presence attracted the admiration of all of Paris. It was sold to M. Glucq. It is presently on view in the collection of M. Jullienne.[88] (Emphasis added.)

Despite Gersaint's own testament, and the corroborating statement in the *Mercure* to the effect that the *Signboard* was immediately recognized as a masterpiece, Gersaint, for whatever reasons, parted with this token of friendship. That Gersaint so insistently focuses on the sterling quality of his relationship to the artist, and that he would like the reader to believe the work was a mere trifle, hastily dashed off, suggests that somehow Watteau's gift caused him a discomfort; something about the *Signboard* did not sit well with Gersaint. I would hypothesize that what bothered Gersaint about the *Signboard* was not the quality of the finished product, for his account reveals a certain amount of pride in this, but its status as a signboard. Gersaint makes it clear that he was humoring his friend by accepting the offer of a signboard. "I was not in favor of the idea because I would have preferred him to work on something more substantial; but seeing that it would give him pleasure, I consented."[89] Gersaint's pride in the work is tempered by his reservations, and even by some disappointment; in the end, Watteau's gift was only a signboard.

Oliver Banks nods in this direction when he conjectures why Gersaint wished to pass off the *Signboard* as an "inspired improvisation." "He [Gersaint] may also have been sensitive to the parallels that could be drawn by malicious people to Watteau's earlier employment on the Pont Notre-Dame, when he was subjected to rank exploitation by shady dealers. It seems to have been important to Gersaint that he appear in his narrative as Watteau's friend and intimate, rather than as a dealer."[90] Banks is right to focus upon Gersaint's fastidiousness about his relation to Watteau as a dealer; however, I would take his insights further. Banks's argument about Gersaint's reluctance to be compared to those traffickers who exploited artists and art is plausible.

Yet exploitation alone was not the issue, for status was also at stake. Gersaint did not wish to be linked to shady dealers for whom art was a mere commodity, to be bought and sold without appreciation of its aesthetic merit. Gersaint, it would seem, wished to set himself up in the role of friend and enlightened patron and to play down his role as a mere *commerçant*. The *Signboard* compromised Gersaint, not only because it evoked uncomfortable comparisons but also because it evoked philistine associations: signboards, as a form of painting, were not considered art.

Gersaint's reservations about Watteau's gift may in part be attributed to the accepted ways of thinking about the practice of painting and, ultimately, to the way this practice was controlled and regulated both by the Royal Academy and the lowlier Academy of St. Luke. Signboards were part of commercial culture, not of high culture. It was a kind of painting done by unskilled hacks, certainly not by someone of Watteau's artistic standing as a member of the Royal Academy. Gersaint was disappointed with the *Signboard* because of its lowly status: Watteau had not produced a legitimate painting as his parting gift and tribute to his friend.

While this interpretation is tempting, it ultimately proves insufficient and oversimplifies a more complex state of affairs. This interpretation might explain Gersaint's ambivalence toward the *Signboard,* but it is not in keeping with the subtext of the substitute father figure and great guide that Gersaint weaves into the biography. I would argue that Gersaint was working on the same fabric when he stated: "I would have preferred him to work on something more substantial; but seeing that it would give him pleasure, I consented." Here is a reversal in the role of gift giver. The creation of Watteau's masterpiece was made possible only through Gersaint's "gift" of indulgence. Moreover, this account of the painting of a masterpiece in an impossibly short period of time represents the reworking of another trope found in artists' biographies – the artist as magician.[91] The display of "supernatural powers" through the speed with which an artist works is standard in artists' biographies; for example, Tiepolo "painted a picture in less time than it took someone else to grind his colors."[92] Moreover, this kind of virtuoso performance could be likened to a kind of painterly *sprezzatura*. Like Fragonard's fantasy portraits of the 1760s and 1770s, which were valued precisely because they were so quickly done, Watteau's *Signboard* would have been seen as more valuable because of its quick execution.[93] I have suggested that Watteau knew exactly what he was up to when he created a masterpiece masquerading as a signboard; I conclude that Gersaint also knew what Watteau was doing with the *Signboard*, as his account of its creation demonstrates. Gersaint's uneasiness about the artistic standing of a signboard is more than compensated for by pride in his own role in its production, as well as, one could imagine, by his pride in the painterly apotheosis of his own business.

It must be remembered that when Watteau painted the *Signboard*, Gersaint's business was only two years old and not the established success it was to become. Watteau's gift – his image of a well-appointed shop filled with important paintings and a bustling business – must have been a flattering one for Gersaint. The *Signboard*, in this sense, should indeed be viewed as Watteau's parting tribute to his friend and dealer, embodying his affection for Gersaint and his hopes for Gersaint's future success. For Gersaint, the masterly signboard must have represented the fulfillment of a wish. Watteau's strategy of working within the format and conventions of a lowly commercial genre, only to transcend, transform, and, ultimately, elevate the genre, could only have been perceived by Gersaint as an act of faith, friendship, and affirmation. This "apotheosis" of Gersaint's establishment, however, was not mere wish fulfillment on Watteau's part. Watteau, and Gersaint too, must have been fully aware of the new position that paintings and other luxury items occupied in defining social status. As Gersaint articulated it in 1744, "in the capacity of *Curieux* he becomes equal to those same people given over to this noble passion whose rank or condition is beyond his: as such he is invited to and received with pleasure at their gatherings."[94] The ennoblement of commerce implicit in Watteau's *Signboard* aptly reflects the new status enjoyed by those dealers and collectors who shared a common *nobilité d'esprit*. Moreover, this ennoblement of commerce may have carried a particularly pointed meaning for Gersaint at the time the work was painted.

For him to sell paintings and other luxury items legally, Gersaint had to become a member of the *corps de la mercerie*, one of the six *corps de marchands* in Paris.[95] Members of this *corps* sold a wide variety of objects: ribbons, rugs, jewelry, fabrics, lace, gloves, toys, snuff boxes, fans, and parasols, to name just a few. *Merciers* were divided into twenty classes, according to the type of merchandise they sold. Gersaint would have been classified under "*Merchants of art objects,* [selling] paintings, prints, statues, sconces, girandoles, chandeliers, time-pieces, chests, etc."[96] Despite the diversity of merchandise, the *merciers* were unified as a *corps* in that they did not fabricate what they sold. That the *mercier* did not engage in what was legally defined as manual labor had been long recognized, witness the French proverb describing *merciers* as "merchants of everything, makers of nothing."[97]

The *corps de la mercerie* traditionally enjoyed an elevated position among the other *corps de marchands*. The *corps* profited from a greater degree of official privileges and protections and was wealthier than the other five corps; according to Sauval's *Antiquités de Paris,* the *corps de la mercerie* paid as much in taxes each year as the other five *corps* combined.[98] Of greater significance was the distinguished status accorded to the *mercier* in relation to the members of the other *corps*. Because the *marchand merciers* neither fabricated the objects they sold nor engaged in manual labor, they were considered superior, metaphorically more "noble" (if not in actual fact), than the members of the other *corps,* who produced the objects they sold. Savary, in his *Dictionnaire du commerce* of 1723, describes this elevated rank:

> The corporation of haberdashery is considered as the most noble and most excellent of all the *corporations* of merchants, in the measure that its members *do not work at all and fabricate no objects by their own hand,* except to embellish objects which are already made and fabricated. Also those who are admitted into this *corporation* are received nobly; *they are permitted neither to make nor to manufacture any merchandise,* but only to embellish; this is not the case with the other *corporations,* which are regarded as mixed, that is to say, that they perform as merchant and as artisan.[99]

The business of the *mercier* was not that of an ordinary *commerçante,* but of a *noblesse commerçante,* an appellation dating back to the early seventeenth century.[100] This appellation was apt not only because the *marchand mercier* did not engage in manual labor but also because of the kind of luxury items he sold and the clientele who purchased his wares.

The *Signboard* and Gersaint

When Watteau painted the *Signboard,* sometime during the last months of 1720 and the first months of 1721, Gersaint was in the process of becoming a member of the *corps de la mercerie.* A letter dating to October 1720 documents the "reception of Gersaint, in the capacity of *Marchand mercier.*"[101] In this context, Watteau's ambitious signboard might be seen as reinforcing the idea of the *noblesse commerçante,* perhaps specifically acknowledging Gersaint's new status as a *marchand mercier.*

The hypothesis that the *Signboard*'s status as a signboard caused Gersaint's ambivalent response is also insufficient because it is based on the assumption that the distinctions between high culture and popular culture were rigid and static. It does not account for the nuances of cultural categories, such as official high culture, unofficial high culture, and popular culture, or for the shifting relationships among them and for what these shifts signified. I believe this is important since so much of Watteau's art was concerned with breaking the boundaries between traditional cultural categories.

More broadly, Watteau's *Signboard* should be seen as giving form to the aspirations of an emergent class and as a refashioning of the meaning of the term "nobility" within a social order changing its structure from one based on estates to one based on class.[102] "Refashioning" is an apt term here, for part of the signifying code that defined this "new nobility" had to do with fashionability. Keeping up with the fashions counted a great deal and knowing the correct manner in which to display one's fashionability counted even more. This conspicuous display of leisure, of having the time to savor the sensual and sensuous things in life, is bound up with the cult of *honnêteté* and with the rise of the consumption of luxury items – including art objects. In 1699 the English visitor Martin Lister commented on the Parisian vogue for collecting art: "Everyone, that has anything to spare, covets to have some good pictures or sculpture of the best Artists; the like in the ornaments of their Gardens, so that it is incredible what pleasure that vast quantity of fine things give the curious stranger."[103] Several pages later, Lister noted that "there are no people [the Parisians] more fond of coming together to see and be seen."[104] As Robert Neuman and others have pointed out, what we see in the *Signboard* is a contemporary image of social display – the *promenade à la mode.* That it takes place in Gersaint's shop attests both to the power of art as a commodity in conferring social status and to the importance of the dealer – Gersaint – as an intermediary within this milieu.

The subtext hinted at by inconsistencies in Gersaint's biography thus emerges. Gersaint's remarks that the *Signboard* was tossed off by Watteau may thus plausibly be seen as self-consciously transparent artifice; his clientele recognized the painting as a masterpiece, as did Gersaint. His profession that the *Signboard* was a lowly work, despite the evidence and opinion to the contrary, might be seen as a masquerade, but one as "convincing" as was Marie Antoinette playing a milkmaid: it was intended not to succeed, but to put his clients on notice that he, too, participated in the cult of *honnêteté.* Gersaint was displaying the signs of nobility, both figuratively, through his demeanor, and literally, through the *Signboard,* that proclaimed him a noble *commerçant,* thereby demonstrating to potential patrons that he was a worthy intermediary between a noble public and an ennobling art.

If Gersaint's account is any indication, the *Signboard* achieved an instant notoriety; "it attracted the attention of passersby: even highly skilled painters came several times to admire it."[105] Certainly a part of the novelty and attraction of the *Signboard* must have had to do with its contradictory status as both a masterpiece and a signboard. Watteau's transformation of a lowly, "artless," genre into something self-consciously "artistic" would have had a particular appeal; for part of the signifying code of nobility was the ability to take lowly forms of popular culture and transform them tastefully. In this sense, Watteau's *Signboard,* with its breaking down of the boundaries between high and low culture, clearly fits into the larger pattern of cultural transformation and subversion of traditional cultural categories that the participants of *fêtes* and *foires* engaged in and that Watteau regularly put into practice in his paintings.[106]

The Meaning of *Gersaint's Signboard*

In *Gersaint's Signboard,* Watteau, I would argue, self-consciously employed the genre of a low, commercial art form as a means of displaying his skill at a fashionable cultural one-upmanship. Gersaint's biography of Watteau may be seen in a similar light; Gersaint has provided an "artful" commentary within the context of a commercial catalogue. Moreover, the audience who would have viewed the *Signboard,* as well as the audience to whom Gersaint addressed his catalogue, would have appreciated these transformational tactics. But beyond this kind of witty display, Watteau's *Signboard* gives monumental form to the positions of art, collecting, and artifice within the ideological constructs of an emergent social class and its signifying practices. In the *Signboard,* Watteau creates a new genre of painting, as he did in his *fêtes galantes,* in his military paintings, and in *Departure,* by playing the cultural conventions and assumptions of official "high" art against those of popular "low" expression. As a result, he implicitly calls into question traditional, institutionally determined categories, as well as those persons who determined and defined them and their reasons for doing so. I would argue that, ultimately, Watteau was trying to create an alternative to, or a substitute for, what had been traditionally understood as a "meaningful," or important, class of images – history painting. Watteau's new genres represent the artist's quest to create contemporary history paintings: paintings with subjects that could meaningfully represent contemporary experience, yet would not fall within the category of pure genre painting or, as in the case of the *Signboard,* mere commercial art. In the *Signboard,* Watteau redeems and transcends pure genre by embedding allusions to larger, more important meanings – the stuff and substance of traditional history painting – within the specific time, space, and experience of modern life.

Conclusion

One art history survey textbook juxtaposes the image of Hyacinthe Rigaud's magisterial (9 ft. 2 in. × 6 ft. 3 in.) *Portrait of Louis XIV* (fig. 69) with Watteau's diminutive (10 in. × 7 in.) image of an unknown dancing man, titled *L'Indifférent (The Nonchalant One)* (fig. 70). This juxtaposition invites us also to compare the two works. Both paintings show artfully posed, full-length figures in fancy costumes. Rigaud's painting, however, is clearly a portrait. In this portrait, Louis XIV's role as king is signaled overtly by the coronation robes that he wears and by implication through the background of drapery and columns, which, within the conventional language of portraiture, signified nobility.[1] In contrast, whether *L'Indifférent* is a portrait is questionable, since by definition a portrait is a likeness of a particular person. In *L'Indifférent* we are given no indication of who the sitter is, either through the painting's title or through any other traditional markers of identity. The model's costume is theatrical, and his pose is clearly from the repertoire of the dance; yet other indicators, such as a stage, which would identify him as an actor or would indicate a performance, are absent.[2] The ambiguity of place in *L'Indifférent* is intensified by Watteau's sketchy, unfinished facture, which contrasts with Rigaud's highly finished, academic surface in the portrait of Louis XIV. The student looking at this page in the art history text cannot help but compare these two "actors"; the student who actually reads the text will have the nature of this comparison made explicit: "[*L'Indifférent*'s] mincing minuet might be seen as mimicking the monarch's solemn pacing."[3] *L'Indifférent* was painted in 1716, one year after Louis XIV's death. The abundance of commemorative portraits of the king at that time would have made the connection the student is encouraged to draw all but automatic for the eighteenth-century viewer, for as I have attempted to argue in this book, lurking behind many of Watteau's paintings – as he lurks behind *L'Indifférent* – is Louis XIV.

This presence, this unarticulated but commonly understood reference to Louis XIV, was about more than just the deceased king, however; it was about the crisis of authority that Louis XIV had come to represent during Watteau's lifetime. Watteau lived during the so-called sunset years of Louis XIV's reign, when the edifice of state and monarchical authority was reduced to a shell, and during the regency of Philippe d'Orléans, when the locus of power was unstable. The crisis of authority during Watteau's lifetime gave rise to what I will call here a system of subterfuge. This system permeated the upper reaches of French society and culture and was articulated by Watteau in a variety of ways in his paintings.

Rigaud's *Portrait of Louis XIV* again provides a starting point, this time for talking about this system of subterfuge. If Louis XIV could magically step out of the Rigaud painting, he would be a commanding six feet, eight inches tall; if we subtracted five inches to compensate for the elevator wig and heels, he would be six feet, three inches tall, still a commanding height even by today's standards. Of course, the Louis XIV in Rigaud's painting is an image – an image that was deliberately prepared for public consumption and one in which the king was purposely presented as larger than life. Because we are used to looking at such carefully managed images of Louis XIV, it comes as something of a shock to learn that Louis XIV was only five feet, three inches tall in his stocking feet, which was not unusually short for the time. The control of the royal image evident here was an essential feature of the effort to represent a royal ideology. The image and the ideology became difficult to maintain during the last twenty years of Louis XIV's seventy-two-year reign, and the gap between the real Louis and his image is important; I suggest that this gap defined one of the spaces in which Watteau chose to work.

This gap between the real Louis and his image had not always been so egregious. France was the victor during Louis XIV's first two military campaigns, the War of Devolution (1667–68) and the Dutch Wars (1672–79), and artists and writers celebrated, embellished, and inflated Louis XIV's role as the great warrior king and legitimated his imperialistic ambitions. The system of mercantilism implemented by Colbert provided the economic surplus necessary – or at least the means for managing credit – for the display of royal *gloire* and *éclat*.

Colbert established the king as a great and glorious patron of science, culture, and the arts through the founding of various academies on the model of the Académie Française: the Académie des Inscriptions, which grew out of a committee of the Académie Française called the Petite Académie; the Académie Royale de Peinture et de Sculpture; the Académie de Danse; the Académie Française de Rome; the Académie des Sciences; the Académie d'Architecture; and the Académie Royale de Musique. Well known for his pragmatism, Colbert mobilized culture and the arts to serve a dual duty: to present the king as the great benefactor and to provide an effective and efficient propaganda machine. The academies constituted the means to control

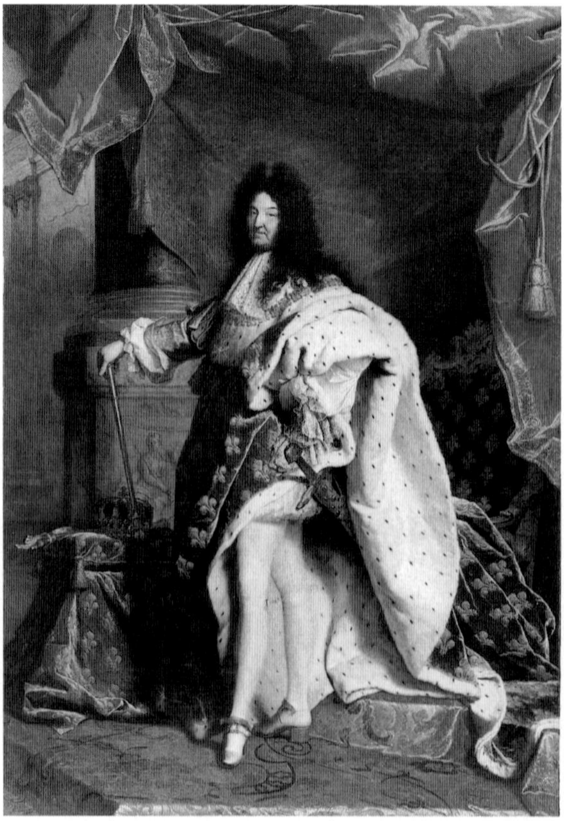

69. Hyacinthe Rigaud, *Portrait of Louis XIV*, 1701, Musée du Louvre, Paris. Cliché, Réunion des musées nationaux.

cultural production. Moreover, Louis and his culture machine prohibited the competition of others who might rival his splendor. The affair of Nicolas Fouquet, whom the king had imprisoned for life for having dared to outshine the king as a patron of the arts at his sumptuous, costly château, Vaux-le-Vicomte (among other presumptions), served as an example for nobles and became a symbol of their subservience to the king and state.

Versailles, too, became a symbol of noble subservience. Louis's consolidation of the nobility around him provided both an audience for and performers of the daily rituals and ceremonials that perpetuated the royal myth and the courtiers' stake in it. At Versailles, Louis provided his courtiers with entertainments that put those of Fouquet to shame, and he dispensed ritual favor there in the form of proximity to his majesty on the basis of a courtier's success in currying the king's good will. But the setting and scenario did not provide the courtier with access to real political power. Those who made decisions about affairs of state were the robe nobles – the hired hands whom Louis XIV increasingly appointed to positions of responsibility, influence, and rank. As long as the image-making machine had the economic and ideological fuel to keep producing, and as long as there was an audience with a stake in believing in it, for whatever reason, then the image could ring true.

But during Louis XIV's sunset years (1690–1715) that image rang increasingly false. France and the king became diminished versions of earlier incarnations of themselves. Beneath the image of the omnipotent ruler was another figure, a less-than-perfect man whose self-aggrandizing state making, whose unremitting imperial ambitions, and whose relentless drain of the resources of his country and countrymen finally concluded in widespread exhaustion – of energy, of treasury, of a way of life. The Louis who retreated into domesticity and piety by the end of the seventeenth century was not the same man who had quipped, "l'état, c'est moi." The image no longer fit the man, yet like the subjects of the emperor who wore no clothes in the Hans Christian Andersen fairy tale, Louis's subjects – noble and commoner alike – dared not speak the truth about their ruler.

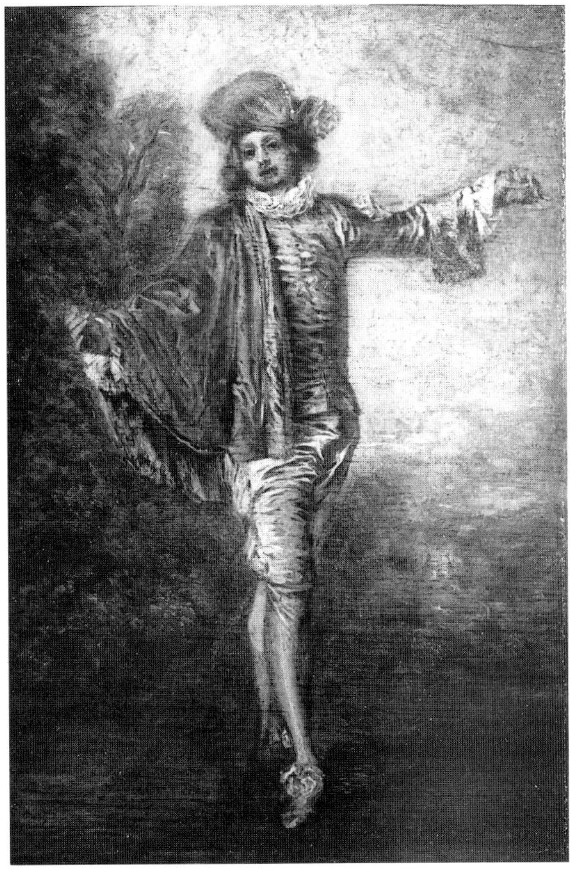

70. Antoine Watteau, *The Nonchalant One (L'Indifférent)*, c. 1717, Louvre, Paris. France. Photo, Erich Lessing/Art Resource, NY.

Instead, they found ways to compliment the king while acknowledging among themselves the true state of the king's "wardrobe." The modus operandi became a system of subterfuge in which the ambivalence surrounding diminution and the glaring gaps between royal, official ideology and lived experience could be expressed only circumspectly; Watteau was masterfully circumspect. Indeed, Watteau's technique was to use the formal vocabulary of official ideology to comment, albeit ambiguously, on contemporary subjects so as to simultaneously gratify the emperor in his vanity and amuse those who saw that he wore no clothes.

The military paintings, for example, represent an experience and understanding of war at odds with the ideology of the *Roi de Guerre* encoded within the official topographical tradition of military painting. In *Departure,* Watteau depicts one of the great cultural skirmishes of the sunset years – Louis XIV's banishment of the Italian Comedians. He painted this work, about an affair that symbolized the dispute over the king's control of culture, at a time when the Comedians had won out over the king's authority. It is worth mentioning that one of Philippe d'Orléans' first acts as regent was to reinstate the banished Italian Comedians, an event that was foreshadowed in Watteau's tribute in *Departure* to the persistent resistance to authority.

After the death of Louis XIV in 1715, this system of subterfuge adapted to a different set of circumstances. Louis XIV's death freed people, including Philippe d'Orléans, the nephew of Louis XIV who reigned as regent from 1715 to 1723, to be more openly critical of the dead monarch and to question more vigorously the institution of monarchy itself. Respect for Louis XIV evaporated after his death, and an outpouring of grossly disrespectful and satirical verse overflowed. The regent not only had to absorb the negative legacy of Louis XIV but also had to preserve the rights and prerogatives of the monarchy for the future. The regent found himself in an untenable situation, negotiating between various factions competing for power: the parlements, the disenfranchised high nobility, the Maine and Orléans factions within the court, and the upwardly mobile class of wealthy entrepreneurs. With the great patriarch out of the picture each faction tried to carve out its own position of power and prestige for the future. There was still a system of subterfuge, but its raison d'etre had disappeared; the sun was gone from the solar system, leaving the planets to revolve around a void.

Complicating this sense of disarrangement was the reevaluation of commerce and business necessitated by the enormous state debt the regency inherited. There was a greater rapport between businessmen and nobility during the regency than there had been during Louis's reign which had heightened social tensions at the time. Yet also during the regency, businessmen sought to legitimate their position in the social hierarchy, whereas the nobility tried ever harder to distinguish themselves from the mere moneymakers. John Law's *système*, in effect from 1718 until the crash of 1720, based on paper currency backed by projected income from colonial trade, made and broke the fortunes of nobles and bourgeois alike. Everything, it seemed, functioned by and through a system of subterfuge with nothing substantial behind it.

The crisis of authority manifested during the regency is aptly illustrated by the "question of the hat." The regent, in an attempt to implement an aristocratic reform, appointed peers of France (nobles of the state) to seats on various state councils. These men had no training and little interest in making executive decisions about matters of law, trade, currency, and agricultural economics. They were, however, greatly interested in questions of etiquette and precedence. One question in particular, whether a duke or a parlementary president should first take off his hat, excited their interest. The dukes and parlement members both lobbied the Duc d'Orléans on this matter, and Orléans, who wished to retain the support of both groups, made no decision. The "question of the hat" was heatedly discussed for years, and while this debate preoccupied the minds of some, others stepped in to fill the void in responsible civil activity and to take care of the nation's business.

I cite the "question of the hat" because it reflects another dimension of the institutional collapse that enabled Watteau to define his own artistic practices – another of the spaces in which Watteau worked. Watteau's productive mixing and mutating of genres was possible precisely because of the diminished authority within the institutions of Louis XIV's formerly well-oiled culture machine: following form no longer mattered. Just as in political matters surrounding the "question of the hat" others stepped in to fill the void, in the absence of authority in cultural matters, others who were outside the official framework, such as the group of collectors and connoisseurs centered around Pierre Crozat, stepped in to take the reins of culture production and consumption.

This group – the new captains of culture – consisting of wealthy financiers, members of the robe nobility, and, to a lesser degree, members of the sword nobility, constituted an "unofficial" Academy. Moreover, this group also represented a new elite, one whose status was not necessarily determined by traditional standards of rank. Watteau's paintings were appreciated by this group: his works represented new categories of social experience in a way that older forms could not. Watteau created new categorical modes to explain the new world. *Gersaint's Signboard,* for example, celebrated the roles of the dealer and the connoisseur and the power of art and luxury items to confer status during the regency.

The *fête galante* also gave form to the economy of leisure, self-display, and masquerade within the construction of social status. In addition, the acceptance of the *fête galante* as a genre within the Academy's hierarchy of genre had other repercussions: it represented the bankruptcy of past institutional authority within a profoundly different present. It should be mentioned that although a member of the Royal Academy of Painting and Sculpture Watteau did not embrace the institution, nor did the institution embrace him. Twice, he competed for the prestigious Prix de Rome, and twice, he was the runner-up; if his biographers are to be trusted, in each case favoritism rather than merit determined the first-prize winner. Furthermore, he submitted his Academy reception piece five years late, he never attended an Academy meeting (at least according to the records kept by the secretary in the *Procés Verbaux*), and he received no official commissions through the Academy. Watteau was never a beneficiary of royal favor, and the official culture did not provide him with a realistic arena in which to make a living as an artist.

Watteau's long-in-the-making reception piece, *Pilgrimage to Cythera,* did not fit within traditional generic categories of the Royal Academy of Painting and Sculpture. The creation of a new category to accommodate his painting suggests how boundaries were being redrawn to try to patch the gap between past and present practices. For the Academy to accept *Pilgrimage* as a history painting would have required it to reformulate the definition of a history painting; by creating a new category instead, the *fête galante,* Academicians evaded this thorny problem. But their creation of a new category ended by subverting the immutable authority of the hierarchy of genre and its relationship to other official hierarchies.

Throughout this book I have emphasized how Watteau worked against and through existing artistic genres and conventions – how he mixed things up. Watteau stretched some boundaries and broke up others; in all cases, however, he exposed the arbitrary nature of genres and categories in general. The breakdown and transformation of artistic forms and conventions were symptomatic of larger breakdowns and transformations that were occurring throughout French society. Watteau's new categorical modes legitimized and articulated commonly understood situations, practices, and aspirations – which is precisely why his hybrid forms were so well received, and why they became the artistic rule rather than the exception. Witness to this is the flood of *fêtes galantes* by Pater and by Lancret. Lancret was accepted into the Academy as a printer of *fêtes galantes,* and he consistently received important royal commissions. The rococo style developed by Watteau became a symbol of royal power, widely imitated by other European courts.

As I stated in the introduction, I do not wish to reduce Watteau to the sum of his social experiences, but I do not want to ignore the influence of those experiences either. Watteau lived and worked within a fascinatingly elaborate and complex social and cultural milieu. I have argued that Watteau participated successfully in that milieu and that the painterly strategies he chose were effective responses to it. Implicit in this argument is that the same case may be made for Watteau as is made for any artist who exists powerfully within an epoch: not only did the times influence Watteau, but Watteau influenced the times. Watteau used strategies that enabled him to paint in the visual vocabulary of one era to help articulate the emerging vocabulary of another.

Watteau worked in a period when the question of who defined and controlled culture mattered a great deal. Watteau's painterly skirmishes on the eighteenth-century French battlefield of cultural and political power offer a reflection of the complicated relationship that continues today between art and power, culture and society. The management of the image of the king and the state in the eighteenth century belonged to the realm of official culture – dictated from above through institutional channels by a select group of powerful individuals. During the last years of Louis XIV's reign and the regency, this task became quite difficult, given the dearth of funds in the state treasury and the reality of a king who was more in need of having his reputation protected than glorification. Official culture was diminished, and painters within the Academy became adept at skirting sensitive issues and seeking commissions from outside the official venues.

We cannot discuss Watteau's new categorical modes or his breaking of boundaries without addressing his use of elements from popular, or low, culture and from commercial culture. Although Watteau understood and could manipulate a variety of cultural discourses, I would not argue that his inclusion of low elements necessarily reflects his class allegiance or embrace of the values associated with these cultural forms. Rather, their inclusion by Watteau is a part of the larger crisis of authority wherein cultural forms and discourses were fluid and shifting. The boundaries that defined official culture did not allow for a wide range of forms or modes of expression; moreover, the ideological assumptions that gave official culture its force and rationale were no longer in place by the end of the reign of Louis XIV and during the regency that followed. Low culture (which itself is such a slippery category) provided a means to a much wider range of expression than was available within the strictures of official culture. References to street language that Watteau frequently incorporates in the objects he depicts and juxtapositions that create a symbolic subtext in his work function both apart from and against the edifice of official culture.

Watteau's multiple references also articulate a practice that was already widespread – the self-conscious appropriation of low cultural forms as a sign of elite superiority. Elite participation in the uncultivated world of the Parisian fairs, in entertainments, and at public balls certainly had something to do with a Bakhtinian revelry where the lofty and the low all participated in a shared physical existence. Much of the signifying power of these social experiences, however, lay in the act of returning from this undifferentiated realm and in knowing that one had played the role of the "other" well. The elite appropriation of popular cultural forms and practices, such as their amateur theatrical performances modeled after those at the fairs, and the vogue for fairy tales, provided a signifying frame that reminded the participants of who they were not. For the crisis in authority extended to some formerly powerful members of the nobility as well as to the monarch; nobles in straitened circumstances of power could take comfort in aspects of their superiority that were not directly political. This signifying frame also allowed for the display of skills of dissimulation that were bound up with the residual cult of *honnêteté,* the refuge of a politically impotent nobility. In Watteau's paintings we are never sure if the theatrically costumed figures are real actors or not, or if the peasants are authentic peasants or masqueraders, but this pointed ambiguity nicely recapitulates the value of dissimulation within the cult of *honnêtété.*

There is a similar pointed ambiguity in *Gersaint's Signboard* in which a shop's signboard, normally considered the lowest type of commercial art, is really a work of art. Boundaries among cultural, economic, and social categories are negotiated within this framework in response to the crisis of authority. The dealer's shop, and not the Academy, came to function as an institutional fulcrum of artistic taste. Art was produced to please connoisseur-clients and not to perpetuate the power and glorify the demands of the monarch and state. The great commercial ventures that marked the regency, and the great speculative fortunes that were won and lost overnight, endowed commercial activity with a new respectability. The consumption and display of luxury items, including paintings, took on the power to confer status. Watteau's *Gersaint's Signboard* disrupted the traditional boundaries to rearticulate these emerging relationships.

Thus far I have suggested here that Watteau was good at being difficult to nail down: that he deployed painterly strategies that produced sufficient ambiguity to construct narratives and simultaneous commentaries upon them; that he communicated to his contemporaries with an ambiguity they understood about matters no one acknowledged directly; that he articulated his communications in forms of representation that reflected not only the dominant discourse but also the emergent one. Moreover, I have suggested that Watteau seemed to be working toward something in particular, that the means of expression available to an artist of Watteau's breadth were too limited for him to say what he wanted to say, and he had to figure out a way to express himself. The fact of Louis XIV's decline, the need for circumspection, the availability of genres as limited formal means of painterly expression, and the experience of Watteau's particular education all created an environment in which Watteau might come into his own as an artist. He synthesized the times and his talents to address his milieu. And because his milieu was what it was, the only way he could address it was by subverting it.

Many of those who have written about Watteau's work have fastened on an indefinable *tristesse* in it and have pronounced this tone the centrality of his work. I would argue that this tone, which is undeniably present in his work, is neither indefinable nor precisely central; rather, it is a specific expression of the world-weariness of the early-eighteenth-century France that the decline of Louis XIV produced and that Watteau best captured because it was he who grew most adept at negotiating between the compliment and the truth. The means by which Watteau negotiated that space and its significance for reading Watteau's work have been central to this book. I have argued here that Watteau created his paintings by adopting strategies of representation that relied upon thoroughly defined and generally accepted genres – visual formulae freighted with ideological content – but that he deployed the genres only to undermine the message they were supposed to convey. In the political, social, and cultural climate of early-eighteenth-century France, Watteau chose strategies of subversion because they were the only ones that enabled him to express his version of the truth.

Notes

Introduction

1 Thomas Crow, *Painters and Public Life in Eighteenth-Century Paris* (New Haven: Yale University Press, 1985); Norman Bryson, *Word and Image: French Painting of the Ancien Régime* (Cambridge: Cambridge University Press, 1981); and Robert Neuman, "Watteau's *L'Enseigne de Gersaint* and Baroque Emblematic Tradition," *Gazette des beaux-arts* 104 (November 1984): 153–64.

2 Hans-Robert Jauss, "Literary History as a Challenge to Literary Theory," *New Literary History* 2 (1970): 14–15. For an elaboration of his theory of reception, see, Hans-Robert Jauss, *Towards an Aesthetic of Reception* (Minneapolis: University of Minnesota Press, 1982).

3 Roger Chartier, *Forms and Meanings: Texts, Performances, and Audiences from Codex to Computer* (Philadelphia: University of Pennsylvania Press, 1995); Roger Chartier, *Cultural History between Practices and Representations* (Cambridge: Polity, in Association with Blackwell, 1988); Roger Chartier, *Cultural Uses of Print in Early Modern France* (Princeton: Princeton University Press, 1987); and Roger Chartier, *On the Edge of the Cliff: History, Language, and Practices* (Baltimore: Johns Hopkins University Press, 1997).

4 Raymond Williams, *The Sociology of Culture* (New York: Schocken Books, 1982).

5 Chartier, *Cultural History,* 13 ff.; and Robert Darnton, "The Symbolic Element in History," *Journal of Modern History* 58 (1986): 218–34.

6 Robert Darnton, *The Great Cat Massacre and Other Episodes in French Cultural History* (New York: Basic Books, 1984).

Chapter One. Watteau's *Departure of the Italian Comedians in 1697* and the Battle of the Theaters

1 The other copy is #231 in the catalogue of the *Vente des Floralies,* 1970, 4 Juin, Versailles, p. 88, and reproduction on p. 89. Two other sales catalogues list a painting by Watteau titled "Les Acteurs italiens chassés de l'hôtel de Bourgogne par ordonnance de Louix XVI"; Vente Anonyme, 1837 and the Vente Berre, 1839. See Jean Ferré, ed., *Watteau,* 4 vols. (Madrid: Athena Editions, 1972), 3:928–29.

2 This is the standard work on the engravings done after Watteau's paintings. Émile Dacier and Albert Vuaflart, *Jean de Jullienne et les graveurs de Watteau au XVIIIe siècle,* 4 vols. (Paris: La Société pour l'étude de la gravure française à l'occasion du bi-centenaire de la mort de Watteau, 1921–29), 2:59.

3 Watteau's other historical subject, *Louis XIV Presenting the Cordon Blue to M. de Bourgogne,* was painted c. 1710. This work is now lost, but we know of its composition through the engraving done by Nicolas de Larmessin in 1729.

4 Dacier and Vuaflart, *Graveurs de Watteau,* 2:59: "scènes familières, champêtres, théâtrales ou galantes & des figures de caractère, c'est-à-dire qu'ils représentent l'art de Watteau dans ce qu'il a de plus original & de plus personnel."

5 Marianne Roland-Michel is the only Watteau scholar to my knowledge to question the subject of this work. "[T]here is an unusual painting, known only from its print (DV 184), representing *Le Départ des comédiens italiens* (The Departure of the Italian Actors), an event which Watteau cannot have witnessed as the banning of the commedia del'arte occurred in 1697. In fact we know nothing of this work – neither its date, nor its intentions, and even the subject may not correspond to the title of the print." Marianne Roland-Michel, *Watteau: An Artist of the Eighteenth Century* (New York: Alpine Fine Arts, 1984), 173.

6 Norman Bryson, *Word and Image: French Painting of the Ancien Régime* (Cambridge: Cambridge University Press, 1981), 58–88.

7 Edmond and Jules de Goncourt, *French Eighteenth-Century Painters,* trans. Robin Ironside (Ithaca, NY: Cornell University Press, 1948), 5–7.

8 Even Donald Posner, who claims that the meaning of Watteau's *fêtes* are not at all mysterious or melancholy, falls back on the assumptions that mark this sort of writing:

> They [the *fêtes*] do not show real life veiled in fantasy, but a fantasy in the shape of everyday reality. . . . In Watteau's work the momentary disappears as permanent reality; the placid city park is all of nature, amorous play is the center of man's universe. It is none of it true, but it is lovely to believe for an instant – as lovely today as in the days of Watteau.
>
> One might say that Watteau dreamed better than his contemporaries, and that he refined and heightened their dreams; in a sense he dreamed for them. Donald Posner, *Antoine Watteau* (Ithaca, NY: Cornell University Press, 1984), 181.

9 The dates attributed to Watteau's *Departure* in the major works that discuss the image are as follows: Ettore Camesasca and Pierre Rosenberg, *Tout l'oeuvre peint de Watteau* (Paris: Flammarion, Les Classiques de l'Art, 1970), 89 (1705); Dacier and Vuaflart, *Graveurs de Watteau,* 1: 58–59 (during his apprenticeship with Claude Gillot); Hélène Adhémar and René Huyghe, *Watteau, sa vie – son oeuvre* (Paris: Tisné, 1950), 72 (1704–9); François Boucher, "A propos d'une récente acquisition du Louvre: Gillot et Watteau," *Gazette des beaux-arts* 8 (September-October 1923): 170 (1704–5); Paul Mantz, *Antoine Watteau* (Paris: Librairie Illustrée, 1892), 92 (1716); Virgile Josz, *Antione Watteau: Moeurs du XVIIIe siècle* (Paris: Société du Mercure de France, 1903), 26 (toward 1716); Marianne Roland-Michel and Daniel Rabreau, *Les arts du théâtre de Watteau à Fragonard* (Bordeaux: Galerie des Beaux-Arts, 1980), 118 (1705); Posner, *Antoine Watteau,* 49 (possibly under Gillot).

10 The engraving was first announced in the *Mercure de France,* July 1729, p. 1603. The following text appears on the lower-left-hand side of the engraving, and on the right, a Latin translation.

> Departure des Comédiens Italiens en 1697
>
> Gravé d'Après le Tableau Original peint par Watteau haut de
>
> 1 pied 7 pouces sur 1 pied 11 pouces de large.

In smaller print, between the French and Latin texts, is "Tirée du Cabinet de M. L'Abbé Penety."

11 Mariette frequently cites the name of Penetti in his letters to Italian correspondents. See G. Bottari and S. Ticozzi, eds., *Raccolta di lettere sulla pittura, scultura, ed architectura scritte da più celebri personnaggi che dette arte fiorirono dal secoto XV al XVII,* 8 vols. (Milan: G. Silvestri, 1822), 2:passim.

12 Unfortunately, no copy of this pamphlet is known to have survived. However, there is a reference to it in Thomas-Simon Gueullette, *Notes et souvenirs sur le théâtre italien au XVIIIe siècle,* ed. J. E. Gueullette (Paris: E. Droz, 1938), 23. Gueullette recounts Mezzetin's comments about this pamphlet: "C'étoit selon lui, l'histoire de feue Madame de Maintenon et elle contenait une satire des plus sanglantes contre cette dame. Le Roi en avait été outre et avait donné les ordres les plus rigoureux pour la suppression de ce livre, et pour empêcher qu'il ne devint public."

13 Elisabeth Charlotte d'Orléans, *Correspondance,* 2 vols., trans. Runet (Paris, 1853), 2:296. Letter to M. de Harling, 20 December 1720, cited in Pierre Mélèse, *Le théâtre et le public à Paris sous Louis XIV, 1659–1715* (Paris: Droz, 1934), 54: "Ils avaient disait-on représenté la vieille guenipe de la façon la plus drôle."

14 Anne-Marguerite Du Noyer, *Lettres historiques et galantes,* 9 vols. (LaHay: Pierre Husson, 1761), 1:50, cited in Mélèse, *Théâtre et public,* 54.

15 Saint-Simon, *Mémoires* (Paris: Hachette, 1921) 4:124, cited in Mélèse, *Théâtre et public,* 54. Charles Pinot Duclos, *Mémoires secrets,* 2 vols. (Paris: Cotin, 1808), 2:507: "on les a chassés pour avoir joué *La Fausse Prude,* dans laquelle on dit que Mme de Maintenon s'est reconnue."

16 The argument is explicated and documented most clearly in Gueullette, *Notes et souvenirs,* 23–25. See also Émile Campardon, *Les comédiens du roi de la troupe italienne pendant les deux derniers siècles,* 2 vols. (Paris: Berger-Levrault, 1880; reprint, Geneva: Slatkine Reprints, 1970), 1:xxii–xxiv; and Pierre Mélèse, "A propos de l'expulsion des Comédiens Italiens en 1697," *Revue historique et littéraire* 44 (1937): 553–37.

17 See Gueullette, *Notes et souvenirs,* 22–24. The play is sometimes attributed to Le Noble; see *Mercure historique et politique de la Haye,* June 1697, cited in Mélèse, *Théâtre et public,* 52–53. For further discussion on the question of the authorship of this piece and on the closure of the Italian theater, see Giacomo Cavallucci, "Fatouville, auteur dramatique," *Revue d'histoire littéraire de la France* 43 (1936): 481–512.

18 Claude and François Parfaict, *Histoire de l'ancien théâtre italien depuis son origine en France, jusqu'à sa suppression en l'année 1697,* 2 vols. (Paris: Lambert, 1753), 2:129–30. This work is one of the most complete and reliable for the history of the theater.

> M. d'Argenson, Lieutenant-général de Police, depuis le 9 Janvier, précédent, en vertu d'une lettre de cachet du Roi, à lui addressée et accompagné d'un nombre de commissaires et d'Exempts, et de toute la Robe courte se transporte à onze heures du matin au théâtre de l'hôtel Bourgogne, et y fit apposer les scelles sur toutes les portes, non seulement des rues Mauconseil et Françoise, mais encore sur celles des loges des acteurs, avec défense à ces derniers de se présenter pour continuer leurs spectacles, Sa Magesté ne jugeant plus à propos de les garder à son service.

19 The troupe at the time of its banishment consisted of Angelo Constantini (Mezzetin); Michel Angelo Fracanzani (Polichinelle); Evariste Gherardi (Harle-

quin); Jean-Joseph Jeraton (Pierrot); Giovanni Battista Constantini (Octave); Marc Antonio Romagnesi called Cinthio (Docteur); Carlo Virgile Romagnesi, de Belmont (Leandre); Giuseppe Tortoriti, called Pascariel (Scaramouche); Catarina Biancolelli (Colombine); Angelica Toscano (Marinette): Elisabeth Daneret (Babet-la Chanteuse); Unknown (Spinette); Cadet (scene designer).

20 The best discussion of this type of image is provided by Pierre Marcel, *La peinture française au début du dix-huitième siècle* (Paris: Ancienne Maison Quantin, 1906), 207–16. For engravings of this kind of image, see Émile Dacier, *La gravure française* (Paris: Larousse, 1944); Francois Courboin, *Histoire illustrée de la gravure en France*, 4 vols. (Paris: Maurice Le Garrec, 1923–28), vol. 2; and Marianne Grivel, *Le commerce de l'estampe à Paris au XVIIe siècle* (Geneva: Librairie Droz, 1986).

21 The most detailed sources for information on the history and collection of the *cabinet du roi* are Georges Duplessis, "Le Cabinet du Roi: Collection d'estampes commandées par Louis XIV," *Le bibliophile français* 4 (1869): 87–105; Andre Jammes, "Louis XIV, sa bibliothèque et le cabinet du roi." *Library* 20, no. 1 (March 1965): 1–12; and Grivel, *Le commerce de l'estampe à Paris au XVIIe siècle.* More recently, Katie Scott has argued that the presentation of these images as diplomatic gifts allowed a means by which "French propaganda entered an international court economy as a political commodity to be circulated and exchanged." *The Rococo Interior: Decoration and Social Spaces in Early Eighteenth-Century Paris* (New Haven:Yale University Press, 1995), 178.

22 This painting by Watteau is lost; it is known through the enraving by Nicolas de Larmessin. Watteau did the painting as a favor for his friend Antoine Dieu, who had been commissioned to paint this subject for the series *L'histoire du roi.* This series, undertaken by Le Brun in 1663, represented the important moments from the king's life. Le Brun made sketches for nineteen subjects, fourteen of which were painted by various artists and then made into tapestries. Subsequently, the tapestries were engraved and made up part of the *cabinet du roi.* In the early eighteenth century a series of seven supplementary images was commissioned, only three of these images were made into tapestries; Watteau's image was not one of these. For a discussion of the collaboration between Dieu and Watteau, see Mantz, *Antoine Watteau,* 154–55. Pierre Rosenberg discusses Dieu's images in "Dieu as Draughtsman," *Master Drawings* 17, no. 2 (1979): 161–69. For more information on *L'histoire du roi,* see Daniel Meyer, *L'histoire du roy* (Paris: Editions de la Réunion des Musées Nationaux, 1980), and Maurice Fenaille, *Etat général des tapisseries de la manufacture des Gobelins depuis son origine jusq'à nos jours,* 3 vols. (Paris: Imprimerie Nationale, 1903).

23 For the various versions of Le Brun's *Conférence sur l'expression* and its influence in the eighteenth century, see Jennifer Montagu, *The Expression of the Passions: The Origin and Influence of Charles Le Brun's "Conférence sur l'expression générale et particulière"* (New Haven: Yale University Press, 1994), esp. 85–100, and Thomas Kirchner, *L'expression des passions. Ausdruck als Darstellungsproblem in der fransösischen Kunst und Kunst theorie des 17. und 18. Jahrhunderts* (Mainz: Philipp von Zabern, 1991).

24 Sarah Cohen discusses the awareness of the nuances of gesture, pose, and character in the eighteenth century. Her discussion of character and corporeal gestures in relation to Watteau's *Figures de différents caractères* is useful as well in understanding how the viewers would have been particularly sensitive to the conven-

tions of character and expression in the works under consideration here. See "Body as 'Character' in Early Eighteenth-Century French Art and Performance," *Art Bulletin* 78 (September 1996): 454–66.

25 The major maps of Paris that I have consulted include Boisseau, 1650; Gomboust (the most detailed seventeenth-century plan), 1652; Rochefort, 1675; Bullet and Blondet, 1676; Jaillot, 1713; La Caille (by 20 neighborhoods), 1714; De Largrive, 1728; Roussel, 1730; and Turgot (Bretez), 1739. On the seventeenth-century plans, the east facade is the one shown, whereas in the eighteenth-century plans, the south facade is shown. In the plan Gomboust, the south portion of the hôtel is separated from the main portion of the building whereas in the Plan de la Caille, they are clearly a single building.

26 David Illingworth, "Documents inédits et nouvelles précisions sur la théâtre de l'hôtel de Bourgogne," *Revue d'histoire du théâtre* 22 (1970): 129–30. See also David Illingworth, "L'hôtel de Bourgogne: Une salle de théâtre à l'italienne à Paris en 1647?" *Revue d'histoire du théâtre* 23 (1971): 40–49. Two other studies on the hôtel Bourgogne are Deierkauf-Holsboer, *Le théâtre de l'hôtel de Bourgogne,* 2 vols. (Paris: Editions A. G. Nizet, 1970); and W. L. Wiley, "The Hôtel Bourgogne," *Studies in Philology* 70 (December 1973): 3–109.

27 Characters of the Italian Comedy employed conventionalized gestures and movements. William Hogarth describes the individual natures of these characters in *Analysis of Beauty* (Oxford: Clarendon Press, 1955), 158–59.

> The attitudes of the harlequin are ingeniously composed of certain little quick movements of the head, hands and feet, some of which shoot out as it were from the body in straight lines, or are twirled about in little circles.
>
> Scaramouche is gravely absurd as the character is intended in over-stretched tedious movements of unnatural lengths of lines: these two characters seem to have been contrived by conceiving a direct opposition of movements. Pierrot's movements and attitudes are chiefly in perpendiculars and parallels, so is his figure and dress.
>
> Pulcinello is droll by being the reverse of all elegance, both as to movement, and figure, the beauty of variety is totally, and comically excluded from this character in every respect; his limbs are raised and let fall almost altogether at one time, in parallel directions as if his seeming fewer joints than ordinary, were no better than the hinges of a door.

28 For the gestures appropriate to the *amoureuse,* see Gustave Attinger, *L'esprit de la commedia dell'arte dans le théâtre français* (Paris: Librairie Théatrale, 1950), 39–41; and François Riccoboni, *L'art du théâtre* (Paris, 1750; reprint, Geneva: Slatkine Reprints, 1971), 4–14.

29 The figures have been identified in the catalogue entry for this painting in Roland-Michel and Rabreau, *Les arts du théâtre,* 117–18.

30 In Riccoboni's *L'art du théâtre,* 13; the author, a former Comedian in the Italian tradition, advises that performers never elevate their hands above their eye with this exception: "Mais quand une violent passion le transporte, l'Acteur peut oublier toutes les règles."

31 *Arlequin Jason ou la toison d'or* was first performed on 9 September 1684. The horse property appeared in the *Scene de triomphe.* For this scene, see Evaristo Gherardi, ed., *Théâtre italien de Gherardi, ou recueil général de toutes les comédies et scènes françoises jouées par les comédiens italiens du roi pendant tout le temps qu' ils ont été au service,* 6 vols. (Amsterdam: A. Braakman, 1701), 1:175–79. This play has been attributed to Fatouville and is discussed in Henry

Carrington Lancaster, *The Period of Racine, 1673–1700,* part IV, *A History of Dramatic Literature* (Baltimore: Johns Hopkins University Press, 1940), 617–18.

32 Bibliothèque Nationale, Collection Hénin, vol. 67, pièce no. 5873.

> Ces spectacles sont fort nouveaux
> de voir dans le siècle ou nous sommes
> des hommes porter des chevaux
> ou des chevaux changer en hommes

33 The only monograph on Gillot is Bernard Populus, *Claude Gillot (1673–1722): Catalogue de l'oeuvre gravé,* 2 vols. (Paris: Société pour l'étude de la gravure française, 1930).

34 Pierre-Jean Mariette states that Gillot designed scenes for the Opéra; see Pierre-Jean Mariette, *Abecedario de P. J. Mariette et autres notes inédites de cet amateur,* ed. Ph. de Chennevières and A. Montaiglon, 10 vols. (Paris: J. B. Dumoulin, 1859), 2:307. The scenarios written by Gillot are preserved at the Bibliothèque Nationale, manuscrit français 9312. For the marionette theater, see Émile Campardon, *Spectacles de la foire St. Germain,* 2 vols. (Paris: Berger-Levrault, 1877), 1:381. For a general discussion of Gillot's relationship with the Italian Comedians, see Populus, *Claude Gillot,* 24–37.

35 For *Livre de scènes comiques,* see Populus, *Claude Gillot,* 28 and 193–200; for *Suite de quatre scènes comiques du Théâtre Italien,* 91–95. The four paintings, reproduced in engraved form, in the latter series are *Scène de Deux Carosses* (Musée du Louvre), *Le Tombeau de Maître André* (Musée du Louvre), *Arlequin Empereur de la Lune* (Musée de Nantes), and *Le Cheval de Troie* (Musée de Langres).

36 *Arlequin Gourmand,* also commonly titled *Arlequin Soldat Gourmand,* or *Le Tombeau de Maître André,* painting (Musée du Louvre), drawing (Musée du Louvre), engraving, Populus, catalogue numbers 19 and 343. The drawing and engraving differ from the painting. The scenery in the painting is clearly italianate, whereas the scenery in the drawing and engraving shows a simple inn. *Scène de deux carosses,* also commonly titled *Deux femmes pour le pas se mettent en colère,* or *La rencontre des porteurs de chaise,* painting (Musée du Louvre); drawing (Musée du Louvre); engraving, Populus, catalogue number 348.

37 Regnard, *La foire St. Germain,* in Gherardi, *Théâtre italien,* 6:265–68.

38 *Le Tombeau de Maître André,* in Gherardi, *Théâtre italien,* 5:369–72.

39 See the useful semiotic analysis of Gillot's theatrical scenes in Norman Bryson, *Word and Image: French Painting of the Ancien Régime* (Cambridge: Cambridge University Press, 1981), 75–79.

40 Roland-Michel and Rabreau, *Les arts du théâtre,* 29–47, especially 30–31.

41 For the importance of the theater in one's social education, see Henri Lagrave, *Le théâtre et le public à Paris de 1715–1750* (Paris: Klinckseik, 1972), 613–53.

42 Roland-Michel and Rabreau, *Les arts du théâtre,* 31. For more on theatrical iconography, see François Moreau, "Iconographie théâtrale," in Margaret Grasselli and Pierre Rosenberg, *Watteau: 1684–1721* (Paris: Éditions de la Réunion des Musées Nationaux, 1984), 509–28.

43 Roland-Michel and Rabreau, *Les arts du théâtre,* 30–31. Posner, *Watteau,* 49, suggests that theatrical scenes were not part of the "high quality art business," but that these scenes grew in popularity at the beginning of the eighteenth century, and the market for them grew, too.

44 On compositional method, see Anne-Claude Philippe de Caylus, "Vie de Watteau," in Pierre Rosenberg, ed., *Vies anciennes de Watteau* (Paris: Hermann, 1984), 78–79. "Sa coutume étoit de dessiner ses études dans un livre relié, de façon qu'il en avoit toujours un grand nombre sous sa main . . . Quand il lui prenoit en gré de faire un tableau il avoit recours à son recueil. Il y choisissoit les figures qui lui convenoient le mieux pour le moment. II en formoit ses groupes, le plus souvent en consequence d'un fonds de paysage qu'il avoit conçu ou préparé. Il étoit rare même qu'il usât autrement."

45 For a discussion of this type of image and its history, see Victor Fournel, *Les cris de Paris, types et physionomies d'autrefois* (Paris: Firmin-Didot, 1887).

46 For the stage at the Hôtel Bourgogne, see Wiley, "The Hôtel Bourgogne," 77–78, and Deierkauf-Holsboer, *Théâtre de l'hôtel de Bourgogne.*

47 Mantz, *Antoine Watteau,* 92 and Josz, *Watteau,* 26 and 143–45.

48 Mantz, *Antoine Watteau,* 92: "on peut même considérer comme certain que, pour raconter cette ancienne aventure, Watteau s'est servi des figures et des accoutrements que la nouvelle troupe mettait sous ses yeux."

49 Dacier and Vuuflart, *Graveurs de Watteau,* 1:58.

50 See Georges Monval, *Les collections de la Comédie Française: Catalogue historique et raisonné* (Paris: Société de propagation des livres d'art, 1897), 69–75.

51 Monval, *Comédie Française,* 72–73.

52 For a discussion of the Gillot drawing and its relationship to *Departure,* see Martin Eidelberg, "Watteau and Gillot: A Point of Contact," *The Burlington Magazine* 116 (September 1974): 232–39. I find the relationship between the figure in the drawing and the figure in *Departure* to be generic, representing a pose commonly used in comedy. The *Departure* figure leans forward at a greater angle and appears to be moving forward. Watteau uses this pose again in *Les Comédiens Italiens,* 1716–18.

53 See note 19.

54 Tiberio Fiorelli (1604–94) made the role of Scaramouche famous in France. He played the role until the age of 80, when he died from an injury he received after falling off the stage during a performance. See Campardon, *Comédiens du roi,* 1:222–34.

Guiseppe Tortoriti took over the role of Scaramouche after the death of Fiorelli. He had played the role of Pascariel with the troupe since 1685. See Campardon, *Comédiens du roi,* 2:165–69.

55 Angelo Lolli (1622–1702) played Docteur Baloardo from 1653 until 1694, when he retired because of his age and infirmities. Campardon, *Comédiens du roi,* 1:294–96. Marc Antonio Romagnesi (1633–1703) joined the troupe in 1667 under the name of Cinthio. He played this role of *amoureux* until 1694 when he replaced Lolli as the Docteur until the banishment. Campardon, *Comédiens du roi,* 2:107–14.

56 The drawing for this frontispiece is by Pierre-Paul Sevin. See Roland-Michel and Rabreau, *Les arts du théâtre,* 169–70.

57 *Mercure Historique et Politique de la Haye,* June 1697, cited in Mélèse, *Théâtre et le public,* 52–53.

> La disgrâce des Comédiens Italiens arriva si à l'improviste qu'il eût peu de gens qui n'en fussent surpris. Chacun a raisonné là-dessus, mais les raisonnements qui ont été faits sont forts differéns. Les uns prétendent que le principal sujet de leur disgrâce, et

parce-qu'ils n'ont pas voulu supprimer, certaines expressions impures et quantité de postures indécentes dont les représentations de leur Pièces étoient remplies, quoi qu'on leur en eût plusieurs fois fait réitérer les ordres. D'autres disent que la cour de France veut absolument donner dans la dévotion; qu'après la publication de la Paix [de Ryswick], elle a résolu de supprimer toutes sortes de spectacles, et qu'elle commence par chasser les Comédiens Etrangers. Quelques-uns soutiennent qu'ils ont voulu représenter une nouvelle Pièce de Sr. Le Noble, intitulée *La Fausse Prude,* où il fait un portrait fort peu avantageux d'une Dame fort estimée du Roi. Il y en a enfin qui ne croyent pas se tromper avançant que S.M. ne les chasse que parce-que c'étoit des impudens, qui ne se faisoient quelquefois nul scruple de jouer jusqu'aux personnes de la Famille Royale, comme ils firent un jour Mme la Dauphine. Quelcune de ses raisons pouroit bien y avoir contribué. Mais je crois que la principale, ou plutôt l'unique est que par là le Roi épargne 18.000 livres tous les ans à quoi bon une si grosse dépense pour faire divertir les Parisiens dans un temps où la Cour a tant besoin d'argent?

58 *Gazette d'Amsterdam,* 23 May 1697, cited in Mélèse, *Théâtre et public,* 52. "On ne sait pas la véritable cause de cette disgrâce."

59 Germain Brice, *Description de Paris,* (Paris, 1698) 1:229, cited in Mélèse, *Théâtre et public,* 52, n. 3: "pour des raisons que l'on n'a point publiées."

60 Orléans, *Correspondance,* 1:277 (letter to Duchess de Hanover, 2 November 1702), cited in Mélèse, *Théâtre et public,* 5–6. "Depuis que le Roy n'y va plus [à la comédie], c'est devenu un péché."

61 For a discussion of this antitheatre movement, see Mélèse, *Théâtre et public,* 2–6; Lancaster, *Period of Racine,* 5–9. For the official seventeenth-century point of view, see Jacques Benigne Boussuet, *Maximes et réflexions sur la comédie* (Paris: J. Anisson, 1694).

62 Mélèse, *Théâtre et public,* 51.

63 Philippe de Courcillon Dangeau, *Journal de la Cour de Louis XIV,* 19 vols., ed. Eudore Soulié (Paris: Firmin-Didot, 1854–60), 2:101, cited in Mélèse, *Théâtre et public,* 51: "tous les mots à double-entendre qui sont trop libre."

64 Mélèse, "Expulsion des Comédiens," 535–37.

65 *Relations véritables,* 31 December 1694, cited in Mélèse, *Théâtre et public,* 51, n. 3: "la Sorbonne [s'étant] assemblée au sujet des Comédies et des Opéras . . . [a fait] remontrer à M. l'Archevêque que les Comédiens Italiens étoient trop libres sur leur pièces."

66 See Mélèse, *Théâtre et public,* 52–54, for these journals and gazettes.

67 For a concise history of the Comédie Française, see Georges Mongrédien, *Daily Life in the French Theater at the Time of Molière,* trans. Claire Elaine Engel (London: George Allen & Unwin, 1969), 97–104.

68 *Lettre de Cachet pour l'établissement des Comediens du Roi,* October 1680, cited in Mélèse, *Théâtre et public,* 421. "Sadite Magesté veut que ladite seule Troupe puisse représenter les Comédies dans Paris faisant deffenses à tous autres Comédiens François de s'establir dans la Ville et Fauxbourgs de Paris sans ordre exprès de S.M."

69 For a brief history of the Opéra, see Mongrédien, *French Theater,* 113–20.

70 *Ordannance portant défense aux Comédiens de se servir dans leurs représentations de plus de deux voix et de six violins,* cited in Mélèse, *Théâtre et public,* 417–18: "apporter un préjudice considérable à l'execution des ouvrages par le théâtre du St. Jean-Baptiste de Lully."

71 For a brief history of the Italian Comedy in France there are many sources; see, among them Virginia Scott, *The Commedia dell'Arte in Paris: 1644–1697* (Charlottesville: University of Virginia Press, 1990); Mongrédien, *French Theater,* 105–12; G. Attinger, L'esprit de la commedia dell'arte dans le théâtre français (Paris: Librairie théâtrale, 1950); Isadore Schwarz, *The Commedia dell'Arte and Its Influence on French Comedy* (Paris: H. Samuel, 1933). For more detailed chronicles, see Campardon, *Comédiens du roi,* and Parfaict and Parfaict, *Ancien théâtre italien.*

72 In act 4, scene I, of *Les Chinois* by Regnard and Dufresny, Colombine proclaimed: "Nos équipages seroient aussi superbes que les vôtres, si nous voulions faire des exactions sur le public, & mettre, comme vous, nos premières Représentations au double." Gherardi, *Théâtre italien,* 4:205.

73 Lancaster, *Period of Racine,* 605.

74 *Mémoire pour les Comédiens du Roy contre Chas. Dolet,* Archives Nationale, AD VIII 10, cited in Mélèse, *Théâtre et public,* 54, n. 1. "En l'année 1698, les Comédiens italiens ayant plusieurs fois désobéi aux Ordres que le Roy leur avoit fait donner, de ne point mêler de scènes françoises dans leurs Pièces, parce que les Comédiens François s'en estoient plaints, et que cela estoit contraire à leurs privilèges, Sa Majesté informée de leurs fréquents désobéissances, les congédia, et M. le Duc de Beauvilliers de faire fermer leur Théâtre, ce qui fut exécuté."

75 *Nouvelles extraordinaires de Leide,* 6 June 1697, cited in Mélèse, *Théâtre et public,* 55, n. 2: "ils ne pourront plus parler François, mais toujours Italien dans leurs pièces."

76 Mongrédien, *French Theater,* 110.

77 *Retour de la Foire de Bezons,* in Gherardi, *Théâtre Italien,* 6:135–72.

78 *Lettre de Pontchartrain à la reynie,* 8 January 1696, cited in Georges-Bernard Depping, ed., *Correspondance administrative sous le règne de Louis XIV,* 4 vols. (Paris: Impr. Impérial, 1850–55), 2:711: "s'il leur arrivoit de faire quelques postures indécentes, ou de dire des mots équivoques et quelque chose que soit contre l'honnêteté S.M. les cassera, et les renvoyera en Italie. Elle veut qu'à cet effet vous envoyiez tous les jours de Comédie quelqu'un de confiance qui vous rendre compte de ce qui se passera, enfin qu'à la première contravention, vous fassiez fermer leur théâtre."

79 Saint-Simon, *Mémoires,* 4:124, cited in Mélèse, *Théâtre et public,* 54, n. 3.

> Le Roi chassa fort précipitamment toute la troupe des Comédiens Italiens, et n'en voulut plus d'autre. Tant qu'ils n'avaient fait que se déborder en ordures sur leur théâtre, et quelquefois en impiétés, on n'avoit fait qu'en rire; mais ils s'avisèrent de jouer une pièce qui s'appelait, *La Fausse Prude,* où Mme de Maintenon fut aisément reconnue. Tout le monde y courut: mais après trois ou quatre représentations qu'ils donnèrent de suite, parce que le gain les y engagea, ils eurent ordre de fermer leur théâtre et de vuider le Royaume en un mois. Cela fit grand bruit, et si ces comédiens y perdirent leur établissement par leur hardiesse et leur folie, celle qui les fit chasser n'y gagna pas, par la licence avec laquelle ce ridicule événement donna lieu d'en parler.

80 Orléans, *Correspondance,* 2:295, cited in Mélèse, *Théâtre et public,* 54.

81 Jeffrey Ravel discusses the importance of the printed editions of the Italian Comedians' plays by Evaristo Gherardi in *The Contested Parterre: Public Theater and French Political Culture, 1680–1791* (Ithaca: Cornell University Press, 1999), 113–118.

82 For an excellent synthesis of the materials on the fairs, and a description of them, see Robert Isherwood, "Entertainment in the Parisian Fairs in the Eighteenth Century," *Journal of Modern History* 53 (March 1981): 24–48; and Robert Isherwood, *Farce and Fantasy: Popular Entertainment in Eighteenth-Century Paris* (New York: Oxford University Press, 1986), 22–59. Other classic works on fairs and carnivals include Emmanuel Le Roi Ladurie, *Carnival at Romans* (New York: Braziller, 1970); and M. Bakhtin, *Rabelais and His World* (Cambridge, MA: MIT Press, 1968).

83 For the variety of performances to be seen at the Parisian fairs, see Campardon, *Spectacles de la foire*; and François Parfaict, *Mémoires pour servir à l'histoire des spectacles de a foire,* 2 vols. (Paris: Briasson, 1743).

84 Campardon, *Spectacles de la foire,* 1:xviii.

85 Parfaict, *Spectacles de la foire,* 1:11. "La suppression de la troupe des Comédiens Italiens offrit un vaste champs aux entrepreneurs des jeux de la Foire, que se regardeant comme héritiers leurs pièces de théâtre, en donnèrent plusieurs fragmens à cette foire, ajoutant à leur troupe des acteurs propres à les représenter. Le public qui regrettoit les Italiens courut en foule à voir les copies & s'y divertit beaucoup."

86 Joachim C. Nemeitz, *Séjour de Paris: C'est-à-dire instructions fidèles pour le voiageurs de condition* (Leiden: Jean van Abcoude, 1727), 170: "tout y est pêle mêle, les maistres avec les valets & laquais, les filoux avec les honnêtes gens. Les courtisans les plus raffinez; les plus jolies filles, les filoux les plus subtils, sont comme entrelacez ensemble."

87 Isherwood, "Entertainment in the Parisian Fairs," 27.

88 Nemeitz, *Séjour de Paris,* 174. "J'ai vu souvent avec étonnement que même des Dames de condition ont pu entendre & voir des saltez sans rougir de honte; que dis-je, elles n'ont pas pu cacher le contentement qu'elles en ressentoient puisqu'elles rioient de bonne coeur."

89 Isherwood, "Entertainment in the Parisian Fairs," 27.

90 The political dimension of Parisian theater and entertainments is thoughtfully discussed in Isherwood, *Farce and Fantasy,* 81–97.

91 An interesting discussion of how difficult it was to control the fair *spectacles* can be found in Arthur Heulhard, *La foire Saint Laurent: Son histoire et ses spectacles* (Paris: A. Lemerre, 1878), 193.

92 Henry Carrington Lancaster, *Sunset: A History of Parisian Drama in the Last Years of Louis XIV* (Baltimore: Johns Hopkins Press, 1945), 311–31; Maurice Albert, *Les théâtres de la foire* (1900; reprint, New York: Burt Franklin, 1970), 35–36.

93 The details and documents concerning these theatrical battles for the years 1697–1715 are best chronicled in Parfaict, *Spectacles de la foire,* 1:4–175.

94 Parfaict, *Spectacles de la foire,* 1:17–18: "défense a tous particuliers de représenter aucune Comédie ni farce, & pour y avoir contrevenu, condamnation de quinze cens livres de dommages & interests envers les Comediens du Roi."

95 Parfaict, *Spectacles de la foire,* 1:48.

96 Parfaict, *Spectacles de la foire,* 1:63–64, and Campardon, *Spectacles de la foire,* 2:176–77.

97 Parfaict, *Spectacles de la foire,* 1:100–101.

98 Parfaict, *Spectacles de la foire,* 1:108–10.

99 Parfaict, *Spectacles de la foire,* 1:137.

100 For a discussion of Watteau's iconographical substitutions, see Ronald Paulson, *Emblem and Expression: Meaning in English Art of the Eighteenth Century* (Cambridge, MA: Harvard University Press, 1975), 95–104. Similar ideas, and the notion that Watteau creates a modern allegory, are discussed in a roundabout manner in Calvin Seerveld, "Tell-tale Statues in Watteau's Painting," *Eighteenth-Century Studies* 14 (Winter 1980–81): 151–80. See also a semiological discussion of rococo iconography that has bearing on Watteau's works in Alain Guillerm, "Le système de l'iconographie galante," *Dix-huitième siècle,* no. 12 (1980): 177–94.

101 Bryson, *Word and Image,* 58–88.

102 This point and other interesting observations are brought to the fore in Linda Nochlin, "Watteau: Some Questions of Interpretation," *Art in America* 73 (January 1985): 68–87.

103 Bryson, *Word and Image,* 84.

104 Édouard Fournier and Francisque Michel, *Le livre d'or des métiers. Histoire des hôtelleries, cabarets, hôtels garnis et des anciennes communautés* (Paris: Seri, 1859), 121.

105 Édouard Fournier, *Histoire des enseignes de Paris* (Paris: E. Dentu, 1884), 149; and Albert-André Patin de La Fizelière, *Vins à la mode et cabarets au XVIIe siècle* (Paris: René Pincebourde, 1866), 51 and 62.

106 Fournier, *Histoire des enseignes,* 149; Charles Fedgal, *Les vieilles enseignes de Paris* (Paris: Eugène Figuière, 1913), 155; Édouard Fournier, "Les cafés sous Louis XIV," *La siécle,* 30 November 1854 and 3 March 1855.

107 "Ode a la louange de tous les cabarets de Paris," in F. Lachèvre, ed., *Oeuvres libertines de Ch. le Petit* (Paris: H. Champion, 1918), vol. 5, *Disciples et successeurs de Théophile de Viau. Les oeuvres de Claude le Petit.* For a discussion of poetry about cafes, and cabarets, as well as poetry about places in Paris, see Pierre Citron, *La poesie de Paris dans la littérature française: De Rousseau à Baudelaire* (Paris: Éditions de Minuit, 1961).

108 *Arlequin Protée,* in Gherardi, *Théâtre Italien,* 1:73–112.

109 *Arlequin Protée,* in Gherardi, *Théâtre Italien,* 1:78.

Aubergist I: Venez loger chez nous Monsieur.
Bon logis à pied et à cheval.
C'est Au Croissant.
Arlequin: Au Croissant? Voila une Enseigne
de mauvaise augure.

110 A number of books treat signboards and their lore and history. The most comprehensive is Fournier, *Histoire des enseignes;* other useful sources include Henry Baudin, *L'enseigne et l'affiche* (Geneva: Fédération des Sociétés Artistiques de Geneva, 1905); Jean-Daniel Blavignac, *Histoire des enseignes d'hôtelleries, d'auberges et de cabarets* (Genève: Grosset & Trembley, 1874); Clément de Ris, Louis, "Les enseignes de Paris," *Mélanges de littérature et d'histoire* vol. 6 (Paris: La Société des bibliophiles, 1877); Fedgal, *Vieilles enseignes;* E. La Quérière, *Recherches historiques sur les enseignes des maisons particulières* (Paris: V. Didron, 1852); Rosine Grange, "Enseignes anciennes, un langage perdu," *Arts et decoration,* no. 184 (1975): 90–95, and an interesting work by Balzac, [Honoré Balzac], *Batteur de pavé: Petit dictionnaire critique et anecdotique des enseignes de Paris* (Paris: Marchand de nouveautés, 1826). This work focuses on nineteenth-century signs, but also makes useful references to the older traditions of signboards.

111 For a discussion of this literature, see Fournier, *Histoire des enseignes,* 285–87.
112 Cited in Fournier, *Histoire des enseignes,* 286.

> Nous choisîmes, pour le roy, *Le Mouton;*
> Monsieur fut logé *Au Papillon,* et la reine
> *Au Chapeau Rouge;* mais parce que le logis
> et principalement les chambres étoient mal
> accommodés, nous y logeâmes son train, et
> sa personne eût pour elle, *La Saucisson d'Italie.* . . .
> les filles furent logées à *La Petite Vertu*; . . .

"*Mouton*" not only refers to sheeplike qualities in a person (someone who is a ninny) but also is slang for a decoy or prison spy. "*Au Papillon,*" in this context, refers to a person who behaves in a flighty manner and who is attracted to glittery, bright objects. "*Chapeau Rouge*" is slang for someone who openly advertises his or her "hot-blooded" nature.

113 *Le nouveau fourrier de la Cour. Reformant les autres logemens & les accommodant mieux au temps & aux lieux & logeant accommodément ceux qui avoient été oubliez* (Paris: Privately published, 1652), 3. "Puis que la cour change souvent de quartier et que ce n'est pas d'aujourdhui qu'on a marqué les appartemens des personnes illustres qui la composent, dans les logis où pendant pour Enseignes des images qui se rapportent le mieux à l'état de leur fortune présente, ou à leur humeur; il me doit être permis d'enchérir sur celui dont le caprice vient d'assigner la demeure de chacun, en des lieux dont le séjour est mal agréable à quelques-uns."
114 Philibert-Joseph Le Roux, *Dictionnaire comique, satirique, critique, burlesque, libre et proverbial,* 2 vols. (Lyon: Chez les héritiers Berringos, 1735), 1:171: "les cornes que porte un homme qui est cocu."
115 Le Roux, *Dictionnaire comique,* 1:171: "être logé au croissant signifie être de la confrérie d'Acteon, être au nombre des cocus."
116 Regnard, *La baguette de Vulcain,* in Gherardi, *Théâtre italien,* 4:213–38.
117 Regnard, *La baguette de Vulcain, L'augmentation,* in Jean-François Regnard, *Oeuvres complètes de Regnard,* 6 vols. (Paris: Lefèvre, 1810), 6:101–19.
118 Bibliothèque Nationale, Collection Hénin, vol. 68, pièce no. 6016.

> Le Soleil vagabond jamais ne
> se repose il va toujours de maison
> en maison, que de maris feroient la
> même chose s'il leur étoit permis de
> sortir de prison mais d'un époux
> la demeure est certain quelque
> chemin qu'il prenne qu'il aille qu'il
> vienne son ascendant
> toujours l'entraîne
> loger au corissant.

119 This view is presented in the unflattering biography of Mme. de Maintenon, Laurent de La Beaumelle, ed., *Mémoires pour servir à l'histoire de Mme de Maintenon et à celle du siècle passé,* 6 vols. (Amsterdam: By the author, 1755).
120 Gilles Boileau, cited in La Beaumelle, *Mémoires,* 1:167.

> Voi, sur quoi ton erreur se fond
> Scarron! de croie que le monde

Te va voir pour ton entretien
Quoi? ne vois-tu pas, grosse bête,
Si tu gratois un peu ta tête
Que tu le devinerois bien?

121 La Beaumelle, *Mémoires,* 3:41.

122 Du Noyer, *Lettres,* 1:6. "Je Voudrais bien que ce fût dans ces climats où l'on jouit d'une liberté, où l'on peut chanter la Maintenon & Noailles [Mme. de Maintenon's favorite at court] sans craindre la Bastille."

123 The most important of these is R. Bussy Rabutin, *Histoire amoureuse des Gaules, suivie de La France galante, romans satiriques du XIIe siècle attribués au comte de Bussy,* 2 vols. (Paris: Garnier frères, 1868). The work is a collection of libels. Madame de Maintenon is the subject of *La France galante, La suite de France galante,* and *Le divorce roial.*

124 *The Cabinet Open'd; or, the Secret History of the Amours of Madame de Maintenon with the French King,* trans. from the French (London: Printed for Richard Baldwin, 1690), preface. (This work was later printed in France as part of Bussy Rabutin's *Histoire amoureuse des Gaules.)*

125 *Secret History,* 139.

Chapter Two. Watteau's Military Paintings: Conflicts and Confluences

1 E. F. Gersaint, "Abrégé de la vie d'Antoine Watteau," in Pierre Rosenberg, ed., *Vies anciennes de Watteau* (Paris: Hermann, 1984), 33–34:

> Ce fut chez lui [Audran] qu'il prit du goût pour les ornements dont nous avons plusieurs échantillons dans les morceaux de ce genre que l'on a gravés d'après lui. Watteau cedpendant qui ne voulait pas en demeurer là, ni passer sa vie à travailler pour autrui, et qui se sentait en état d'imaginer, hasarda un tableau de génie qui représente un départ de troupes, et qui fit à ses temps perdus: il le montra au sieur Audran, habile homme, et en état de juger d'une belle chose, fut effrayé du mérite qu'il reconnut dans ce tableau; mais la crainte de perdre un sujet qui lui était utile, et sur lequel il se reposait assez souvent pour l'arrangement, et même pour la composition des morceaux qu'il avait à exécuter, lui conseilla légèrement de ne point passer son temps à ces sortes de pièces libres et de fantaisies, qui ne pourraient que lui faire perdre le goût dans lequel il donnait. Watteau n'en fut point la dupe; le parti ferme qu'il avait pris de sortir, joint à un petit désir de revoir Valenciennes, le déterminèrent totalement. Le prétexte d'aller voir ses parents lui servit de moyen honnête; mais comment faire? L'argent lui manquait, et son tableau devenait son unique ressource: il ignorait comment il fallait s'y prendre pour s'en procurer le débit. Dans cette occasion il eut recours à M. Spoude. actuellement vivant, peintre à peu près de mêmes Cantons que lui, et son ami particulier: le hasard conduisit M. Spoude chez le sieur Sirios mon beau-père à qui il montra ce tableau. Le prix était fixé à 60 livres, et le marché fut conclu sur le champ. Watteau vint recevoir son argent; il paritit gaiement pour Valenciennes comme cet ancien sage de la Grèce; c'était là toute sa fortune, et sûrement il ne s'était jamais vu si riche. Ce marché fut l'origin de la liaison que feu mon beau-père a toujours eue avec lui jusq'à sa mort; et il fut si satisfait de ce tableau, qu'il le pria instamment de lui en faire le pendant qu'il lui envoya effectivement de Valenciennes. C'est le second morceau que le sieur Cochin a gravé; il represente une halte d'armée; le tout en était d'après nature: il en demanda 200 livres qui lui furent données. Ces deux tableaux ont toujours passé pour deux des plus belles chose qui soient sorties de sa main.

2 For a discussion of the conventions in artists' biographies, see Ernst Kris and Otto Kurtz, *Legend, Myth, and Magic in the Image of the Artist* (New Haven: Yale University Press, 1979). I discuss more specifically how Gersaint manipulates the conventions of artists' biographies to showcase his own relationship with Watteau in chapter 4 of this book and in "Gersaint's Biography of Antoine Watteau: Reading between and beyond the Lines," *Eighteenth-Century Studies* 25 (Summer 1992): 545–60.

3 *Dictionnaire abrégé de peinture et d'architecture* (Paris: 1746), 2:375–76, reprinted in Rosenberg, *Vies de Watteau,* 41.

4 In "Une réponse anonyme" that appeared in the *Dictionnaire abrégé de peinture et d'architecture* of 1746, reprinted in Rosenberg, *Vies de Watteau,* 40–42, the anonymous author implies that the *Départ des Troupes* was ultimately responsible for his initial entrée into the Royal Academy of Painting and Sculpture. "La Fose, peintre célèbre de l'Académie, l'ayant vu, en fut si content qu'il présenta Watteau à ses confrères, qui s'empressèrent de le recevoir parmi eux." The Comte de Caylus's biography also cites the military paintings as marking a turning point in his development: "Il fit des marches et des repos de soldats, d'un faire absolument opposé à celui de ce maître [Claude Gillot], et ces premiers tableaux ont peut-être églé ce qu'il a fait de plus beau dans la suite." "La vie d'Antoine Watteau peintre de figures et de paysages sujets galants et modernes," in Rosenberg, *Views de Watteau,* 62.

5 "La vie d'Antoine Watteau," in Rosenberg, *Vies de Watteau,* 62.

6 There has been disagreement in past scholarship over which work is actually the "60 livre painting" and which the "200 livre painting." Since Gersaint's descriptions are somewhat generic and since almost all the military paintings represent either halts or marches, this disagreement is not surprising. I am swayed by the identification of the two paintings as *Return from the Campaign (Retour de campagne)* and *Bivouac (Le camp volant)* on the basis of formal and thematic similarities: that they were both engraved by Cochin, which Gersaint specifies in his account; their similarities in size suggesting that they were intended as pendants; and Mariette's confirmation in his Pierre-Jean Mariette, *Abecedario* (Paris: F. de Nobele, 1966), 109. For dissenting views, see Hélène Adhémar and René Huyghe, *Watteau, sa vie – son oeuvre* (Paris: Tisné, 1950); Émile Dacier and Albert Vuaflart, *Jean de Jullienne et les graveurs de Watteau au XVIIIe siècle,* 4 vols. (Paris: La Société pour l'étude de la gravure française à l'occasion du bi-centenaire de la mort de Watteau, 1921–29); and Paul Foucart, *Antoine Watteau à Valenciennes* (Paris: E. Plon, 1892).

7 Oliver Banks, *Watteau and the North: Studies in the Dutch and Flemish Baroque Influence on French Rococo Painting* (New York: Garland Press, 1972), 143–50; and Donald Posner, *Antoine Watteau* (Ithaca, NY: Cornell University Press, 1984), 31–40.

8 I am indebted to Susan Siegfried's discussion of the relationship between ideologies of war and traditions in military painting in "Naked History: The Rhetoric of Military Painting in Postrevolutionary France," *Art Bulletin* 75 (June 1993): 235–58, for both confirming and expanding the direction of my thoughts on the subject.

9 A recent exhibition catalogue on northern military subjects is arranged according to generic types. Michel Van Maarseveen, Jos W. L. Hilkhijsen, and Jacques Dane,

Beelden van een strijd: Oorlog en kunst vóór de Vrede van Munster (Delft: Waanders Uitgevers, Zwolle Stedelijk Museum Het Prinsenhof, Delft, 1998).

10 F. C. Legrand, *Les peintres Flamands de genre au XVIIe siècle* (Brussels: Editions Meddens, 1963), 15.

11 It might even be useful to view this kind of image as a visual analog to official military histories, such as Charles Sevin Quincy, *Histoire militaire du regne de Louis le Grand,* 8 vols. (Paris: Chez Denis Mariette at autres, 1726). This chronicle is framed by a panegyric; it includes a *récit* of the major battles, followed by a recapitulation with the principal facts.

12 The *Petites Conquêtes du Roi* is a series that is smaller in format than the *Conquêtes du Roi* by Van der Meulen. The appellation *"petite"* has nothing to do with the importance or ranking of the military victory.

13 For Van der Meulen, see L'administration générale du mobilier national des manufactures nationales des Gobelins, de Beauvais, et de la Savonnerie, *La Route du Nord. Van der Meulen. Dessins et soies peintes,* exh. cat. (Paris, 1990); Charles Mauricheau-Beaupré, "Un peintre de Louis XIV aux armées: Van der Meulen," *Jardin des Arts* 37 (November 1957): 1–10; Isabelle Richefort, "Nouvelles précisions sur la vie d'Adam François Van der Meulen, peintre historiographe de Louis XIV," *Bulletin de la société de l'histoire de l'art français* (1986): 57–80; Isabelle Richefort, "Adam François Van der Meulen: L'homme, l'oeuvre et l'art," Thèse, Ecole des Chartres, 1980; Maurice Le Maire, *Adam Frans Van der Meulen et la guerre de Holland (1672–1678),* 2 vols. (Mémoire, University of Paris IV-Sorbonne, 1992).

14 Joël Cornette insightfully explores the complex relationship between war, the state, and royal power in *Le roi de guerre: Essai sur la souveraineté dans la France du Grand Siècle* (Paris: Editions Payot & Rivages, 1993). Peter Burke more specifically discusses the making of the king's image in *The Fabrication of Louis XIV* (New Haven: Yale University Press, 1992).

15 Van der Meulen's images are frequently found as truthful illustrations in texts on the period and on military history. For a discussion of the documentary use of paintings in military history, see Olle Cederlöf, "The Battle Painting as a Historical Source: An Inquiry into the Principles," *Revue internationale d'histoire militaire* (1967): 119–44. I thank Pia Cuneo for bringing this article to my attention.

16 Paul Sonnino discusses the economic basis of war in the early modern period in "Louis XIV and the Dutch War," in *Louis XIV and Europe,* ed. Ragnhild Hatton (New York: Macmillan Press, 1976), 153–78.

17 Richefort, "Nouvelles précisions sur Van der Meulen," 61: "c'est cela, je me retrouve."

18 Antoine Schnapper, "Le Grand Dauphin et les tableaux de Meudon," *Revue de l'art* 1–2 (1968): 57–64.

19 I discuss the *Cabinet du Roi* and its ideological function in chapter 1.

20 Richefort, "Nouvelles précisions sur Van der Meulen," 61.

21 The major producers of the *almanachs royaux* include the family business of the Jollains, de Larmessin, the Moncornets, the Landrys, Robert Nanteuil, the Bonnarts, and the Langlois. See Roger-Armand Weigert, "Les almanachs royaux," *Médecine de France* no. 215 (1970): 25–40.

22 Although referred to as the Italian tradition, a strong, active tradition of this tumultuous type of painting could also be found in the north. Painters such as Alt-

dorfer, de Vinck, and Snayers (who was Van der Meulen's teacher) emphasized, sometimes in a most fantastic manner, the tumult of battle.

23 Etienne Parrocel, *Monographie des Parrocel* (Marseille: Imprimerie, 1861); Antoine Schnapper, "Quelques oeuvres de Joseph Parrocel," *La Revue des arts,* 4 and 5 (1959): 163–76; Antoine Schnapper, "Deux tableaux de Joseph Parrocel au Musée de Rouen," *La revue du Louvre et des musées de France* 20 (1970): 78–82.

24 The *Collection Hennin* and the series *Histoire de France,* both at the Bibliothèque Nationale, are useful sources for imagery dealing with current events.

25 At the Battle of Malplaquet, 90,000 allied troops fought against 65,000 French troops; 6,500 allies were killed and 14,000 wounded, while 4,000 French were killed and 8,000 wounded. See Philippe Contamine, ed., *Histoire militaire de la France. 1 Des origines à 1715* (Paris: Presses Universitaires de France, 1992), 533–35.

26 We cannot be certain when in 1709 Watteau left Paris for Valenciennes. Most likely, he left after the results of the Prix de Rome competition in which he participated were announced on 31 August. It is unlikely that he left any earlier that year because of the military turmoil in the area and because of a long hard winter that had lasted, by all accounts, well into April. For a discussion of his departure date, see Marianne Roland-Michel, *Watteau: An Artist of the Eighteenth Century* (London: Trefoil Books, 1984), 30–32.

27 On Valenciennes during the period, see Jules Loridan, *Valenciennes au XVIIIe siècle* (Robaix: Imprimerie Reboux, 1913) and H. Lancelin, *Histoire de Valenciennes depuis ses origines* (Valenciennes: Pierre Giard, 1939), 200–25.

28 See Loridan, *Valenciennes,* 32.

29 The division of Posner's *Antoine Watteau* into three parts – the Flemish Watteau, the French Watteau, and the Great Watteau – illustrates this point. Tom Crow makes the point as well in *Painters and Public Life* (New Haven: Yale University Press, 1985), 72. "The career of Watteau . . . put him, in an almost uncanny way, at the intersection of all the major components of artistic culture after 1700." Another example can be found in Victor Chan, "Watteau's *Les Comediens Italiens* Once More," *Canadian Art Review* 5 (1978–79): 107–12. "In effect, what Watteau has done [in *Les Comediens Italiens*] is to constitute a new subject by combining no fewer than three traditions – a conventional symbol, a pictorial heritage, and a number of identifiable characters – into a configuration illustrating those central forces which govern human existence."

30 Katie Scott, *The Rococo Interior: Decoration and Social Spaces in Early Eighteenth-Century Paris* (New Haven: Yale University Press), 185–200. See also, Katie Scott, "D'un siècle à l'autre: History, Mythology, and Decoration in Early Eighteenth-Century Paris," *The Loves of the Gods: Mythological Painting from Watteau to David,* exhibition catalogue by Collin Bailey, Kimball Art Museum (Fort Worth, TX: Rizzoli, 1992), 32–59.

31 For the Romeyne de Hooghe scenes in relation to Van der Meulen paintings, see Scott, *Rococo Interior,* 184–85; and for the imagery of the countermythology, see Scott, *Rococo Interior,* 177–81, and Burke, *Fabrication of Louis XIV,* 135–49.

32 Hal Opperman, "The Theme of Peace in Watteau," in *Antoine Watteau (1684–1721): Le peintre, son temps et sa légende,* ed. François Moureau and Margaret Morgan Grasselli (Paris: Champion-Slatkine, 1987), 23–28.

33 Opperman, "Peace in Watteau," 24.

34 For a discussion of the different types of camps and military assemblies, see Antoine Feuquieres, *Memoirs Historical and Military Containing a Distinct View of all the Considerable States of Europe,* 2 vols. (London: 1735), vol. 1, chapter XI, "Of the Manner of Assembling an Army," 262 ff. This work was first published in Amsterdam in 1730.

35 Posner, *Watteau,* 33.

36 Mary Vidal, *Watteau's Painted Conversations* (New Haven: Yale University Press, 1992).

37 Claude Sturgill, *Marshal Villars and the War of Spanish Succession* (Lexington: University of Kentucky Press, 1965), 10–11.

38 Claude Sturgill, *Marshal Villars,* 42–43.

39 Albert Babeau, *La vie militaire sous l'ancien régime,* 2 vols. (Paris: Firmin-Didot, 1890), 1:197–209, for a general discussion of women, children, and servants in the army.

40 Babeau, *La vie militaire,* 1:207.

41 For the pacifism of Fénelon, see Nicole Ferrier-Caverivière, "La guerre dans la litterature française depuis la traité des Pyrénées jusqu'à la mort de Louis XIV," *Dix-Septième Siècle* 27, no. 3 (1985): 233–47; Henri Gaston Gouhier and Denise Leduc-Fayette, *Fénelon, philosophie et spiritualite: Actes du colloque* (Geneva: Librairie Droz, 1996); Françoise Gallouédec-Genuys, *Le prince selon Fénelon* (Paris: Presses Universitaires de France, 1963), especially 263–83; and Marguerite Haillant, *Culture et imagination dans les oeuvres de Fénelon: "Ad useum delphini"* (Paris: Les Belles Lettres, 1983), 297–332.

42 Opperman, "Peace in Watteau," 28.

43 The original painting by Van Der Meulen was intended for Marly. It is now in Brussels, Musée Royale des Beaux-Arts. There are two copies by J. B. Martin, one in Versailles and another in Nancy, Musée des Beaux-Arts. The image is discussed in Helge Siefert, *Zum Ruhme des Helden* (Munich: Bayerische Staatsgemäldesammlungen, 1993), 94–95. Two preliminary drawings for the painting are reproduced and discussed in Laure C.-Starcky, *Paris, mobilier national dessins de Van der Meulen et de son atelier,* (Paris: Editions de la réunion des musées nationaux et du centre national des arts plastiques, 1988), 53–55. Another drawing is in the Louvre, and a copy of an engraving after this work can be found in the Bibliothèque Nationale, B.N. Est, Cc 60a.

44 Siefert, *Zum Ruhme des Helden,* 94.

45 The literature on the evolution of the army in the seventeenth century is vast. For a reliable and clear overview of this topic, I recommend Ronald Martin, "The Army of Louis XIV," in *The Reign of Louis XIV: Essays in Celebration of Andrew Lossky,* ed. Paul Sonnino (Atlantic Highlands, NJ: Humanities Press International, 1990), 111–26.

46 Two useful studies of material life in the army are A. Navereau, *Le logement et les ustensiles de gens de guerre de 1439 à 1789* (Poitiers: Société Française d'Imprimerie, 1924); and Albert Babeau, *La vie militaire sous l'ancien régime,* 2 vols. (Paris: Firmin-Didot, 1890).

47 François M. Nodot, *Le munitionaire des armées de France* (Paris: N.p., 1697).

48 The tradition of indicating a cabaret or a wine shop by a wreath dates back to antiquity. For more on this tradition, see Édouard Fournier, *Histoire des enseignes de Paris* (Paris: E. Dentu, 1884), 138–40.

49 For a discussion of the officer problem during the war of Spanish succession, see Émile Léonard, *L'armée et ses problèmes au XVIIIe siècle* (Paris: Plon, 1958); Contamine, *Histoire militaire de la France;* and André Corvisier, *Un problème social de l'ancien régime: La composition de l'armée* (Paris, 1958).

50 The three secretaries of war are Marquis de Barbézieux (Louvois's son), 1691–1701; Michel de Chamillart, 1701–9; and Daniel-François Voisin, 1709–14.

51 See Louis Susane, *Histoire de l'ancienne infanterie française,* 8 vols, (Paris: Corréad, 1849), 8:244; and Maxime Weygand, *Histoire de l'armée française* (Paris: Flammarion, 1961), 155–57.

52 Joseph Quincy's *Mémoires* are extremely useful because they provide an unofficial version of military life – what we might call the everyday life of a *sous officier.* Quincy (1678–1749) was the second son in a not-well-to-do family of the *petite noblesse.* He began his military career in 1697 and, like many *sous officiers,* never rose above a certain rank. During his military career he bemoaned that he was never given a regiment. In compensation, he received the Cross of St. Louis. He composed his *Mémoires* between 1738 and 1742 to distract himself from the death of his wife. The day-to-day accounts were probably gleaned from letters he had written to his eldest brother, Charles Sevin, Marquis de Quincy. Joseph Quincy, *Mémoires du Chevalier de Quincy,* 3 vols., ed. Léon Lecestre (Paris: Librairie Renouard, 1898–1900). For a sampling of these complaints see: 1:90 (about excessive luxury); 2:73–81 (complaint that the lesser ranking officers never get the credit they deserve; the *officiers généraux* take all the credit); 2:222, 287, 3:98 (lack of experience); 2:162, 280, 354 (poor judgment and incompetence); 2:357 (exposes soldiers unnecessarily to danger to further their own ends); 3:140–41.

53

> L'abus qu'il y a en France d'acheter les régiments est la véritable cause qu'il y a si peu de bons officers généraux. On donne l'agrément à un enfant qui sort du collèg, d'acheter un régiment. Il se dit à lui même: Dans huit ans, je serai brigadier, dans quatorze maréchal de camp, dans vingt ans lieutenant général par l'ordre du tableu. Grand dieu, quel officier général! J'ai entendu dire une fois à un jeune colonel: «j'aimerois mieux faire mille fautes à la tête de mon régiment, que de consulter mon lieutenant-colonel.» Bel disposition pour devinir un grand homme!

(Quincy, *Mémoires,* 2:287.)

54 Quincy, *Mémoires,* 1:211.

55 Quincy, *Mémoires,* 3:140–41. "Quel diables d'officiers généraux avons-nous donc aujourd'hui? que sont devenujs les Turenne, les Condé, les Luxembourg, les Catinat et les Vendôme?"

56 A painting in the York Museum of Art is either the original Watteau or a copied version. For further on its attribution, see *Watteau: 1684–1721* (Paris: Editions de la réunion des musées nationaux, 1985), 250–52.

57 For this tapestry series, see Daniel Meyer, *L'histoire du roy* (Paris: Editions de la Réunion des Musées Nationaux, 1980); and Maurice Fenaille, *Etat général des tapisseries de la manufacture des Gobelins depuis son origine jusq'à nos jours,* 3 vols. (Paris: Imprimerie Nationale, 1903).

58 The *cabinet du roi* was a series of royally commissioned engravings gathered in twenty-three bound volumes. Propagandistic in function, they documented the vastness and greatness of Louis XIV's reign and realm and were given as gifts to diplomats and distinguished persons. To compensate for the expense of produc-

tion, the plates for the images in the *cabinet du roi* were sold to print dealers, who in turn sold the individual prints to the public. For more on the *cabinet du roi*, see Georges Duplessis, "Le Cabinet du Roi: Collection d'estampes commandées par Louis XIV," *Le bibliophile français* 4 (1869): 87–105; and André Jammes, "Louis XIV, sa bibliothèque et le cabinet du roi," *Library* 20, no. 1 (March 1965): 1–12.

59 For a discussion of Le Brun and rhetorical use of the body in academic art of the seventeenth and eighteenth centuries, see Jennifer Montagu, *The Expression of the Passions: The Origin and Influence of Charles Le Brun's "Conférence sur l'expression générale et particulière* (New Haven: Yale University Press, 1994). For the notion of the body as a legible text, see Norman Bryson, *Word and Image: French Painting of the Ancien Régime* (Cambridge: Cambridge University Press, 1981), 29–57.

60 Bryson's semiological analysis of Watteau's figures within an overall narrative structure in his chapter "Watteau and Reverie" has become a landmark in art-historical scholarship. Bryson, *Word and Image,* 58–88.

61 The entry on *The Defilade* in Margarel Graselli and Pierre Rosenberg, *Watteau: 1684–1721* (Paris: Editions de la Réunion des Musées Nationaux, 1984, 251–52) suggests that the painting has the quality of an experiment that seems a bit forced.

62 ". . . non seulement il a excellé dans les compositions galantes et champêtres, mais encore dans les sujets d'armée, de marches et des haltes de soldats, dont le charactère simple et naturel rend ces sortes de tableaux très précieux." Jean de Jullienne, "Abrégé de la vie d'Antoine Watteau, peintre du roy en son Académie Royale de Peinture et de Sculpture," in Pierre Rosenberg, *Vies anciennes de Watteau* (Paris: Hermann, 1984), 17.

63

> Nôtre Père qui êtes a Versailles, votre nom n'est plus glorifié
> votre royaume n'est plus si grand! Votre volonté n'est plus fait sur la terre
> ni sur l'onde!
> Donnez-nous notre pain qui nous manque de tous côtes!
> Pardonnez à nos ennemis qui nous ont battus et non à nos généraux qui
> les ont laissez faire!
> Ne succombez pas à toutes les tentations de la Maintenon, mais
> déliverez-nous de Chamillard!

In Maurice Sautai, *La bataille de Malplaquet d'après les correspondants du duc du Maine à l'armée de Flandre* (Paris: Librairie Militaire R. Chapelot, 1904), 2.

64 André Corvisier, "Le moral des combattant panique et enthusiasme: Malplaquet 11 Septembre 1709," *Les hommes, la guerre et la mort* (Paris: Economica, 1985): 228–311.

65

> On se persuada, dans les deux armées, que la paix étoit faite. Une joie universelle se répandit promptement dans les deux camps; nous nous embrassions, les officers ennemies et nous. Les soldats des alliés apportoient du pain aux nôres, qui en avoient grand besoin; car il y avoit trois jours qu'on ne leur en avoit donné: aussi, dès qu'un cheval étoit tué, ils en coupoient des ranches, qu'ils mettoient sur le braisier, et les mangeoient ensuite. Les soldats françois leur donnoient de l'eau-de-vie.
>
> Quelle surprise pour le maréchal de Villars, lorsqu'il revint à l'armée! Il demanda la cause de cette suspension d'armes. Il n'en fut pas plus tôt informé, qu'il fi dire oux officiers généraux des ennemis de se retirer promptement; sinon, qu'il alloit faire

tirer sur eux. . . . Ainsi notre joie ne dura pas longtemps. Le canon recommença de parte et d'autre."

(Quincy, *Mémoires,* 2:359.)

66 There is some debate about the pairing of these two images as pendants. For this discussion, see Grasselli and Rosenberg, *Watteau,* 250–54; and Ettore Camesasca and Pierre Rosenberg, *Tout l'oeuvre peint de Watteau* (Paris: Flammarion, 1970), 95.

67 For uniforms in the military, see Dunoyer de Noirmont and Marbot, *Costumes militaires français depuis l'organisation des. . . .* 3 vols. (N.p., n.d.); Constant Lienhart and René Humbert, *Les uniforme d l'armée française depuis 1690 jusqu'à nos jours,* 8 vols. (Leipzig: M. Ruhl, 1897); and Montigny, *Uniformes militaires* (Paris: Chez l'auteur, 1772).

68 Scott, *Rococo Interior,* especially part 2, explores decorative painting within the context of the construction of social space. Mary Sheriff discusses the complexities of subject and facture in decorative painting in *Fragonard: Art and Eroticism* (Chicago: University of Chicago Press, 1990), 58–116.

69 For Vidal's discussion of the women in *The Halt,* see Mary Vidal, *Watteau's Painted Conversations: Art, Literature, and Talk in Seventeenth- and Eighteenth-Century France* (New Haven: Yale University Press, 1992), 46–47.

70 Vidal, *Watteau's Painted Conversations,* 46–47.

71 Vidal, *Watteau's Painted Conversations,* 46–47.

72 For a brief overview of the decline of *l'esprit militaire,* see Léonard, *L'armée,* 15–54.

73 Quincy, *Mémoires,* 1:73–74, recounts about the Marquis Boissimelle (he was actually a dancing master who impersonated an officer): "Il a fait un équipage de Jean de Paris of [great luxury] – maître d'hôtel, cuisinier, 2 valet de chambre, quantité de gens de livrée qu'il avoit inventée." See 2:20–21 and 81 for a description of the excesses of the officers' table.

74 Quincy, *Mémoires,* 2:198: "paré comme s'il alloit au bal: il avoit un habit d'écarlate brodé en or su toutes les coutures, ses chevaux étoient bien poudrés, il monit un beau cheval gris."

75 Quincy, *Mémoires,* 2:219.

76 For a discussion of the construction of nobility and its relation to the military in the seventeenth century, see Ellery Schalk, *From Valor to Pedigree: Ideas of Nobility in France in the Sixteenth and Seventeenth Centuries* (Princeton: Princeton University Press, 1986).

77 Louis de Rouvroy, Duc de Saint-Simon, *Mémoires du Duc de Saint-Simon,* 20 vols. (Paris: Boislisle): 13:343–44 and 14:414–15, cited in Quincy, *Mémoires,* 2:20.

78 C. F. Brucourt (d'après Barbier), *Essai sur l'education de la noblesse* (Paris: Chez Durand, 1747), 244–45.

Le luxe, la mollesse & la volupté ne doivent point accompagner les Officiers dans l'armées. Le Roi a donné sur cela de sage reglemens: Ne seroit-il pas honteux à des Guerriers de se traiter comme de voluptueuses femmellettes? Il y a eu des Compagnes où chaque officier voulait que les vins les plus exquis & les ragouts les plus fins le suivisent. On a vu des Mulets chargés de ustenstile de cuisine en plus en plus grande quantitée que n'étoit le train d'artillery. Un éclat fastueux d'équipages, un attirail d'opulence & de Volupté, qui excitoient l'avidité des ennemis & souvent en étoient la porie: une multitude de valets inutiles, une quantité de bêtes superflues qui augmentoient considerablement les armés sans en augmenter la force.

79 Joan Kelly, *Women, History, and Theory* (Chicago: University of Chicago Press, 1984); Sherry Ortner, "Is Female to Male as Nature Is to Culture?" in *Women, Culture, and Society,* ed. Michell Zimbalist Rasaldo (Stanford, CA: Stanford University Press, 1974), 67–87; Joan Scott, *Gender and the Politics of History* (New York: Columbia University Press, 1988); and Maria Warner, *Monuments and Maidens: The Allegory of the Female Form* (London: Weidenfeld & Nicholson, 1985).

80 Mary Garrard, Artemisia Gentileschi: *The Image of the Female Hero in Italian Baroque Art* (Princeton: Princeton University Press, 1989).

81 Jacqueline Lichtenstein, *The Eloquence of Color: Rhetoric and Painting in the French Classical Age,* trans. Emily McVarish (Berkeley and Los Angeles: University of California Press, 1993).

82 I thank Pia Cuneo for bringing this idea to my attention.

83 For a discussion of the representation of prostitutes in military scenes, see J. R. Hale, *Artists and Warfare in the Renaissance* (New Haven: Yale University Press, 1990); and Legrand, *Les peintres flamands de genre,* chap. 5.

84 F. Ingersoll-Smouse, *Pater* (Paris: Les beaux-arts éditions d'étude et de documents, 1928), 11–13 and 69–74.

85 Quincy, *Mémoires,* 2:382:

> Je ne puis m'empêcher de fire ici l'éloge de Mlle Chevalier, fameuse et très belle courtisane suivant l'armée. Elle s'étoiat emmourachée d'un officier du régiment; elle le suivoit partout. Malgré la canonnade de trois jours et la bataille, elle resta constamment à nos drapeaux. On ne peut oublier sans ingratitude les services importants qu'elle rendit au Régiment. Dès qu'un officier ou un soldat étoit blessé, elle le faisoit transporter sur-le-champ, et elle l'accompagnoit jusqu'à l'endroit où étoit notre chirurgien-major; ensuite elle revenoit au régiment. Elle nous sauva beaucoup de soldats.

86 The terms *"belle capitulation"* and *"belle retraite"* are often used interchangably, although *"belle capitulation"* seems to emphasize skill in calling for and negotiating a surrender, and *"belle retraite"* seems to refer more to the formal action of the retreat. Léonard brings together much useful information documenting the lack of *esprit de combat* and the elevation of *belle retraite* during this period: *L'armée et ses problèmes,* 15–32.

87 Quincy, *Mémoires,* 2:372, "Si notre infanterie fit une belle retraite, on peut dire aussi que notre cavalerie, que je voyaois sur notre droite dans une belle plaine, la fit dans le plus belle ordre du monde."

88 Louis Pelet, *Mémoires militaires relatifs à la succession d'Espagne sous Louis XIV,* 10 vols. (Paris: Collection de documents inédits sur l'histoire de France, 1835–55), 9:287. "La retrait se fit avec un ordre qu'on n'aurait osé attendre battue, et une tranquilité dont on ne devait pas se flatter devant une armée victorieuse."

89 Quincy, *Mémoires,* 3:90, "Nous admirâmes la valeur de ce corps respectable; mais la retraite précipitée de la troupe dorée dans nos retranchements nous fit éclater de rire."

90 The correspondence between Villars and Secretary of War Chamillard paints a picture of the sad state of the army in the Flemish campaign during 1708–9: "En effet, je trouvai les troupes dans un état déplorable, point d'habits, point d'armes, point de pain," in Claude Louis Hector Villars, *Vie du Maréchal de Villars,* 4 vols. (Paris: Chez Moutard, 1784), 2:30. Fenelon found this state of affairs

so distressing that in his correspondence he continually pleads for peace since the army could not possibly win the war.

91 Léonard, *L'armée,* especially, 33–54; Albert Babeau, *La vie militaire sous l'ancien régime,* 2 vols. (Paris: Firmin-Didot, 1890), and André Corvisier, *L'armeé française de la fin du XVIIe siècle au ministère de Choiseul,* 2 vols. (Paris: Presses universitaires de France, 1964.)

92 Quincy, *Mémoires,* 3:137. "On a beau me parler des spectacles, des comédies, des opéras, des carrousels, enfin de tous les plus beaux spectacles du monde, il n'y en a point certainement qui frappe plus les yeux qu'une armée en bataille qui attend l'ennemi, ou qui est en march pour le combattre."

93 J.-B. Du Bos, *Réflexions critiques sur la poésie et sur la peinture,* 7th ed., 1770. Reprint (Geneva: Slatkine Reprints, 1967), 11–12.

94 See Babeau, *La vie militaire,* 9–21, for these reviews.

95 Quincy, *Mémoires,* 1:79.

> Le roi voulant faire voire à toute l'europe que, malgré la Guere qu'il venoit de soutenir contre presque toutes les puissance de cette partie du monde, la France n'étoit nullement épuisé, ni en hommes ni en argent, il fit assemblés aux environs de Compiègne une armée considerable, dont toutes es troupes qui la composeront étoient d'une magnificence extraordinare. . . . Le duc de Bourgogne en fut nommé généralissme, et le maréchal de Boufflers général.

96 For Quincy's description of the *luxe* displayed at this event, see *Mémoires,* 1:79–97.

97 Saint-Simon, 2:105–17. "Il n'y eut point de régiment qui qui n'en fût ruiné pour bien des années, corps et officiers" (117).

98 Frédérick Masson, *Le Marquis de Grignan: Petit-fils de Madame de Sévigné* (Paris: Librairie Plon, 1887), 230. "Ce fut une magnificence ruineuse: du 31 août, où il en repartit, il est difficile de compter ce que cette fête militaire put coûter à la France et à tous ceux qui, par métier, furent tenus d'y prendre part."

99 Cornette, *Roi de guerre,* 156–58, for an account of this event.

100 For the *luxe* of Boufflers: Quincy, *Mémoires,* 1:90; and Masson, *Marquis de Grignon:* "Tout ce qu'on a dit de sa défense surpasse tout imagination. Il a changé d'habit tous les jours, de chevaux, de selles, de housses, de fourreaux de pistolets, et toute la suite de ceux qui l'ont visité et ont mangé chez lui ont été défrayés" (231–32).

> Voici, d'après le *Mercure de France,* le menu d'un diner de Boufflers: «La table fut servie à trente-cinq plats, y compris la machine du milieu: quatre plats de douze marcs, savoir: quatre moyennes entrées et six potages, seize hors-d'oeuvre en des plats de quatre marcs. Les grands et les peitits potages furent relevés de hors d'oeuvres en pareil nombre qui furent aussi relevés de trent-quatre plats d'entremets et de rôts. Huit hors-d'oeuvres d'entremets furent encore relevés devant le Roi, dont il y avait deux assiettes de trent-six ortolans chacune. Le fruit était au delà de tout ce qu'on peut imaginer pour la profusion et l'arrangement. On y but les vins les plus exquis et les liqueurs les plus rares.»

101 François Nodot, *La rivale travestie ou les avantures galantes arivées au camp de Compiègne avec tous les mouvemens de l'armée* (Paris: Chez Brunet, 1699).

102 For Nodot's descriptions, see *Camp de Compiègne,* 80–92. I discuss the conventional nature of visual and verbal representation of *fêtes* in chapter 3.

103 Nodot, *Campe de Compiègne,* 180: "On ne peut voir un plus beau feu, que celuy qui se fit de part & d'autre. Le canon étoit servi aussi promptement que la mous-

queterie. Les Grenades lancées des deux côtez, faisoient mille & mille cercles en l'air, qui étant sans cesse reiterez, formoient un berceau de feu, depuis la rivière, jusqu'à la porte Chapelle."

104 Babeau, *La vie militaire,* 2:193.

105 Quincy, *Mémoires,* 3:123–25.

106 Quincy, *Mémoires,* 3:19.

> Les lieutenants de plusieurs régiments d'infanterie, ennuyés d'avoir toujours les bras croisés, imaginèrent de s'habillier à la housarde. Ainsi déguisé, moitié à cheval, moitié à pied, ils s'avançoient près des retranchements des alliés. Ils étoient au nombre de deux cents dans ces deux troupes. Auparavant d'en approcher, ils avoient la précaution d'embusquer ceux qui étoit à pied. Les housards ennemis ne manquoient pas de sortir promptement de leur camp pour courir après. Nos faux housards feignoient de fuir, et insensiblement ils les attiroient dans l'embuscade, d'où il partoit un feu de mousqueterie qui en culbuoit toujours quelques-uns. Ensuite, nos faux housards à pied se joignoient à ceux qui étoit à cheval, et ils marchoient ensemble avec rapidité sur les ennemis, qui ne demandoient point leur reste. Ces combats duràent pendant quelques jours; mais notre général, qui en craignoit les suites, ordonna sous peine de prison, à ces officers, d'abandonner cette petite guerre.

107 Quincy, *Mémoires,* 3:23.

> M. du Cheray, alors conseiller au Parlement de Paris, mon parent et mon ami, et fils de M. d'Ormesson, intendant de la généralité de Soissons, vint me voir. La curiosité seule l'avait engagé à s'y rendre; il resta quelques jours dans notre armée. Il me pria un jour très instamment de lui faire voir de près les ennemis du roi. Je le menai à une de nos grandes gardes. . . . Il y avait vis-à-vis un poste des ennemis de 600 hommes, qui n'était séparé de nous que par le Censet, et qui était sur une chaussée. Je savais parfaitement qu'il y avait ordre de part et d'autre de ne pas tirer. . . . Il eut le temps de les voir et de leur parle bien à son aise sans aucune crainte et sans aucun risque.

108 Most of the information about the *Maison militaire* or *Gardes du Corps de Louis XIV* is from André Corvisier, "Les Gardes du Corps de Louis XIV," in *Les hommes, la guerre et la mort* (Paris: Economica, 1985), 17–143; M. F. Sicard, *L'histoire des institutions militaires des français,* 4 vols. (Paris: J. Correard Jeune, 1834), 2:53–87; and André Corvisier, *A Dictionary of Military History and the Art of War* (Cambridge, MA: Blackwell, 1994).

109 A 1708 ordinance stipulated only that they not be valets. See Corvisier, "Les Gardes du Corps," 131.

110 Anon., *La parfait homme de guerre ou l'idée d'un heros* (Amsterdam: Jacques Desbordes, 1699).

111 The legend on the print:

> Malgré les bombes et boulets
> Le feu le sant et le Carnage
> L'homme de guerre à pour objets
> De selever par son courage
> jusqu'ux Emplois de Commandant
> Ou de perir Chemin faisant

112 S. Rocheblave, *Essai sur le Comte de Caylus, l'homme, l'artiste, l'antiquaire* (Paris: Hachette, 1889).

113 Scott, *The Rococo Interior,* 153. The identity of a M. Bougi, identified by Mariette as the owner of a concert scene by Watteau, may be the Marquis de Colonges, who was a brigadier in the king's army. Grasselli and Rosenberg, *Watteau,* 35.

114 The most comprehensive account of La Roque's life can be found in H. Guénot, "La Roque," in Grenoble, Centre de recherche sur les sensibilités université des langues et lettres de Grenoble, *Dictionnaire des journalistes, supplément* 4 (Paris: Presses Universitaires de France, 1984), 91–102. The *Dictionnaire* entry on La Roque includes references to other biographies and archival sources. It also points out the discrepancies between the various sources. Two other useful and frequently consulted biographies include Clément de Ris, *Les amateurs d'autrefois* (Paris: Plon, 1877), 209–28; and Edme Gersaint, *Catalogue raisonné des differens effets curieux & rares contenus dans le cabinet de feu M. La Roque* (Paris: J. Barois, 1745), avertissement.

115 Corvisier, "Malplaquet," 228–311. All the *rélations* and other accounts of the Battle of Malplaquet have been gathered and published by Maurice Sautai in *La bataille de Malplaquet.*

116 Corvisier, "Malplaquet," 307: "Nous avons perdu le champ de bataille par la poltronerie qui règne depuis longtemps dans ce régiment du Roie et gardes françaises qui ont laché pied dans cette dernière affaire."

117 Camesasca brings together numerous documentary sources concerning the dating of Watteau's trip to Valenciennes. See Camesasca and Rosenberg, *Watteau,* 84. Opinion in scholarship seems equally divided about the meeting of La Roque and Watteau; some argue that they met later in Paris, most likely at the theater.

118 Quincy was in Valenciennes from the Battle of Malplaquet in September 1709 until May 1710. *Mémoires,* 3:12.

119 Quincy, *Mémoires,* 3:7.

120 La Roque wrote a *"notice nécrologique"* that appeared in the *Mercure de France* in August 1721. Gersaint's biography appeared in the catalogue for the *vente après-décès* of Quentin de Lorangère in 1744. Both are reproduced in Rosenberg, *Vies de Watteau,* 5–7 and 29–44.

121 His *opéras* are Antoine La Roque, *Théoné, Tragédie* (Paris: Chez Pierre Ribou, 1715) and, cowritten with Pellegrin, *Medée et Jason Tragédie* (Paris: Chez Christophe Ballard, 1713).

122 Edme Gersaint, *La Roque,* avertissement: "Sa passion dominante a toujours été pour les beaux Arts. Il les aimoit en galant homme, qui encourage ceux qui les cultivent, qui les connoît; & qui se fait un plaisir d'en rassembler des échantillons proportionnez à ses facultés. Aussi laisse-t-il après lui un assemblage de plusieurs sortes de *Curiosités* très-considerables pour un simple Particulier."

123 Gersaint, *La Roque,* avertissement, "Tableaux de choix; Desseins; Estampes; Bronzes & autres ouvrages de Sculpture; Porcelaines; Lacqs de toute espece; Diamans & autres Pierres fines d'une coleur parfaite; Pierres gravés en creux & en relief; coquilles."

124 There were also 41 Watteau drawings. Gersaint, *La Roque,* 168–70.

125 In 1921 the painting was noted at the Château de Vézenobres, where it belonged to Bernis-Calvières, one of La Roque's descendants. For the provenance, see Camesasca and Rosenberg, *Watteau,* 106.

126 Norma Betten made this perceptive observation in "The Military Paintings of Antoine Watteau," Master's thesis, University of Washington, 1974, 15.

127 Vidal, *Watteau's Painted Conversations,* 43.

128 For the iconography of tobacco, see Simon Schama, *The Embarrassment of Riches: An Interpretation of Dutch Culture in the Golden Age* (New York: Alfred A. Knopf, 1987), 193–215.

129 Edgar Munhall, *Little Notes Concerning Watteau's "Portal of Valenciennes"* (New York: The Frick Collection, 1992), 30.

130 Munhall, *"Portal of Valenciennes,"* 22.

131 The most comprehensive accounting of the attribution is in Betten, *Military Painting of Antoine Watteau,* 38–46. For a briefer account, see Camesasca and Rosenberg, *Watteau,* 96.

132 The first state of this print is completely by Watteau and is quite rare. There is a copy at the Cabinet des Estampes at the Bibliothèque Nationale. The second state, finished by Thomassin, is far more common; it is the one that was included in the Jullienne collection. See Dacier and Vuaflart, *Graveurs de Watteau,* 3:86–87.

133 For recruiting and recruiting practices, see Georges Girard, *La service militaire en France à la fin du regne de Louis XIV: Racolage et milice, 1701–1715* (Paris: Plon, 1921); and Roger Vaultier, *"Le racolage et le recruitment sous l'ancien régime."* Extrait de *Vert et Rouge,* no. 27 (May 1950): 8–13.

134 For the distance between the official image of troop movement and what we see represented in Watteau's image, see Pierre Briquet, *Code militaire ou compilation des ordonnances des roys de France concernant le gens de guerre,* 3 vols. (Paris: Pierre Gandoüin, 1728), 1:102–8; G. Giffart, *L'art militaire française pour l'infanterie* (Paris: Chez Giffart, 1696); and Joseph Frédéric Leopold (engravings by Guerard), *Les Exercices de Mars* (1700).

135 To my knowledge, Jacques Mathey, *Peintures répparues* (Paris: F. de Nobele, 1966), was the first to make this association between Watteau's *Recruits on the Way to Join the Regiment* and Van der Meulen's *Siege of Dole.*

136 The original painting is today at Versailles, and there are five known copies – in Schleisheim, Basel, Dôle, Lille, and Paris; see Siefert, *Zum Rhume des Helden,* 98. The engraving, by Huchtenburg and Baudouins, is not a copy of the painting; it is a more panoramic image. It was part of the *cabinet du roi,* vol. 16, Van der Meulen, *Conquêtes du Roi.* In 1669, Louis XIV granted Van der Meulen the *lettres patentes* of the privilege to engrave and sell works after his paintings. We know that he made a substantial addition to his income from the sale of his engraved images at the Gobelins. See Richefort, "Nouvelles précisions sur Van der Meulen," 62–64.

137 Opperman, "Peace in Watteau," 26.

138 Philibert-Joseph Le Roux, *Dictionnaire comique, satirique, critique, burlesque, libre et proverbial,* 2 vols. (Lyon: Chez les hériters Berringos, 1735), "fig. Etre dans le, ou du Régiment de l'Arc en ciel. C'est, être laquais, porter les coleurs." The *arc-en-ciel* is also cited in Paul Émile Littré, *Littré Dictionnaire de la Langue Française* (Chicago: Encyclopaedia Britannica, 1994), 1:277. I thank Lise Leibacher and Louis Godbout for their help in tracking down the colloquial meaning of *"l'arc-en-ciel."*

139 Jean-François Regnard, *Foire St. Germain,* 6:221–22, in Evariste Gherardi, *Le théâtre italien de Gherardi,* 6 vols (Paris: Briasson, 1741). The play was first performed in 1695.

Arlequin: J'y ai éte trois ans cuirassier du Guet, après avoir servi volontaie dans le régiment de l'arc-en ciel.
Colombine: J'en ai jamais ouï paler de ce régiment-çà.
Arlequin: C'es pourtant un des gros régimens du Royaume; les soldats y sont tantôt fantassins et tantôt carrossiers et sont habillés de verd. de rouge et de jaune, suivant la fantasie des capitaines.

Colombine: Je commence prèsentement à voir quelque teinture de votre regiment.
Arlequin: Comment Diable! C'est la milice la plus nécessaire à l'état, et c'est le regiment qu' l'on fait le plus vite son chemin: c'est de-la qu'on tire des officiers pour remplir les postes les plus lucratifs. Je connais vingt commis en chef qui n'ont jamais fait leurs exercises que dans ce corps-là.

140 Delosme de Monchenai, *Le Phénix,* in Gherardi, *Théâtre italien,* 3:359–61. The play was first performed in 1699.

141 "Ils maudissent entre eux sans doute, / La dure et fatiguante Route: / Mais au gite allant heberger / Aux depense du premier Village / Ils sauront se dedommager / De la fatigue du Voiage."

142 Opperman, "Peace in Watteau," 26.

143 Opperman, "Peace in Watteau," 27, n. 15.

Chapter Three. The *Fête Galante* and the Cult of *Honnêteté*

1 E. F. Gersaint, "Abrégé de la vie d'Antoine Watteau," in Pierre Rosenberg, ed., *Vies anciennes de Watteau* (Paris: Hermann, 1984), 35.

2 Anatole de Montaiglon, ed., *Procès-verbaux de l'académie royale de peinture et de sculpture, 1648–1793,* 10 vols. (Paris: Charavay Frères for the Société de l'Histoire de l'Art Français, 1875–92), 4:252.

3 Joachim C. Nemeitz, *Séjour de Paris: C'est-à'dire instructions fidèles pour le voiageurs de condition* (Leiden: Jean van Abscourde, 1727), 235–36.

Tout le jardin qui est très spacieux, fut illuminé par une infinité de lampes & de bougies suspenduës en partie entre les arbres, en partie placées à platte terre. Le Théâtre pour la comédie composée par Dancourt & intitulée *L'Impromptu de Surène,* fut construit au fond du Jardin. L'on y laissa à entrer tout le monde, sur tout les Masques, & on en 4 endroits du Jardin. Le nombre des masques qu'il y eut là, est inexprimable: & d'autant qu'il faisoit alors le tems de monde le plus beau, ce Bal dura jusqu'à 6 heures du matin.

4 Anne-Marguerite Du Noyer, *Lettres historiques et galantes,* 9 vols. (LaHaye: Pierre Husson, 1761), 6: 485–86: "un jardin enchanté avec plusieurs allées d'orangers, du milieu desquelles sortoient quatre jets d'eau de fleur d'orange, dont l'odeur embauma toute la chambre & qui surprient agréablement la Compagnie."

5 Du Noyer, *Lettres,* 6:362–63.

Pendant le fort de danse, une personne de ma connoissance apperçût à terre quelque chose de blanc, qui avoit l'air d'une Lettre, & laissant tomber son mouchoir, dessus, elle ramassa l'un & l'autre sans qu'on s'aperçût de la trouvaille qu'elle venoit de faire, qui étoit éffectivement une Lettre ou du moins un Billet dans lequel il n'y avoit que ces quatre vers:

Depuis que mon coeur est charmé
Comment vous-trouvez du plaisir
  d'être aimée?
Ah! s'il en est pour vous qui lui soit
  comparable.
Vous êtes plus aimée que vous n' êtes aimables.

6 Du Noyer, *Lettres,* 6:364–65.

7 Nemeitz, *Séjour de Paris,* 219. "Il ne faut point être Misanthrope. Il faut badiner, rire, jouër, chasser & faire ce qui est semblable. Un homme journalier ou bizarre donne bientôt du dégoût; un tel tempérament ne convient point du tout avec celui d'un François, bien moins de ceux qui sont accoûtmez de vivre dans les délices & dans la joie & qui sont toujours en bonne humeur."

8 Terry Castle, *Masquerade and Civilization: The Carnivalesque in Eighteenth-Century English Culture and Fiction* (Stanford: Stanford University Press, 1986).

9 There is a rich body of scholarship on the concept of the *honnête homme* and the cult of *honnêteté.* For the history of the cult of *honnêteté,* see Maurice Magendie, *La politesse mondaine et les théories de l'honnêteté en France au XVIIe siècle de 1600 à 1660* (Paris: Presses universitaires de France, 1925), and more recently, Domna Stanton, *The Aristocrat as Art* (New York: Columbia University Press, 1980). Mary Vidal, *Watteau's Painted Conversations: Art, Literature, and Talk in Seventeenth- and Eighteenth-Century France* (New Haven: Yale University Press, 1992), addresses the relationship between the visual arts and the cult of *honnêteté,* focusing on the function of conversation; see especially, 75–98. For an insightful summary, see Thomas Crow, *Painters and Public Life in Eighteenth-Century Paris* (New Haven: Yale University Press, 1985), 67–69.

10 Katie Scott's discussion of the formation of what she calls "projected ideals," such as nobility, has informed my thinking about the history of *honnêteté*; see *The Rococo Interior: Decoration and Social Spaces in Early Eighteenth-Century Paris* (New Haven: Yale University Press, 1995), 8.

11 Baldassare Castiglione, *The Book of the Courtier,* trans. Charles Singleton, in *The Renaissance Man* (New York: Franklin Watts, 1959).

12 Nicolas Faret, *L'honneste homme ou l'art de plaire à la cour,* ed. M. Magendie (Paris: Presses universitaires de France, 1925).

13 Stanton, *The Aristocrat as Art,* 19–20.

14 Stanton, *The Aristocrat as Art,* 95.

15 Antoine Gombard, Chevalier de Méré, *Oeuvres posthumes,* ed., Charles Boudhors, 3 vols. (Paris: F. Roches, 1930), see especially vol. 3, *De la vraie honnêteté* and *Suite de la vraie honnêteté.*

16 Méré, cited in Stanton, *The Aristocrat as Art,* 81.

17 Méré, cited in Stanton, *The Aristocrat as Art,* 47.

18 For an account of Hôtel Rambouillet and the literary circle there, see Émile Magne, *Voiture et l'hôtel de Rambouillet: Les origines, 1597–1635, portraits et documents inédites* (Paris: Émile Paul, 1929–30). Other works of interest for seventeenth-century *salon* society include the now classic work, Carolyn Lougee, *Le Paradis des Femmes: Women, Salons, and Social Stratification in Seventeenth-Century France.* (Princeton: Princeton University Press, 1976). I would also recommend Erica Harth, *Cartesian Women: Versions and Subversions of Rational Discourse in the Old Regime* (Ithaca, NY: Cornell University Press, 1992).

19 Stanton, *The Aristocrat as Art,* 48.

20 Routrou, *Saint–Genest,* cited in Stanton, *The Aristocrat as Art,* 175.

21 Warren Roberts, *Mortality and Social Class in Eighteenth-Century French Literature and Painting* (Toronto: University of Toronto Press, 1974), 42–43.

22 The *appartements* were held Monday, Wednesday, and Friday, from six o'clock until ten o'clock, when the court would meet in a salon for dancing, cards, concerts, and refreshments. They are an example of "formal" domestic life. To chart the decline in entertainments and *fêtes,* consult Pierre François Godart de

Beauchamps, *Recherches sur les théâtres de France depuis l'année onze cens soixante et un jusques à présent* (Paris: Prault Père, 1735), 3:1.

23 Elborg Forster, ed., *A Woman's Life in the Court of the Sun King: Letters of Liselotte von der Pfalz, 1652–1722* (Baltimore: Johns Hopkins University Press, 1984), 53–54.

24 Marie-Madeleine de La Fayette, *Mémoires de la cour de France pour les années 1688–1689* (Paris: E. Flammarion, n.d.), 329. "Les bals de la cour étaient si tristes qu'ils ne commençaient qu'à près de minuit, et ils étaient toujours finis avant deux heures."

25 La Fayette, *Mémoires,* 329.

26 La Fayette, *Mémoires,* 328. "Le Roi ne l'approuva pas, disant que jamais on n'allait à ces sortes d'endroit qu'il n'eût quelque conte désagréable, et que les femmes d'un certain air n'y devaient pas aller. Cela fit que la princesse, qui aime bien les plaisirs, s'en priva, à son grand regret."

27 Du Noyer, *Lettres,* 6:261. "Nous en avons eu une [fête] d'une autre espèce: car ce n'a eté qu'une procession pompeuse, qui s'est faite par ordre du Roi, lors que le ministre du Grande-Maître de Malte a fait ici son entrée publique."

28 Du Noyer, *Lettres,* 6:106.

29 Chevalier de Mailly, *Diverses aventures de France et d'Espagne* (Paris: P. Ribou, 1707), 153.

30 Jean Paul Marana, *Lettre d'un Sicilien à un de ses amis* (Paris: Pierre Maubal, 1710), 31. "L'or et l'argent est devenu si commun, comme j'ai déjà dit, qu'il brille sur les habits de toutes sortes de personnes, & le luxe démésuré a confondu le maître avec la valet, & les gens de la lie du peuple avec les personnes les plus élevés. Tout le monde port l'épée, & Paris resemble à l'Utopie de Thomas Morus, où l'on ne distinguoit personne."

31 Katie Scott provides an excellent discussion of the construction of noble identity for this period in Scott, *Rococo Interior,* 81–120.

32 *Gravure de mode* were quite generic and often rather crudely done, although in the eighteenth century they became more elaborate and finely detailed. Frequently, the model was identified as a member of the court, which presented a certain psychological appeal for the buyer. According to Grivel, the fashions were inspired by descriptions given in the *Mercure Galant* of the *fêtes* given at court. See Marianne Grivel, *Le commerce de l'estampe à Paris au XVIIe siècle* (Geneva: Librairie Droz, 1986), 143–44. For fashions in general, see Aileen Ribeiro, *Dress in Eighteenth-Century Europe: 1715–1789* (London: Batsford, 1984). Although this book addresses a later time period. Ribeiro's insights provide a useful framework for an analysis of fashion in general; see Aileen Ribeiro, *The Art of Dress: Fashion in England and France, 1750–1820* (New Haven: Yale University Press, 1995). Most recently, Sarah Cohen has discussed some of Watteau's works related to fashion plates in "Body as 'Character' in Early Eighteenth-Century French Art and Performance," *Art Bulletin* 78 (September 1996): 454–66.

33 J. H. Marchand, *Testament histori-morali politique de Monsieur Rauponeau: Écrit et publié par lui-même* (Paris: By the author, 1760), 241. "Je vis pareillement que les caractères alphabetiques de cette langue sont aussi mutipliés que chaques pièces de nos habits, où que chaque instrument de nos moeurs: que ces caractères symboliques changeants encore plus rapidement de form que ceux des langues ordinaires."

34 For sumptuary laws, see Scott, *Rococo Interior,* 81–82. Richard Sennett, *The Fall of Public Man* (New York: Vintage, 1978), 66, and Jacques Saint-Germaine, *La vie quotidienne en France à la fin du grand siècle* (Paris: Hachette, 1965), 68–69.

Related to this is a discussion of the absolute value of change in Raymonde Robert, *Le conte de fées littéraire en France de la fin du XVIIe à la fin du XVIIIe siècle* (Nancy: Presses universitaires de France, 1982), 295 ff.

35 For a discussion of this masquerade of everyday dress and its meaning, see Sennett, *Fall of Public Man,* 66–72.

36 Marana, *Lettre,* 16. "Ils ont toutes le privilege d'aller masquées en tout tems, de se cacher & de se faire voir quand il leur plaît; & avec un masque de velours noir, elles entrent quelque fois dans les Eglises, comme au Bal & à la Comédie, inconnuës à Dieu & à leurs maris."

37 A. J. Dezallier D'Argenville, *Voyage pittoresque de Paris ou indication de tout ce qu'il y'a de plus beau dans cette ville en peinture, sculpture & architecture* (Paris: De Bure, 1749), 226: "qui entreroient dans les maisons et prendroient place aux repas sans y être invités."

38 For a discussion of Sceaux within the context of *salon* society, see Georges Mongrédien, *La vie de société au XVIIe et XVIIIe siècles* (Paris: Hachette, 1950); Léo Claretie, *Histoire des théâtres de société* (Paris: Librarie Molière, 1906), 41 ff.; and Leonce de Piepape, *Une petite-fille du Grande Condé: La duchess du Maine, reine de Sceaux et conspiratrice* (Paris: Plon, 1910).

39 Two entertaining biographies of the Duchesse du Maine are Francis Birrell, *La Duchesse du Maine* (London: G. Howe, 1929); and Arvede Barine, *Princesses et grandes dames* (Paris: Hachette, 1890).

40 Louis de Rouvroy, Duc de Saint-Simon, *Mémoires du Duc de Saint-Simon,* 20 vols. ed. Adolphe Chéruel and Adolphe Regnier (Paris: Librarie Hachette, 1873–87), 10:358, "Sceaux étoit plus que jamais le théâtre des folies de la duchesse du Maine, . . . Nuits blanches en loteries, jeux, fêtes, illuminations, feux d'artifice, en un mot fêtes et fantaisies de toute les sortes, et de tous les jours."

41 Saint-Simon, *Mémoires,* 5:134, "On ne comprenoit pas la folie de la fatigue de s'habiller en comédienne, d'apprendre et de déclamer les plus grands rôles, et de se donner en spectacle public sur un théâtre. . . . Outre le ridicule, ces plaisirs n'étoient pas à bon marché."

42 Beauchamps, *Recherches sur les théâtres,* 3:156.

43 For the aristocratic status of the theater, see Claretie, *Théâtres de société.*

44 Mme. de Stael, cited in Birrell, *Duchess du Maine,* 41.

45 Beauchamps, *Recherches sur les théâtres,* 3:154.

46 Charles Claude Genest, *Les divertissements de Sceaux* Paris: Etienne Ganneau, 1712), aij.

47 Genest, *Divertissements de Sceaux,* aij. "Ce sont de purs amusemens, des jeux imprévus, non pas des compositions méditées; & jusqu'aux divertissemens qui paroissent le mieux suivis, ce ne sont à vrai dire que des espèces d'impromptu, propres seulement pour les occasions que les ont fait naître."

48 René Démoris, "Les fêtes galantes chez Watteau et dans le roman contemporain," *Dix-huitième siècle,* no. 3 (1971): 339.

49 Robert, *Le conte de fées,* 344–45.

50 Du Noyer, *Lettres,* 6:492:

> il (Comte Taroucu) a présenté divers retranchemens: dans l'un on jouoit à la Bassette, l'autre étoit le Théâtre du Bal, dans un autre on voyoit huit boutiques qui formoient une espèce de Foire St. Germain, & qui étoient remplis de tout ce qu'on pouvait souhaiter de plus exquis. . . . Ces prétendus Marchands crioient & appelloient les Passans comme on est accoûtumé de faire dans les foires: & pour rendre leurs fonds intarissables, on avoit fait un Magasin dans des autres Retrenchemens de la

Salle, d'où l'on tiroit à tous momens dequoi regarnir les Boutiques, & remplacer ce qui avoit été consumé: . . . ainsi quelque grande que fût la foule qu'il y eut à cette Foire; car on y laissa entrer tous les masques, & quoi qu'elle dûrat jusqu'à six heures du matin les boutiques furent toujours également bien fournies.

51 A very useful analysis of the *contes de fées* is provided by Robert, *Le conte de fées*; Mary Elizabeth Storer, *La mode des contes de fées* (Paris: Librairie Ancienne Honoré Champion, 1928).

52 Henriette Julie de Casteluau, Comtesse de Murat, *Epître aux fées modernes*, preface to *Histoires sublimes et allegoriques* (Paris: J. & P. Delaune, 1699), cited in Robert, *Le conte de fées*, 401.

53 Henriette Julie de Casteluau, Comtesse de Murat, *Le voyage de campagne*, vol. 29, *Voyages imaginaires, songes, visions et romans cabalistique* (Paris: Privately published, 1788); Catherine Durand [Bédacier], *Les petits soupers de l'été de l'année 1699, Ou aventures galantes avec l'origine des fées*, 2 vols. (Paris: J. Musier et J. Rolin, 1702). Robert, *Le conte de fées*, 328–49, discusses the ideological and literary function of the framing device in these and other works.

54 Murat, *Le voyage de campagne*, cited in Robert, *Le conte de fées*, 338.

55 The process of appropriation functions in a number of situations. Recently, it has been discussed within the context of postmodernist culture. For example, modern art's appropriation of popular culture was the focus of the 1990 exhibition at the Museum of Modern Art, New York; see the catalogue, Kirk Varnadoe, *High and Low: Modern Art and Popular Culture* (New York: Museum of Modern Art, 1990), and the response to it that appeared in *October* 56 (1991). An excellent account of appropriation of "primitive cultures" by Western cultures can be found in James Clifford, *The Predicament of Culture: Twentieth-Century Ethonography, Literature, and Art*, (Cambridge, MA: Harvard University Press, 1988).

56 Paul LaCroix, *Mémoires curieux sur l'histoire des moeurs et de la prostitution en France aux dix-septième et dix-huitième siècles*, 2 vols. (Brussels: Librairie Universelle de J. Rozez, 1861), 2:260.

57 Marie-Madeleine de La Fayette, *Mémoires de la cour de France pour les années 1688–1689* (Paris: Flammarion, n.d.), 329. "Le goût de Monseigneur aux bals est de changer souvent d'habit, par le seul plaisir de n'être pas reconnu et de parler à des personnes indifférentes."

58 Saint-Simon, *Mémoires*, cited in Nicolas de Blégny, *Le livre de commodes des adresses de Paris pour 1692*, ed. Édouard Fournier, 2 vols. (Paris: P. Daffis, 1872), 2:135. "Pendant l'hyver précédant, plusieurs masques de cire de personnes de la cour, au naturel, qui les portoient sous d'autres masques, en sorte qu'en démasquant on y étoit trompé en prenant le second masque pour le visage, et c'en étoit un véritable, tout différent qui étoit dessous; on s'amusa fort à cette badinerie."

59 At the opera the public balls were sponsored by the Royal Academy of Music in 1715 in an attempt to offset production expenses. To a great extent these balls must have served as a replacement for the royally sponsored balls after the dissolution of the court at Versailles in 1715. The number of private balls dropped off after the establishment of these public balls.

60 [Louis Liger,] *Le voyageur fidèle ou le guide des étrangers dans la ville de Paris* (Paris: Pierre Ribou, 1716), 261.

On y donne le Bal, ce qui y attire une foule prodigieuse de monde de tout état, de tout âge & de tout sexe, & fait faire des parties de masques pour y goûter le divertissement avec plus de liberté; car pour lors on y prend des grisettes pour les dames de conséquences & des Bourgeois pour des Seigneurs. . . . Là, n'ayant pour tout siège que le gazon on s'y asseoit sans cérémonie; comme le hazard dans ces rencontres préside toujours plus que tout autre chose, il me tomba en lot une jeune femme, . . . nous continuons nôtre entretien; la plaisanterie fait d'abord son personnage, les mots d'esprit & à la double entente viennent s'y mêler: & enfin l'amour qui est toujoûrs le Héros de la pièce, voulut y paraître.

61 Nemeitz, *Séjour de Paris,* 185–200, for his discussion of balls and masquerades.

62 Nemeitz, *Séjour de Paris,* 186–87. "L'on a ici la liberté de paroître en toutes sortes de masques, des hommes en habits de femme, & des femmes en habit d'homme, en des masques de toutes sortes de Nations, et tout âge & de toutes façons quelques étranges & droles qu'ils soient. Tout est ici permis, & plus bizzare qu'un masque est, plus on l'admire."

63 Nemeitz, *Séjour de Paris,* 194: "près de 20 personnes, qui ont péri par quelque mort violent à l'occassion de ces divertissements."

64 Nemeitz, *Séjour de Paris,* 194.

65 For another discussion of the elite appropriation of the *parade* see Crow, *Painters and Public Life,* 53–55.

66 See J. E. Gueullette, *Un magistrat de XVIIIe siécle, ami des lettres, du théâtre, et des plaisirs, Thomas-Simon Gueullette* (Paris: E. Droz, 1938).

67 Gueullette, *Thomas-Simon Gueullette,* 63.

Nos divertissements, toujours nouveaux et variés, nous attirèrent, outre nos amis priès, un concours étonnant de spectateurs du premier rang. Comme nous n'ouvrions la scène qu'à onze heures du soir, quantité de seigneurs et de dames partaient en poste de Versailles, après le souper du Roi, pour venir prendre part à nos plaisirs. A l'example de ce qui se passe à Venise, nous admettions les masques à nos spectacles. Nous donnions le bal ensuite: cela formait des nuits blanches dont on paraissait fort content.

68 Genest, *Divertissements de Sceaux,* 49.

69 Démoris, "Fêtes galantes chez Watteau," 354. "L'habit italien, dès qu'on n'est plus sur la scène, devient donc moins la marque d'une profession que la marque d'un divertissement noble, que le signe d'un être capable de donner à sa vie la dimension d'une fiction."

70 Donald Posner, *Antoine Watteau* (Ithaca, NY: Cornell University Press, 1984), 163.

71 Gueullette, *Thomas-Simon Gueullette,* 69.

Sous le nom de Bertrand, et sous l'habit du vrai paysan, il copiait avec tant de naturel et de perfection les gens de ce caractère, pour le chant et pour la danse, que n'ayant qui que ce soit au monde qui l'égalât, il pouvait passer pour un original d'autant plus excellent qu'ayant passé trois au quatre heures dans son habit ordinaire avec des personnes qui ne l'avaient vu que cette fois-là, et changeant de figure et de vêtement, on le faisait souper avec ces mêmes personnes qui ne le reconnaissaient pas, et qui, lorsqu'on le demasquait pour ainsi dire, ne pouvaient croire que ce fut le même qu'elles avaient vu dans l'après midi.

72 Henri Nicolle, "Thomas-Simon Gueullette," *Revue de France* 10 (1874): 782–83.

73 Genest, *Divertissements de Sceaux,* 52.

74 For Crozat, see Louis Clément de Ris, *Les amateurs d'autrefois* (Paris: E. Plon, 1877), 183–207; and Margaret Stuffman, "Les tableaux de la collection de Pierre Crozat; historique et destinée d'un ensemble célèbre, établis en partant d'un

inventaire après décès inédit (1740)," *Gazette des beaux-arts* 72 (July 1968): 1–144.

75 Comte de Caylus, "Vie de Watteau," in Pierre Rosenberg, *Vies anciennes de Watteau* (Paris: Hermann, 1984), 78–79. "Il avoit des habits galans, quelques-uns de comiques, dont il revetoit les personnes de l'un et de l'autre sexe, selon qu'il en trouvoit qui vouloit bien se tenir, et qu'il prenoit dans les attitudes que la nature lui presentoit, en preférant volontiers les plus simples aux autres."

76 Norman Bryson, *Word and Image: French Painting of the Ancien Régime* (Cambridge: Cambridge University Press, 1981), 82.

77 Ronald Paulson, *Emblem and Expression: Meaning in English Art of the Eighteenth Century* (Cambridge, MA: Harvard University Press, 1975), 96. Also see my interpretation of this painting in Julie Plax, "Watteau's *Voulez-Vous Triompher les Belles:* An Interpretation and Inquiry into the Theme of Love," Master's thesis, University of Missouri, Columbia, 1979.

78 For the importance of gesture and its social significance in Watteau's paintings, see Sarah Cohen, "*Un Bal Continuel*: Watteau's Cythera Paintings and Aristocratic Dancing in the 1710's," *Art History* 17 (June 1994): 160–81.

79 Bryson, *Word and Image,* 82–83.

80 Hélène Adhémar and René Huyghe, *Watteau, Sa vie–son oeuvre* (Paris: Tisné, 1950), 117, see nothing suggestive about these hands.

81 Méré, *Oeuvres,* 3:158.

82 Nicholas Mirzoeff, "Seducing our Eyes: Gender, Jurisprudence, and Visuality in Watteau," *The Eighteenth Century: Theory and Interpretation* 35 (Summer 1994): 135–54.

83 Watteau was not a painstaking painter, nor was he academically trained. According to Comte de Caylus, "Vie de Watteau," cited in Rosenberg, *Vies des Watteau:* "Watteau pensoit profondement sur la peinture, et combien son execution étoit inferieure a ses idées. En effet, n'ayant aucune connaissance de l'anatomie" (72). "Watteau pour accélérer son effet et son execution, aimoit à peindre gras. Cette manoeuvre a eu toujours beaucoup de partisans, et les plus grands maitres en ont fait usage. Mais pour l'emploier avec success il faut avoir de grandes et d'heureuses preparations, et Watteau n'en faisoit presque jamais" (76).

84 Mary Sheriff's linking of genius, aesthetics, and the notion of the courtier, in the chapter "Easel Painting and the Aesthetics of Brushwork," is important for understanding the often overlooked significance of Watteau's technique. See Mary D. Sheriff, *Fragonard: Art and Eroticism* (Chicago: University of Chicago Press, 1990), 117–52.

85 Katie Scott has remarked upon a similar perspectival ambiguity in Watteau's *La Perspective.*

> French theorists, as disparate in their views as Roger de Piles, the champion of colour, and Henri Testelin, the tireless defender of Le Brun, were inclined to agree that the function of perspective was principally to facilitate the legibility of a pictorial narrative by so judiciously aligning the point of central perspective with the object or action of the composition's primary focus, that the spectator was enlightened in a single, instantaneous *coup d'oeil.* On the surface *The Perspective* promises no less, but where the diagonals converge is found only a carcass; an empty centre.

(*Rococo Interior,* 158–59.)

86 Plax, "Watteau's *Voulez-Vous.*"

87 Posner, *Watteau,* 174–76.

88 Posner, *Watteau,* 174.

89 A. P. de Mirimonde, "Les sujets musicaux chez Antoine Watteau," *Gazette des beaux-arts* 58 (November 1961): 249–88.

90 A. P. de Mirimonde, "Statues et emblèmes dans l'oeuvre d'Antoine Watteau," *La Revue du Louvre et des Musées de France,* 12, no. 1 (1962): 11–20; and Calvin Seerveld, "Tell-tale Statues in Watteau's Painting," *Eighteenth-Century Studies* 14 (Winter 1980–81): 151–80.

91 As Seerveld has pointed out in "Tell-tale Statues" and as Crow further develops, in *Painters and Public Life,* 57–65, the arabesque form reveals the foundations of Watteau's *fêtes.* Another related study on *galante* iconography is Alain Guillerm, "Le système de l'iconographie galante," *Dix-huitième siècle,* no. 12 (1980): 177–94.

92 Seerveld, "Tell-tale Statues," 152.

93 Emblem 3, *The Voluntary Prisoner,* in Philip Ayres, *Emblemata Amatoria* (1683), depicts a field of caged birds and birds willingly flying into cages. For a discussion of the iconography of the caged bird, see Elise Goodman-Soellner, "L'oiseau pris au piège: Nicolas Lancret *Le Printemps* and the *Prisionnier Volontaire* of P. Ayres," *Gazette des beaux-arts* 107 (March 1988): 127–30.

94 Seerveld, "Tell-tale Statues," 155.

95 For a discussion of the transposition from the decorative form of the arabesque to easel paintings, see Crow, *Painters and Public Life,* 58–65.

96 For an explanation of Watteau's painterly and compositional problems, see Crow, *Painters and Public Life,* 265, n. 57.

97 Crow, *Painters and Public Life,* 45–74, for a discussion of the *fêtes galantes.*

98 Crow, *Painters and Public Life,* 57.

99 This passsage is discussed in Gérard Le Coat, "*Le pèlerinage à l'isle de Cithère:* Un sujet «aussi galant qu'allegorique»," *Canadian Art Review* 2, no. 2 (1975): 9–23. The full text of the announcement, which appeared in the *Mercure de France,* April 1733, 772, is as follows:

> une estampe nouvellement gravée d'après un des plus beaux tableaux de feu Watteau, peintre flamand de l'Académie royale de peinture & sculpture. Le sujet aussi galand qu'allégorique représente *L'Embarquement des pellerins pour l'Isle de Cithère.* Le tableau original est d'une grande composition & d'un effet charmant; il est dans le Cabinet de M. de Jullienne, lequel continüe, depuis plus de douze années, à faire graver tous les ouvrages de ce gracieux peintre; nous pouvons assurer que celuy-ci est un de ceux qui fait le plus de plaisir. Il est très heureusement gravé par le Sr. Tardieu, grande estampe en largeur.

(Cited in Émile Dacier and Albert Vuaflart, *Jean de Jullienne et les graveurs de Watteau a XVIIIe siècle,* 4 vols. [Paris: La Société pour l'étude de la gravure francaise à l'occasion du bi-centenaire de la mort de Watteau, 1921–29], 3:52.)

100 Comte de Caylus, "Vie de Watteau," 79–80. "En un mot, à la reserve de quelques-uns de ses tableaux tels-que *L'Accordée* ou *La Noce de Village, Le Bal, L'Enseigne* faite pour le Sieur Gersaint, *L'Embarquement pour Cythère* qu'il peint pour sa réception dans votre Académie, et qu'il a répétée, ses compositions n'ont aucun object. Elles n'expriment le concours d'aucune passion et sont part conséquent, déporvues d'une des plus piquantes parties de la peinture, je veux dire l'action."

101 For a discussion of the "coming or going" question and references to the pertinent scholarship on the painting, see Michael Levey, "The Real Theme of Watteau's

Embarkation for Cythera," *Burlington Magazine* 13 (May 1961): 180–85. Joseph Sloane provides a novel solution to this question in "Watteau's *Embarkation for Cythera:* A Suggested Solution," *Studies in Iconography* 7 and 8 (1981–82): 289–99. Sarah Cohen explores the function of gesture and the dance in the economy of the painting in "*Un Bal Continuel:* Watteau's Cythera Paintings," and Nicholas Mirzoeff examines the relationship between representation and laws concerning gender and sexual practices in "Seducing Our Eyes," 135–54.

102 For this tradition, see Émile Dacier, "Autour de Watteau – L'Île de Cythère avant *l'Embarquement,*" *Revue de l'art ancien et moderne* 71 (1937): 247–50; and Mary Louise Ennis, "The Voyage to Cythera: From Courtly Allegory to Erotic Utopia in French Literature, 1700–1750," Ph.D. diss., Yale University, 1989.

103 Louis de Fourcaud, "A. Watteau, scènes et figures théâtrales," *Revue de l'art ancien et moderne* 15 (February 1904): 135–50 and (March 1904): 193–213. Dancourt described the *mise en scene* as "the young men and women of the village, dressed as pilgrims, prepare for a voyage to the Temple of Love."

104 For works dealing with the possible theatrical sources for *Pilgrimage,* see Fourcaud, "Scènes et figures théâtrales"; Charles de Tolnay, "*L'Embarquement pour Cythère* de Watteau au Louvre," *Gazette des beaux-arts* 46 (July 1955): 91–102; Hélène Adhémar, "*L'Embarquement pour l'île de Cythère*" – *Watteau* (Paris: Le musée des chefs-d'oeuvre, 1947); Edmond Pilon, "Les origines de *l'embarquement pour l'isle de Cythère,*" *Revue de l'art ancien et moderne* 40 (July–August 1921): 83–94; Jean Locquin, "Contributions à l'étude des sources d'inspiration d'Antoine Watteau," *Bulletin de la société de l'histoire de l'art français* (1949): 49–52; and Robert Tomlinson, *La fête galante: Watteau et Marivaux* (Geneva: Droz, 1981), 110–26 and 174–75.

105 For a discussion of the Cythera novels, see Locquin, "Étude d'Antoine Watteau"; and Hélène Adhémar, "Watteau, les romans et l'imagerie de son temps," *Gazette des beaux-arts* 90 (November 1977): 165–72.

106 Tomlinson, *La fête galante,* 116–18.

107 Nemeitz, *Séjour de Paris,* 566. "Mais [c'est] surtout le Dimanch que beaucoup le monde y va se divertir."

108 Antoine Furetière, *Voyage de Mercure* (first published in 1659), in Edouard Fournier and Francisque Michel, *Le livre d'or des métiers. Histoire des hôtelleries, cabarets, hôtels garnis et des anciennes communautés* (Paris: Seri, 1859), 280–81.

109 Tomlinson, *La fête galante,* 117.

110 J. H. Marchand, *Testament histori-morali-politique de Monsieur Rauponeau* (Paris: By the author, 1760), 19.

111 The notion of compositionally suggesting temporality in *Pilgrimage* is discussed in A. Rodin, *L'art, entretiens réunis par Paul Gsell* (Paris: Grasset, 1911), 91ff. A more detailed analysis can be found in Evanghélos Moutsopoulos, "Les structures de la temporalité chez Watteau," in *Antoine Watteau (1684–1721): Le peintre, son temps et sa légende,* ed. François Moureau and Margaret Morgan Grasselli (Paris: Champion-Slatkine, 1987), 143–48.

112 Levey, "Watteau's *Embarkation for Cythera,*" 180–85.

113 This device was common in the numerous *Emblemata Amatoria,* or emblems of love. Examples include Otto van Veen's *Amorum Emblemata,* first published in 1608; Philip Ayres's *Embemata Amatoria,* published in 1683; and Daniel Heinsius's *Emblemata Amatoria,* published in 1608.

114 This detail was first brought to my attention by Normal E. Land.
115 Tolnay, "*L'Embarquement,*" 96.
116 Tolnay, "*L'Embarquement,*" 96.
117 Although the scallop shell is more specifically associated with Venus and the Pilgrim's badge, other types of shells, such as the oyster, did refer to the female genitalia in French slang. "*Coquille*" in general, without reference to the species, was also a common slang term for this part of the female anatomy. See John S. Farmer and W. E. Henley, *A Supplemental Glossary of Colloquial English*, 5 vols. (London: Privately printed, 1896), 4:341–42 and 5:119.
118 Tomlinson, *La fête galante,* 122–23.
119 Tomlinson, *La fête galante,* 122.

> Ma gourde sera toujours pleine
> D'un just divin,
> Je te rafraîcherai sans pein soir et matin,
> Et pendant le cours du chemin,
> Aimable fille
> Quand je te verserai du vin,
> Présente ta coquille.

120 Tomlinson, *La fête galante,* 122.

> Ma foi, pauvre pèlerin,
> Tu vas perdre tes coquilles,
> Et tu serais bien heureux
> Si tu sauves ton bourdon.

121 Mario Praz, *Studies in Seventeenth-Century Imagery* (Rome: Edizioni di Historia e Litteratura, 1964), 92–93. Examples of this emblematic motif can be found in Daniel Heinsius, *Emblemata Amatoria;* Otto van Veen (Vaenius), *Amoratum Emblemata* (1608); and Junius Hadrianus, *Emblemata* (1565).
122 Posner, *Watteau,* 194–95.
123 Levey, "Watteau's *Embarkation for Cythera,*" 185.

Chapter Four. The Meeting of High and Low Culture in Watteau's *Gersaint's Signboard*

1 Louis-Sébastian Mercier, *Tableau de Paris,* 12 vols. (1782; reprint, Geneva: Slatkine Reprints, 1979), 1:215–16. "Ces enseignes avoient pour la plupart un volume colossal et en relief; elles donnoient l'image d'un peuple gigantesque, aux yeux du peuple le plus rabougri de l'Europe. On voyoit une garde d'épée de six pieds de haut, une botte grosse comme un muid, un éperon large comme une roue de carrosse; un gant qui auroit logé un enfant de trois ans dans chaque doigt." The English translation is from Daniel Roche, *The People of Paris: An Essay in Popular Culture in the Eighteenth Century,* trans. Marie Evans, in association with Gwynne Lewis (Berkeley and Los Angeles: University of California Press, 1987).
2 The documentary and laboratory evidence for the alterations to the painting are exhaustively examined in Hélène Adhémar, "*L'Enseigne de Gersaint* par Antoine Watteau. Aperçus nouveaux," *Bulletin du laboratoire du Louvre* 9 (1964): 7–18. It should be noted that the original height of the painting was 11 cm less (155 cm) than it was after the alterations.

3 Ettore Camesasca and Pierre Rosenberg, *Tout l'oeuvre peint de Watteau* (Paris: Flammarion, Les Classiques de l'Art, 1970), 123; and Margaret Grasselli and Pierre Rosenberg, *Watteau: 1684–1721* (Paris: Editions de la Réunion des Musées Nationaux, 1984), 447–50.

4 On the basis of her examination, Adhémar is convinced that the signboard was originally done on two separate canvases that were joined together. This repudiates Paul Alfassa's earlier argument that the work was divided at the time that the painting entered the collection of Frederick of Prussia, around 1744, in response to Frederick's desire to have two large pendants to decorate his newly created music room. See Adhémar, *"L'Enseigne de Gersaint,"* and Paul Alfassa, *"L'Enseigne de Gersaint," Bulletin de la société de l'histoire de l'art français* (1910): 146–47.

5 Édme Gersaint, *Catalogue raisonné des diverses curiosités du cabinet de feu M. Quentin Lorangère* (Paris: Barois, 1744), 3–4: "le tout étoit fait après nature; les attitudes en étoit si vraies et si aisées; l'ordonnance si naturelle; les groupes si bien entendus, qu'il attiroit les yeux des passans." Scholars who argue for the "realist" view of *Gersaint's Signboard* include Kenneth Clark, "Watteau – *L'Enseigne de Gersaint,*" in *Looking at Pictures* (New York: Holt, Rinehart & Winston, 1960), 75–87; and most recently, Marianne Roland-Michel, *Watteau: An Artist of the Eighteenth Century* (New York: Alpine Fine Arts, 1984), 109.

6 Comte de Caylus, *"La vie d'Antoine Watteau peintre de figures et de paysages, sujets galantes et modernes"* (1748), in Pierre Rosenberg, ed., *Vies anciennes de Watteau* (Paris: Hermann, 1984), 79–80.

7 The first scholarly work to argue this position is Alfassa, *"L'Enseigne de Gersaint."* Hélène Adhémar has elaborated upon this interpretation in Hélène Adhémar and René Huyghe, *Watteau, sa vie – son oeuvre* (Paris: Tisné, 1950), and Adhémar, "*L'Enseigne de Gersaint* par Watteau," 7–18. Donald Posner carries this interpretation to a logical conclusion when he states that, in adopting the form of a signboard, Watteau was paying tribute to his artistic roots as a painter of signboards. "Now, at the end of his life, Watteau wanted to remember the beginning." In *Antoine Watteau* (Ithaca, NY: Cornell University Press, 1984), 276.

8 L. Aragon, *'L'Enseigne de Gersaint'* (Paris: Ides et Calendes, 1946). Hélène Adhémar has elaborated upon Aragon's observation in Adhémar, *"L'Enseigne de Gersaint."* Adhémar discusses the two halves as a diptych, representing the old and the new taste in painting. Jean Ferré, ed., *Watteau,* 4 vols. (Madrid: Athena Editions, 1972), 1:223, carries this argument even further, to suggest that the two halves of *L'Enseigne* were originally two separate, independent works. Most recently, Mary Vidal has suggested that Watteau brought the best of the old and the new together, not in conflict, but in a dialogue about the art of painting; see Vidal, *Watteau's Painted Conversations: Art, Literature, and Talk in Seventeenth- and Eighteenth-Century France* (New Haven: Yale University Press, 1992), especially the chapter titled "*L'Enseigne de Gersaint* and the Conversational Structure of the Artistic Sign," 143–96.

9 Oliver Banks, *Watteau and the North: Studies in the Dutch and Flemish Baroque on French Rococo Painting* (New York: Garland Press, 1977), 241–52.

10 Gérard Le Coat, "Modern Enchantment and Traditional Didacticism in Watteau's *L'Enseigne de Gersaint* and Couperin's *Folies Françaises,*" *Gazette des beaux-arts* 41 (November 1978): 169–72.

11 Le Coat, "Watteau's *L'Enseigne de Gersaint,*" 172.

12 Robert Neuman, "Watteau's *L'Enseigne de Gersaint* and Baroque Emblematic Tradition," *Gazette des beaux-arts* 104 (November 1984): 153–64.

13 Neuman, "Watteau's *L'Enseigne de Gersaint,*" 155–57.

14 Neuman, "Watteau's *L'Enseigne de Gersaint,*" 156.

15 See chapter 2 on Watteau's military paintings.

16 An announcement for the engraving after *L'Enseigne de Gersaint* informs us that "Cette fameuse Enseigne ne fut exposée que quinze jours," *Mercure de France,* November 1732, p. 2449, cited in Alfassa, *"L'Enseigne de Gersaint,"* 136.

17 Mercier, *Tableau de Paris,* 2:204. "Il seroit plus commode & plus facile d'aller tout de suite chez M. un tel, no. 87, que de trouver M. un tel au *Cordon bleu,* ou à la *Barbe d'argent,* la quinzième porte cochère à droite ou à gauche aprés telle rue."

18 Roche, *People of Paris,* 224–28, provides insightful analysis of the multitextual role of signboards in eighteenth-century Paris.

19 Edouard Fournier, *Histoire des enseignes de Paris* (Paris: E. Dentu, 1884), 77–78. Fournier recounts this charming tale in his discussion of the various streets that derived their names from well-known signs.

20 Henri Sauval, *Histoire et recherches des antiquités,* 1:285; cited in Fournier, *Histoire des enseignes,* 77–78.

> Avec le temps, son nom (puits-d'amour) a passé à une maison proche de là, et comme ce nom a paru galant à un marchand qui la loue, il a fait repeindre l'ensiegne et l'a rehaussée de couleurs fort vives, et même, afin de mieux représenter la fable, il y a figuré un puits, tout entouré de belles filles et de jeunes garçons, avec un petit Amour qui décoche des flèches sur eux, et ces paroles au bas: *Au Puits d'Amour.* Or, comme d'autres marchands ont trouvé cette enseigne fort à leur gré, et d'autant plus qu'ils s'imaginent que les enseignes plaisantes, ou que se font remarquer, attirent les chalands, les uns l'ont tout à fait copiée, les autres se sont contentés de l'imiter.

21 In jargon, "well of love" refers to the vagina. See John S. Farmer and W. E. Henley, *A Supplemental Glossary of Colloquial English,* 5 vols. (London: Privately printed, 1896), 4:343.

22 The most comprehensive work covering the iconography, lore, and history of Parisian signboards is Fournier, *Histoire des enseignes.* For other useful works about signboard history and imagery, see chapter 1, n. 110, and John Grand-Carteret, *L'histoire – la vie – les moeurs – et le curiosité par l'image, le pamphlet, et le document (1450–1900),* 4 vols. (Paris: Librairie de la curiosité et de beaux arts, 1928). More recently, Richard Wrigley critically examines signboards in "Signs and the Spaces of Professionalism in the Eighteenth and Early Nineteenth Century," *Oxford Art Journal* 21, #1 (1998): 43–67.

23 For a discussion of some of these long-standing devices, see Rosine Grange, "Enseignes anciennes, un langage perdu," *Arts et decoration,* no. 184 (1975): 90–95.

24 Fournier, *Histoire des enseignes,* 391.

25 Mercier, *Tableau de Paris,* 1:215. "Quand le vent souffloit, toutes ces enseignes, devenues gémissants, se heurtoient & se choquoient entr'elles; ce qui composoit un carillon plaintif & discordant, vraiment incroyable pour qui ne l'a pas entendu."

26 Alfred Franklin, *Dictionnaire historique des arts, métiers et professions* (1906, reprint; New York: Burt Franklin, 1968), 304–5. "La réduction des enseignes à une même grandeur, hauteur et avance sur les rues est à désirer pour la décoration

de la ville et pour empêcher l'abus de plusiers marchands et artisants qui attachent à leur maisons des enseignes d'une dépense et d'une grandueur excessives."

27 Fournier, *Histoire des enseignes,* 16.

28 Fournier, *Histoire des engsignes,* 17: "exerça toute espèce de vexations contre les propriétaires de ces enseignes."

29 Fournier cites the principal 1693 articles concerning signboards; *Histoire des enseignes,* 17–18.

Article XII – Pour les enseignes grandes ou petites, y compris la potence, s'il y en a, ou autres accompagnements, qu'elles soient suspendues au-dessus ou au-dessous de l'auvent, en quelque nombre qu'il y en ait à la même maison, un seul droit de quatre livres; mais pareil droit pour chaque marchand ou artisan, dans la même maison. Si, après l'anné révolue, il était fait ou exposé quelque nouvelle enseigne, nouveau droit de quatre livre.

Article XIII – Pour tous les tableaux appliqués sur les trumeaux et jambages des portes, ou de la boutique, en quelque nombre qu'ils soient à la même maison, pour le même marchand, un seul droit de quatre livres.

Article XXI – Pour les bustes aux maisons ou encoignures, indiquant la profession, quelque nombre qu'il y en ait, le tout en une même maison, un seul droit de quatre livres.

Article XXII – Pour les cadrans indiquant la profession, un seul droit de quatre livres.

Article XXVIII – Aucun propriétaire ou locataire des maisons, boutiques ou échoppes ne pourra faire poser, établir ou échanger aucune desdites choses ou espèces, qu'il n'ait obtenu préamblement la permission, par écrit, desdits commissaires.

30 Mercier, *Tableau de Paris,* 1:215. "Elles donnoient l'image d'un peuple gigantesque, aux yeux du peuple le plus rabougri de l'Europe."

31 Roche, *People of Paris,* 226.

32 The most comprehensive account of these punning signboards can be found in Fournier, *Histoire des enseignes,* 218–28 and 269–78.

33 Fournier, *Histoire des enseignes,* 220.

34 Tallement des Réaux, *Les histoirettes de Tallemant des Réaux,* 2nd ed. (Paris: Delloye, 1840), 10:42, cited in Fournier, *Histoire des enseignes,* 224.

Un commis borgne ayant exigé d'un cabaretier des droits qu'il ne lui devoit pas, le cabaretier, pour se venger, fit représenter le portrait du commis, à son enseigne, sous la forme d'un voleur, avec cette inscription: *Au Borgne qui prend.* Le commis, s'en trouvant offensé, vint trouver le cabaretier et lui rendit l'argent des droits en question, à la charge qu'il feroit réformer son enseigne. Le cabaretier, pour y satisfaire, fit seulement ôter de son enseigne le *p,* si bien qu'il resta: *Au Borgne qui rend,* au lieu du *Au Borgne qui prend.*

35 Fournier, *Histoire des enseignes,* 206.

36 Fournier, *Histoire des enseignes,* 222.

37 Mercier, *Tableau de Paris,* 5:109, cited in Fournier, *Histoire des enseignes,* 193. Là, tous les rois de la terre dorment ensemble: Louis XIV and Georges III se baisent fraternellement, le roi de Prusse couche avec l'impératrice de Russie, l'Empereur est de niveau avec les Électeurs; là, enfin, la tiare et le turban se confondent. Un cabaretier arrive, remue avec le pied toutes ces têtes couronnées, les examine, prend au hasard la figure du roi de Pologne, l'emporte, l'accroche et écrit dessous: *Au Grand Vainqueur.*

38 Fournier, *Histoire des enseignes,* 398–99.
39 E. La Quérière, *Recherches historiques sur les enseignes des maisons particulières* (Paris: V. Didron, 1852), 25. "On disait d'un méchant portrait, d'un méchant tableau, qu'il était bon à faire une enseigne."
40 Philibert-Joseph Le Roux, *Dictionnaire comique, satirique, critique, burlesque, libre, et proverbial,* 2 vols. (Lyon: Chez les héritiers Berringos, 1735), 1:239. "On dit aussi d'un méchant portrait, d'un méchant tableau, qu'il est bon à faire une enseigne à bière. Parce que ces sortes d'enseignes sont toujours très mal faites."
41 Le Roux, *Dictionnaire comique,* 2:132. "On dit autrefois, Gueux comme un peintre. Mais ce proverbe est devenue faux en ces dernier jours, où la peinture a été cultivée & annoblie. On doit plutôt dire Glorieux comme un peintre."
42 Franklin, *Dictionnaire,* 559, and Louis Vitet, *L'académie royale de peinture et de sculpture, étude historique* (Paris: Michel Levy Frères, 1861), 18–20.
43 Franklin, *Dictionnaire,* 559: "que pour relever les plus beaux de tous les arts, sans aucun dessein de préjudicier à quoi que ce puisse estre au corps de la maistrise."
44 Jacques Wilhelm, "François Le Moyne and Antoine Watteau," *Art Quarterly* 14, no. 3 (1951): 216–30. In this article, Wilhelm discusses Le Moyne's signboard for a hairdresser's shop and its relation to Watteau's oeuvre.
45 Dezallier D'Argenville, *Abrégé de la vie des plus fameux peintres* (Paris, 1762), 4:417–28, cited in Wilhelm, *"François Le Moyne,"* 225.
46 Edmond and Jules de Goncourt, *French Eighteenth-Century Painters,* trans. Robin Ironside (Ithaca, NY: Cornell University Press, 1948), 110.
47 Goncourt, *French Painters,* 111.
48 Manuscript notes of Pierre-Jean Mariette's *Abecedario,* cited in Émile Dacier and Albert Vuaflart, *Jean de Jullienne et les graveurs de Watteau au XVIIIe siècle,* 4 vols. (Paris: La Société pour l'étude de la gravure française à l'occasion du bicentenaire de la mort de Watteau, 1921–29), 3:14: "qui a servi pendant quelque temps de montre à la boutique d'un peintre du pont Nôtre Dame à Paris." In eighteenth-century usage, *"montre,"* which more properly refers to a window display, could also refer to a sign.
49 Roland-Michel, *Watteau,* 151.
50 Louis de Fourcaud, "Antoine Watteau, peintre d'arabesques," *Revue de l'art ancien et moderne* 25 (January 1909): 49–59, and (February 1909): 129–40.
51 Fourcaud, "Peintre d'arabesques" (February 1909): 134–35.
52 Margaret Grasselli and Pierre Rosenberg, *Watteau: 1684–1721* (Paris: Editions de la Réunion des Musées Nationaux, 1984), 62–63, and 69. For further discussion of these drawings, see François Boucher, "Les sources d'inspiration de *L'Enseigne de Gersaint,*" *Bulletin de la société de l'histoire de l'art français* (1958): 123–29; Gustave Lebel, "A propos de deux equisses d'enseignes du XVIIIe siècle," *Bulletin de la société de l'histoire de l'art français* (1921): 55–61; Martin Eidelberg, *Watteau's Drawings: Their Use and Significance* (New York: Garland Press, 1977), 236–52.
53 Grasselli and Rosenberg, *Watteau,* 450.
54 For a discussion of the history of these commercial images, and the conventions they employed, see Boucher, "Sources d'inspiration," 123–29.
55 For a useful summary of the provenance and bibliography concerning *Gilles* see Grasselli and Rosenberg, *Watteau,* 430–36.
56 Hélène Adhémar, "Watteau, les romans et l'imagerie de son temps," *Gazette des beaux-arts* 90 (November 1977): 165–72. See also, Donald Posner, "Another Look at Watteau's *Gilles,*" *Apollo* 117 (February 1983): 97–99.

57 Charles and François Parfaict, *Mémoires pour servir à l'histoire des spectacles de la foire,* 2 vols. (Paris: Briasson, 1743), 2:36–37, "mit pour enseigne son portrait habillé en Pierrot."

58 Jeannine Baticle, "Pierrot, Gilles et les autres," in *Antoine Watteau (1684–1721): Le peintre, son temps et sa légende,* ed. François Moureau and Margaret Morgan Grasselli (Paris: Champion-Slatkine, 1987), 39.

59 Watteau may have known Belloni through Gillot, who was involved with the theatrical entrepreneurs and performers at the fairs. See Bernard Populus, *Claude Gillot (1673–1722): Catalogue de l'oeuvre gravé,* 2 vols. (Paris: Société pour l'étude de la gravure française, 1930), 1:24–27.

60 Rosalba Carriera, *Journal de Rosalba Carriera pendant son séjour à Paris en 1720–1721,* trans. Alfred Sensier (Paris: J. Techener, 1865). Carriera's *Journal* provides a glimpse into this group and its members.

61 Andrew McClellan discusses Gersaint's business in relation to the new position of art and the dealer in constructing elite status in "Watteau's Dealer: Gersaint and the Marketing of Art in Eighteenth-Century Paris," *Art Bulletin* 78 (September 1966): 439–53. Katie Scott's work, *The Rococo Interior: Decoration and Social Spaces in Early Eighteenth-Century Paris* (New Haven: Yale University Press, 1995), explores the coding of interior decoration in relation to social status.

62 For an insightful examination of the literature of eighteenth-century sales catalogues see Krzysztof Pomian, *Collectors and Curiosities: Paris and Venice, 1500–1800,* trans. E. Wiles-Portier (Cambridge: Polity Press, 1990). In the second half of the century a profusion of works provided advice for the collector, for example, Carl Heinrich Heinecken, *Idée général d'une collection complète d'éstampes* (Leipzig: J. P. Kraus, 1771). Monographs, such as Charles Antoine Jombert, *Catalogue raisonné de l'oeuvre de Sebastien Le Clerc, chevalier romain, dessinateur & graveur du cabinet du Roi* (Paris: Chez l'auteur, 1774), also included extensive advice on collecting. For example: xxvij–xxxij, an "Avis aux marchands d'estampes sur la distinction des vignettes, culs de lampes, frontispieces & autres ornemens qu'on met dans les livres."

63 Raymonde Robert, *Le conte de fées littéraire en France de la fin du XVIIe à la fin du XVIIIe siècle* (Nancy: Presses universitaires de France, 1982), 363–64.

64 Édme Gersaint, *Catalogue raisonné des diverses curiosités du cabinet de feu M. Quentin Lorangère* (Paris: Barois, 1744), 2–3.

> Quels avantages un Curieux ne tire-t-il pas de suites ordinaires de sa curiosité? . . . son titre de Curieux lui donne l'entrée dans les Cabinets les plus fameux et il peut aller s'y récréer; en qualité de Curieux, il devient égal à ceux-mêmes qui livrés à cette noble passion se trouvent au-dessus de son état par leur rang ou par leur condition: comme tel il est appelé et reçu avec plaisir dans leurs assembleés établieés à dessein de se communiquer leurs découvertes ou leurs acquisitions; il profite et jouit avec eux de ces nouveautés et il acquiert ainsi journellement des lumières et des connoissances en s'amusant avec fruit.

65 Édme Gersaint, *Catalogue de Lorangère,* 183–84.

> A son retour à Paris, qui étoit en 1721, dans les premières années de mon établissement, il vint chez moi pour me demander si je voulais bien le recevoir, et lui permettre, *pour se dégourdier les doigts* ce sont ses termes, je voulois bien, dis-je, lui permettre de peindre un plafond que je devois exposer en dehors; j'eus quelque répugnance à le satisfaire, aimant beacoup mieux l'occuper à quelque chose de plus solide; mais voyant que cela lui feroit plaisir, j'y consentis. L'on scait la réussite

qu'eut ce morceau; le tout étoit fait après nature; les attitudes en étoit si vraies et si aisées; l'ordonnance si naturelle; les groupes si bien entendus, qu'il attiroit les yeux des passans; et même les plus habiles Peintres vinrent à plusiers fois pour l'admirer: ce fut le travail de huit journées, encore n'y travailloit-il que les matins, sa santé délicate, ou pour mieux dire, sa foiblesse, ne lui permettant pas de s'occuper plus longtems. C'est le seul ouvrage qui ait un peu aiguisé son amour propre; il ne fit point difficulté de me l'avouer.

(The English translation is from Anita Brookner, *Watteau* [Twickenham, Eng.: Hamlyn, 1967], 22.)

66 Gersaint, *Catalogue de Lorangère,* 187. "Watteau espéroit de jour en jour gagner assez de force pour pouvoir entrenprendre ce voyage où je devois l'accompagner; mais sa défaillance augmentant de plus en plus & la nature manquant chez lui tout-à-coup il mourut entre mes bras audit Nogent, peu de temps après, le 18 Juillet 1721, âgé de 37 ans." (The English translation is from Brookner, *Watteau,* 22.)

67 The most thorough investigation of the mythic conventions in artists' biographies is Ernst Kris and Otto Kurtz, *Legend, Myth, and Magic in the Image of the Artist* (New Haven: Yale University Press, 1979).

68 Banks, *Watteau and the North,* 235.

69 My use of psychoanalytic theory in understanding and interpreting works of art and biographical texts has been guided by the work of Ellen Handler Spitz, *Art and Psyche: A Study in Psychoanalysis and Aesthetics* (New Haven: Yale University Press, 1985). Spitz thoughtfully explores the potential and limitations for psychoanalytic theory for the art historian. In particular, see "Liebert and the Documentary Approach," 65–75.

70 Gersaint had made the first payment on the inventory of Antoine Dieu's "commerce de tableaux, cadres, etc" on 15 April 1718. On 28 April 1718, a fire on the Petit Pont destroyed the shop from which Dieu had conducted business and its contents. See Dacier and Vuaflart, *Graveurs de Watteau,* 1:106.

71 The *Mercure de France* announced Gersaint's buying trips to Holland in 1734, 1736, 1739, and 1740. See Dacier and Vuaflart, *Graveurs de Watteau,* 1:108.

72 For Gersaint's role in merchandising the *goût chinois,* see Francis Watson, "Beckford, Mme. de Pompadour, the Duc de Bouillon and the Taste for Japanese Lacquer in Eighteenth-Century France," *Gazette des beaux-arts* 61 (February 1963): 101–27.

73 Gersaint, Marchand Jouaillier sur le Pont Nôtre Dame, Vend toute sorte de Clainquaillerie Nouvelle et de Gout, Bijoux, Glaces, Tableaux de Cabinet, Pagodes, Vernis et Porcelaines du Japon, Coquillages et autres morceaux d'Histoire Naturelle, Cailloux, Agathes, et généralement toutes Marchandises Curieuses et Étrangères.

74 Several useful sources for the relationships among economics, the luxury trade, and institutions of artistic production include Christopher Berry, *The Idea of Luxury* (Cambridge: Cambridge University Press, 1994); John Brewer and Roy Porter, eds., *Consumption and the World of Goods* (London: Routledge, 1993); Katie Scott, "Hierarchy, Liberty and Order: Languages of Art and Institutional Conflict in Paris," *Oxford Art Journal* 12 (1989): 59–70; Michael Sonenscher, *Work and Wages: Natural Law, Politics and the Eighteenth Century French Trades* (Cambridge: Cambridge University Press, 1989); Steven Laurence Kaplan and Cynthia J. Koepp, eds., *Work in France, Representations, Meaning, Organization, and Practice* (Ithaca, NY; Cornell University Press, 1986); W. McAllister

Johnson, "Paintings, Provenance and Price: Speculations on the Eighteenth-Century Connoisseurship Apparatus in France," *Gazette des beaux-arts* 115 (May–June 1986): 28–42. See also the art forum, "Work, Leisure, and Art," that I organized for *Eighteenth-Century Studies* 29 (Winter 1995–96): 211–28. This includes four essays: Candace Clements, "Noble Liberality and Speculative Industry in Early Eighteenth-Century Paris: Charles Coypel," 213–18; Andrew McClellan, "Edme Gersaint and the Marketing of Art in Eighteenth-Century Paris," 218–22; Paula Rea Radisich, "Deconstructing Dissipation," 222–25; and Wendy Wassyng Roworth, "Painting for Profit and Pleasure: Angelica Kauffman and the Art Business in Rome," 225–28.

75 For a discussion of the documentary evidence, see Paul Alfassa, *"L'enseigne de Gersaint,"* 130–34. More recently, Marianne Roland-Michel has painstakingly reexamined the documentary evidence, concluding that Watteau most probably returned to Paris in the early summer of 1720. See Roland-Michel, *Watteau,* 45–46.

76 Alfassa, *"L'Enseigne de Gersaint,"* 140–42. For the equivalent English measurements of the shop I have relied on Oliver Banks's calculations in Banks, *Watteau and the North,* 235.

77 For the attempted identification of these works, see O. Fischel, "Altes und neues vom *Schild de Gersaint,*" *Zeitschrift für Kunstgeschichte* 1 (1932): 341–53; Adhémar, *"L'enseigne de Gersaint,"* 16; and Dacier and Vuaflart, *Graveurs de Watteau,* 1:110.

78 Grasselli and Rosenberg, *Watteau,* 452.

79 Here I rely on the dimensions provided by Banks, *Watteau and the North,* 234.

80 Banks, *Watteau and the North,* 234–35.

81 Gersaint, *Catalogue de Lorangère,* 183. "J'ai vécu assez longtemps avec Watteau, et nous étions assez amis pour avoir appris quelques particularités dont je ferai part au public avec plaisir."

82 Gersaint, *Catalogue de Lorangère,* 183. "Watteau ne fut alors occupé qu'à ces ouvrages médiocres; il fut cependant distingué des autres parce qu'il se trouva propre à tout, en même temps d'expédition: il répétait souvent les mêmes sujets; il avait surtout le talen de rendre si bien son "Saint Nicolas, qui est un Saint que l 'on demandait souvent, qu'on le réservait particulièrement pour lui; *je savais* (me dit-il un jour) *mon Saint Nicolas par coeur,* et je me passais d'original."

83 Kris and Kurtz, *Legend, Myth, and Magic,* 30–38.

84 Giorgio Vasari, *Lives of the Artists* (Baltimore: Penguin Books, 1965), 57–81.

85 Of the eighteen French eighteenth-century biographies included in Pierre Rosenberg's *Vies anciennes de Watteau* (Paris: Hermann, 1984), only three, all published after Gersaint's biography, mention the *Signboard.* Comte de Caylus, *La vie d'Antoine Watteau: Peintre de figures et de paysages sujets galants et modernes* (Paris, 1748), cited in Rosenberg, *Vies de Watteau,* 79–80: "En un mot, à la réserve de queques-uns de ses tableaux tels que l'Accordée de village, le Bal, l'Enseigne faite pour le sieur Gersaint, l'Embarquement de Cythère qu'il a peint pour sa réception dans votre Académie et qu'il a répétée, ses compositions n'ont aucun object. Elles n'expriment le concours d'aucune passion et sont, par conséquent, dépourvues d'une des plus piquantes parties de la peinture, je veux dire l'action." Jacques Lacombe, "Note sur Watteau," in *Dictionnaire portatif des beaux-arts* (Paris: 1755), cited in Rosenberg, *Vies de Watteau,* 95: "il peignit pour le sieur Gersaint, son ami, marchand sur le Pont Nôtre-Dame, le plafond de sa boutique.

Ce morceau travaillé avec soin, attirait les regards des curieux, et faisait un spectacle pour les passants." Ulla Tessin, "Antoine Watteau," in *Portraits des hommes illustres, avec un abrégé historique de leurs vies* (1762), cited in Rosenberg, *Vies de Watteau,* 97: "De son vivant, ses tableaux étaient prisés plus qu'ils ne le sont aujourd'hui: l'enseigne de la boutique, peinte par Watteau, pour Gersaint, brocanteur et marchand de tableaux, fut vendu, si je ne me trompe, 3 ou 4,000 francs: c'est qu'elle était plus vigoureusement peint, et mieux empâtée, que le commun de ses ouvrages." The only other reference to Gersaint is indirect, probably alluding to the "death scene" in Gersaint's biography. A.-J. Dezallier d'Argenville, *Abrégé de la vie des plus fameux peintres* (Paris: 1945), cited in Rosenberg, *Vies de Watteau,* 46: "On lui conseilla de prendre l'air, et un ami le mena au village de Nogent près de Paris, où sa santé s'affaiblissant de jour en jour, il mourut en 1721, âgé de trente-sept ans."

86 Gersaint, *Catalogue de Lorangére,* 183–84: "et même les plus habiles Peintres vinrent à plusieurs fois pour l'admirer:"

87 For the provenance of *L'Enseigne,* see Dacier and Vuaflart, *Graveurs de Watteau,* 3:56–57; and Graselli and Rosenberg, *Watteau,* 452.

88 *Mercure de France,* November 1732, 2449, cited in Alfassa, *"L'Enseigne de Gersaint,"* 135–36, n. 1.

Ce Morceau qu' a 9 pieds de large, sur 5 pieds de haut, a toujours été regardé comme le Chef-d'oeuvre de cet excellent Peintre. Il représente le Magasin d'un Marchand, qui est rempli de différens Tableaux des plus grands Maîtres; on y reconnoît le caractère de et le goût de chacun de ces Maîtres.

Cette fameuse Enseigne ne fut exposée que quinze jours; elle fit l'admiration de tout Paris Elle fut vendue à M. Glucq. On la voit à présent dans le cabinet de M. Jullienne.

89 Édme Gersaint, *Catalogue de Lorangère,* 183, "j'eus quelque répugnance à le satisfaire, aimant beaucoup mieux l'occuper à quelque chose de plus solide; mais voyant que cela lui feroit plaisir, j'y consentis." The English translation is from Anita Brookner, *Watteau,* 22.

90 Banks, *Watteau and the North,* 235.

91 Kris and Kurtz, *Legend, Myth, and Magic,* 61–98.

92 Kris and Kurtz, *Legend, Myth, and Magic,* 94.

93 For a discussion of the fantasy portraits and the significance of painterly execution, see Mary Sheriff, *Fragonard: Art and Eroticism* (Chicago: University of Chicago Press, 1990).

94 Gersaint, *Catalogue de Lorangère,* 2, "il (the Curieux) devient égal à ceux-mêmes qui livrés à cette noble passion se trouvent au-dessus de son état par leur rang ou par leur condition: comme tel il est appelé et reçu avec plaisir dans leurs assemblées."

95 For more on the *corps de marchands* and the *corps de la mercerie,* see Carolyn Sargentson, *Merchants and Luxury Markets: The Marchands-Merciers of Eighteenth-Century Paris* (Santa Monica, CA: J. Paul Getty Museum, 1996); Franklin, *Dictionnaire,* 645–47, and 478–80; and for a general overview of the role of the *marchand-mercier,* see Francis Watson, "Les marchands-merciers et le gout français au XVIIIe siècle," *L'oeil* 153 (September 1967): 12–21.

96 *Dictionnaire de Trévoux* (1771 ed.), 5:944, cited in Franklin, *Dictionnaire,* 508. "*Les Marchands d'objets d'art.* [selling] tableaux, estampes, statues, candélabres,

girandoles, lustres, pendules, coffres, etc." Franklin notes that at the end of the seventeenth century there were twenty-one classes of *marchand merciers.*

97 Trévoux, *Dictionnaire,* cited in Franklin, *Dictionnaire,* 480: "marchands de tout, faiseurs de rien."

98 Sauval, *Antiquités de Paris,* 2:475, cited in Franklin, *Dictionnaire,* 480.

99 Savary, *Dictionnaire du Commerce* (ed. 1723), 2:711, cited in Franklin, *Dictionnaire,* 501.

Le corps de la mercerie est considéré comme le plus noble et le plus excellent de tous les corps marchands, d'autant que ceux qui le composent *ne travaillent point et ne font aucun ouvrage de la main,* si ce n'est pour enjolivier les choses qui sont déjà faites et fabriquées. Aussi ceux qui sont admis dans ce corps sont-ils reçus noblement, *ne leur étant pas permis de faire ni de manufacturer aucunes marchandises,* mais seulement de les enjoliver, ce qui n'est pas des autres corps, qui sont regardez comme mixtes, c'est-à-dire qu'ils tiennent du marchand et de l'artisan.

100 For a discussion of the history of the usage of the term "*noblesse commerçante,*" see Franklin, *Dictionnaire,* 500–502.

101 Dacier and Vuaflart, *Graveurs de Watteau,* 1:107, "réception de Gersaint, en qualité de Marchand mercier" and an act of 1721 qualified Gersaint as a *mercier.*

102 For a good discussion of the shift from an estate structure to a class structure that was occurring, see Amanda Arriaza, "Mousnier and Barber: The Theoretical Underpinnings of the 'Society of Orders' in Early Modern Europe," *Past and Present* 89 (November 1980): 39–57. For the relationship between the nobility and commerce, see Henri Lévy-Bruhl, "La noblesse de France et le commerce à la fin de l'ancien régime," *Revue d'histoire moderne* 8 (1933): 209–35.

103 Martin Lister, *A Journey to Paris in the Year 1698* (London: Jacob Tonson, 1699), 9.

104 Lister, *Journey to Paris,* 14.

105 Gersaint, *Catalogue de Lorangère,* 183–84, "qu'il attiroit les yeux des passans; et même les plus habiles Peintres vinrent à plusieurs fois pour l'admirer:" The English translation is from Brookner, *Watteau,* 22.

106 This same pattern appears in the vogue for *contes de fées,* in the amateur *parades* that imitated those at the *foires,* and, as Robert Isherwood has pointed out, in the incorporation of street cries and popular vaudevilles into the salon, by men such as Collé, and into the Opéra Comique by writers such as Charles Favart and Panard. Robert Isherwood, *Farce and Fantasy: Popular Entertainment in Eighteenth-Century Paris* (New York: Oxford University Press, 1986).

Conclusion

1 Ann Hollander, *Seeing through Clothes* (New York: Avon books, 1980), 138–48, for the tradition of drapery use in portraiture.

2 JoLynn Edwards, "Watteau and the Dance," in *Antoine Watteau (1684–1721),* ed. François Moureau and Margaret Moran Grasselli (Paris: Champion-Slatkine, 1987), 138–148. Edwards identifies the dance pose in *L'Indifférent* and notes its similarity to the Rigaud portrait of Louis XIV.

3 Horst de la Croix and Fred S. Kleiner, eds., *Gardner's Art through the Ages,* 10th ed. (New York: Harcourt Brace College Publishers, 1996), 890.

Bibliography

Adhémar, Hélène. "*L'Enseigne de Gersaint* par Antoine Watteau. Aperçus nouveaux." *Bulletin du laboratoire du Louvre* 9 (1964): 7–18.

"Watteau, les romans et l'imagerie de son temps." *Gazette des beaux-arts* 90 (November 1977): 165–72.

Adhémar, Hélène, and René Huyghe. *Watteau, sa vie – son oeuvre.* Paris: Tisné, 1950.

Administration générale du mobilier national des manufactures nationales des Gobelins, de Beauvais, et de la Savonnerie. *La Route du Nord. Van der Meulen. Dessins et soies peintes.* Exh. cat. Paris, 1990.

Albert, Maurice. *Les théâtres de la foire.* 1900. Reprint, New York: Burt Franklin, 1970.

Alfassa, Paul. "L'Enseigne de Gersaint." *Bulletin de la société de l'histoire de l'art français* (1910): 126–72.

Alméras, Henri, and Paul d'Estrées. *Les théâtres libertins au XVIIIe siècle.* Paris: H. Daragon, 1905.

Aragon, Louis. *L'Enseigne de Gersaint.* Paris: Ides et Calendes, 1946.

Arriaza, Amanda. "Mousnier and Barber: The Theoretical Underpinnings of the 'Society of Orders' in Early Modern Europe." *Past and Present* 89 (November 1980): 39–57.

Arsène, Alexandre. *Histoire de la peinture militaire.* Paris: Librairie Renouard, Henri Laurens Editeur, 1889.

Attinger, G. *L'esprit de la commedia dell'arte dans le théâtre français.* Paris: Librarie théâtrale, 1950.

Babeau, Albert. *La vie militaire sous l'ancien régime.* 2 vols. Paris: Firmin-Didot, 1890.

Bahktin, M. *Rabelais and His World.* Cambridge, MA: MIT Press, 1968.

[Balzac, Honoré]. *Batteur de pavé: Petit dictionnaire critique et anecdotique des enseignes de Paris.* Paris: Marchand de nouveautés, 1826.

Banks, Oliver. *Watteau and the North: Studies in the Dutch and Flemish Baroque Influence on French Rococo Painting.* New York: Garland, 1977.

Bapst, Germain. "La décoration théâtrale sous Louis XIV." *Gazette des beaux-arts* 7 (1891): 484–95.

Essai sur l'histoire du théâtre: La mis en scène, le décor, le costume, l'architecture, l'eclairage, l'hygiène. Paris: Imprimerie générale, 1893.

Barine, Arvède. *Princesses et grandes dames.* Paris: Librairie Hachette, 1890.

Baticle, Jeannine. "Pierrot, Gilles et les autres." In *Antoine Watteau (1684–1721): Le peintre, son temps et sa légende,* ed. François Moureau and Margaret Morgan Grasselli, 37–41. Paris: Champion-Slatkine, 1987.

Baudin, Henry. *L'enseigne et l'affiche.* Geneva: Auspices de la Fédération des Sociétés Artistiques de Génève, 1905.

Beauchamps, Pierre-François Godart de. *Recherches sur les théâtres de France depuis l'année onze cens soixante et un jusques à présent.* 3 vols. 1735. Reprint Geneva, Slatkine Reprints, 1968.

Bellier de la Chavignerie. "Notes pour servir à l'histoire de l'Exposition de la Jeunesse." *Revue universelle des arts* 19 (1864): 38–67.

Berry, Christopher. *The Idea of Luxury.* Cambridge: Cambridge University Press, 1994.

Berthelemy, Jean Simon. "Poeme sur la Galerie de Monsieur de Jullienne." Manuscript. Paris, Bibliothèque d'Art et d'Archéologie (Foundation Doucet).

Betten, Norma. "The Military Paintings of Antoine Watteau." Master's thesis, University of Washington, 1974.

Birrell, Francis. *La Duchesse du Maine.* London: G. Howe, 1929.

Black, Jeremy. *The Origins of War in Early Modern Europe.* Edinburgh: John Donald Publishers, 1987.

Blanc, Charles. *Historie des peintres de toutes les écoles.* Paris: Jules Renouard, 1865.

Le trésor de la curiosité. 2 vols. Paris: J. Renouard, 1857.

Blanc, Hippolyte. *Bibliographie des corporations ouvrières avant 1789.* Paris: Librarie de la Société Bibliographique, 1875.

Blavignac, Jean-Daniel. *Histoire des enseignes d'hôtelleries, d'auberges et de cabarets.* Genève: Grosset & Trembley, 1874.

Blégny, Nicolas. *Le livre de commode des adresses de Paris pour 1692.* 2 vols. Ed. Edouard Fournier. Paris: Paul Daffis, 1872.

Bonnet, Jacques. *Histoire de la danse sacrée et prophane: Sa progrès & ses révolutions, depuis son origine jusq'à présent. Avec un supplement de l'histoire de la musique & le parallèle de la peinture & de la poesie.* Paris: Chez Houry, 1732.

Boquet, Guy. "Les Comédiens italiens à Paris au temps de Louis XIV." *Revue d'histoire moderne et contemporaine* 26 (July–September 1979): 422–38.

Bossuet, Jacques Benigne. *Maximes et réflexions sur la comédie.* Paris: J. Anisson, 1694.

Bottari, G., and S. Ticozzi, eds. *Raccolta di lettere sulla pittura, scultura, ed architecttura scritte da più celebri personnaggi che dette arte fiorirono dal secoto XV al XVII.* 8 vols. Milan: G. Silvestri, 1822.

Boucher, François. "A propos d'une récente acquisition du musée du Louvre: Gillot et Watteau." *Gazette des beaux-arts* 8 (September–October 1923): 165–78.

"Les sources d'inspiration de *L'Enseigne de Gersaint.*" *Bulletin de la société de l'histoire de l'art français* (1958): 123–29.

Bouyer, Raymond. "Watteau et la musique." *Revue de l'art ancien et moderne* 40 (July-August 1921): 95–99.

Boyer, Jean-Claude. "Les représentations guerrières et l'evolution des arts plastiques en France au XVIIe Siècle." *XVIIe siècle,* #148 (July–September 1985): 291–305.

Brewer, John, and Roy Porter, eds. *Consumption and the World of Goods.* London: Routledge, 1993.

Briggs, Robin. *Early Modern France: 1560–1715.* Oxford: Oxford University Press, 1977.

Briquet, Pierre. *Code militaire ou compilation des ordonnances des roys de France concernant le gens de guerre.* 3 vols. Paris: Pierre Gandoüin, 1728.

Brucourt, C. F. *Essai sur l'education de la noblesse.* Paris: Chez Durand, 1747.

Bryson, Norman. *Word and Image: French Painting of the Ancien Régime.* Cambridge: Cambridge University Press, 1981.

Burke, Peter. *The Fabrication of Louis XIV.* New Haven: Yale University Press, 1992.

Popular Culture in Early Modern Europe. London: Temple Smith, 1978.

Bussy Rabutin, R. *Histoire amoureuse des Gaules, suivie de La France galante, romans satiriques du XIIe siècle attribués au comte de Bussy,* 2 vols. Paris: Garnier frères, 1868.

The Cabinet Open'd; or, The Secret History of the Amours of Madame de Maintenon with the French King. Trans. from the French. London: Printed for Richard Baldwin, 1690.

Cailleux, Jean. "Four Studies of Soldiers by Watteau." *Burlington* 101 (December 1959): supplement.

Camesasca, Ettore, and Pierre Rosenberg. *Tout l'oeuvre peint de Watteau.* Paris: Flammarion, Les Classiques de l'Art, 1970.

Campardon Émile. *Les comédiens du roi de la troupe italienne pendant les deux derniers siècles.* 2 vols. 1880. Reprint, Geneva: Slatkine Reprints, 1970.

Spectacles de la foire St. Germain, 2 vols. Paris: Berger-Levrault, 1877.

Caraccioli, L. A. *Dictionnaire critique, pittoresque et sentencieux: Propre à faire connoître les usages du siècle, ainsi que les bisarres.* 2 vols. Lyon: Benoit Duplain, 1768.

Carriera, Rosalba. *Journal de Rosalba Carriera pendant son séjour á Paris en 1720–1721.* Trans. Alfred Sensier. Paris: J. Techeuer, 1865.

Cary, Melbert B. *War Cards.* New York: Press of the Woolly Whale, 1937.

Castiglione, Baldassare. *The Book of the Courtier.* Trans. Thomas Hoby. In *The Renaissance Man,* 131–512. New York: Franklin Watts, 1959.

Castle, Terry. *Masquerade and Civilization: The Carnivalesque in Eighteenth-Century English Culture and Fiction.* Stanford, CA: Stanford University Press, 1986.

Catalogue des tableaux de cabinet de M. Crozat Baron de Thiers. Paris, 1755.

Caylus, Comte de. "*Le bordel ou Le Jean Foutre punis. . . .*" Manuscript. Bibliothèque de l'Arsenal, Paris.

Cederlöf, Olle. "The Battle Painting as a Historical Source: An Inquiry into the Principles." *Revue international d'histoire militaire* (1967): 119–44.

Champeaux, A. de. *Histoire de la peinture décorative.* Paris: Renouard, 1890.

Champier, Victor, and R. Sandoz. *Le Palais-Royal d'après des documents inédits, 1629–1900.* 2 vols. Paris: Société de propagation des livres d'art, 1900.

Champion, Pierre. " Watteau à Nogent." *Revue de l'art ancien et moderne* 40 (July-August 1921): 109–14.

Chan, Victor. "Watteau's *Les Comédiens Italiens* Once More." *Canadian Art Review* 5 (1978–79): 107–12.

Chartier, Roger. *Cultural History between Practices and Representations.* Trans. Lydia G. Cochrane. Cambridge: Polity Press, 1988.

Forms and Meanings: Texts, Performances, and Audiences from Codex to Computer. Philadelphia: University of Pennsylvania Press, 1995.

On the Ege of the Cliff: History, Language, and Practices. Trans. Lydia G. Cochrane. Baltimore: Johns Hopkins University Press, 1997.

Chatelus, Jean. "Themes picturaux dans les appartements des marchands et artisans parisiennes au XVIIIe siècle." *Dix-huitième siècle,* #6 (1974): 309–24.

Citron, Pierre. *La poésie de Paris dans la litterature française: De Rousseau à Baudelaire.* Paris: Les Éditions de Minuit, 1961.

Claretie, Léo. *Histoire des théâtres de société.* Paris: Librairie Molière, 1906.
Clark, Kenneth. "Watteau – *L'Enseigne de Gersaint.*" In *Looking at Pictures.* New York: Holt Rinehart & Winston, 1960, 75–87.
Clement, Pierre. *La police sous Louis XIV.* Paris: Didier, 1866.
Clément de Ris, Louis. *Les amateurs d'autrefois.* Paris: E. Plon, 1877.
"*Les enseignes de Paris.*" *Mélanges de litterature et d'histoire.* Vol. 6. Paris: La société des bibliophiles, 1877.
Clements, Candace. "Noble Liberality and Speculative Industry in Early Eighteenth-Century Paris: Charles Coypel." *Eighteenth-Century Studies* 29 (Winter 1995–96): 213–18.
Clifford, James. *The Predicament of Culture: Twentieth-Century Ethnography, Literature, and Art.* Cambridge, MA: Harvard University Press, 1988.
Cohen, Sarah. "*Un Bal Continuel:* Watteau's Cythera Paintings and Aristocratic Dancing in the 1710's." *Art History* 17 (June 1994): 160–81.
"Body as 'Character' in Early Eighteenth-Century French Art and Performance." *Art Bulletin* 78 (September 1996): 454–66.
Dance and the Body in the French Court of the Ancien Régime. New York: Cambridge University Press, 2000.
Colletet, François. *La ville de Paris contenant les noms de ses rues de ses faubourgs, eglises, monasteries, chapelles & colleges. . . .* Paris: Jean Musier, 1699.
Colombey, Émile. *Ruelles, salons et cabarets.* 2 vols. Paris: E. Dentu, 1892.
Contamine, Philippe, ed. *Histoire militaire de la France.* Vol. 1, *Des origines à 1715.* Paris: Presses universitaires de France, 1992.
Cooer, Gabriel François. *Trois pièces sur cette question les nobles doivent-ils commercer.* Paris: S.p., 1758.
Cornette, Joël. *Le roi de guerre: Essai sur la souveraineté dans la France du Grand Siècle.* Paris: Editions Payot & Rivages, 1993.
Corvisier, André. *L'armée française de la fin du XVIIe siècle au ministère de Choiseul.* 2 vols. Paris: Presses universitaires de France, 1964.
A Dictionary of Military History and the Art of War. Cambridge, MA: Blackwell, 1994.
Les hommes, la guerre et la mort. Paris: Economica, 1985.
Louvois. Paris: Fayard, 1983.
"Un problème social de l'ancien régime: La composition de l'armée." Extrait de *Actualité d'Histoire,* #22 (February 1958).
Courboin, François. *Graveurs et marchands d'estampes au XVIIIe siècle.* Paris: Société pour l'étude de la gravure française, 1911.
Histoire illustrée de la gravure en France, 1600–1800. Vol. 4. Paris: Maurice Le Garrec, 1928.
Courboin, François, and Marcel Roux. *La gravure française: Essai de bibliographie.* 3 vols. Paris: Maurice Le Garrec, 1928.
Courcy, Charles. "Les cafés de Paris." Extrait de *La Revue de Poche* (July 15, 1867).
Crow, Thomas. *Painters and Public Life in Eighteenth-Century Paris.* New Haven: Yale University Press, 1985.
Dacier, Émile. "Autour de Watteau – L'île de Cythère avant *l'Embarquement,*" *Revue de l'art ancien et moderne* 71 (1937): 247–50.
La gravure de genre et du moeurs. Paris: G. van Oest, 1925.
La gravure française. Paris: Larousse, 1944.
"Les premiers amateurs de Watteau." *Revue de l'art ancien et moderne.* 40 (July-August 1921): 115–30.

Dacier, Émile, and Albert Vuaflart. *Jean de Jullienne et les graveurs de Watteau au XVIIIe siècle.* 4 vols. Paris: La Société pour l'étude de la gravure française à l'occasion du bi-centenaire de la mort de Watteau, 1921–29.

Darnton, Robert. *The Great Cat Massacre and Other Episodes in French Cultural History.* New York: Basic Books, 1984.

"The Symbolic Element in History." *Journal of Modern History* 58 (1986): 218–34.

Dauvergne, Robert. "Les surnoms militaire en France au XVIIIe siècle." *Onomastica* 2 (1948): 237–45.

Deierkauf-Holsboer, Sophie Wilma. *Le théâtre de l'hôtel de Bourgogne.* 2 vols. Paris: Éditions A. G. Nizet, 1970.

Delamare, Nicolas. "Description historique & topographique de la ville de Paris." In *Traité de la police.* 4 vols. Paris: Jean & Pierre Cot, 1705.

Démoris, René. "Le corps royal et l'imaginaire au 17e siècle: *Le portrait du roi* par Felibien." *Revue des sciences humaine* 14, #172, 9–30.

"Les fêtes galantes chez Watteau et dans le romans contemporain." *Dix-huitième siècle,* no. 3 (1971): 337–57.

Le roman à la première personne du classicism aux lumières. Paris: A. Colin, 1975.

Depping, Georges-Bernard, ed. *Correspondence administrative sous le règne de Louis XIV entre le cabinet du roi les secretaires d'état, le chancelier de France.* 4 vols. Paris: Imprimerie Impériale, 1850–55.

Depréaux, Albert. *Les affiches de recrutement du XVIIe siècle à nos jours.* 2 vols. Paris: Leroy & cie, 1911.

Des bons mots et des contes. Paris: Claude Barbin, 1699.

Desrat, G. *Histoire de la danse: Historique, théoretique, pratique et bibliographique.* Paris: Libraries-Imprimeries Réunies, 1895.

Dezallier D'Argenville, A. J. *Abrégé de la vie des plus fameux peintres.* 1762. Reprint, Genève: Minkhoff Reprints, 1972.

Voyage pittoresque de Paris ou indication de tout ce qu'il y a des plus beau dans cette ville en peinture, sculpture & architecture. Paris: De Bure, 1749.

Dorbec, Prosper. "L'exposition de la jeunesse." *Gazette des beaux-arts* 33 (June 1905): 456–70, and 34 (July 1905): 77–86.

Douai, Musée de la Charreuse de Douai. *Van der Meulen peintre des conquêtes de Louis XIV.* Douai, 1967.

Du Bois de Saint-Gelais, Louis-François. *Description des tableaux du Palais Royale avec la vie des peintres à la tête.* Paris: Chez d'Houry, 1737.

Histoire Journalière de Paris. Ed. M. Tourneaux. Paris: Pour la Société des bibliophiles françois, 1885.

Du Bos, Jean-Baptist. *Réflexions critiques sur la poésie et sur la peinture.* 7th ed. 1770. Reprint, Geneva: Slatkine Reprints, 1967.

Duclos, Charles Pinot. *Mémoires secrets.* 2 vols. Paris: Colin, 1808.

Du Fresnoy, Charles Rivière. *Oeuvres de Monsieur Rivière du Freny.* Paris: Briasson, 1731.

Du Gérard. *Tables alphabetique: Chronologique des pièces representés sur l'ancien théâtre italien depuis son établissement jusqu'en 1697 qu'il a été fermé.* Paris: Prault, 1750.

Dumesnil, M. J. *Histoire des plus célèbres amateurs français et leurs relations avec les artistes.* 3 vols. Paris: E. Dentu, 1856–58.

Dumont, Jean. *Histoire militaire de Prince Eugène de Savoie du Duc de Marlborough et du Prince de Nassau-Frise.* 3 vols. La Haye: Isaac van den Kloot, 1729.

Dumont-Royal, Antoine. *Les glorieuse antiquitez de Paris.* 1660. Reprint, Paris: A Quantin, 1879.

Du Noyer, Anne-Marguerite Petit. *Lettres historiques et galantes.* 9 vols. La Haye: Pierre Husson, 1761.

Dunoyer de Noirmont and Marbot. *Costumes militaires français depuis l'organisation des. . . .* 3 vols. N.p., n.d.

Duplessis, Georges. "Le Cabinet du Roi: Collection d'estampes commandées par Louis XIV." *Le bibliophile français* 4 (1869): 87–105.

Catalogue de la collection de pièces sur les beaux-arts imprimées et manuscrites recueillie par Jean-Pierre Mariette, Charles-Nicolas Cochin et M. Deloynes, auditeur des comptes, et acquise récemment par le départment des Estampes de la bibliothèque nationale. Paris: A Picard, 1881.

Les ventes de tableaux, dessins, estampes et objets d'art, 1611–1800. Paris: Rapilly, 1874.

Durand, Catherine [Bédacier]. *Les petits soupers de l'été de l'année 1699. Ou aventures galantes avec l'origine des fées.* 2 vols. Paris: J. Musier et J. Rolin, 1702.

Edwards, JoLynn. "Watteau and the Dance." In *Antoine Watteau (1684–1721): Le peintre, son temps et sa légende,* ed. François Moureau and Margaret Morgan Grasselli, 138–48. Paris: Champion-Slatkine, 1987.

Eidelberg, Martin. "Watteau and Gillot: A Point of Contact." *Burlington Magazine* 116 (September 1974): 232–39.

Watteau's Drawings: Their Use and Significance. New York: Garland Press, 1977.

"Watteau's *Le Rendez-Vous.*" *Gazette des beaux-arts* 70 (November 1967): 285–94.

Eisenberg, Baron. *L'art de monter à cheval.* [Engraved by B. Picart]. La Haye: P. Gosse & J. Neaulue, 1727.

Ekberg, Carl. *The Failure of Louis XIV's Dutch War.* Chapel Hill, NC: University of North Carolina Press, 1979.

Encyclopédia methodique: Art militaire. Paris: Panckoocke, 1784.

Engerand, Fernand. *Inventaire des tableaux commandés et achetées par la direction des bâtiments du roi: 1709–1792.* Paris: Ernest Leroux, 1901.

Ennis, Mary Louise. "The Voyage to Cythera: From Courtly Allegory to Erotic Utopia in French Literature, 1700–1750." Ph.D. diss., Yale University, 1989.

Faret, Nicolas. *L'honneste homme ou l'art de plaire à la cour.* Ed. M. Magendie. Paris: Presses universitaires de France, 1925.

Favart, Charles. *Cythère assiègée: Opéra comique.* Paris: Duchesne, 1760.

Fedgal, Charles. *Les vieilles enseignes de Paris.* Paris: Eugene Figuière, 1913.

Felibien, André. *Conférences de l'académie royale de peinture et de sculpture.* Amsterdam: Estienne Roger, 1706.

Fenaille, Maurice. *Etat général des tapisseries de la manufacture des Gobelins depuis son origine jusq'à nos jours.* 3 vols. Paris: Imprimerie Nationale, 1903.

Fer, Nicolas. *L'atlas curieux ou le monde dressé et dédié à nos seigneurs les enfans de France.* Paris: Chez l'auter, 1700.

Introduction à la fortification. Paris: Chez l'auteur, 1684.

Ferré, Jean, ed. *Watteau,* 4 vols. Madrid: Athena Editions, 1972.

Ferrier-Caverivière, Nicole. "La guerre dans la litterature française depuis le traité des Pyrénées jusqu' a' la mort de Louis XIV." *Dix-Septième Siècle* 37, no. 3 (1985): 233–47.

Fetis, Edouard. "Van der Meulen." *L'artiste* 6 (15 May 1851): 8–11.

Feuquieres, Antoine. *Memoirs Historical and Military Containing a Distinct View of All the Considerable States of Europe.* 2 vols. London: T. Woodward & C. Davis, 1735.

Fischel, O. "Altes und neues vom *Schild de Gersaint.*" *Zeitschrift für Kunstgeschichte* 1 (1932): 341–53.
Forster, Elborg, ed. *A Woman's Life in the Court of the Sun King: Letters of Liselotte von der Pfalz, 1652–1722.* Baltimore: Johns Hopkins University Press, 1984.
Fosca, François. *Histoire des cafés de Paris.* Paris: Firmin-Didot, 1934.
Foucart, Paul. "Antoine Watteau à Valenciennes." *Société des beaux-arts des départments* 16 (1892): 529–60.
Fourcaud, Louis de. "A. Watteau, scènes et figures théâtrales." *Revue de l'art ancien et moderne* 15 (February 1904): 135–50 and (March 1904): 193–213.
"Antoine Watteau, peintre d'arabesques." *Revue de l'art ancien et moderne* 25 (January 1909): 49–59, and (February 1909): 129–40.
Fournel, Victor. *Les cris de Paris, types et physionomies d'autrefois.* Paris: Firmin-Didot, 1887.
Curiosités théâtrales anciennes et modernes, françaises et étrangers. Paris: Adolphe Delahaye, 1859.
Les rues de vieux Paris: Galerie popularie et pittoresque. Paris: Firmin-Didot, 1879.
Fournier, Edouard. "Les cafés sous Louis XIV." *La siècle,* 30 November 1854, and 3 March 1855.
Chroniques et légendes des rues de Paris. Paris: E. Dentu, 1864.
Histoire des enseignes de Paris. Paris: E. Dentu, 1884.
Fournier, Edouard, and Francisque Michel. *Le livre d'or des métiers. Histoire des hôtelleries, cabarets, hôtels garnis et des anciennes communautés.* Paris: Seri, 1859.
Franklin, Alfred, *Le café, le thé, & le chocolat.* Vol. 13, *La vie privée d'autrefois.* Paris: Librarie Plon, 1893.
Les corporations ouvrières de Paris du XVIIe au XVIIIe siècle. Paris: Firmin-Didot, 1884.
Dictionnaire historique des arts, métiers et professions. 1906. Reprint, New York: Burt Franklin, 1968.
Furetière, Antoine. *Dictionnaire Universel. . . .* 3 vols. Rotterdam: Reinier Leers, 1718.
Gallouédec-Genuys, Françoise. *Le prince selon Fénelon.* Paris: Presses Universitaires de France, 1963.
Garrard, Mary. *Artemisia Gentileschi: The Image of the Female Hero in Italian Baroque Art.* Princeton: Princeton University Press, 1989.
Gaston, Jean. *Les images des confréries parisienne avant la revolution.* 2 vols. Paris: A. Marty, 1909.
Gauthier, Maximilien. *Watteau.* Paris: Librairie Larousse, 1959.
Genest, Charles Claude. *Les divertissements de Sceaux.* Paris: Etienne Ganneau, 1712.
German, Louis de, ed. *Mémoires du Marquis de Franclieu.* Paris: Honore Champion.
Gersaint, Edme F. *Catalogue d'une collection de coquilles appartenant à M Sevin, conseiller au Parliament.* Paris: Prault, 1749.
Catalogue d'une grand collection de tableaux des meilleurs maistres d'Italie, de Flandres et de France qui doivent etre vendus dans. . . . Paris: P. Prault, 1749.
Catalogue raisonné de coquilles et autres curiosités naturelles. Paris: Flahault et Prault, 1736.
Catalogue raisonné de toutes les pièces qui forment l'oeuvre de Rembrandt. Paris: Hochereau l'aîné, 1751.
Catalogue raisonné des bijoux, porcelaines, bronzes, lacqs, lustres de cristale, roche et de porcelaine . . . etc . . . provenans de la succession de M. Angan Vicomte de Fonspertius. Paris: Pierre Prault & Jacques Barois, 1747.

Catalogue raisonné des differens effets curieux & rares contenus dans le cabinet de feu M. La Roque. Paris: J. Barois, 1745.

Catalogue raisonné des diverses curiosités du cabinet de feu M. Quentin de Lorangère. Paris: Barois, 1744.

Catalogue raisonné des tableaux, diamans, bagues de toute espèce, bijoux & autres effets provenant de la succession de feu Monsieur Charles Godefroy, banquier & joüaillier. Paris: Pierre Prault & Jacques Barois, 1744.

Catalogue raisonné d'une collection considerable de diverses curiosités en tous genres contenuës dans les cabinets de feu Bonnier de la Moisson, Bailly & Capitaine des Chasses de la Varenne des Thuilleries & Ancien Colonel du Regiment Dauphin. Paris: Jacques Barois & P. G. Simon, 1744.

Gherardi, Evaristo, ed. *Le théâtre italien de Gherardi, ou receuil général de toutes les comédies et scènes françoises jouées par les comédiens italien du roi pendant tout le temps qu' ils ont été au service.* 6 vols. Amsterdam: A. Braakman, 1701.

Giffart, G. *L'art militaire française pour l'infanterie.* Paris: Chez Giffart, 1696.

Girard, Georges. *La service militaire en France à la fin du regne de Louis XIV: Racolage et milice, 1701–1715.* Paris: Plon, 1921.

Godard d'Aucourt, Claude. *L'académie militaire ou les héros subalternes.* Amsterdam: Par la Société, 1749.

Godart de Beauchamps, Pierre François. *Recherches sur les théâtres de France depuis l'année onze jusqu'à présent.* Paris: Prault Père, 1735.

Goncourt, Edmond de, and Jules de Goncourt. *French Eighteenth-Century Painters.* Trans. Robin Ironside. Ithaca, NY: Cornell University Press, 1948.

Goodman, Elise. "Rubens's 'Conversatie à la Mode': Garden of Leisure, Fashion and Gallantry." *Art Bulletin* 64 (June 1982): 247–59.

Goodman-Soellner, Elise. "L'oiseau pris au piège: Nicolas Lancret *Le Printemps* and the *Prisionnier Volontaire* of P. Ayres." *Gazette des beaux-arts* 107 (March 1988): 127–30.

Goubert, Pierre. *Louis XIV and Twenty Million Frenchmen.* New York: Pantheon Books, 1966.

Gouhier, Henri Gaston, and Denise Leduc-Fayatte. *Fénelon, philosophie et spiritualité: Actes du colloque.* Geneva: Librairie Droz, 1996.

Grand-Carteret, John. *Les almanachs français, 1600–1895.* Paris: J. Alislié, 1896.

L'histoire – la vie – les Moeurs – et la curiosité par l'image, le pamphlet, et le document (1450–1900). 4 vols. Paris: Librairie de la curiosité et de beaux-arts, 1928.

Grange, Rosine, "Enseignes anciennes, un langage perdu." *Arts et décoration,* no. 184 (1975): 90–95.

Grasselli, Margaret, and Pierre Rosenberg. *Watteau: 1684–1721.* Paris: Editions de la Réunion des Musées Nationaux, 1984.

Grivel, Marianne. *Le commerce de l'estampe à Paris au XVIIe siècle.* Geneva: Librarie Droz, 1986.

Guénot, H. "La Roque." In Grenoble, Centre de recherche sur les sensibilités université des langues et lettres de Grenoble, *Dictionnaire des journalistes, supplément* 4. Paris: Presses universitatires de France, 1984.

Guérin, Nicolas. *Description de l'académie royale de peinture et sculpture.* Paris: Jacques Collombat, 1715.

Gueullette, J. E. *Un magistrat du XVIIIe siècle, ami des lettres, du théâtre, et des plaisirs, Thomas-Simon Gueullette.* Paris: E. Droz, 1938.

Guiffrey, Jules. *Les Gobelins et Beauvais.* Paris: Librarie Renouard, n.d.

Les modèles et le musée des Gobelins. 2 vols. Paris: Musées nationaux, n.d.
Notes et documents inédits sur les expositions du XVIIIe siècle. Paris: J. Baur, 1873.
"Van der Meulen: Mémoire de ses travaux pour le roi depuis le 1er Avril 1664 – Inventaire des tableaux et dessins trouvés chez lui, aux Gobelins, le 6 Mai 1691." *Nouvelles archives de l'art français,* 2nd series, vol. 1 (1879–81): 119–45.
ed. *Collection des livrets des anciennes expositions depuis 1673 jusqu'en 1800.* 4 vols. Paris: Liepmannssohn & Dufour, 1869–71.
ed. *Comte de batiments du roi sous le regne de Louis XIV.* 5 vols. Paris: Imprimerie nationale, 1881–94.
Guignard, M. de. *L'Ecole de Mars ou mémoires instructifs sur toutes les parties qui composent le corps militaire en France, avec leurs origines & les differentes manoeuvres ausquells elles sont employées.* Paris: Chez Simart, 1725.
Guillerm, Alain. "Le système de l'iconographie galante." *Dix-huitième siècle* (1980): 177–94.
Haillant, Marguerite. *Culture et imagination dans les oeuvres de Fénelon: "Ad useum delphini.* Paris: Les Belles Lettres, 1983.
Haldane, Charlotte. *Mme. de Maintenon: Uncrowned Queen of France.* New York: Bobbs-Merrill, 1970.
Hale, J. R. *Artists and Warfare in the Renaissance.* New Haven: Yale University Press, 1990.
Hallays-Dabot, Victor. *Histoire de la censure théâtrale.* Paris: E. Dentu, 1862.
Harth, Erica. *Cartesian Women: Versions and Subversions of Rational Discourse in the Old Regime.* Ithaca, NY: Cornell University Press, 1992.
Hatton, Ragnhild, ed. *Louis XIV and Europe.* London: Macmillan Press, 1976.
Heinecken, Carl Heinrich. *Idée général d'une collection complète d'estampes.* Leipzig: J. P. Kraus, 1771.
Heulhard, Arthur. *La foire Saint Laurent: Son histoire et ses spectacles.* Paris: A. Lemerre, 1878.
Hillairet, Jacques. *Dictionnaire historique des rues de Paris.* Paris: Editions de Minuit, 1961.
Hogarth, William. *Analysis of Beauty.* Oxford: Clarendon Press, 1955.
Hollander, Ann. *Seeing through Clothes.* New York: Avon Books, 1980.
Hurtaut, Pierre-Thomas-Nicolas, and Magny. *Dictionnaire historique de la ville de Paris et ses environs.* 4 vols. Paris: Moutard, 1779.
Illingworth, David. "Documents inédits et nouvelles précisions sur le théâtre de l'hôtel de Bourgogne." *Revue d'histoire du théâtre* 22 (1970): 129–30.
"L'hôtel de Bourgogne: Une salle de théâtre à l'italienne à Paris en 1647?" *Revue d'histoire du théâtre* 23 (1971): 40–49.
Illustre (L') mousquetarie: Nouvelle galante. Paris: n.p., 1697.
Ingersoll-Smouse, F. *Pater.* Paris: Les beaux-arts éditions d'étude et de documents, 1928.
Isherwood, Robert M. "Entertainment in the Parisian Fairs in the Eighteenth Century." *Journal of Modern History* 53 (March 1981): 24–47.
Farce and Fantasy: Popular Entertainment in Eighteenth-Century Paris. New York: Oxford University Press, 1986.
Jaillot, Jean. *Recherches critiques, historiques et topographiques sur la ville de Paris.* 5 vols. 1778–79. Reprint, Paris: Berger-Levrault, 1977.
Jal, A. *Dictionnaire critique de biographie et d'histoire.* 2nd ed. Paris: Henri Plon, 1872.

Jallut, Marguerite. "Les peintres des batailles des XVIIe et XVIIIe siècles." *Archives de l'art française* 22 (1950–57): 115–25.

Jammes, André. "Louis XIV, sa bibliothèque et le cabinet du roi." *Library* 20, no. 1 (March 1965): 1–12.

Jauss, Hans-Robert. "Literary History as a Challenge to Literary Theory." *New Literary History* 2 (1970): 7–37.

Towards an Aesthetic of Reception. Minneapolis: University of Minnesota Press, 1982.

Johnson, W. McAllister. "Paintings Provenance and Price: Speculations on the Eighteenth-Century Connoisseurship Apparatus in France." *Gazette des beaux-arts* 115 (May–June 1986): 191–99.

Jombert, Charles Antoine. *Catalogue raisonné de l'oeuvre de Sebastien Le Clerc, chevalier romain, dessinateur & graveur du cabinet du roi.* Paris: Chez l'auteur, 1774.

Josz, Virgile. *Antoine Watteau: Moeurs du XVIIIe siècle.* Paris: Société du Mercure de France, 1903.

Kaplan, Steven Laurence, and Cynthia J. Koepp, eds. *Work in France, Representations, Meaning, Organization, and Practice.* Ithaca, NY: Cornell University Press, 1986.

Kelly, Joan. *Women, History, and Theory.* Chicago: University of Chicago Press, 1984.

Klein-Rebour, F. "Les femmes soldats à travers les ages." *Revue historique de l'armée* 16 (February 1960): 3–20.

Kris, Ernst, and Otto Kurtz. *Legend, Myth, and Magic in the Image of the Artist.* New Haven: Yale University Press, 1979.

Lachèvre, Frederic, ed. *Les oeuvres libertines de Claude le Petit.* Paris: H. Champion 1918.

Lacordaire, A. L. *Notice historique sur les manufactures impériales de tapisseries des Gobelins et de tapis de la Savonnerie.* Paris: A la Manufacture des Gobelins, 1855.

La Croix, Paul [Dufour, Pierre]. *Histoire de la prostitution chez tous les peuples du monde depuis l'antiquité la plus reculée jusqu'à nos jours.* 6 vols. Paris: Serée, 1853.

Mémoires curieux sur l'histoire des moeurs et de la prostitution en France au dix-septième et'dix-huitième siècles. 2 vols. Brussels: Librarie Universelle de J. Rozez, 1861.

Ladurie, Emmanuel Le Roi. *Carnival at Romans.* New York: Braziller, 1970.

La Fayette, Marie-Madeleine de. *Mémoires de la cour de France pour les années 1688–1689.* Paris: E. Flammarion, n.d.

Lancelin, H. *Histoire de Valenciennes depuis ses origines.* Valenciennes: Pierre Giard, 1939.

La Quérière, E. *Recherches historiques sur les enseignes des maisons particulières.* Paris: V. Didron, 1852.

La Roque, Antoine de. *Théoné, Tragédie.* Paris: Chez Pierre Ribou, 1715.

Lavergne, Georges-Claudius, ed. *Archives des corporations des arts et métiers.* Paris: Librairie Charavay: 1879.

Lebel, Gustave. "A propos de deux equisses d'enseignes du XVIIIe siècle," *Bulletin de la société de l'histoire de l'art français* (1921): 55–61.

Lebeuf, Abbé. *Histoire de la ville et de touts les diocise de Paris.* 5 vols. Paris: Librairie de Fechoc et Letouzey 1883.

Le Coat, Gérard. "*Le pèlerinage à l'isle de Cithère:* un sujet «aussi galant qu'allégorique»." *Canadian Art Review* 2, no. 2 (1975): 9–23.

Lecomte, Florent. *Cabinet des singularities d'architecture, peinture, sculpture et gravure,* 3 vols. Paris: n.p., 1699.

Legrand, D'Aussy. *Histoire de la vie privée des françois depuis l'origine de la nation jusqu à nos jours.* 3 vols. Paris: Laurent Beaupré, 1815.

Legrand, F. C. *Les peintres Flamands de genre au XVIIe siècle.* Brussels: Editions Meddens, 1963.

Le Grand, Marc-Antoine. *La foire St. Laurent.* Paris: Ribou, 1709.

Le Maire, Maurice. *Adam Frans Van der Meulen et la guerre de Holland (1672–1678).* 2 vols. Mémoire, University of Paris IV-Sorbonne, 1992.

Le Maire. *Paris ancien et nouveaux.* Paris: Theodore Girard, 1685.

Lemonnier, Henry. "Au Musée Condé." *Gazette des beaux-arts,* #771 (November 1926): 279–87.

Léonard, Émile. *L'armée et ses problèmes au XVIIIe siècle.* Paris: Plon, 1958.

Leopold, Joseph Frédéric. *Les exercices de mars.* [Engravings by Guérard]. 1700.

Le Rouge, Georges. *Les curiositez de Paris, de Versailles, de Marly, de Vincennes, de St. Cloud et de ses environs.* Paris: Chez Saugrin, 1716.

Le Roux, Philibert-Joseph. *Dictionnaire comique, satirique, critique, burlesque, libre et proverbial.* 2 vols. Lyon: Chez les hériters Berringos, 1735.

Levey, Michael. "The Real Theme of Watteau's *Embarkation for Cythera.*" *Burlington Magazine* 13 (May 1961): 180–85.

Lévy-Bruhl, Henri. "La noblesse de France et le commerce à la fin de l'ancien régime." *Revue d'histoire moderne* 8 (1933): 209–35.

Lichtenstein, Jacqueline. *The Eloquence of Color: Rhetoric and Painting in the French Classical Age.* Trans. Emily McVarish. Berkeley and Los Angeles: University of California Press, 1993.

Lienhart, Constant, and René Humbert. *Les uniformes de l'armée française depuis 1690 jusqu'à nos jours.* 8 vols. Leipzig: M. Ruhl, 1897.

[Liger, Louis.] *Le voyageur fidèle ou le guide des étrangers dans la ville de Paris.* Paris: Pierre Ribou, 1716.

Lister, Martin. *A Journey to Paris in the Year 1698.* London: Jacob Tonson, 1699.

Livio, Robin. *Tavernes estaminets, guinguettes et cafés d'antan et de naguère.* Paris: Port Royal, 1961.

Locquin, Jean. "Contributions à l'étude des sources d'inspiration d'Antoine Watteau." *Bulletin de la société de l'histoire de l'art français* (1949): 49–52.

"Le paysage en France au début de XVIIIe siècle et l'oeuvre de J. B. Oudry." *Gazette des beaux-arts,* #617 (November 1908): 353–80.

Loridan, Jules. *Valenciennes au XVIIe siècle.* Robaix: Imprimerie Reboux, 1913.

Lougee, Carolyn. *Le Paradis des Femmes: Women, Salons, and Social Stratification in Seventeenth-Century France.* Princeton: Princeton University Press, 1976.

Louis XIV. *Mémoires.* Ed. Jean Longnon. Paris: Librairie Jules Tallndier, 1978.

Luria, Keith. *Territories of Grace: Cultural Change in the Seventeenth-Century Diocese of Grenoble.* Berkeley and Los Angeles: University of California Press, 1991.

Magendie, Maurice. *La politesse mondaine et les théories de l'honnêteté en France au XVIIe siècle de 1600 à 1660.* Paris: Presses universitaires de France, 1925.

Magne Émile. *Le Château de Saint-Cloud.* Paris: Calman-Lévy, 1932.

Les fêtes en europe au XVIIe siècle. Paris: Martin Dupis, 1930.

Images de Paris. Paris: Calman-Lévy, 1939.

Les plaisirs et les fêtes en France au XVIIe siècle. Genève: Editions de la Frigate, 1949.

Voiture et l'hôtel de Rambouillet: Les origines, 1597–1635, portraits et documents inédites. Paris: Émile Paul, 1929–30.

Mailly, Chevalier de. *Les entretiens des cafés de Paris et les diférens qui y surviennent*. Trévaux: E. Ganeau, 1702.

Maintenon, Françoise d'Aubigné de. *Mémoires pour servir à l'histoire de Mme de Maintenon & à celle du siècle passé*. 6 vols. Ed. Laurent de La Beaumelle. Amsterdam, 1789.

Mandrou, Robert. *De la culture populaire aux 17e et 18e siècles*. Paris: Éditions Stock, 1975.

La France au XVIIe et XVIIIe siècles. Paris: Presses universitaires de France, 1974.

Louis XIV et son temps, 1661–1715. Paris: Presses universitaires de France, 1973.

Mantz, Paul. *Antoine Watteau*. Paris: Librarie Illustrée, 1892.

Marana, Jean Paul. *Lettre d'un Sicilien à un de ses amis*. Paris: Pierre Maubal, 1710.

Marcel, Pierre. *La peinture française au début du dix-huitième siècle, 1690–1721*. Paris: Ancienne Maison Quantin, 1906.

Marchand (d'après Barbier), J. H. *Testament histori-morali-politique de Monsieur Rauponeau: Écrit et publié par lui-même*. Paris: A la courtile aux dépense de l'auteur, 1760.

Mariette, Pierre Jean. *Abecedario*. Paris: F. de Nobele, 1966.

Description sommaire des dessins de grands maistres d'Italie, des pays bas et de France au cabinet de feu Crozat. Paris: P. J. Mariette, 1741.

Marolles, Michel. *Paris ou déscription de cette ville*. 1677. Reprint, Paris: A Quantin, 1879.

Martin, Ronald. "The Army of Louis XIV." In *The Reign of Louis. XIV: Essays in Celebration of Andrew Lossky*, ed. Paul Sonnino, 111–26. Atlantic Highlands, NJ: Humanities Press International, 1990.

Masson, Frédéric. *Le Marquis de Grignan: Petit-fils de Madame Sévigné*. Paris: Librairie Plon, 1887.

Mathey, Jacques. "The Early Compositions of Antoine Watteau in the Style of the Dutch and Flemish Painters." *Art Quarterly* (Autumn 1957): 244–58.

Peintures réapparues. Paris: F. de Nobele, 1966.

Mauclair, Camille. "La maladie de Watteau." *Revue de l'art ancien et moderne*. 40 (July–August 1921): 100–108.

Mauricheau-Beaupré, Charles. "Un peintre de Louis XIV aux armeés: Van der Meulen." *Les jardin des arts*, #37 (November 1957): 1–10.

McClellan, Andrew. "Edme Gersaint and the Marketing of Art in Eighteenth-Century Paris." *Eighteenth-Century Studies* 29 (Winter 1995–96): 218–22.

"Watteau's Dealer: Gersaint and the Marketing of Art in Eighteenth-Century Paris." *Art Bulletin* 78 (September 1996): 439–53.

Mélèse, Pierre. "A propos de l'expulsion des Comédiens Italiens en 1697." *Revue historique et littéraire* 44 (1937): 533–37.

Répertoire analytique des documents contemporains d'information et de critique concernant le théâtre à Paris sous Louis XIV, 1659–1715. Paris: E. Droz, 1934.

Le théâtre et le public à Paris sous Louis XIV, 1659–1715. Paris: Droz, 1934.

Mémoire historique de la vie d'un Fantassin de vingt-cinq ans de service. N.l.: n.p., 1711.

Mémoires pour sevir à l'histoire de la Calotte. 3 vols. Aux Etats Calotins, D'l'mprimerie Calotine, 1752.

Menilglaise, Godefroy. "Voyage d'un Hollandoise en France, 1713–1714." *Mémoires de la société des sciences de l'agriculture et des arts de Lille* 2 (1873): 22–48.
Mention, Léon. *L'armée de l'ancien régime de Louis XIV à la revolution.* Paris: L. H. May, n.d.
Mercier, Louis-Sébastian. *Tableau de Paris.* 12 vols. 1782. Reprint, Geneva: Slatkine Reprints, 1979.
Méré, Antoine Gombard, Chevalier de. *Oeuvres posthumes.* Ed. Charles Boudhors. 3 vols. Paris: F. Roches, 1930.
Méthivier, Hubert. *Le siècle de Louis XIV.* Paris: Presses universitaires de France, 1950.
Meyer, Daniel. *L'histoire du roy.* Paris: Editions de la Réunion des Musées Nationaux, 1980.
Meyer, Jean. *La vie quotidienne en France au temps de la Régence.* Paris: Hachette, 1979.
Michaux, Monique. "La gravure militaire française du XVe au XVIIe siècle." *Revue historique de l'armée* 16 (September 1960): 3–14.
Mirimonde, A. P. "La musique dans les allégories de l'amour: II Eros." *Gazette des beaux-arts* 69 (May–June 1967): 319–46.
"La musique dans les allégories de l'amour: I Venus." *Gazette des beaux-arts* 68 (November 1966): 265–90.
"Les opinions de M. Lebrun sur la peinture hollandois." *Revue des arts,* #4 (1956): 207.
"Statues et emblèmes dans l'oeuvre d'Antoine Watteau." *La revue du Louvre et des Musées de France* 12, no. 1 (1962): 11–20.
"Les sujets musicaux chez Antoine Watteau." *Gazette des beaux-arts* 58 (November 1961): 249–88.
Mirzoeff, Nicholas. "Seducing our Eyes: Gender, Jurisprudence, and Visuality in Watteau." *The Eighteenth Century: Theory and Interpretation* 35 (Summer 1994): 135–54.
Mongrédien, Georges. *Daily Life in the French Theater at the Time of Molière.* Trans. Claire Elaine Engel. London: George Allen & Unwin, 1969.
La vie de société au XVIIe et XVIIIe siècles. Paris: Hachette, 1950.
Montagu, Jennifer. *The Expression of the Passions: The Origin and Influence of Charles Le Brun's "Conférence sur l'expression générale et particulière."* New Haven: Yale University Press, 1994.
Montaiglon, Anatole de. *Catalogue raisonné de l'oeuvre de Claude Mellan.* Abbeville: Les P. Briez, 1856.
"Petits pièces: Extraits de différents recueils de poésies et relatives à des artists." *Nouvelles archives de l'art française* (1872): 109–23.
ed. *Procès-verbaux de l'académie royale de peinture et de sculpture, 1648–1793.* 10 vols. Paris: Charavay Frères for the Société de l'Histoire de l'Art Français, 1875–92.
Monval, Georges. *Les collections de la Comédie Française: Catalogue historique et raisonné.* Paris: Société de propagation des livres d'art, 1897.
Moussalli, Ulysse. "Les sources flamandes du Watteau." *La révue belge de l'archaeologie et de l'histoire de l'art* 24 (1955): 75–80.
Moutspoulos, Evanghélos. "Les structures de la temporalité chez Watteau." In *Antoine Watteau (1684–1721): Le peintre, son temps et sa légende,* ed. François

Moureau and Margaret Morgan Grasselli, 143–48. Paris: Champion-Slatkine, 1987.
Munhall, Edgar. *Little Notes Concerning Watteau's "Portal of Valenciennes."* New York: The Frick Collection, 1992.
Murat, Henriette Julie de Casteluau, Comtesse de. *Le voyage de campagne.* Vol. 29, *Voyages imaginaires, songes, visions et romans cabalistique.* Paris: Privately published, 1788.
Navereau, A. *Le logement et les ustensiles de gens de guerre de 1439 à 1789.* Poitiers: Société Française d'Imprimerie, 1924.
Nemeitz, Joachim C. *Séjour de Paris: C'est-à-dire instructions fidèles pour le voiageurs de condition.* Leiden: Jean van Abcoude, 1727.
Neuman, Robert. "Watteau's *L'Enseigne de Gersaint* and Baroque Emblematic Tradition." *Gazette des beaux-arts* 104 (November 1984): 153–64.
Nicolle, Henri. "Thomas-Simon Gueullette." *Revue de France* 10 (1874): 768–95.
Nisard, Charles. *Histoire des livres populaire ou de la litterature de colportage.* 2 vols. Paris: Librairie d'Amyot, 1854.
Nochlin, Linda. "Watteau: Some Questions of Interpretation." *Art in America* 73 (January 1985): 68–87.
Nodot, François. *Le munitionaire des armées de France.* Paris: N.p., 1697.
La rivale travestie ou les avantures galantes arivées au camp de Compiègne avec tous les mouvemens de l'armée. Paris: Chez Brunet, 1699.
Le nouveau fourrier de la Cour. Reformant les autres logemens & les accomodant mieux au temps & aux lieux & logeant acommodément ceux qui avoient été oubliez. Paris: Privately published, 1652.
Opperman, Hal. "The Theme of Peace in Watteau." In *Antoine Watteau (1684–1721): Le peintre, son temps et sa légende,* ed. Françoise Moureau and Margaret Morgan Grasselli, 23–28. Paris: Champion-Slatkine, 1987.
Ortner, Sherry. "Is Female to Male as Nature Is to Culture?" In *Women, Culture, and Society,* ed. Michell Zimbalist Rasaldo, 67–87. Stanford, CA: Stanford University Press, 1974.
Parfaict, Claude, and François Parfaict. *Histoire de l'ancien théâtre italien depuis son origine en Fiance, jusqu'à sa suppression en l'année 1697.* 2 vols. Paris: Lambert, 1753.
Parfaict, François. *Mémoires pour servir à l'histoire des spectacles de la foire.* 2 vols. Paris: Chez Briasson, 1743.
La parfait homme de guerre ou l'idée d'un hero. Amsterdam: Jacques Desbordes, 1699.
Paris, Galerie Cailleux. *Peintures de dix-huitième siècle au musée des beaux-arts de Bordeaux.* Paris: 1970.
Paris, Manufacture nationale des Gobelins. *Exposition Antoine-François Van der Meulen.* Paris: Manufacture nationale des Gobelins, n.d.
Paris, Musée de l'Armée. *Les Invalides: Trois siècles d'histoire.* Paris: Musée de l'Armée, 1974.
Paris, Musée du Louvre, Galerie Mollien. *Catalogue le cabinet d'un grand amateur: P.J. Mariette, 1694–1774. Dessins du XVe siècle au XVIIIe siècle.* Paris: Réunion des Musées Nationaux, 1967.
Parrocel, Charles. *Differentes attitudes de la cavalerie et de l'infanterie dessinée et partie gravée par Parrocel, peintre ordinaire du roi.* N.p., nd.
Parrocel, Etienne. *Monographie des Parrocel.* Marseille: Imprimerie, 1861.

Paulson, Ronald. *Emblem and Expression: Meaning in English Art of the Eighteenth Century.* Cambridge, MA: Harvard University Press, 1975.
Pelet, Louis. *Mémoires militaires relatifs à la succession d'Espagne sous Louis XIV.* 10 vols. Paris: Collection de documents inédits sur l'historie de France, 1835–55.
Pellegrin, *Medée et Jason tragédie.* Paris: Chez Christophe Ballard, 1713.
Perrault, Charles. *Les hommes illustrés qui ont paru en France pendant ce siècle.* Paris: Antoine Dezallier, 1697.
Piépape, Léonce de. *Une petite-fille du Grande Condé: La duchess du Maine, reine de Sceaux et conspiratrice.* Paris: Plon, 1910.
Piganiol de La Force, Jean-Aimar. *Description de Paris, de Versailles, de Marley, de Meudon, de St. Cloud, de Fontainbleu et toutes les autres belles maisons & chateaux des environs de Paris.* 8 vols. Paris: Chas-Nicolas Poirion, 1742.
Pilon, E. "Les origines de *l'embarquement pour l'isle de Cythère.*" *Revue de l'art ancien et moderne* 40 (July-August 1921): 83–94.
Plax, Julie Anne. "Gersaint's Biography of Antoine Watteau: Reading between and beyond the Lines." *Eighteenth-Century Studies* 25 (Summer 1992): 545–60.
Pöete, Marcel. *La promenade à Paris au XVIIIe siècle: L'art de se promener, les lieux de promenade dans la ville et aux environs.* Paris: Armand, 1913.
Pomian, Krzysztof. *Collectors and Curiosities: Paris and Venice, 1500–1800.* Trans. E. Wiles-Portier. Cambridge: Polity Press, 1990.
Poncheville, A. de. "Watteau à Valenciennes." *Revue de l'art ancien et moderne* 40 (July-August 1921): 75–82.
Populus, Bernard. *Claude Gillot (1673–1722): Catalogue d'oeuvre gravé.* 2 vols. Paris: Société pour l'étude de la gravure française, 1930.
Le portefeuille galant, ouvrage mêlé de prose & de vers. Paris: Jean Moreau, 1700.
Portet, Mariette. *St-Cloud les hauts-de-Seine.* Condé-sur-Noireau: Ch. Corlet, 1966.
Posner, Donald. "Another Look at Watteau's *Gilles.*" *Apollo* 117 (February 1983): 97–99.
———. *Antoine Watteau.* Ithaca, NY: Cornell University Press, 1984.
Praz, Mario. *Studies in Seventeenth-Century Imagery.* Rome: Edizioni di Historia e Letteratura, 1964.
Préaud, Maxine, Pierre Casselle, Marianne Givel, and Corinne Le Bitouzé. *Dictionnaire des éditeurs d'estamps à Paris sous l'ancien régime.* Promodis: Editions des Cercle la Librairie, 1987.
Prechac, Jean de. *L'illustre Parisienne, histoire galante & véritable.* Paris: Pierre Witte, 1714.
Puységar, Jacques de Chastenet de. *L'art de la guerre.* La Haye: Chez Frederic-Henri Scheurleer, 1749.
Quincy, Charles Sevin. *Histoire militaire du regne de Louis le Grand.* 8 vols. Paris: Chez Denis Mariette at autres, 1726.
Quincy, Joseph. *Mémoires du Chevalier de Quincy.* 3 vols. Ed. Léon Lecestre. Paris: Librairie Renouard, 1898–1900.
Radisich, Paula Rea. "Deconstructing Dissipation." *Eighteenth-Century Studies* 29 (Winter 1995–96): 222–25.
Rahir, Edouard. *Watteau, peintre d'arabesques.* Paris: Henri Laurens, n.d.
Ravel, Jeffrey. *The Contested Parterre: Public Theater and French Political Culture, 1680–1791.* Ithaca: Cornell University Press, 1999.
Regnard, Jean-François. *Oeuvres complètes de Regnard.* 6 vols. Paris: Lefèvre, 1810.

Relation de ce qui s'est passé à la bataille donnée le 11 Septembre 1709 auprès de Mons. Paris: De l'imprimerie de Frederick Leonard, n.d.

Relation de la bataille donné près des forêts de Sart & de Jansart dans le Hainaut le 11 Septembre 1709 avec plusieurs circonstances qui l'ont précedée & suivie depuis le 9 jusqu'au 17 du même mois avec la liste des morts et des Blessés, and *La lettre de'un officer de distinction de l'armée de France contenant aussi une relation fort curieuse de la dite bataille.* Paris, 1711.

Remy, P. *Catalogue des tableaux, miniatures . . . de cabinet de M. . . . [Caylus].* Paris, Didot, 1773.

Catalogue raisonné de tableaux . . . de feu M. Aved. Paris: Didot, 1766.

Catalogue raisonné de tableaux . . . feu Monsieur Dezallier D'Argenville. Paris: Didot, 1766.

Revol, J. *Histoire de l'armée française.* Paris: Librairie Larouse, 1929.

Rey, Robert. *Quelques satellites de Watteau.* Paris: Librairie de France, 1931.

Ribeiro, Aileen. *The Art of Dress: Fashion in England and France, 1750–1820.* New Haven: Yale University Press, 1995.

Dress in Eighteenth-Century Europe, 1715–1789. London: Batsford, 1984.

Riccoboni, François. *L'art du théâtre.* 1750. Reprint, Geneva: Slatkine Reprints, 1971.

Richefort, Isabelle. "Nouvelles précisions sur la vie d'Adam François Van der Meulen, peintre historiographe de Louis XIV." *Bulletin de la société de l'histoire de l'art français* (1986): 57–80.

Robert, Raymonde. *Le conte de feés littéraire en France de la fin du XVIIe siècle à la fin du XVIIIe siècle.* Nancy: Presses universitaires de France, 1982.

Roberts, Warren. *Morality and Social Class in Eighteenth-Century French Literature and Painting.* Toronto: University of Toronto Press, 1974.

Roche, Daniel. *The People of Paris: An Essay in Popular Culture in the Eighteenth Century.* Trans. Marie Evans, in association with Gwynne Lewis. Berkeley and Los Angeles: University of California Press, 1987.

Rocheblave, S. *Essai sur le Comte de Caylus, l'homme, l'artiste, l'antiquaire.* Paris: Hachette, 1889.

Rodin, A. *L'art, entretiens réunis par Paul Gsell.* Paris: Grasset, 1911.

Roland, Henri. "An Early Watteau." *Phoebus* 1 (1946): 173–75.

Roland-Michel, Marianne. *Watteau: An Artist of the Eighteenth-Century.* New York: Alpine Fine Arts, 1984.

Watteau et sa génération. Paris: Galerie Cailleux, 1968.

Roland-Michel, Marianne, and Daniel Rabreau. *Les arts du théâtre de Watteau à Fragonard.* Bordeaux: Galerie des Beaux-Arts, 1980.

Romi. *Maisons closes: L'histoire l'art la litterature les moeurs.* Paris: Romi, 1952.

Rosenberg, Pierre. "Dieu as Draughtsman." *Master Drawings* 17, no. 2 (1979): 161–69.

ed. *Vies anciennes de Watteau.* Paris: Hermann, 1984.

Rousset, Camille. *Le Comte de Gisors.* Paris: Didier et C., 1868.

Saint Aubin, Auguste de. *Exercise de l'infanterie françoise ordonné le 6 Mai 1755 copié d'après l'original executé et presenté par Baudouin.* Paris: Fessart & Chaubert, 1759.

Saint-Germain, Jacques. *La vie quotidienne en France à la fin du grand siècle.* Paris: Hachette, 1965.

Saint-Simon, Louis de Rouvroy, Duc de. *Mémoires du Duc de Saint-Simon.* 20 vols. ed. Adolphe Chéruel and Adolphe Regnier. Paris: Librarie Hachette, 1873–87.

Saisselin, Remy. *Taste in Eighteenth-Century France.* Syracuse, NY: Syracuse University Press, 1965.

Sargentson, Carolyn. *Merchants and Luxury Markets: The Marchands-Merciers of Eighteenth Century Paris.* Santa Monica, CA: J. Paul Getty Museum, 1996.

Sarraméa, François. *Lettres d'un cadet de Gascogne sous Louis XIV.* Paris: Champion, 1740.

Sautai, Maurice. *La bataille de Malplaquet d'après les correspondants du duc du Maine à l'armée de Flandre.* Paris: Librairie Militaire R. Chapelot, 1904.

Sauval, Henri. *La chronique scandaleuse de la cour et de Paris.* Paris: H. Daragon, 1910.

Histoire et recherches des antiquities de Paris. 3 vols. Paris: Charles Moette & Jacques Chardon, 1724.

Scarron aparu à Madame de Maintenon et les reproches qu'il lui fait, sur ses amours avec Louis le Grand. Cologne: Chez Jean le Blanc, 1694.

Schalk, Ellery. *From Valor to Pedigree: Ideas of Nobility in France in the Sixteenth and Seventeenth Centuries.* Princeton: Princeton University Press, 1986.

Schefer, Jean-Louis. "Notes sur les systèmes représentatifs." *Tel-Quel* 41 (Spring 1970): 44–71.

Scénographie d'un tableau. Paris: Collection Tel Quel, aux éditions de Seuil, 1969.

Schnapper, Antoine. "Deux tableaux de Joseph Parrocel au Musée de Rouen." *La revue du Louvre et des musées de France* 20 (1970): 78–86.

"Le Grand Dauphin et les tableaux de Meudon." *Revue de l'art* 1–2 (1968): 57–64.

"Quelques oeuvres de Joseph Parrocel." *La revue des arts* 4–5 (1959): 163–76.

Schwarz, Isadore. *The Commedia dell'Arte and Its Influence on French Comedy.* Paris: H. Samuel, 1933.

Scott, Katie. "Hierarchy, Liberty and Order: Languages of Art and Institutional Conflict in Paris." *Oxford Art Journal* 12 (1989): 59–70.

The Rococo Interior: Decoration and Social Spaces in Early Eighteenth-Century Paris. New Haven: Yale University Press, 1995.

Scott, Virginia. *The Commedian dell'Arte in Paris: 1644–1697.* Charlottesville: University of Virginia Press, 1990.

Seerveld, Calvin. "Tell-tale Statues in Watteau's Painting." *Eighteenth-Century Studies* 14 (Winter 1980–81): 151–80.

Sennett, Richard. *The Fall of Public Man.* New York: Vintage Books, 1978.

Sheriff, Mary D. *Fragonard: Art and Eroticism.* Chicago: University of Chicago Press, 1990.

Sicard, M. F. *L'histoire des institutions militaires des français.* 4 vols. Paris: J. Corréard Jeune, 1834.

Siefert, Helge. *Zum Ruhme des Helden: Historien und Genremalerei des 17. und 18. Jahrhunderts aus den Beständen der Alten Pinakothek.* Munich: Bayerische Staatsgemäldesammlungen, 1993.

Siegfried, Susan. "Naked History: The Rhetoric of Military Painting in Postrevolutionary France." *Art Bulletin* 75 (June 1993): 235–58.

Sloane, Joseph. "Watteau's *Embarkation for Cythera:* A Suggested Solution." *Studies in Iconography* 7 and 8 (1981–82): 289–99.

Sonenscher, Michael. *Work and Wages: Natural Law, Politics and the Eighteenth-Century French Trades.* Cambridge: Cambridge University Press, 1989.

Sonnino, Paul, ed. *The Reign of Louis XIV: Essays in Celebration of Andrew Lossky.* Atlantic Highlands, NJ: Humanities Press International, 1990.

Spitz, Ellen Handler. *Art and Psyche: A Study in Psychoanalysis and Aesthetics.* New Haven: Yale University Press, 1985.

Stanton, Domna, *The Aristocrat as Art.* New York: Columbia University Press, 1980.

Starky, Laure. *Desseins de Van der Meulen et de son atelier.* Paris: Mobilier National, 1988.

Stephane, Bernard. *La dictionnaire des noms de rues.* Paris: Editions Mengés, 1977.

Stewert, Philip. "Representations of Love in the French Eighteenth Century." *Studies in Iconography* 4 (1978): 125–48.

Storer, Mary Elizabeth. *La mode des contes de fées.* Paris: Librairie Ancienne Honoré Champion, 1928.

Stuffman, Margaret. "Les tableaux de la collection de Pierre Crozat; historique et destinée d'un ensemble célèbre, établis en partant d'un inventaire après décès inédit (1740)." *Gazette des beaux-arts* 72 (July 1968): 1–144.

Sturgill, Claude. *Marshal Villars and the War of Spanish Succession.* Lexington: University of Kentucky Press, 1965.

Susane, Louis. *Histoire de l'ancienne infanterie française.* 8 vols. Paris: Librarie Militaire de J. Corréad, 1849.

Tableau et liste de toutes les jolies marchands de quarante-huit divisions de Paris. . . . Paris: N.p., n.d.

Tolnay, Charles de. "*L'Embarquement pour Cythère* de Watteau au Louvre." *Gazette des beaux-arts* 46 (July 1955): 91–102.

Tomlinson, Robert. *La fête galante: Watteau et Marivaux.* Genève: Librairie Droz, 1981.

Vallée, Hélène. "Sources de l'art de Watteau: Claude Simpol." *Promethée (L'Amour de l'Art)* 20 (April 1939): 67–74.

Valotaire, M. "La recrue allant joindre le regiment." *Gazette des beaux-arts* 15, #701 (October–December 1919): 401–6.

Van Maarseveen, Michel, Jos W. L. Hilkhijsen, and Jacques Dane. *Beelden van een strijd: Oorlog en kunst vóór de Vrede van Munster.* Delft: Waanders Uitgevers, Zwolle Stedelijk Museum Het Prinsenhof, Delft, 1998.

Varnadoe, Kirk. *High and Low: Modern Art and Popular Culture.* New York: Museum of Modern Art, 1990.

Vauban, Sebastien Le Prestre de. *Oisivetés.* Paris: J. Corréad, 1843.

Vaultier, Roger. "*Le racolage et le recrutement sous l'ancien régime.*" Extrait de *Vert et Rouge* no. 27 (Mai 1950): 8–13.

Versailles. *Charles Le Brun, 1619–1690: Peintre et dessinateur.* Exh Cat. Château de Versailles, 1963.

Vidal, Mary. *Watteau's Painted Conversations: Art, Literature, and Talk in Seventeenth- and Eighteenth-Century France.* New Haven: Yale University Press, 1992.

Villars, Claude Louis Hector. *Vie du Maréchal de Villars.* 4 vols. Paris: Chez Moutard, 1784.

Visions admirables d'un pèlerin de Parnasse. Paris: Jean Gesselin, 1635.

Vitet, Louis. *L'académie royale de peinture et de sculpture, étude historique.* Paris: Michel Levy Frères, 1861.

Voltaire, François-Marie Arouet de. *Siècle de Louis XIV.* In *Oeuvres complètes de Voltaire,* vols. 14 and 15. Paris: Garner Frères, 1878.

Warner, Maria. *Monuments and Maidens: The Allegory of the Female Form.* London: Weidenfeld & Nicholson, 1985.

Watson, Francis. "Beckford, Mme. de Pompadour, the Duc de Bouillon and the Taste for Japanese Lacquer in Eighteenth-Century France." *Gazette des beaux-arts* 61 (February 1963): 101–27.

"Les marchands-merciers et le gout français au XVIIIe siècle." *L'oeil* 153 (September 1967): 12–21.

Weigert, Roger-Armand. "Les almanachs royaux." *Médecine de France,* no. 215 (1970): 25–40.

Weygand, Maxime. *Histoire de l'armée française.* Paris: Flammarion, 1961.

Wildenstein, Georges. "Le gout pour la peinture dans le cercle de la bourgeoisie parisienne autour 1700." *Gazette des beaux-arts* 48 (1956): 113–20.

Mélanges. Paris: Les Beaux-Arts, Editions d'Etudes et de Documents, 1926.

Wiley, W. L. "The Hôtel Bourgogne." *Studies in Philology* 70 (December 1973): 3–109.

Wilhelm, Jacques. "François Le Moyne and Antoine Watteau." *Art Quarterly* 14, no. 3 (1951): 216–30.

Wrigley, Richard. "Between the Street and the Salon: Parisian Shop Signs and the Spaces of Professionalism in the Eighteenth and Early Nineteenth Century." *Oxford Art Journal* 21, no. 1 (1998): 43–67.

Zetter, C. *Évolution des foires et marchés à travers les siècles.* Paris: Comité de la Foire de Paris, 1923.

Index